Folktales from Northern India

ABC-CLIO CLASSIC FOLK AND FAIRY TALES

Jack Zipes, Series Editor

Collectors in the nineteenth and early twentieth centuries unearthed a wealth of stories from around the world and published them in English translations for the delight of general readers, young and old. Most of these anthologies have been long out of print.

The ABC-CLIO Classic Folk and Fairy Tales series brings back to life these key anthologies of traditional tales from the golden age of folklore discovery. Each volume provides a freshly typeset but otherwise virtually unaltered edition of a classic work and each is enhanced by an authoritative introduction by a top scholar. These insightful essays discuss the significance of the collection and its original collector; the original collector's methodology and translation practices; and the original period context according to region or genre.

Certain to be of interest to folklorists, these classic collections are also meant to serve as sources for storytellers and for sheer reading pleasure, reviving as they do hundreds of folk stories, both reassuringly familiar and excitingly strange.

Folktales from Northern India

William Crooke
and Pandit Ram Gharib Chaube

Edited and with an Introduction
by Sadhana Naithani

Library of Congress Cataloging-in-Publication Data

Folktales from northern India / by William Crooke and Pandit Ram Gharib Chaube ; edited and with an introduction by Sadhana Naithani.
    p. cm.—(ABC-CLIO classic folk and fairy tales)
Translated from the Hindi.
Includes index.
  ISBN 1-57607-698-9 (hardcover: alk. paper)
1. Tales—India. 2. Folklore—India. I. Crooke, William, 1848–1923. II. Gharib Chaube, Ram, Pandit. III. Naithani, Sadhana. IV. North Indian notes and queries. V. Indian antiquary. VI. Series.
  GR305 .F6485 2002
  398.2'0954—dc21

                            2002009495

06 05 04 03 02   10 9 8 7 6 5 4 3 2 1 (cloth)

This edition reprints in its entirety and retains the original publication sequence of folktales from Northern India, collected and edited by William Crooke and Pandit Ram Gharib Chaube, published in North Indian Notes & Queries *and in* Indian Antiquary *between September 1892 and March 1926. The text of this edition has been altered only to fit an increased page dimension and to reflect contemporary typographical conventions.*

ABC-CLIO, Inc.
130 Cremona Drive, P.O. Box 1911
Santa Barbara, California 93116-1911

This book is also available on the World Wide Web as an e-book. Visit http://www.abc-clio.com for details.

Contents

Contents

Contents

CONTENTS

Contents

Contents

Contents

Contents

CONTENTS

Contents

CONTENTS

Contents

From the *Indian Antiquary*

1924

Contents

Contents

Contents

CONTENTS

ॐ

1NTRODUCTION

I

One of the new forms of generation and communication of knowledge in colonial India was the emergence of ethnographic periodicals, instituted by colonial officers, in the second half of the nineteenth century. They were printed at the government presses and, though not official publications, they were quasi-official in their scope and objective. They were largely "miscellanist" in nature, carrying small notes of information on subjects around which the journal was conceptualized; were generally ethnographic; and were meant essentially for the use of the British residents of India who were also their major contributors and subscribers. One of the first such journals was the *Punjab Notes and Queries* (*PNQ*), instituted by Captain R. C. Temple in 1885. From the onset, the journal refused to accept any writing critical of the government. *PNQ* wished to inform readers about various aspects of India and Indian life, ranging from archaeology to ethnography (Morrison 1984). When the editor of *PNQ*, Captain Temple, was called to lead the military campaign against Burma in 1885, he handed over the journal to his contemporary in the Indian Civil Service, William Crooke.

In William Crooke's hands the periodical was renamed *North Indian Notes and Queries* (*NINQ*). Though it was intended, even by William Crooke, to be a continuation of *PNQ*, *NINQ* differed from its predecessor in many ways. At a time when the study of India was based more and more in philological and archaeological sciences dealing with ancient texts, edicts, coins, and other material remains of ancient India, *NINQ* was to concern itself with the living India, the contemporary India. And in its concern with the real, it placed itself in the rural society—its everyday culture, its age-old customs, its local gods and godlings whose fame remained within the boundaries of the village and around whom no great religious institution existed or had grown—and in the fictional narratives that the rural society enjoyed, transmitted, and produced (Crooke, *NINQ* 1891). Though William Crooke in his theoretical writings advocated a survivalist approach, we see in the organization of *NINQ* that a modern paradigm of anthropology and folktale study was emergent. And this is the first feature in which *NINQ* was unprecedented by any other journal, including *PNQ*.

The difference is not merely formal, but essential to the perspective. And while William Crooke did not write another lengthy editorial after the first "Introductory," the concern with the live and the popular religion and narratives of the rural populace of northern India was a belief that grew with him. Three decades later he held the opinion "that our (British) ignorance of many important aspects of Hinduism is stupendous. Most of the existing manuals are based on the analysis of the sacred books, and the much more vital question, the working everyday faith of the immense rural population, has been studiously ignored." (Crooke Papers, MS 132). While *PNQ* had a rather muddled perspective, *NINQ* was clear and conscious to begin with, and radical in its more matured stages.

Following from this perspective, the clear format of *NINQ* emerged. Unlike its predecessor, it was not a jumble of little notes sent by various British residents of India. After 1893, *NINQ* had only four sections: Popular Religion, Anthropology, Folktales, and Miscellania. The differentiation between Popular Religion and Folktales shows once again the modernity of *NINQ*'s paradigm. Popular religion was also based on storytelling, but *NINQ* differentiated between the religious lore and the social, secular narrative—the folktale, which may have a religious basis but is still essentially different from a religious story.

The fact is that in the Indian context, the western scholars were faced with an overwhelmingly oral culture. Orality cut across the boundaries between the so-called classical and folk cultures. And it is within orality that various types of discourses were located. As Lutz Röhrich has shown in his *Märchen und Wirklichkeit* (*Folktale and Reality*, 2001), legend, myth, and folktale not only are different types of narratives but create different relations between the tellers and narrative. One may "believe" in a legend, but one "enjoys" a folktale. Both are fiction, but they affect people's relation to their reality in different ways at different historical times. And therefore, I consider the differentiation achieved in the format of *NINQ*, and the independence it granted to the folktale, a step that has remained unappreciated for its relative modernity.

The format and perspective of *NINQ* were not the only factors that distinguished it from other colonial ethnographic writing. A crucial difference lies in the fact that almost all the entries in *NINQ* were by Indians. There are hardly any contributions by common British residents. Its section "Folktales" carried narratives told and recorded exclusively by Indians. This is probably the most important distinguishing feature of *NINQ*: A discourse is created here and it is a discourse partly created by Indians themselves. Although there are a vast variety of narrators—cooks, attendants, water carriers, peons, traders (actually small shopkeepers), and others—some of the narrators and those who recorded tales are rather constant and appear again and again. Let me recount a few of those in the following and attempt to place them in their sociohistorical context.

There are many recorded tales that were told by one Akbar Shah Manjhi. As the name reveals, he was a Muslim of the Manjhi, or Manjhwar, community, which is one of the biggest tribes in the Mirzapur District. At the time of collecting these tales, William Crooke was posted as the Revenue Collector of District Mirzapur, which had a large tribal population. These tribes had been of immense interest to Crooke and were the focus of his four-volume work *Tribes and Castes of North India,* published later in 1896. It is therefore not surprising that William Crooke came in contact with Akbar Shah Manjhi in the early 1890s. In his short article written a decade later (Crooke 1902, 302–307) Akbar Shah Manjhi was the only narrator whom he mentioned by name. Crooke described him as

> a quaint old blind man, Akbar Shah Manjhi, who used to support himself by going about to marriages and other feasts and amusing the people by his tales. This old man came readily to my camp, and was quite pleased to stay there indefinitely so long as the camp suttler had an order to provide him with food. He would sit at my tent-door at night and reel off tales ad libitum. The difficulty of understanding his curious patois was successfully overcome, and a large number of tales were taken down in the usual way and translated as opportunity occurred. (Crooke 1902, 306)

True to the repertoire of a professional storyteller, Akbar Shah Manjhi's stories are limited neither by religion nor by themes. He tells tales of Hindu Gods, which are his folk versions of mythological stories, and he tells tales from a famous cycle of tales—like those of Emperor Akbar and his witty Minister Bîrbal—but these are rather unusual tales from the cycle. He narrates about the "virtue of faith" as well as "a tale of two queens." These tales show that Akbar Shah Manjhi's repertoire was very varied. It carried secular narratives, stories based on religion, long legends, and cyclical stories, and he must have been able to narrate to a variety of listeners on a variety of occasions. The North Western Provinces and

Oudh, the present state of Uttar Pradesh, had a mixed population comprising Hindus and Muslims. Though the former were in majority, the influence of Islam in the region has extended beyond the religious, as it was one of the major areas of Mughal rule. And thus the region had been open to Persian influences, from language to stories, since the sixteenth century at least. At the same time the region also comprised the main locales of two great Indian epics—the *Ramayana* and the *Mahabharata*. Akbar Shah Manjhi's name and tales are like a catalog of all these factors. His last name shows his tribal origin, while the first and the middle show that his tribe had converted to Islam. His stories show that the boundaries between all these were fluid, especially as far as a professional storyteller was concerned. His narration to William Crooke is, however, symbolic of his contemporary world: that Akbar Shah Manjhi, a tribal professional storyteller, was narrating to an Englishman, who was the highest colonial official of the district and a representative of the biggest colonial empire. In this moment of narration mentioned by Crooke, when Akbar Shah Manjhi, "the quaint old blind man," must have come either to Crooke's residence in Mirzapur or to his jungle camp, there were centuries of global trade and politics that had made this moment possible—both for William Crooke and for Akbar Shah Manjhi. And in the same moment the tales of this "quaint old blind man" were to be immortalized and communicated across seven seas. The act of the narration of a folktale by an Indian storyteller to a British civil servant was not such a simple, day-to-day event as it seemed. It is not possible to know what the "quaint old blind man" thought of the not-so-young British civil servant, and how much of the communication was really one-to-one. Yet the fact that Akbar Shah Manjhi came back again and again, narrated so many tales, and was remembered by Crooke shows that there was something interesting for him as well, and he probably enjoyed telling his tales to yet another new listener, probably without questioning what the returns were and for whom. In that respect he was certainly "quaint," while Crooke was part of the global economy and power structure. And the process in which they were involved, though from very different positions, connected them in an inseparable manner. Akhbar Shah Manjhi's narrative will always be known in Crooke's mother tongue.

The case of Akbar Shah Manjhi brings many important issues of folkloristics to the fore: one, that the narration of even a traditional oral narrative is an act based in contemporary reality; two, that the collection of folktales by colonial British administrators in India was essentially different from that of their contemporary European folklorists in Europe who were at best differentiated/distanced by class from their narrators and not necessarily by language and culture; and three, that the transformation of orality in the colonial context was transformation not only into literacy but also into another language. The question here is: How was the linguistic transformation achieved? To this we shall return later.

A particular group of people also appears again and again in *NINQ*, though not as a group but as individuals—these are the village schoolteachers. Their recurrence is not accidental, but part of Crooke's plan to collect folktales from village schoolteachers. They were part of the village society but were literate. They could be contacted through the official network of the Education Ministry under whom the village schools functioned. In 1892, Crooke had Mr. Nesfield, director of the Education Department, issue a circular to village schoolteachers asking that they contribute folktales to William Crooke's collection (Rouse 1899, vii). Whether in response to this or due to personal contact with Pandit Râm Gharîb Chaube, a large number of tales were received from all across the province. Though only some of these were published in *NINQ*, they formed an important part of the larger collection. The Village School system was a network of schools established by the colonial state. It was replacing the traditional systems of education, which were based in religious communities and, at least theoretically, provided the same education to everyone. On the other hand, the Village School system was scanty and poorly funded. The teachers in these schools generally did not know English. Since the nineteenth-century urban collector saw the rural populace as the only source of "authentic" folklore, village schoolteachers were considered good allies because they were rural like the narrators and literate enough to communicate with the collectors. In the context of *NINQ*, the teachers were both Hindu and Muslim, though in the case of the former they were invariably upper caste. Colonial India was far away from the integration of lower castes into the education system.

Lower-caste people also form a large number of the narrators in *NINQ*. These were generally service-class people in the civil servant's large staff: cooks, attendants, peons, tailors, and orderlies. This class of people formed the majority of narrators in the overall colonial folktale collection. They were the most approachable, were of rural background, were often illiterate, and could be considered "folk" as per any criterion.

One group of narrators is completely missing from this collection— that of women. William Crooke and Pandit Chaube were conscious of this. Crooke even later lamented the fact that, except for Flora Anne Steel, no British woman had taken to collecting folktales from the best narrators in India—the women: "If we had more ladies as well versed in the native ways and language as Mrs. Steel, no doubt much might be learned from the women, who are the main depositories of knowledge of this kind" (Crooke 1902, 304). Chaube recorded the only tale from a woman narrator to be published in *NINQ*. However, she was only identified as "wife of Ramai Kharwar of Dudhi, Mirzapur District" (*NINQ* 5, no. 12: 210). Woman narrators were not within the reach of male collectors. Interestingly, other sections of *NINQ*—popular religion, anthropology, and folk medicine—carried many notes about women, and even about very intimate practices like cures for swollen breasts or charms against miscarriage. At this point we are only taking note of the absence of women narrators in this folktale collection. However, a century later, I must note, it finds a woman editor in me.

The above listing of narrators is made possible by another unique feature of *NINQ*, which was also found in all other unpublished manuscripts ascribed to William Crooke in two different archives. Every tale carried the following credits and details: tale told by, tale recorded by, their designation or caste or both, and the place where it was recorded. This systematic record of narrators and places is not a characteristic of colonial folklore scholarship and is not followed in such a consistent manner in any other collection. It was generally assumed that the tales were recorded by the British collectors themselves, and the narrators were generally identified as "rustic," "rude," "unlearned," "folk completely free of European influence," etc. A missionary folktale collector had his entire collection illustrated by local artists and the only credit he gave them was "illustrated by native hands" (Swynnerton 1892). No body, no mind, no face, and, of course, no gender.

Like that of people, the identification of place had very limited importance. Generally, the collectors identified only the large regions and their names, like "folktales of Panjab," or "of Deccan," or "of Central India," etc. Beyond this they described the geography in romantic terms. So India had rivers, jungles, mountains, and plains, but not administrative units like the province, the district, the tehsil, or the village. Here again, *NINQ* differs from other colonial folktale collections. It gives dry facts like district, tehsil, and village. And yet, these are the most important facts as they let us see from how many places the tales were sent or collected and how many different dialects were involved, and therefore how representative the collection can be considered. This important feature of *NINQ* gains in meaning when we find that a very large number of districts of the province are represented here by at least a few of their villages. There are a larger number of tales from Mirzapur, where Crooke and Pandit Chaube were based.

This descriptive analysis raises many questions: If there are so many villages, people, and dialects involved, then in what language were the materials received? If Crooke heard the tales, as it seems likely in the case of Akhbar Shah Manjhi, then who was recording it? Did Crooke understand Hindi, and dialects of Hindi? Did he understand them so well as to be able to translate from them? What accounts for the uniqueness of *NINQ*?

In the next section of this introduction, I will study the printed journal with its manuscript materials in order to be able to answer the above questions.

II

NINQ made its first appearance in April 1891. Its editor, William Crooke, Esq., C. S., of Mirzapur (*NINQ*) saw it as a continuation of *PNQ*, yet renamed it and spelled out a new program and perspective in the first and the only editorial "Introductory," which appeared in the first issue. He listed out eight subjects of interest, adding especially those types of information on subjects that did not already form parts of the official information-gathering bodies like the Archaeological Survey of India. He also lamented the inaccessibility of information contained in regularly produced volumes like the *Settlement Reports*.

However, the first issue of *NINQ* was not exactly in keeping with the intentions expressed in the "Introductory." Though there were a lot of entries by William Crooke himself, these mainly about the tribal peoples of south Mirzapur, the majority of the entries were taken from already published settlement reports, from gazetteers of various districts, and even from the report of the inspector general of police. Some entries were taken from major works on India by British authors. The selections were interesting and published in a readable format, but at this stage *NINQ* lacked the spark of originality and clarity that characterizes its post–September 1892 issues. In 1891, *NINQ* seemed to be clearing the materials collected for *PNQ* and striving to generate materials for itself. It thus carried information about any part of India, and very little about the North Western Provinces. This format of *NINQ* continued almost unchanged for the first six months. In subsequent issues some sections from the original plan were dropped, such as Numismatics and Ethnology, and reappeared only occasionally. The constant sections of *NINQ* were Popular Religion, Anthropology, Anglo-India, and Folklore. In the first five months of *NINQ* there was no clear and scientific differentiation between Popular Religion and Folklore. The Folklore section carried not folktales but notes on omens, agricultural practices, charms against diseases, etc.

The first "folktale" appeared in the September 1891 issue, was titled "The Barber and the Demon. A Folktale told by Lachhman Ahir, cultivator of Mirzapur," and carried an important footnote from the editor William Crooke: "This is the first of a series of original folktales recorded from the lips of peasants in Mirzapur and literally translated" (*NINQ*, Sept. 1891: 99).

This declaration is the only sign that, starting late in 1891, Crooke was trying to make a systematic collection of the folktales. This collection was to be original and tales were to be collected from the cultivators. Who else could be the first choice of narrators for a District Revenue Collector if not the cultivators from whom the agricultural revenue was already being "collected" and toward which the entire bureaucracy of the Indian Civil Service was organized? However, as it turned out in the following issues, this declaration was more a sign of Crooke's intentions at this point than a working plan. *NINQ*'s section "Folklore" continued to carry a confused jumble of notes, and only a few folktales appeared, those also erratically. In the next ten issues (October 1891–July 1892) some carried one or two, at best three, folktales, while others carried none. By July 1892, it would have seemed to an interested reader of *NINQ* that the "original series" declared in September 1891, ten months earlier, had been forgotten. However, the few tales that were published had names of narrators and those who recorded them. One of the two people recording the tales was Karam-ud-din of Mirzapur, who seems to be from Crooke's clerical staff and who collected a few tales from a Muslim cook woman, also of the staff. The other was E. David, in all probability the same person whom Crooke mentioned in his article a decade later as "a native Christian clerk in my own office, who, of course, knew the vernacular Hindustani, but little or no English. . . . This man had the excellent quality of being too great a fool and possessed of too little imagination to render it possible for him to do much harm. He got me a number of tales from an old cook-woman" (Crooke 1902, 305).

And Crooke "could not suffer fools" (grandson Patrick Crooke, 2001). Temple says the same, that Crooke was not "able to bear fools" (Temple 1924, 4). One of Crooke's notebooks has the following quote in his own handwriting: "Blessed is the man who having nothing to say, abstains from firing us with wordy evidence of the fact. G. Elliot Theophrastus" (Crooke Papers, MS 134). Crooke's conversations with this Indian-Christian assistant must have been reflective of a sinister colonial comedy in which identities were enmeshed between racial, religious, cultural, and administrative hierarchies.

However, what Crooke had to say about the cook woman is interesting in the way he refers to his narrator as "friend," and the comment specifies his theoretical understanding of folktales and their dispersion:

> I have never read a stronger instance in support of my old arguments, that in the incidents of the story and not in the thread of a story is to be found the true folklore tradition. Our friend Mahtabo, the cook, has jumbled together, in the most interesting fashion to the 'folklorist', an extraordinary number of incidents properly belonging to different classes of tales. (Crooke Papers, MS 124; Offprint of a folktale published by Crooke in *Indian Antiquary*, June 1892)

One of the other frequent narrators was a weaver. It is obvious that Crooke would have gotten to know all these people in connection with his official position and duties, and they were all subordinates of one kind or another.

If we connect Crooke's listed frustrations in the collection of folklore with the erratic pace of folktale publication in *NINQ*, we realize that in 1891 Crooke was intending and trying to begin a systematic collection of folktales, but was largely unable to do so with his own capabilities, which were limited by a lack of knowledge of the language and dialects of the region, and by the kind of assistance available to him. Moreover, there seemed to be no growth in the theoretical differentiation between folktales and other narratives. His intention had been to collect from the cultivators (who would have been living outside the town of Mirzapur), but a majority of the handful of tales had been narrated by a Muslim cook woman and a Christian Ayah, and a couple by a cultivator. The cooks, ayahs, peons, orderlies, and even cultivators formed the regular stock of narrators for the British collectors because of contact with them through work or domestic labor, and were thus those most easily accessible. The pace of the publication of the declared "series" shows that those who were collecting and presenting an English version were either too slow or presented such crude versions that the editor needed to work a lot on them, or both. And thus, the intended folktale series was not able to take off for twelve months, until August 1892.

In September 1892, *NINQ* had a new entry—that of a new name: Pandit Râm Gharîb Chaube. There was a contribution by him, titled "Eastern Districts, NWP—Spells used by village exorcisors" (94–95) in the section Popular Religion. The text had been transcribed in Roman script and translated into English. It was "scientific" in its linguistic and anthropological approach. The writer of this text, Râm Gharîb Chaube, was to appear with an ever increasing number of entries in all the sections of *NINQ*. And although in this September 1892 issue of the periodical this was his "only" entry, two of the three folktales in the section "Folklore" carry the unmistakable style of Râm Gharîb Chaube as seen in the hundreds of manuscripts in his handwriting. This issue also had a remarkable news item in the section "Anglo-India"—that G. Lawrence Gomme had taken over as president of the Folklore Society in London from Andrew Lang, the bitter critic of Benfy's theory that European folktales had their origin in the Indian folktales (Dorson 1968, 282, 305–306). Interestingly, the corresponding entry of Pandit Râm Gharîb Chaube in *NINQ*, though as a nondistinguishable contributor at this stage, was to mark a turning point in the story of the colonial periodical *NINQ*. In the following months there were more and more original articles by Chaube and Crooke and an increasing numbers of folktales. Chaube was missing from the immediately following issues, but Crooke suddenly started publishing folk songs recorded by him but credited to Crooke. These were given in the dialect and in translation. In January 1893, just three months later, Pandit Râm Gharîb Chaube became a regular feature of *NINQ*, having among his contributions a long legend, an explanation of prefixes, and a popular Hindi verse/song. *NINQ* also began to have an increasing number of "folktales," mainly credited to E. David and Karam-ud-din.

In March 1893, *NINQ* was published with major changes in its format: It now had only four sections: Popular Religion, Anthropology, Folktales, and Miscellanea. This overall change reflects a sharper focus on areas of interest, as well as a clear distinction between closely related areas like popular religion, anthropology, and folktales. The changes in *NINQ* were limited not only to classification, but also to the contents. In the past few months, *NINQ* had been publishing more and more original entries, and from March 1893 this is the defining characteristic of *NINQ*. Both in content and in style, the baggage of *PNQ* had been dropped.

The most significant of these changes for us is the change of the section titled "Folklore" to "Folktales." In the same issue tales narrated by Akbar Shah Manjhi were begun and recorded by Pandit Râm Gharîb Chaube. As these continue through the following issues, it can be said that the publication of the series of "original" folktale recordings that Crooke had announced took off only in March 1893 and that Chaube, who had joined Crooke in 1892, was the major difference between Crooke's earlier and later attempts to collect folktales. And as I reconsidered Crooke's memory of the narrator Akbar Shah Manjhi and juxtaposed Chaube's recordings of Akbar Shah Manjhi's narratives in the colonial situative context of folktale collection, I realized that in that historical moment when Akbar Shah Manjhi came again and again to narrate his tales in the presence of a British administrator, it was Râm Gharîb Chaube who was recording Akbar Shah Manjhi for posterity!

From March 1893 onward every issue of *NINQ* carried many folktales with and without crediting Chaube. Folktales published in *NINQ* had not only one consistent format, but also a style of narrating that is unmistakably his. However, *NINQ* carried in its other sections a large number of entries by Chaube and Crooke, and these were original recordings too, no longer culled from settlement reports and similar official documents. With the added participation of Pandit Chaube, *NINQ* had really come into its own.

These "Folktales of Northern India" were collected, translated, and compiled in the contemporary state of Uttar Pradesh. The main language of the region is Hindi, but dialects abound and change every few hundred kilometers. Uttar Pradesh is one of the largest Indian states, where the fertile plains of major rivers have been the basis of a largely agricultural society. The region was also the epicenter of a peasants' and soldiers' revolt against British rule in 1857. The tales of this collection reflect the tapestry of social and personal lives and beliefs of the population, albeit colored by late-nineteenth-century colonial anthropological perceptions. In other words certain aspects of social life, like the caste, and of personal life, like superstitions, are emphasized to correspond with the larger belief in the primitive and survivalist nature of Indian village life. And yet, in Râm Gharîb Chaube's articulation, the tales connect back to their native roots, moods, and meanings.

The first three issues of 1893 (January through March) show a very quick transformation of *NINQ* from an advanced version of *PNQ* to a periodical unparalleled in its time. The changes in this period reflect both the real possibilities and the intended plan. By March 1893, a plan emerges that remains constant until the last issues of *NINQ* in 1896. And within this plan, a major shift in the study of India happens: Not only did *NINQ* carry original entries, but it was henceforth constituted of entries by Indians. Entries by British residents were either specific ones, like the studies by R. Greeven, or only occasional. Any other colonial periodical, such as *Indian Antiquary* (*IA*) or even *PNQ*, always had an overwhelming number of entries, if not the entire issue, written by Europeans. *NINQ* not only generated information about "Indians," but also involved some of them in the process of its articulation. It is obvious from the details of the narrators and those who recorded them that the narratives could not have been sent as English language texts. The question arises as to how and by whom *NINQ* was "written" or authored. This question can be answered only by a study of the manuscript papers and other documents archived as the "William Crooke Papers" in the Royal Anthropological Institute (RAI), London.

III

There are two types of manuscript materials for *NINQ*: one, the texts of folktales; and two, the texts and notes related to all other sections of *NINQ*. Along with these are Crooke's diaries and notebooks. In the following we shall consider these in the above sequence.

Almost all the tales published in *NINQ* carry names of those who narrated and recorded them. The placement of this information varies: it appears along with the title, at the end of the tale, or as footnotes. This has been kept as such in this volume to reflect the evolution of the *NINQ* pattern. Some tales also carry comments by William Crooke, which are signed "Ed." Comments signed "Ed." in the second portion of this volume, tales from the *Indian Antiquary,* are from Richard Carnac Temple, the editor of that journal. The study of the manuscripts reveals additional realities about this folktale collection. The most striking of these, which lends a new meaning to this folktale collection, is that all the information regarding the tellers, the folktale texts, and the comments are in the handwriting of Pandit Râm Gharîb Chaube. The titles in the left margin, however, are in William Crooke's handwriting.

Not all of these texts were even published in *NINQ*, like some long versified legends that Chaube is known to have specially collected for William Crooke from singers in the western parts of the province. Crooke also acknowledged in *IA* that Râm Gharîb Chaube had been collecting folk songs for him for some years. We find some folk songs published in *NINQ*, but not too many. In the manuscripts we find long versified legends that could also be loosely called folk songs. These have probably remained unpublished. One of them, titled by Chaube "The Legend of Raja Karuk," runs one hundred fifty handwritten pages, and is transcribed and translated, interspersed with Chaube's explanatory commentary. It opens with a personal note:

> In the western districts of North Western Provinces there is a
> class of people who sing the songs of Raja Karuk. They are
> chiefly jogis but sometimes other men who are as illiterate and
> beggarly as the jogis also sing those songs. I have managed to
> collect them and give them below with their English translation
> for the readers of *North Indian Notes and Queries* hoping that
> they would find them interesting. (Crooke Papers, MS 124)

Unfortunately, the text seems not to have reached the readers of *NINQ*. It is, however, an exuberant model of Pandit Chaube's linguistic and literary sensitivity and folkloric knowledge. It shows why William Crooke's plan of "original" recordings of folktales was realized and expanded from being a collection from cultivators of Mirzapur to one of folktales from the entire province and from specific groups, including professional storytellers, after Chaube joined him in 1892.

The other manuscript materials relate to all other sections of *NINQ*. Most of these exist as typed texts on paper of various sizes, because strips of notes were torn away as per the length of the note. They are kept as bunches whereby notes around a subject are stuck together at the margins. Let us consider some of these "bunches" as examples:

Example 1: On the theme of "Marriage, rituals, kinship and joking relationships" there are many handwritten texts by Chaube and Crooke, and also typed texts sourced at other works and related to China, Africa, and Melanasia.

Example 2: A handwritten note by Râm Gharîb Chaube on "Children's

Teeth." To this are stuck many typed notes that are references to similar or comparable practices elsewhere in the world.

Example 3: A large bunch of papers has a long text by Pandit Râm Gharîb Chaube titled "Popular prayer and legends about the Sun-God or Surya Narayan." The text has small stylistic changes made in red ink. So Chaube's "They have much faith in the Sun-God in the N. W. Provinces . . ." is changed to "Natives of Northern India have. . . ." There is a note in brackets below the main text in Crooke's handwriting: "[The conception of sun as the giver of offspring and remover of leprosy is interesting. In many countries women expose themselves naked to the sun in the hope . . .]."

Example 4: One text in Chaube's handwriting. Title written on another piece of paper and stuck on top, in Crooke's handwriting "Bihar: the legend of a saint." In the left margin a note in Chaube's handwriting "To the Editor of *North Indian Notes and Queries.* 19/3/95" is struck off in Crooke's ink. At the end of the text appears the name "Bhupendra Nath Gupta." The process is clear: the text had been contributed by Gupta, translated and prepared for *NINQ* by Chaube, and sent to Crooke with the note. Crooke had pasted a new title on the original, struck off the note to himself—"Editor,"—and sent it for publication. The text is even dated (Crooke Papers, MS 131).

Other types of related materials are Crooke's diaries and notebooks. All these are full of bibliographical references to various anthropological, ethnological, and folkloristic works. Crooke wrote on any type of paper and in any type of notebook. One of them is especially interesting: references on small bits of paper are pasted over the female models in a booklet advertising fur coats (Crooke Papers, MS 134). In the war years, 1914 to 1917, Crooke wrote on any paper he could find, including letters of information from rail and gas companies and from publishers.

Though these three types of papers can clearly be divided into two types—original texts and bibliographical references—they are part of the same whole because they are related to each other. In the original texts, which are often the final texts meant for publication, there is a communication between the two types of materials and the two men in whose handwriting/typed scripts the entire materials of *NINQ* are. It is possible that some of the texts have remained unpublished. But all these English language texts of Indian folklore are the work of Pandit Râm Gharîb Chaube and William Crooke. The papers leave no doubt that, when *NINQ* got free of the need to publish from elsewhere, the two of them did the work for every issue. This is probably why, apart from the editor, it is only Pandit Râm Gharîb Chaube as contributor whose independent tone is part of his contributions. In the following comments on texts, Chaube's style is indistinguishable from that of the editor of *NINQ*, William Crooke:

> This is one of the "Faithful Animal" type of tales. The Ahir is in the proverbial wisdom of the country-side universally regarded as treacherous and ungrateful. The reference to the human sacrifice in honour of the goddess Devi is noteworthy. (Crooke Papers, MS 124)

> The tale is interesting in two ways especially. It is an example of the old custom of polyandry. "It is an illustration of the popular belief that the houses which are not illuminated in the evening are cursed. . . . It is an instance of marriages between high-castes and low-castes which was of common occurrence in olden times" (Crooke Papers, MS 124).

There are also some notes interesting in themselves, and reflective of some lighter sides of the collectors.
By Crooke:

> Rural incantations. This morning I visited the hermitage of a saint named Gulab Shah at Faizabad in Sahâranpur District. He says he is two hundred years old and has high reputation in the neighborhood. Not long ago he was seen walking over Jamuna (river) while it was in high flood with his bundle of grain which he had obtained as alms on his head. He tells me that when they bring sick children to him he breaks off a leaf from the Bel tree which overhangs his hermitage and flinging it into the air says to the disease—*Bhago haramzada*—"Clear out you rascal." This is always effectual. W. Crooke.

By Chaube:

> A Charm to turn wine into milk. Faqirs have a charm for turning wine into milk. They get an ounce of the flowers of the mango and two ounces of cow hoofs. These ground together and a little put into country (illicit) liquor will turn it into milk. (Crooke Papers, MS 131/14)

NINQ changed with the entry of Râm Gharîb Chaube, and the archival papers show none other than he as coauthor and coeditor of *NINQ* with William Crooke. The papers catalogued as "William Crooke Papers" in the RAI Archive in London contain more folkloric texts in the handwriting of Pandit Râm Gharîb Chaube than in that of William Crooke and bear testimony to the fact that Chaube was an unusually prolific scholar. He knew languages; his English translations were poetic; he collected oral songs, stories, narratives of beliefs, superstitions, and herbal medicine (Crooke Papers, MS 131/1; *NINQ* 1893–96); and he translated not only his own collected items, but also all the other texts sent by readers of *NINQ* and respondents to the Department of Education circular. The number of these runs into the thousands, and together they overwhelm a postcolonial researcher who knows that Râm Gharîb Chaube does not exist in the catalog of any library or archives, neither in the United Kingdom nor in India.

IV

The tales collected by Chaube and Crooke were later also published in *Indian Antiquary* (*IA*), which was edited by Richard Carnac Temple. A biographical obituary in the *Proceedings of the British Academy* (1924) was written by Temple, wherein we are told that "Crooke left behind him a quantity of undigested material of great worth, songs and tales of the Indian people and the like, now in the hands of myself [Temple], Mr. H. A. Rose, and my colleague in the editing of *Indian Antiquary*, Mr. S. M. Edwardes, and we hope in due course to prepare it all for the press" (Temple 1924, 579). There is no way of knowing whether Temple and others published all of what was left, but it is certain that the tales published in *Indian Antiquary* after Crooke's death and included in this volume are from the materials mentioned by Temple. These tales were collected simultaneously with those published in *North Indian Notes and Queries*. They have the same methodological and structural design and are the results of the combined activity of William Crooke and Pandit Râm Gharîb Chaube. Of course, in *IA*, Pandit Chaube is not mentioned as Crooke's associate and the tales were published as collected by William Crooke.

Temple and Crooke had been contemporaries in India. Both arrived there in 1871, Temple in the army and Crooke in the Indian Civil Service (ICS). More than being contemporaries, their association was due to similar interests—that of studying Indian folklore. Temple instituted the first ethnographic journal—*PNQ*—and is well remembered for his three-volume work *Legends of Punjab* (1884–1885). Temple handed *PNQ* over to William Crooke when he took up the editorship of *Indian Antiquary* in 1887. He remained at this position until his death in 1931, and summed up this experience thus:

> *We've struggled, you and I, for fifty years*
> *To pierce the veil of mystery, that lies*
> *On India's past so heavily, and cries*
> *Aloud for rending with the seracher's shears.*
> (Temple, MSS Eur F, 98/59)

Temple's and Crooke's writings not only differ from each other, but are essentially divergent in their perspective toward the colonized subjects and their folklore. Temple's expansive militaristic and administrative experience on the Indian subcontinent culminated in his reflecting "On the Practical Value of Anthropology":

> [The object of] Anthropological Studies . . . is to add a working knowledge of mankind to the equipment of those already possessed of a matured . . . acquaintance with science or literature generally. . . . What is the good of Prehistoric Anthropology, for instance, or of Comparative Religion, to an undergraduate. . . . Before those freshly passed through an English University there is a very wide field spread. . . . Year by year whole batches of them are destined to go forth to all parts of the world to find a livelihood; to find places where work lucrative, dignified, and useful awaits them; to find themselves also in a human environment, strange, alien and utterly unlike anything in their experience. Will not a sound grounding anthropology be a help to such as these? . . . It matters nothing that they be civil servants, missionaries, merchants, or soldiers.
> (Temple 1904, No. 11, 223–225)

Crooke's experience of intense research in India integrated with his perception of the science and made him realize the need for its development: "Anthropology, a new and progressive science, must occasionally revise its doctrines, and this is particularly the case in India where it is hampered by the use of certain terms which obscure the facts and impede the solution of its cardinal problems. Here, as elsewhere, the fallacy that identity of language implies identity of race still flourishes" (Crooke Papers, MS 132).

Though this comparative is not an essential subject here, it needs to be mentioned because *IA* differed hugely from *NINQ*. *IA* was the high status journal of Indology and oriental studies. Though it concerned itself with ethnography, that was only one of its areas amongst others like archaeology. At retirement Temple was knighted and headed major scholarly bodies and publications. He was the president of the Jubilee Congress of the Folklore Society in 1928 when a journalist-interviewer titled an article "The Chief of Fairy-Tale Men" and introduced Temple thus: "What is he like, the chief of the fairy-tale men? What sort of person would spend so many years hunting after myths and goblins, and tracking to their lairs the fugitive demons and bogeys of legend? A romantic? He would not admit. A dreamer? Nothing of the sort." (Temple, Eur F98/10) Sir Temple could not have been "a romantic and dreamer folklorist" after heading several military campaigns and a tortuous penal settlement for the rebels of the British Raj in India.

When Crooke died in 1923 in England, Temple wrote his biography for the British Academy and seemed to know better when he recorded that Crooke had been "too outspoken a critic of the Secretariats—the ruling power in India in his day . . ." (Temple: 1924, 1):

> Despite his [Crooke's] intimate knowledge of India and its inhabitants, his was an uneventful career officially, though it was a strenuous one, and he could not win the promotion to which his usual acquirements entitled him. . . . But official disapproval cannot affect a man's capabilities for putting the result of his researches on paper, and here Crooke was beyond the reach of his superiors in office. . . . He was always willing to help research in these directions in any way open to him, and he loved it for its own sake. But in this side of his life—its unofficial side—he was never in any way pushing and reaped but little renown or recognition, and what of these came his way came late in life. . . ." (Temple 1924, 576–577)

Temple's and Crooke's "career" graphs had indeed been rather different, as had also the totality of their scholarly productions. Yet, however Temple may have judged success and failure, Crooke summed up his own experience of studying India thus: "Now as I look back on many happy years spent in India my only regret is that these opportunities were not used to better purpose" (Crooke Papers, MS 132).

V

In 1896, William Crooke applied for retirement, was granted it, and returned to England after twenty-five years of Service in India, all of which were spent in the North Western Provinces and Oudh. Along with the promised high pension of Indian Civil Service, he had earned himself the reputation of a scholar of popular religion and folklore of northern India. His work was known to his contemporaries, and in the writings of many other similarly inclined civil servants immense respect for Crooke's work, especially for his collection of folklore, is evident (Rouse 1899). In other areas of life, however, matters were different. In official circles he had also gained the label of "critic of the Secretariat" and was not a favorite of the colonial state. On the home front, wife and sons remained in awe of him but distanced, leaving him to work in his study. As I investigated the memories of his grandsons, Hugh and Patrick Crooke (1999 and 2001), they told me that they were born in the years following Crooke's death in 1923, but that their grandmother, who was much younger than Crooke, lived with them. She recounted to them that after her marriage to William Crooke they had gone on a winter tour across the district, during which Crooke would be busy with his magisterial duties through the days and in the evenings would sit under a tree where he was visited by village folk who came to tell him songs and stories. Hugh Crooke hesitantly put it, "Well, it was a strange marriage" (1999). And Patrick Crooke said that his grandmother respected her husband's work but did not understand it. Moreover, Crooke spent his retirement years in scholarly production and wrote and edited works specially connected to India. He received an honorary doctorate from Oxford University and was president of the Folklore Society from 1911 to 1912. It is surprising that he did not put his mammoth collection of folktales in a single volume. Some of them were published in *Indian Antiquary*.

Research into Pandit Râm Gharîb Chaube's biography reveals that his life also changed due to Crooke's retirement. Chaube had been on a high salary paid by William Crooke, but he was otherwise not employed. He was as educated as Crooke and had for four years, from 1892 to 1896, dedicated his days and nights not only to *NINQ*, but also to other works of

Crooke. When Crooke left, he tried to work with other "administrator-scholars," but was unable to continue for long because nobody else treated him like Crooke had—with concern and mutual respect (Crooke Papers, MS 139). There had been space for his intellectual expression, even though he did not receive the credit that was due to him. And yet, he could not stop documenting the culture of his land, even though the infrastructures required were no longer at his disposal. Keshavchandra Shukl's biography of Hindi literateur Ram Chandra Shukl (1952) tells us something about Pandit Râm Gharîb Chaube: that through many desperate attempts at employment, and escapes from the same, Chaube realized the historical anonymity that had been imposed on him and his scholarship in the colonial power structures of knowledge. He had admired Crooke for his knowledge and Crooke had appreciated and encouraged his immense capabilities, but for some reason Crooke did not adequately acknowledge Chaube in his published works (1892 and 1896). In a letter from Chaube, written to Crooke in 1900, there is admiration based on the memories of their collecting folklore together in India. When contrasted with the memories of Crooke's family members, it seems ironic that only Chaube's letter brings Crooke out as a very compassionate, intense, and scholarly person. After 1896, Crooke neither published the mammoth collection of folktales nor acknowledged Chaube elsewhere. In spite of their intense scholarly association, which produced a vast amount of scholarship, they were divided by the power structures of nations and colonialism. William Crooke was a British civil servant, and Pandit Râm Gharîb Chaube was a free-spirited intellectual, albeit of a colonized country. His intellectual work had to be expressed via William Crooke, and Chaube was left neither with materials nor with fame. In this historical trap he had found a William Crooke, who allowed him much free space, and to whom he gave his intellectual passion and labor, but Chaube could not escape the pain of this objectively unfair exchange. Pandit Râm Gharîb Chaube is known to have gone insane before his death in 1914. He was a bachelor and had no descendants. *NINQ* and William Crooke also did not find scholarly successors, and the prolific Pandit became anonymous, except in the handwritten manuscripts in the archives in London, where his identity and scholarship have remained concealed for more than a century, and in the collective memory of his village. It is possible that Crooke kept the folktale manuscripts carefully due to their scholarly value, but he also kept Chaube's letter, and these two together lead back to the forgotten Pandit. It makes one wonder whether Crooke too was indeed unaware of the pain of an unfair exchange. "Many of these fields of research are closed to Europeans, partly owing to their defective linguistic training, partly to want of time, partly because they are confronted with a myriad taboos which it is difficult to overcome. Much of this work must be left to the new generation of Indian scholars, who alone have the privilege of admission behind the veil which shrouds these mysteries. *Needless to say, we already owe much to them, and we may confidently expect that they will not fail to utilise the opportunities which they already possess*" (Crooke Papers, MS 132; emphasis added).

Crooke was right. Chaube had given all his intellectual passion in spite of the constraints of the situation. There are probably many more Chaubes buried in "scholarly" files of colonial British administrators, soldiers, missionaries, and women.

Conclusion

What the folktales in this volume and the study of their source—*NINQ* and its manuscripts—show is an unusual example of colonial scholarship, whereby the so-called native is an active agent in the process of globalization of his native culture. In the native's own intellectual history, this is a stage whereby he sees his nativity with a western scientific distance. His nativity merges with the "scientific" method, but his "view" is not that of the western scholar, as can be seen in this note on popular religion by Chaube, wherein the writing on a village goddess becomes a report of the village and the involvement of the writer, a complete documentary format:

> Cholera caused by an offended deity: This year cholera has prevailed in my village Gopalpur in the Gorakhpur District. This is very generally attributed to the anger of the local goddess. . . . I have several times advised people to clean up their houses, so as to please the goddess during her mighty rambles which she takes through the village, but to no avail. No one can say how long she may continue persecuting this unfortunate village. (*NINQ*: V/11 1896, 184)

The personal involvement and emotion of the native scholar subvert the scientific distance of the "imperial gaze" (Pratt 1992). William Crooke was not the only active agent in the process of globalization. This understanding challenges the discourse that has emerged under the influence of Edward Said's *Orientalism* (1977) and has stressed the role of European orientalists alone in the construction of the "orient." And although the differential power position of the orientalists and their native associates cannot be denied, the singularity of agency in this construction cannot be sustained. Widening the scope of postcolonial theory, Ian Adam and Helen Tiffin suggest that "post-colonialism can be characterized as having two archives, related but not co-extensive." One of these is the literary writings from the erstwhile colonized countries that reflect "the subordinating power of European colonialism" and the other "a set of discursive practices involving resistance to colonialism [and] colonialist ideologies . . ." (1991, 5). However, this "useful formulation" of postcolonial writing is based on a certain perception of the colonial constructions. The same has been termed "colonial mower" by Spivak and postcolonialism has been seen as "aftermath" (Adam and Tiffin 1991, 5–6). Based in literary theory, these formulations face a challenge from the processes of textualization of orality in the colonial context. The postcolonial writings in the fields of anthropology and history also see the "native assistants" as lackeys of their British associates (Raheja 1996). The identity of Pandit Chaube does not fit into any established niche of "native assistant," nor William Crooke's into one of an all-powerful, ruthless orientalist. There is, for example, no evidence of William Crooke knowing Hindi beyond a few words. In this situation, how could he control the initial flow of information, or how could he check any censorship that the person recording may have applied? And of course, the narrators as well as all others involved were aware of Crooke also as British administrator. All his constructions would have had to emerge from this premise. Theoretically, this applies to all colonial scholars, though space for individual strategies was probably varied, in a sense akin to what Mary Louis Pratt (1992) has called the "contact zone." In the context of Peru, Pratt's contact zone "refers to the space of colonial encounters, the space in which peoples geographically and historically separated come into contact with each other and establish ongoing relations, usually involving conditions of coercion, radical inequality, and intractable conflict . . ." (Adam and Tiffin 1991, 6). However, the colonial process itself generated knowledge that fused linguistic and geographical boundaries and could be simultaneously available across continents. After the first year of its publication *NINQ* was published simultaneously every month in India and in England. And thus, though his contributions were largely undeclared, readers across the continents were reading Indian folktales in Râm Gharîb Chaube's language.

None of the colonial collections were ever published in the original language, and this folktale record of northern India too is in English only. The prospect of a global village interconnected by information technology in the English language has caused many languages to feel threatened. This linguistic dominance of English in the postmodern and postcolonial cultures is based in the linguistic geography of the colonial world. Indian folklore was textualized in English and made available internationally in the second half of the nineteenth century. This poses both a challenge and an advantage to students of Indian folklore worldwide. The linguistic aspect of the colonial collections of Indian folklore is shared by folklore collections from the entire colonial world. England was the first recipient of vast amounts of folklore from its colonies in Asia and Africa and was thus considered the biggest collector in the late nineteenth century. The modern study of Asian and African folklore is closely connected to the processes of colonialism, especially in the fields of culture and education. These records of oral traditions were most often the first written records of these cultures. Their collection, translation, and compilation could not have been possible without the contribution of native scholars. Yet the language of their publication was English, and British men and women have been considered their "folklorists." This is an unchangeable reality of colonial folklore collections. If the linguistic loss is in any way displacement of culture, then it is irreversible. However, if it is seen as a particular methodological and ideological process of textualizing orality, then the unique features of this particular process appear. First, it is a multilingual process. Second, its essential character is very international and intercultural. Third, it creates new connections between oral cultures of different continents. And finally, the feature that defines all colonial collections from anywhere in the world is that they were intended as international publications.

What got deleted from proper records in this process was the involvement of the native scholars and other people. How far this deletion was intentional, or simply based in the current perceptions, is relatively a meaningless question, that is, relative to the fact of the deletion itself and its consequences. It seems that half a century of independence for many of the erstwhile colonized countries has not been long enough to deconstruct their own image. It also seems that postcolonial theory too has not yet been able to deal with the question of such deletions. Pandit Râm Gharîb Chaube is probably the first native scholar and associate of a British folklorist whose identity I have been able to explore, and to the best of my knowledge, no other study of the role of a native scholar in colonial folklore collection has appeared. The consequences of the deletion have apparently been severe, as it is now difficult to reconstruct the identities. Pandit Chaube's insanity not only is a personal tragedy, but is symbolic of the consequential nature of certain aspects of colonial scholarships that have either been looked over or not questioned. His emergence also changes the nature of our understanding of these tale texts. They are texts negotiated between Chaube's nativity and Crooke's foreignness. Colonialism linked globally not only trade, but also cultures and knowledge. The voluminous collections of folklore from the Indian subcontinent have been its major expression since the middle of the nineteenth century.

Sadhana Naithani
Jawaharlal Nehru University
New Delhi
April 2002

Bibliography

Adam, Ian, and Helen Tiffin, eds. 1991. *Past the Lost Post: Theorising Post-Colonialism and Post-Modernism.* New York: Harvester Wheatsheaf.

Bonser, Wilfrid. 1961. *A Bibliography of Folklore as Contained in the First Eighty Years of the Publications of the Folklore Society (1878–1957).* London: William Glaisher.

———. 1969. *A Bibliography of Folklore for 1958–1967. Being a Subject Index Vols. 69–78 of the Journal, Folklore.* London: William Glaisher.

Crooke, Hugh. August 6, 1999. Telephone interview, London. Written from immediate memory.

Crooke, Patrick. June 26, 2001. Recorded interview, Wingham, Canterbury.

Crooke, William. 1894. *The Popular Religion and Folklore of Northern India.* 2 vols. Allahabad Government Publication.

———. 1896. *The Tribes and Castes of the North Western Provinces.* 4 Vols. Calcutta: Office of the Superintendent of Government Printing.

———. 1897. *The North Western Provinces of India: Their History, Ethnology and Administration.* London: Methuen.

———. "Correspondence. The Collection of Folklore." 1902. *Folklore* 13: 302–307.

———. William Crooke Papers. Uncatalogued. London: Royal Anthropological Institute. MS 124–139: Letters, Note Books, Diaries, Manuscripts, Miscellaneous Papers.

Crooke, William, ed. 1891–1896. *North Indian Notes and Queries.* A Monthly Periodical Devoted to the Systematic Collection of Authentic Notes and Scraps of Information Regarding the Country and the People. Allahabad: "Pioneer" Press; London: Archibald and Company.

Dorson, Richard M. 1968. *The British Folklorists.* Chicago: Chicago University Press.

Morrison, Charles. 1984 "Three Systems of Imperial Ethnography. British Official as Anthropologist in India." Pp. 141–169 in: *Knowledge and Society. Studies in So-*

ciology of Culture Past and Present. Ed. Henrika Kuklick and Elizabeth Long. Greenwich and Connecticut: JAI Press.

Naithani, Sadhana. 1997. "The Colonizer Folklorist." *Journal of Folklore Research* 34, no. 1: 1–14.

———. 2001. "Prefaced Space. Tales of the Colonial British Collectors of Indian Folklore." Pp. 64–79 in *Imagined States. Nationalism Longing and Utopia in Oral Cultures.* Ed. Luisa Guidice and Gerald Porter. Logan: University of Utah Press.

———. 2002. "To Tell A Tale Untold." *Journal of Folklore Research* 39, no. 2–3 (May–December).

Pratt, Mary Louise. 1992. *Imperial Eyes.* London; New York: Routledge.

Raheja, Gloria Goodwin. 1996. "Caste, Colonialism, and the Speech of the Colonized: Entextualisation and Disciplinary Control in India." *American Ethnologist* 23, no. 3: 494–513.

Röhrich, Lutz. 2001. *Märchen und Wirklichkeit.* 5. Aufl. Baltmannsweiler: Schneider Verlag Hohengehren: 9, 36.

Rose, H. A. 1924. "In Memoriam: William Crooke (1848–1923)." *Folklore* 34: 382–385.

Rouse, W. H. D. 1899. *The Talking Thrush And Other Tales From India.* Collected by William Crooke and Retold by W. H. D. Rouse. London: J. M. Dent.

Shukl, Chandrashekhar. 1952. *Ramchandra Shukl Jeevan aur Krititva.* Varanasi Vanivitan Prakashan.

Shukl, Keshavchandra. 1952. *Acharya Ramchandra Shukl Jeevanvrat evam Sansmaran.* Varanasi Vanivitan.

Swynnerton, Rev. Charles. 1892. *Indian Nights' Entertainment: Folk Tales from the Upper Indus. With Numerous Illustrations by Native Hands.* London: Elliot Stock.

Temple, R. C. 1856–1931. Temple Collection IORL MSS EUR.F.98: Manuscripts of the "Legends of Punjab," Letters, Papers, Newspaper Cuttings, Literary Remains and Maps.

———. 1904. "On the Practical Value of Anthropology." Miscellaneous Papers by Sir R. C. Temple. The British Library 12272.h.17.

———. 1924. "William Crooke (1848–1923)." Published for The British Academy. London Humphrey Milford, Oxford University Press.

Temple, R. C., ed. 1883–1931. *The Indian Antiquary.* A journal of Oriental Research in Archaeology, Epigraphy, Ethnology, Geography, History, Folklore, Languages, Literature, Numismatics, Philosophy, Religion, etc.

꒰

Acknowledgments

The inspiration behind this compilation was the manuscripts in the handwriting of Pandit Râm Gharîb Chaube, which are still unpublished. This volume has been compiled from tales that were collected by Chaube and William Crooke between 1891 and 1896. The majority of the tales contained herein were published in *North Indian Notes and Queries,* a monthly periodical edited by William Crooke. The rest of the tales were published in the famous journal *Indian Antiquary.* They have never appeared as a single volume before, nor were they to be found in any one library or archive. Parts of the published materials existed only in the Nehru Memorial Library, New Delhi, as an old microfilm. I thank the staff of the library who took special care in making photocopies of the same and allowed me to publish them. Professor Jack Zipes obtained the larger part of the materials from libraries in the United States and I thank him for the effort.

The research on *North Indian Notes and Queries* could be done only in London and I was able to undertake it. For this I thank the Charles Wallace (India) Trust, British Council, for a research grant in 2001. In the Oriental and India Office Collections of the British Library the cooperation of the staff has been a pleasure. The Royal Anthropological Institute agreed to show me the William Crooke Private Papers, and in the archives these were shown to me by archivist Beverly Emery with special care as these are not cataloged and not in general use. I thank Mrs. Emery for her patience and cooperation. I thank The Folklore Society in general, and the Joint-Archivists, Mrs. Jean Tsushima and Mr. George Monger, in particular, for granting me access to the Crooke materials in the society's care. I am especially indebted to the society's research assistant, Dr. Caroline Oates. She has been helpful as before, but it is her friendship that made my research so much more memorable. She helped me organize the meeting with the Crooke family in Canterbury and accompanied me on the visit.

William Crooke's grandson Mr. Patrick Crooke met us in July 2001 in Canterbury, showed us the family photographs, and talked freely about his grandfather. I thank him for sharing personal details and also for undertaking a journey to meet me in Canterbury.

I am grateful to Dr. Mary Ellen Brown, Professor Margaret Mills, Professor Anil Bhatti, and Professor Majid Siddiqui for support at various points.

Sudheer's love and frank criticism has been my personal strength throughout the research. I thank him especially for sharing the joys of many discoveries in this research.

For historical reasons much was unknown about the collectors and their methodology and I have tried to piece together the bits from many different sources. I am responsible for any error of judgment or detail.

Sadhana Naithani
New Delhi
April 2002

FROM *NORTH INDIAN NOTES & QUERIES*

1. The Banya Boy and his Four Wives—Told by Lachhman Ahir, a Cultivator at Mirzapur.

There was once a Banya, who had a very sharp son. When he grew up his father did his best to get him married, but several times his proposals were rejected. Finally, with great difficulty, he made the arrangements. The night before the marriage day his son was asleep, when he saw in a dream that a daughter of a Bádsháh, of a Rája, of a Sahukár and of a Nat, were all four attending on him. When he woke his father called to him to come and be married, but he answered that he would not marry until he could marry all these four. His father was enraged that all his trouble should come to nought; so he beat his son, who ran away to a distant land. There it so happened that the daughter of the Bádsháh was carrying on a flirtation with the son of the Wazir. Just at that time they were walking about in the garden and were planning to hire a servant who would keep their doings secret and would carry letters from one to the other. At the moment in came the Banya's son, who said that he had come from far and wanted service. They asked his name, but he said he had forgotten it, and only knew that people called him *murkha* (fool). They decided that he would answer, and gave him the berth. Some time after these two were chatting as usual and *murkha* was listening. At last they asked him what they had been saying. "Well," said he, "I heard you say that *murkha* had no jacket. Let us have one made for him by to-morrow." The girl replied, "Yes. This was just what we were saying;" and next day had a jacket made for him, believing that he was an utter fool. Again they were chatting, and she asked *murkha* what they were saying, and in the same way he wheedled a coat and turban from her. Soon after the lovers planned to run away, because, as the princess said, her father would never let them marry. So she told her lover to go at midnight, that very night, to her stable and bring three horses saddled, ready, near her window. When he came he was to fling a clod at the window. The moment *murkha* heard this he went off to the Wazir and said:—"Your son is planning to run off with the Bádsháh's daughter. You had better be careful, lest the Bádsháh murder you and your family." The Wazir took the hint and promptly locked his son up in a room, where he remained tearing his hair in misery. Meanwhile at midnight *murkha* took the three horses to the window, woke the Bádsháh's daughter, and she and her maid came down, and the three of them started off. When they had gone some way the girl called to the supposed Wazir's son:—" We have gone far enough. Let us halt here as I am dead tired." But all *murkha* replied was "Humph! come along." After some time she again wanted to halt and got the same reply. At last she said:—"Why are you so cruel? You know I never rode a horse in my life, and I am almost tumbling off." But he only gave her the same answer. So it went on till morning when the Bádsháh's daughter discovered that it was with *murkha*, not the Wazir's son, that she had eloped. She was so horrified that she fell off the horse, and when she came to her senses, wept incessantly. Then her maid told her to harden her heart, that it was her fate to go with *murkha* and not with the son of the Wazir, and that she had better trust in Providence. So when evening came the maid gave *murkha* a gold-mohur and told him to go to the bazar and buy some delicate food for her mistress, and hire a comfortable house where they could stay. He went into the bazar and could not find any food he liked, so at last he bought some carrots which he thought would be soft food for the lady, and he also got some *halwa* and *púris*, thinking that she might eat these if she did not fancy the carrots: and he could not find a first-rate house, so he saw a grain-parcher's oven, and thinking that this would be a warm spot, he hired it for the night. When he put the carrots before the Bádsháh's daughter she became insensible at the sight, and when she recovered, she said:—"How can I eat a thing I never saw in my life before?" But the maid hinted to her that *murkha* had a little sense after all and had brought *halwa* and *púris*: so she ate some of these. Then the maid asked him if he had hired a house, and he said:—"Yes; I have got excellent quarters." Then he took them to the grain-parcher's oven, and at the sight the Bádsháh's daughter again lost her senses. But the maid went out and at length found a tolerable house, where they stayed for the night. Next morning *murkha* went into the town, and saw some jewellers testing a diamond. Up came the Rája's jeweller and pronounced the diamond false. Murkha objected and said it was genuine. Then the Rája's jeweller said:—"I will make a bet with you. What will you stake?" The Bádsháh's daughter was wearing a diamond necklace, so *murkha* went and asked her to give it to him. She at first refused to give it, but *murkha* threatened to kill her. So she had to give it to him. Then *murkha* took it to the bazar and said:—"I will stake this."

The king's jeweller answered:—"If the diamond is genuine I stake my house and wealth and my place against the necklace." So the diamond was tested, and they put it on an anvil and struck it with a sledge-hammer. The diamond was not broken, nay, it penetrated the iron. So *murkha* won the house, and wealth and place of the Rája's jeweller. Then he returned to the Bádsháh's daughter and said:—"Come along. I have got another house for you." So he brought her to the jeweller's house. She had no idea how he got it, for she knew nothing of the gamble. Some days after her maid asked *murkha* to call a barber's wife to give her mistress a bath. So he went off and called the woman, who used to bathe the Rája's wife, and she did the same for the Bádsháh's daughter. But when she went back to the Ráni, she mentioned how lovely *murkha*'s wife was. The Ráni told the Rája, and he was anxious to see her. So he gave a general dinner in his garden and *murkha* had to bring his lady. She was wearing her diamond necklace, but oppressed by the heat, she took it off and hung it to a tree, and when she was going away forgot all about it: and only remembered it when she reached home late at night. Then she besought *murkha* to go back and fetch it. So he went back, but the glitter of the diamonds had attracted a black snake. When *murkha* touched the necklace the snake bit him and he died. Next morning the gardener came, and seeing *murkha* dead, threw his body into the river and took the necklace. Now as the corpse of *murkha* went floating down, it so chanced that a number of Nat girls were bathing, and all of them set to tease one girl by saying:—"Here comes your husband floating down." When the body came close by, this girl saw that he had died of the bite of a black snake: so by a spell she knew she revived *murkha*, and tied a string round his neck by means of which he became a parrot. Then she shut him up in a cage, and every night she used to open the string, when he became a man again. Meanwhile she kept him in her hut until it so happened that the party of Nats wandering about, doing their tricks, came below the Rája's palace. The Rája's daughter saw the parrot and sent word to her father to get it for her. At first the Nat girl refused to give it up, but the Rája's daughter was so pressing that she was obliged to give her the bird. The Rája's daughter was delighted and took the parrot out of its cage. By chance she noticed the string round its neck, which, when she untied the parrot, turned at once into a man. This delighted the Rája's daughter still more, particularly as she was obliged to live alone. So she used to keep *murkha* in his parrot shape all day and turn him into a man at night. But one night the guard heard two people talking in the princess's chamber, so they climbed up on the top of the house and seeing *murkha*, tried to arrest him. *Murkha* had to escape, and running into the house of a Sahukár, implored him to save his life. He said that he did not mind helping him, but that he could think of only one plan. "I have," said he, "an only daughter. Now if you are ready to marry her, you may go into the room, and when the guard comes, I will tell them that my son-in-law is the only other man in the house." *Murkha* had to agree to save his life: so when the guard came to search the house the Sahukár put them off, and next day married *murkha* to his daughter. *Murkha* then lived at the Sahukár's house. But one day the maid of the Bádsháh's daughter with whom he first eloped, happened to pass by and saw him. She came and told her mistress, who would not believe her. "Why," said she, "he is dead and the necklace is lost, and some one else must have taken his shape." But the maid insisted that it was he. So she made her mistress come with her, and when she saw him, sure enough it was *murkha*. So she caught him by the arm and said:—"What are you doing here? Come home at once." On this, up comes the Sahukár's daughter and says:—"What are you doing with my husband?" But the Bádsháh's daughter said:—"He is my husband—not yours." As they were disputing thus a policeman (*police-wála*) came up and was carrying all three to the Rája, when on the way the Nat's daughter met them and claimed him. When they got near the Rája's palace, the Rája's daughter recognized him and caught him. So the policeman could do nothing, but take the five of them before the Rája, and said:—"Your Majesty! Here's a curious case. Four young women are fighting over one man." The Rája made an enquiry and heard all their stories. Finally he said:—"There is no doubt all four of you are his wives. So you better all live with him." So all ended happily and *murkha*'s destiny was fulfilled, in that he married the daughters of the Bádsháh, the Rája, the Sahukár and the Nat.

2. The Saint Bo Ali.

"In a town between Brochia (Broach) and Amadabat (Ahmadábád) is buried a certain holy Mahometan called Polle Medoni (Boali *Madani* or of Medina). Hither flock pilgrims from all parts of India, some hoping to obtain wealth, some children, some one thing, some another. One may see these pilgrims travelling hither, some loaded with iron-chains of great weight, others with muzzles on their mouths which they only remove for the purpose of taking food. As soon, however, as they have piously worshipped at the shrine they declare that the chains are miraculously broken and the muzzles drop off of their own accord."—*Joannes de Lact: Topography of the Mogul Empire* quoted in *Calcutta Review, Vol. LI, p. 353.*

3. The Story of the Jinn—A Folktale told by Rahmat, Weaver of Mirzapur.

There was a soldier, who was in great poverty. One day somebody told him that in a certain city a banker in whose house no one could live, and that no matter what clever people used to try and expel the jinn from there, lost their lives. So he determined to risk his life, and leaving all he had in the world with his wife, he started. When he reached the banker's house he found him sitting there in great grandeur. He saluted him, and the banker asked who he was. He replied that he was a magician and had power over the race of the demons (*deo*), the jinn and the fairies (*pari*). The banker replied:—"People who were a hundred years old have attempted this task and failed. What can a youth like you do?" He replied:— I have arrested hundreds such." Then the banker said to a servant:—"Well! show him the house, but be ready at the back door to take his corpse when the jinn flings him out." When he got inside the house, what should he see but a masonry well in the courtyard: the whole place was clean, which was usual in a deserted dwelling. Then with the invocation "Bismillah" he continued his search. He came on a lovely garden full of all kinds of fruits, in the midst of which was a lovely room with twelve doors (*bárahdari*). There was a splendid couch and two jewelled chairs. So he sat down on one of the chairs. Four men in magnificent dresses appeared. One began to sprinkle water about, another to arrange the carpets, one to settle the chairs, one to tie up the mosquito net of the couch. When they had done this, they said:—"Young man, why have you come into this danger, and are in a fair way to lose your life? You had better leave this." So the soldier knowing he must go on with the adventure, made no reply. No time passed when a lovely princess, about sixteen years old, appeared. She came and stood by him. He bowed to her and said:—"Pardon me, my lady." She smiled and seated him by her side. Soon after the jinn appeared in the form of a prince. He was sorely wrath and said:—"What is this princess?" She smiled and said:—"Don't disturb me. Don't you know that this is my brother?" He replied:—"You never had a brother. Where did this one come from?" She said:—"I assure you he is my brother." "Is he older or younger than you," asked the jinn. "He is older than me," she said. So the jinn bowed and sat down in front of them, and asked the soldier all about himself. He said:—"How can I tell where I have been? I have been two days with this banker, and I heard from him that no one could live in his house, but I did not know the reason. So I agreed to clear the house for him in return for a reward. What good luck I had to meet your royal highness!" The jinn said:—"You are a truthful man." Soon after appeared a lovely handmaid. She stood with her hands clasped, and the jinn prince said, "bring." So she came up with a tray of food. He was afraid to eat: so the princess asked, "Brother! why don't you eat?" He made no reply, but the jinn forced him to eat. Then they all three lay down to rest. Then the jinn said in the morning:—"I must go, but the servants will give you a bath and breakfast. When you are done, send back the dishes for me." He went off, and so it happened for some days that the jinn used to return in the evening and the three used to dine together. They all slept together, and in the morning the jinn and the princess used to go away and leave the soldier alone. The soldier determined to see where they went to every day. Next morning as they were going, he watched them. He followed and watched the princess push the jinn towards the well. The jinn pushed her in and jumped in himself after her. The soldier began to lament them both. As usual, the handmaid appeared with his food. When she saw him lamenting, she asked him what was the matter. He said: "Have you not seen, you wretch, that the prince and princess have fallen into the well?" She smiled and said:—"What business have you with tales like these. Mind your own business." He was much displeased, and finally she had to go and tell the princess that her brother was going to kill himself for grief. Then the jinn told the princess to go and look after her brother. She came and found her brother in an evil state. She asked:—"What have you done with yourself?" He began to weep and said:—"I saw you and the prince with my own eyes falling into the well. Why should I not weep." "What a fool you are," she answerd. "Did you ever see one lover push another into a well?" "Well," said he, "how did you fall into the well, and why were you not hurt?" "Why," she answered, "it is in this well I live. When you eat I will tell you all about it." Then they both ate, and when they were done the soldier said:—"Go on with the story." She said:—"Brother, I am the daughter of a merchant in a distant land. My father had a capital of Rs. 4,000. He and his wife had two children. We lived well on his income. I was then eleven years of age. One day I was looking about from the housetop—suddenly a strong wind arose—I sat down to shelter myself.

When the wind stilled, I saw this prince there, armed with all five weapons, in royal attire." I said "How came you on my housetop?" I threatened to complain to my father. He followed me down. I sat down on my bed and thought that my mother would surely see me and tell my father, and have him punished. I asked my mother, "Have you eyes in your head, or don't you notice anything?" She said:—"What is the matter, girl?" So I whispered to the prince, "Don't speak for goodness sake. No one sees you but I." So I kept the matter quiet: and every day when I woke I used to see him standing before me with his hands folded. Then I feared he might be of the race of the jinn or a bhút or pret. I feared he might injure me. I asked him who he was and how he lived without eating. On this he began to weep and said:—"You have well spoken. I am starving for three days: give me some food." I pitied him and told him to wash his hands, and that when I was eating I would give him some too. I called him when I began to eat and wanted to give him a plate of his own. He said:—"Your father and mother will ask to whom you have given the food. Then what will you say. If you allow me I will eat out of a corner of your plate and no one will notice it." I was afraid of him, so I agreed. So it went on for many days. Soon after my father fell into difficulties and his creditors began to threaten him. In those days debtors were hardly treated. My father came home weeping and made me over to my mother, while he went abroad. As I was lamenting the jinn appeared and asked what I wanted. I told him all my troubles. He said:—"Is this all you are lamenting about? Tell your father to open his shop and sell his wares for anything the purchasers will give." Then he asked me to give him myself if he saved my father from his troubles. So I instructed my father as the jinn advised: and my mother asked him to follow these instructions. He went and opened his shop. The jinn said:—"I am going to buy something from your father." He went and bought a lot of things at so high a price that all his debts were paid off. Then my father having become rich again, began to think of getting me married. The jinn hearing this wept and said, "Lady! now I can come here no longer." I asked my mother not to get me married, but she would not mind. Then I told the jinn I would go with him. He was much pleased and agreed to take me off at midnight, but we slept till morning. When I woke and saw it was daylight, I gave him a slap. Then he awoke and reproached himself with his carelessness: and promised to come immediately, when he disappeared at once. Soon after I got a pain in my hand. Physicians came, but could do me no good, and I died in an hour. When my friends lamented me by name, I wondered for whom they were mourning. Then they took my body to the grave. There the jinn appeared and asked me if I was coming. I said, "yes" and he took me in his arms and carried me to this house.

Thus the princess told the soldier her whole story. He said:—"I will tell your friends all about it and bring them to see you." In the evening the jinn again appeared and said:—"You two have had a long talk today." She-said:—"My brother talks of going home." The jinn replied:—"He can go when he pleases. God protect him!" Then the soldier said:—"Please leave this house as I am under an oath to the banker." The jinn said:—"Ask your sister." She told me to tell him that the house was at his service. Then all three left the house, and the jinn gave the soldier a lot of jewels and sent him off: but he was not to look behind him. He obeyed, and in a moment found himself at his own door. He found his house full of gold and silver, and his wife laden with jewels. He said to her:—"Where did you get all these things?" She told him that after he had gone, a person came and called him. He said he was a friend of her husband and had brought food for him. She told her child to tell him that her husband had gone abroad. He said:—"All right. I will leave the food here." He did so and left four plates—two of gold and two of silver. She supposed he would come back for the vessels. Next day he brought a fresh supply and every day brought a fresh lot of vessels with clothes, jewellery, &c. The soldier would not believe her story and threatened to cut her in pieces. That night no food came, and this strengthened his suspicions. Next day he went off to the merchant, the father of the girl. He salaamed to him and asked to speak with him in private. Then he told the merchant the whole story of the girl. He asked:—"When will she come?" The soldier said, "two days hence." So he entertained him. On the third day the jinn came with the girl and the soldier also brought his wife there. Soon after it was rumoured that a jinn was in love with the merchant's daughter, and that the king of the land also loved her. They began to plan to burn the jinn. The soldier agreed to help and soon got the jinn in his power. He began to recite spells: when lo! a youth of twenty years appeared, and said "Why are you keeping me in durance?" The soldier paid no attention to his words: but pulled a feather out of his pocket and threw it on the ground. This turned into a kite, and the jinn rolled about and also became a kite. Both flew away in a cloud of dust. When the dust cleared they found that both had fought and fallen into the fire. One the soldier killed and burnt and the other he put into his bag. Soon the kite was burnt into ashes, from which a smoke arose, and the soldier enclosed it in a bottle, and thus imprisoned the jinn. He showed it to all the people and then buried the bottle into the earth. That night a boy dug up the place, found the bottle and took it with him to the river side where he opened it. As he opened it a blaze of fire issued from the bottle, and the boy was consumed while the jinn escaped. All this time the soldier thought that he had disposed of the jinn. When he appeared he caught the soldier and broke his neck and tried to kill the king. He escaped, but his daughter fell in love with the jinn. So the jinn took both her and the merchant's daughter, and lived with them both ever after.

(To be continued).

4. How the Needle succeeded in killing the Tiger— A Folktale told by Ram Tahal Kahar, a Cultivator of Mirzapur.

Once upon a time a needle set out to kill a tiger. On the road he met first a bludgeon, then a scorpion, then an insect which eats the mango-fruit, and then a piece of cowdung, all of which the needle took with him. All five came to the house of the tiger, and the needle stood up straight on the threshold, the scorpion got into the tiger's oil jar, the insect into the fire-place and the piece of cowdung spread itself on the doorstep. When the tiger came back from the jungle the needle ran into his foot as he was going in: he then put his paw into the oil jar to get some oil to rub on the wound and he was stung by the scorpion: enraged with the pain he ran to the fire-place to light a lamp to see what had happened to him, when the insect got into his eye and blinded him. "Misfortunes never come singly," said the tiger, and he rushed out: but he trod on the cowdung, slipped and broke his back, and this was the end of him.

5. Burial-ground Ghosts.

In Rohilkhand and the western districts of Oudh, one often hears of the "*Shahába.*" In burial-grounds, specially where the bodies of those slain in battle are buried, it is alleged that phantom armies appear in the night. Tents are pitched, horses tethered, and nautches held at which the deceased heroes and jinns attend. One occasionally hears of an ordinary mortal who, attracted by the lights, went and witnessed such a spectacle, the sequel in such cases being that the unwary person had to pay for his temerity with death or loss of reason.—*Jwala Prasada.*

6. *The Legend of Hemavati.*

Hemávatí was daughter of Hemráj, the Bráhman priest of the Gahirwár Rája of Benares. She was very beautiful. One day she went to bathe in the queen's tank, and Chandrama, the Moon God, embraced her. She cursed him, but he promised that her son would be lord of the earth, and from him would spring a thousand branches. She enquired: "How shall my dishonour be effaced when I am without a husband?" "Fear not," he replied:—"Your son will be born on the banks of the Karnávatí river. Then take him to Khajuráya and offer him as a gift and perform a sacrifice. In Mahoba he will reign and become a great king. He will possess the Philosopher's stone and turn iron into gold. On the hill of Kalanjár he will build a fort. When, your son is born you must perform a Bhánda Jag to wipe away your disgrace, and then leave Benares to live at Kalanjár." Her son was born, Chandrama formed a great festival, and Vrihaspati wrote his horoscope. He was called Chundra Varmma. At 16 years of age he killed a tiger, when Chandrama gave him the Philosopher's stone and taught him polity. Then he did sacrifice to remove his mother's sin and built eighty-five temples when the disgrace of Hemávatí was washed away.—*Cunningham: Archeological Reports, Vol. XXI, p. 79*

7. *The Death of Banu Begam, Mumtaz-i-Mahal, the Lady of the Taj at Agra—Infant crying in the womb.*

Just previous to the birth of her daughter Dahrari Begam (the adorner-of-the-world queen), the infant cried while yet in the womb. The mother despaired of life, and at once summoned Sháh Jahán, and said:—"It is a fact well known that when an infant cries in the womb the mother never survives."—*W. Crooke.*

[Does this idea generally prevail?—ED.]

8. *Sneezing—Omens from.*

In both Europe and Asia, not only among Aryan but also among Semetic peoples, some form of blessing is a custom of very general prevalence. Among some people it is the sneezer who is blessed by the bystanders: among others he blesses himself, and among Muhammadans he blesses God. [According to the Muhammadan religion it is a sacred duty to reply to a sneeze (*'utás*). For example, if a person sneeze and say immediately after "God be praised" (*alhamdul Alláh*) it is incumbent upon at least one of the party to exclaim "God have mercy on you" (*yarhamauk Alláh*)—Hughes's *Dictionary of Islám*, sv.] In Italy, for instance, it is common to greet the sneezer with the salutation "may you have children," or "may God preserve you." In Hindi the blessing takes the form of *Sada Jiyo*: "may you live for ever;" and the Jews of Arabia use precisely the same salutation. But another and a totally different significance has been attached to this act in very different places and at very different times. Among the Arabs, for instance, "if while any one is making an assertion regarding which there is any room for doubt, another sneezes, the speaker appeals to the omen as a confirmation of what he was saying." Now this notion seems to have prevailed among the Greeks of the time of Xenophon as appears from the well-known passage in the Anabasis (III, 2). Among the Hindús, sneezing, when it occurs behind one, is considered so unfavourable an omen that they will at once leave off any work they may have commenced: and this notion may be shown to have prevailed among the ancients by a quotation from St. Augustine. The attempts that have been made to explain these customs are as various as the customs themselves. The Muhammadan, for instance, accounts for his *alhamdul Allah* by a reference to the tradition that when the breath of life was inspired into the nostrils of Adam he sneezed and immediately uttered these words; while the custom of blessing the sneezer has been in Europe traced to the occurrence in the middle ages of some fatal epidemic, one of the symptoms of which was sneezing. The first is no explanation at all: the second evidently ignores the extreme antiquity of the custom.—*Calcutta Review, Vol. II*, p. 109.

[Dr. Tylor: *Primitive Culture, Vol. I*, p. *97, sqq.*, shows that it is connected with "the ancient and savage doctrine of pervading and invading spirits, considered as good or evil."—ED.]

9. How the Ahir got the better of the Demon and acquired a Wife—A folktale recorded by E. David, a Native Christian of Mirzapur, from the life of an old Muhammadan Cookwoman.

There was once an Ahír who was a great fool. One day he was ploughing his field when somebody told him that his wife had given birth to a son. He was so pleased that he gave his informant one of his pair of oxen, and going to his mother, told her that his wife had a son. She said—"My son, how can this be when you are not married yet?" But he insisted that it was so, and that his informant would not have told him a lie. So he took some money with him and went in search of the man and said:— "Brother can you tell me where my father-in-law lives?" The man said:— "When you go out of the city you will see a well. The first woman that comes there dressed in yellow clothes is your wife. You have only to ask her where she lives." The Ahír was delighted, and buying a lot of presents in the bázár, went and sat by the well. Finally a woman came up, and she by chance had yellow clothes, and it so chanced that a boy had been born to her lately. The Ahír followed her with the things, and said he had brought them for the baby. She thought they must have been sent from some relation's house, so she gave him tobacco to smoke. As he was smoking the woman's husband came in and was surprised to find a stranger there. But when he went inside and saw the presents he was still more incensed from jealousy and began to thrash his wife. When the Ahír heard her cries he was greatly enraged at any one beating his wife, so he went in and beat the woman's husband soundly and turned him out. Next day he went to the landlord of the village and said:— "Give me a little land and I will cultivate it." The landlord said he had no land to spare except a field which would grow a hundred maunds of rice. "This field, said he, is empty, but in the middle of it is a *pípal* tree in which a demon (*deo*) resides; he won't let any one sow it. If you care for it you may have it." He agreed to take the field, and taking an axe with him began to cut away at the tree. When the demon saw what he was about, he roared at the Ahír and warned him to let the tree alone, but the Ahír said:— "Keep quiet, or I will give you a cut with my axe." Then the demon became afraid and said:— "Well! if you spare this tree you may ask what you please." The Ahír replied:— "I was going to sow rice here and I should have got a hundred maunds of grain: I don't mind letting the tree alone for a hundred maunds of grain." This the demon agreed to give. Next day the demon's nephew (his sister's son, *bhánja*) came to pay him a visit: and the demon told him what had happened. He replied:— "Uncle! if you only give me the order I will go and kill the Ahír." He replied:— "It would be a good job." So his nephew started to kill the Ahír. The Ahír was sleeping at a well in front of his house. When the young demon saw him he got in a panic and hid in the water-tank beside the well. When the Ahír woke he put his foot by chance on the demon's head who shouted out *Bápré! Bápré!* (O father, father). The Ahír asked:— "Who are you." He replied:— "My uncle, the demon, merely sent me to ask whether you will have your hundred maunds in husked or unhusked rice." The Ahír replied:—"Well! I suppose I may as well have it husked." When he came back he told his uncle what a fright he had got. "All right!" said he, "it is true I only promised to give paddy, but I suppose I must give cleaned rice." So the Ahír got the best of the demon, received his tribute of rice regularly, and lived happily with the woman ever after.

[The Ahír is usually the type of the village boor. In this case he gets the best of the demon, who is also generally a fool.—Ed.]

10. *The Legend of the Dhorawat Tank.*

The Ráni had no children; she was induced to make a pilgrimage to the Ganges and bore a son: the minister's wife, who was also childless, had a son. The Rája's son killed his sister's son, but after the battle he could not release the dagger from his hand. One day a thirsty calf came towards him, to which he presented a *lota* full of water, and as the calf drank it up eagerly, the dagger released itself from his hand. Then the Rája determined to make a tank, and it was to be the circuit made by his horse when let loose. The minister turned its head to the south, where it was soon brought to a standstill by the Kunwa Hill. Next day the Rája dug five baskets of earth, and each of his followers did the same except one Rajput, who sat with a sword in his hand. When interrogated, he said he was used only to carry arms and letters. On this the Rája gave him a letter to Bhikham, King of Ceylon, and ordered him to bring back a monolith (*lát*) to place in the centre of the lake. Bhikham accordingly gave up the pillar to the soldier, but as the latter was bringing it, the cock crew and he was obliged to drop it, where it is now six miles from the lake.—*Cunningham: Archæological Reports, Vol. XVI*, p. 41.

[The horse incident in regard to tanks is very common, and other illustrations will be given. These ghostly messengers, like Hamlet's ghost, can never stand the dawn.—Ed.]

11. *Bombay—Expulsion of a Devil.*

The following evidence was recently before the High Court, Bombay, in a poisoning case:—Lala Sundar, the chief witness, in describing the circumstances of the case, said:—"I have been ill for two years. About two months ago I came to the market and met the accused. I did not know him before. He said he would cure me. He stayed that night in my house. Next day he told me that I was possessed by a devil, and that he would drive him out. He said, six or seven rupees would be necessary. I asked Dhulia and two others to come and drive away the devil, as they were my neighbours. Accused said nothing. I paid these men Rs. 5. The three neighbours came. I was made to sit with my head covered, and a burning torch was turned round my head. The accused was there. They beat tom-toms and at last I began to shake. The devil said through my mouth:—"I want $2\frac{1}{2}$ seers of flour and $2\frac{1}{2}$ seers of rice." My wife gave the rice and flour to the accused, who was inside the house. He brought the rice and flour out from the house cooked. The food was waved round my head. Amtha, Rama and others went with the food to the river and ate it there. When they came home I saw them swollen and unconscious; and they were then taken to hospital. Accused was five days in my house. He did nothing. The bag produced, in which were found *dhatura* seeds, is the accused's. He said:— "Why do you send for others? I can drive the devil out." No one but the accused took part in the cooking. The accused was afterwards arrested.

Wahali, wife of Lala Sundar, said among other things:—The accused came to my house and stayed six days. He said:—"My husband had a devil." He said:—"Let them beat a tom-tom," and they did so. My husband sent for Dhulia and other neighbours to drive the devil away. The devil asked for $2\frac{1}{2}$ seers of rice and $2\frac{1}{2}$ seers of flour. I gave the flour and rice to the accused with some molasses. I pounded the rice at that time, and ground the wheat after the devil asked for it. I was outside and accused was inside. I was not to cook it, as it was the food of demons. I could see the accused cook the stuff. He put the food into the pots and threw something into both the pots. I did not eat anything, nor did my-husband. The other people took the food and went to the river.

The medical evidence showed that the five persons, who went to the river and ate the food, were all suffering from *dhatura* poisoning. One of them, Malia Lala, died soon after admission.

12. Hindu Superstition.

It is looked upon as unlucky to sit with one foot placed on the other. What is the origin of this?—*Kanwar Jwala Prasad.*

13. Faizabad—Akbar and the Bridge Builder.

Nawáb Khán Khána, the Prime Minister, sent his favourite slave Fahím to Nepál to purchase elephants. When the latter arrived at Jaunpur, he was so struck with the place that he determined to perpetuate his name in connection therewith by building a bridge. He was told by the builders that he alone could bridge the Gumti, who could pave the foundations with gold. Nothing daunted: Fahím deliberately flung some bags of money into the stream. The builders stayed his hand, and at once acknowledged that he was the man for the situation, and the work was commenced. When funds failed, Fahím addressed the Wazír and procured more, and when the bridge was completed, he wrote and said he had returned as far as Jaunpur, but he could proceed no further until the Emperor came in person to ensure arrangements for the convoy of the elephants to Akbarábád. Akbar came and saw for himself the great work which his slave had constructed, and forgave the deception which had been practised upon him.—*Settlement Report,* p. 172.

14. The Story of Murdan Khan and the Daughter of the Jinn, told by Fateh, a weaver of Mirzapur.

There was once the son of a soldier who fell into poverty and said to his mother:—"If I had Rs. 50 I would go somewhere in search of service." His mother gave him the money out of her savings. When he had gone some distance he saw a corpse lying near the road and a grave ready dug. A large crowd was there, and one man would not allow the corpse to be buried. The people remonstrated, but he would not mind. The Sepáhi enquired why he would not allow the corpse to be buried. He was told that the dead man owed Rs. 50, and that his creditor would not allow him to be buried till he was repaid. No one present could afford to repay the debt. Finally the Sipáhi paid the debt with all the money he had and buried the corpse. Then he returned home. His mother asked him how he came to return so soon. He replied that with this Rs. 50 he had purchased property, worth many lakhs, and had now no money to pay for its carriage. He told his mother that he needed Rs. 50 more for this purpose. She gave it to him and said she had no more. The Sipáhi again started with the money. When he reached the spot where he had buried the corpse, he met a Sipáhi armed with sword and shield. They spoke to each other. The second Sipáhi asked the other where he was going. He replied that he was a Sipáhi and had left home with Rs. 50, and had got a corpse buried in that very spot by paying its debts: and had got Rs. 50 more with which he was going in search of employment. Then the second Sipáhi told him that his name was Murdan Khán, and that he also was in search of service, and that he had also Rs. 50. So they joined and went off together. When they came to a certain city, what did they see but that a river ran in the midst of it, dividing the city into two equal parts. But no one could cross from one bank to the other. They asked why this was so, and the inhabitants told them that in former times people used to cross freely, but no one had crossed for the last fifty years. If any boat put out it was sunk in the river. Then Murdan Khán proposed to his friend that if they could buy goods on this side which were not procurable on the other and take them across the profits would be great. The other agreed, but said it was impossible to convey the goods across. Murdan Khan said he would devise some plan. So they purchased goods worth Rs. 75 and tried to hire a boat, but no boatman would accept the job. Finally Murdan Khán said he would manage the boat himself, so the boatman lent him an old boat. Murdan Khán loaded the boat and the news spread in the city. All the people turned out to see the spectacle. Then Murdan Khán let his boat loose and sat on the bulwarks with his sword drawn. His friend said:—"What use is a sword on the river?" Murdan Khán told him to watch what would happen. When the boat reached half way across, a hand appeared out of the river and caught the boat and tried to drag it under water. Murdan Khán struck at it with his sword and part of the hand fell into the boat. Then the boat got across. Then his friend asked Murdan Khán:—"What is the meaning of this?" Murdan Khán replied:—"This was the hand of a daughter of the Jinn. She had made a vow to marry a man, so she got hold of a man to her liking. By him she bore a daughter. She also wishes to marry a man. For this reason she drags down boats that she may find some one on board to her liking." His friend, astonished, asked:—"How did you learn this?" Murdan Khán replied that he was skilled in the science by which secrets become disclosed. I saw a bracelet (*kangan*), a thumb-ring (*arsi*), and two or three rings which fairies wear on the hand, when it fell into the boat." When this bracelet was shown to the jewellers they declared it was worth the revenue of a kingdom so they asked him whence he had stolen it. Then the jeweller informed the city kotwál. He arrested the two Sipáhis and brought them before the King. He interrogated them about the bracelet. Then Murdan Khán explained how he had cut off the hand of the daughter of the Jinn and acquired the bracelet. He added that he had also a thumb-ring and two finger-rings which he got in the same way. The King was greatly pleased, and presented him with a *khilat* of immense value. Then Murdan Khán offered the fairy jewellery to the King. He presented it to his Queen. She gave it to her daughter. The Princess said:—"What is the use of a single set? I want the pair." The King called all the jewellers and tried to get the pair of these jewels made, but no one could make them. So he sent for Murdan Khán and said:—"If you can get the pair of these jewels you may have my daughter to wife. Murdan Khán said:—"I cannot marry just now, but I am anxious to get my brother, who is with me, married. If you agree to my proposal I will do my best." The King agreed. Then Murdan Khán dived into the river and reached the palace of the Jinn. There he announced himself to be a physician. The Jinn's daughter, who was in great pain from the loss of her hand, sent for him at once and said she would give him anything he pleased if he would cure her. Murdan Khán had the severed hand with him. He told the Jinn's daughter to shut her eyes and he could cure her at once. So she shut her eyes. Then Murdan Khán fixed the severed hand to the stump, and it became as it was before. All the Jinns were astonished at his skill. They offered him all sorts of presents. He said he wanted only the pair of the bracelet. So she gave it to him with a lot of other jewels. So he came up out of the water with the jewellery and brought them to the King, who was much pleased; and according to his promise married the Sipáhi to the Princess: and the King dismissed her with her husband, accompanied by an army and valuable presents. When Murdan Khán and his friend got home all the people wondered how this poor Sipáhi had gained a Princess for his bride. Soon after Murdan Khán took leave of his friend, but the Sipáhi replied:—"What am I that I should take all this wealth. Stay here and we will serve you." But Murdan Khán said:—"It is not in my power to stay." "Why," asked his friend. Then Murdan Khán explained to him:—"I am the corpse which you had buried. You and I are clear, and I can stay no longer. By the order of God I had to stay with you: so now the blessing of the Almighty be on you." Then he disappeared. His friend long lamented him. Finally, he erected a splendid tomb to his memory, and appointed a Háfiz to read the Qurán there, and afterwards spent his life in ease and happiness.

15. Throbbing of Eyes.

Hindús believe that in case of male's throbbing of the right eye is auspicious and that of the left eye, inauspicious. On the contrary, in case of females, the throbbing of the left eye augurs something good, and that of the right eye some evil.—*Kunwar Jwálá Prasád.*

16. Bhimsen—A Legend of—Spirits scared by dawn.

Bhímsen fascinated one of the Devís, who desired to marry him, and instructed him to build a suitable marriage-hall (*chauri*) in one night. He failed to complete it before cock crow, and had to abandon the building. which still lies incomplete at Mokand Dwára.—*Garrick: Archæological Reports, Vol. XXIII,* p. 132.

[The superstition is very common. It attaches, for instance, to the Bijaigarh Fort, in south Mirzapur, and to various other unfinished buildings.—ED.]

17. The Golden-haired Rání and the Jogi.

The following story is literally translated as told by Mansukhi, a Chamár woman, of Mirzapur:—There was a king who had seven sons. When he died and his eldest son succeeded him, the seven brothers determined to marry, but the wife of the youngest was the loveliest of all and her hair was of gold. One day she was sitting on the housetop, drying her hair, when a Jogí passed by and sat down below. When he began to beg the king told his servant to give the Jogí some alms, but he refused to take alms from the hands of the servant. Then he asked the Jogí:—"From whose hand will you take alms?" He replied:—"Let all who are in the king's house come, and I will take the alms from whomever I select." The king was informed of this, and in his anger said:—"Turn him out." But the Jogí said:—"You may kill me, but I won't go." The king at last asked his youngest brother to give the alms, but he would not take it from him: and the same was the case with all the brothers. Then the king and his wife and the wives of all the brothers, except the youngest, went, and they too all failed. At last the Jogí said that if she with the golden hair came he would take alms from her hand. But the king said: "She cannot come," and again gave orders to drive away the Jogí. But the Jogí would not stir. Finally, the servants proposed that a cloth should be hung up and the youngest Ráni be asked to pass out the alms from behind it. Still the Jogí would not agree. At last the golden-haired Ráni came, and the moment the Jogí saw her, he pronounced a spell (*mantra*) that she was turned into a bitch and began to run after the Jogí. Then the Rája seized her and tied her with a golden chain, but the Jogí turned her at once into a horseman (sawar), and took her home, when she became a woman again. Now this Jogí by his spells had killed all the people of the land in which he dwelt, and the only persons who survived were two, who equalled the Jogí in their knowledge of magic—a Bráhman and an old woman—the latter of whom lived in the Jogí's house. The Jogí was a great gambler, and he and the Bráhman used to play. Whenever the Jogí went to gamble he used to cut off the Rání's head and hang it by a rope to the roof, while he put her body to sleep on a couch. When he came back he used to fix her together with a stick, and then she came to life again. Some time after the Rája and his brothers determined to go and recover the little Rání. So with great difficulty they reached the Jogí's house where the old woman met them. They told her the whole story, and asked her to show them the little Rání. She said:—"This is the Jogí's dinner hour. Wait till he goes, and I will do what I can." So she turned them into flies and hid them in the house. When the Jogí returned, he said:—"I smell a man, I smell a man." The old woman said:—"What a fool you are! There is not even a man's shadow here." So the Jogí was pacified and ate his dinner. So when he went away the old woman turned the king and his brothers into men again, and taking the stick ordered the Rání's head to descend and join her body. She came to life again. Then they put her into a carriage and took her home. By ill luck the Jogí saw them departing, so he asked the Bráhman for a grain of sesamum (*sarson*), and with it blew a spell upon them, so they all had to come back to the Jogí's house, and then he killed them all except the little Rání, to whom he gave a sound beating.

Now one of the seven wives had borne a son, and when he was grown up and playing with the other boys, he used to speak of his father and his uncles. But the boys laughed at him and said:—"Where have you a father or uncles?" So he was distressed and asked his mother, and she told him the whole story. Then though all his friends warned him, yet he determined to go and rescue them. So he rode off to the Jogí's house, and there the same old woman met him. She asked his business, and he enquired:—"Have not my aunt and my uncles come here?" So she told him that the Jogí had killed all his uncles, but that his aunt was living. He said:—"Show me my aunt, for I want to take her home." She said:— "I will show her to you, but take her home you cannot." So she showed him the head and body of his aunt, and gave him the magic stick with which he restored her to life. She asked:—"Who are you?" He answered:—"I am your nephew, and I was born after the Jogí carried you off. Now you must come with me." She said:—"This is impossible. Why are you risking your life?" The boy answered:—"Whatever happens I must do it. But when the Jogí comes you must find out from him in what his life remains." So he cut off her head again and hung it up and went and hid himself. So when the Jogí returned the Rání asked him where his life was. First he said it was in the fire, but she would not believe this, and so he tried to deceive her many times. At last he told her:—"Beyond the seven oceans is a forest watched by a tiger and tigress and a guard of nine hundred witches. In the midst is a sandal tree, on which hangs a golden cage containing a diamond parrot. In this is my life." When the boy heard this from his aunt he started at once, and with great difficulty crossed the seven oceans. The moment he came into the forest the tiger rushed at him, to whom the boy said:—"Good morning, uncle! "(*mámu salam.*) Then the tiger said:—"You have been twelve years coming, but still you are my brother:" so he spared him, and conducted the boy as far as his jurisdiction reached. When he got so far the tigress charged him, but she also spared him and conducted him to her borders. When he reached the witches' border they called out:—"We will eat human flesh to-day." But when he approached he bowed to each and said:—"Good morning, aunt." Then all said:—"Why, this is our nephew!" Then he told them that the Jogí had sent him for the diamond parrot. So they gave him the parrot, and when he returned he came to the Jogí's house and called out—"Jogí! buy the parrot?" When the Jogí saw the bird, he saw at once that this contained his life. So he rushed down to seize the bird, but as he was coming down the staircase the boy broke one of the parrot's legs, and immediately one of the Jogí's legs broke too. But he continued to run on one leg, so the boy broke the other leg of the parrot. Then the second leg of the Jogí broke, and he fell on the ground imploring the boy to spare him. Then the boy said:—"You have killed my father and uncles. You must bring them to life." So the Jogí did so. Then he said:—"You must restore to life all the people of the land." This too the Jogí did. Then the boy crushed the parrot to death, and as it died the Jogí died too. Then he took the magic stick and revived his aunt, the golden haired Ráni. So they all went home and lived happily ever after.

18. Saharanpur—The Legend of a Famine.

The great famine happened in this wise. The Rishi Gautama, stern ascetic though he was, could not resist the charms of the beautiful Aha-lyá, and married her. He soon repented of his choice. Indra, the god of the rain, a most unscrupulous deity, previously guilty of stealing King Ságar's horse, conceiving a guilty passion for the sage's wife, proceeded to gratify his desires at the first opportunity afforded by the good man's absence. Gautama unexpectedly returned, and detecting him in the act of adultery, exclaimed:—"Ah! rascal! hast thou come to work evil in my house?" So he cursed the god whose body became infected with sores, and he retired to do penance in the Siwáliks, devoting himself to the worship of Siva. In consequence of his seclusion, no rain fell for one hundred years, and universal famine prevailed. The Munis and Deotas had recourse to Deví, praying for the fulfilment of her prophecy. She regarded them with one hundred eyes, whence her second name *Satákshi*, and kept her promise, nourishing all living creatures in the form of a yam. The fossils found in the Sewáliks are esteemed trophies of Deví's power against the giants, while the *surál* (*pueraria tubarosa*) is a living monument to her beneficence to mankind. This bulb grows abundantly on both sides of the Siwáliks, and being a common article of diet among the poorer classes, is, in their eyes, a voucher of the authenticity of the myth.—*Calcutta Review, Vol. LVII*, p. 203.

19. *Treading on Heel Ropes.*

In the Parganas Bhawapár and Chillupár, district Gorakhpur, it has been observed that the native women very carefully avoid crossing the ropes tied to the hind legs of horses (*pichhári*), under the superstitious belief that by doing so they lose their fertility or become barren.—*Balkrishna Lal.*

20. *Peculiarities of the Jinn.*

The elements, according to popular belief, are four, *viz.*, earth, air, water and fire (*khak, bád, áb, átish*). The first is supposed to be the one of which human beings are made, and the last is supposed to enter largely in the composition of the Jinn. Jinns are, it is believed, very partial to sweet-meats, and for the purpose of procuring these, are supposed to visit the shops of hulváis (confectioners) at night after the hours when men have retired. It is believed they go dressed in green and put their money down at the shop without a word, and receive the sweets in return. Woe be to the hulvái that weighs short!—*Jwalá Prasadá.*

21. *The Legend of Rája Nala.*

Rája Nala, of Narwar, offends the Goddess Lakshmi, and is so reduced to want that he is obliged to go and seek the assistance of his father-in-law. On the way he catches some fish, which he makes over to his wife while he says his prayers. The Ráni in preparing the fish wounds her finger, and a drop of her blood touches the fish, which revive and jump into the water. The Ráni excuses herself by saying that she had eaten it herself. On reaching her father's house they are ignominiously received. A female slave gives them some broken victuals, which at the Rája's request the earth opens and receives. They then depart and go to the house of an old friend who hospitably receives them. While lying awake the Ráni sees a golden statue of a peacock, which was adorned with a necklace worth nine lakhs, open its beak and begin devouring the necklace. Fearing that they would be suspected of theft they leave the house secretly, and go to Garh Pingla, where the Rája earns his living as a grass-cutter. There they stay twelve years, and a son is born to them, and on the same day the Rája of Garh Pingla has a daughter. When the time came for naming the children, Rája Nala is in despair at his poverty, but a Bráhman casts the horoscope of the boy, predicts that he will be a Rája, and that his name should be Dulhan. In the same way the daughter of the Rája is named Márwan, and it is predicted that unless she marries Rája Dulhan she must die, and that her husband had been born on the same day as she in a grass-cutter's cottage. Search is made, and the Rája directs that rations are to be distributed to all the grass-cutters, but no fire to be given to them. The other grass-cutters fail to cook their food, but when Rája Nala approaches the fireplace, fire issues spontaneously from it. The disguise of Rája Nala is then discovered, and his son is married to the Rája's daughter. Being reinstated in his kingdom, Rája Nala visits his wife's relations, but rejects their hospitality, and at his request the earth opens and shows the fragments of food which the slave-girl had given him. The relatives are confounded, and the Rája visits the friend who had received him with hospitality. He questions the Rája, who calls his attention to the peacock image, which is observed disgorging the necklace which it had swallowed. The Rája's integrity being thus established, he returns home. When his son Dulhan comes of age the Bráhmans are consulted to fix an auspicious day on which to claim his bride Márwan. They declare that unless Dulhan can ride in one day to Garh Pingla he will die if he consummates his marriage with Ráni Márwan. The father dreading the oracle, forbids the name of Márwan to be mentioned, and marries Dulhan to two celestial nymphs. Meanwhile Ráni Márwan is told of her marrige, and builds a palace near a tank. She induces her father to order that all foreigners should stay there, but that neither they nor their cattle should be allowed to use the water of the tank. Finally, a merchant arrives, who says he has come from Garb Narwar, 700 kos off. Ráni Márwan induces him to take a letter to Dulhan, but Rája Nala learns of this, destroys the letter, and expells the messenger from the city on pain of death. Ráni Márwan then sends her favourite parrot with a letter to her husband: but his celestial wives destroy the bird with the letter. Finally, Ráni Márwan offers half the kingdom to any one who will take a letter to Dulhan. Finally, a poor wretch undertakes the dangerous mission. He goes to Garh Pingla and takes up his quarters with an old woman who makes garlands. Here he plays before Rája Dulhan and contrives to deliver the letter. Dulhan determines to claim his wife, and informs his father of his intention. His father explains the oracle to him and tries to dissuade him. Dulhan goes to the stables and asks the camels if any one will undertake to convey him in one day to Garh Pingla. All refuse except one old blind camel which had been a native of Garh Pingla, and used to go there still daily to drink water out of its tanks. She undertakes to convey him there in half a day. The suspicions of his nymph wives are excited, and while sleeping each used to put into her mouth one of Dulhan's fingers, so he could not escape without awaking them. He deceives them by making sheaths for his finger of bark, the colour of his skin, and when his wives sleep he withdraws his fingers from their mouths and escapes. He starts on the blind camel. His wives pursue, and overtaking him at the Chumbal river, hold on behind to the camel's tail. The camel advises Dulhan to cut off her tail, so that his pursuers might be thrown into the river. This he does and arrives at Garh Pingla, where he re-claims his bride, and they lived happily ever afterwards.—*Archæological Reports, Vol. VII., p.* 95, *sqq.*

[This is a curious variant of the well-known tale of Nala and Damayanti, for an abstract of which see Mrs. Manning's *Ancient and Medieval India, Vol. II., p.* 85, *sqq.*—Ed.]

22. The Four Princes and the Four Fairies—A Folktale told by Maulavi Karmud-din Ahmad of Mirzapur.

There was once a king who had four sons. One night the king had a dream that there was a platform of silver, a tree of gold with emerald leaves, and fruit of pearls hanging on it. Soon after he saw a peacock rise from the earth and alight on the tree, when it began to eat the pearls. Suddenly all these things disappeared from his view as well as the peacock. On this the king woke and found himself alone. He was confounded at this dream so that he could not attend his council. On this the king's sons said: "Father! what has happened to you to-day?" He told them what he had seen in his dream, and said:—"If I see this sight once again I will live: if not I will die." They promised to arrange for him to witness the sight again if he would give them three months' time. They asked him to be consoled, and to carry on his duties as usual. The four sons then started in four, different directions. The youngest son went off towards Fairyland. When the youngest son reached Fairyland he sat down at the door of a Fairy. Soon after the Fairy saw him and fell in love with him. Now these Fairies were four sisters. They all came up and saw the Prince, and asked him why he had come here. "If a demon (*deo*) chance to see you he will eat you up." He said:—"I have come to your door and now will not leave it." So the Fairies agreed to keep him as their servant. Accordingly he stayed there, and shortly after he himself fell in love with the Fairy who loved him. He told her that he had come on business. She asked him what the business was. He then told her his father's dream, and that he had come in search of the sight which had appeared to his father. So she asked him to explain what it was his father had seen. He explained it fully. The Fairy said:—"All right! When do you wish to go?" He said:—"Only a fortnight remains out of the three months." The Fairy said:—"You can go tomorrow. But remember that we are four sisters. When you reach home, place four chairs in a row, and sit on one yourself and keep a drawn sword in your hand." Further, she gave him a hair and a little box, and said:—"When you burn this hair we, four sisters will appear. But take care that you do this yourself, and do not allow any one else to do it for you. If you fail we will never come. When we come we will dance. As we dance, whichever of us begins to dance and then say "Wah! Wah!" cut off her head with the sword. By doing this the platform of silver will be produced. When the second Fairy dances and says "Wah! Wah!" cut off her head, and out of it will be formed the golden tree. Do the same with the third, and the emerald leaves will be formed, and when you cut off the head of the fourth, the clusters of the pearls will be produced. Soon after open the box which I have given you, and out of it will come a peacock which will sit on the tree and begin to eat the pearls. Every thing will then disappear: and the four Fairies will appear sitting on the four chairs, and the peacock will return to his box." The Prince hearing this went home. As he was near home he saw his three brothers. He asked them if they had brought this wondrous spectacle with them. They said they were unable to find it. Then the three Princes asked the youngest if he had found it. "Yes," said he. The elder brothers thought it very curious that he should have succeeded when they had failed. So they made a plan to learn the secret from him, and then throw him down a well. They asked him to draw a little water for them. So he told them the secret and drew some water for them. Then they pitched him into the well. They went with the secret to the king, and proclaimed through the city that whoever wished to see the spectacle should present himself. A great crowd assembled. One of the Princes then burnt the hair and the four Fairies appeared. They saw, as they were flying through the air, that the young Prince was not there. The Princes put the hair several times on the fire, but the Fairies did not appear, but returned home. On the way back the Fairies were thirsty, and went to draw water from the well into which the little Prince had been thrown. They got a demon to let down a rope to draw water for them. The Prince caught the rope. The demon said:—"Who are you?" He said:—"I am a man. Pull me out." The Fairies told the demon to draw him out. When the Prince came out the Fairies recognized him. When they heard his story they told him to go home and put the hair on the fire, and they would come at once. When he came home his three brothers wondered and said:—"Well, you can display the spectacle. But do not tell our father what has happened." He replied that he would say nothing. He burnt the hair, and the Fairies appeared, and all happened as they promised. The king was delighted at the sight. Then another king who was present saw the sight and wrote him to order him to present the spectacle to him or stand the risk of war. The young Prince told the Fairies that the other king had demanded to get the spectacle. The Fairies said:—"You may prepare to fight." The other king wondered that this inferior king should dare to resist him. When the battle came off the Fairies sent the demon to help the little Prince, and he in a moment disposed of all their enemies. Then the Fairies pardoned the three brothers, and all four married the four Princes.

23. The Crow and the Sparrow—A Folktale recorded by Maulavi Karm-ud-din Ahmad of Mirzapur.

There were once a crow and a sparrow who agreed each to eat the young of the other when they were born. When the crow had young the sparrow ate them: when the sparrow had young ones, the crow wanted to eat

them. The sparrow said:—"Go first and wash your mouth in the tank."
The crow went to the tank. The tank said:—"Go and bring a water vessel (*abkhora*)." The crow went to the potter. The potter said:—"Bring me clay first." The crow went to the cow and asked her to dig some clay. The cow said:—"First bring me some grass." The cow ate the grass and dug the clay. The crow took it to the potter. He made the vessel. The crow came to the tank and was about to draw water when a king, who was sitting there on the watch for sport, slew the crow with an arrow.

24. *A Cure for Piles.*

It is believed by the Muhammadans of Oudh that piles can be cured if the sufferer sits on the skin of a tiger, while the possession of its claws prevents the effect of evil-eye.—*Aziz-ud-din Ahmed.*

25. *Gaya—Charms to procure Offspring.*

At the village of Mírapur Nadera the ruins of a number of Hindú temples have been converted into mosques. The chief object of interest is an old *dargáh,* about half a mile east of the village, ascribed to Sayyad Ahmad Sháh, a local saint. In the *dargáh* is a tree, to which females for miles around come to tie *chillás* with the object of obtaining children. The *chillá* consists of a small piece of the dress of the weaver, which must be torn and tied to one of the branches of the tree. The woman tying the *chillá* must visit the spot quite alone and at night.—*G. A. Grierson.*

26. *Montgomery—The Legend of Dipalpur.*

Dipálpur is a very old city indeed. It is said to have been founded by one Srí Chand, after whom it was called Srínagar. Srí Chand had no children. His priest Chandra Mani stood on one leg for 5 months and 27 days: after which the Goddess Deví gave him his two sons, Bhím and Lallújas Ráj. He brought them to Dipálpur, and two of Srí Chand's wives adopted them. One day on the way to the temple they indulged in a game of tip-cat. The cat struck one of Srí Chand's wives, who expressed in vigorous language her opinion that they ought to be swallowed up by the earth. Almost immediately Bhím disappeared in the ground and Lallújas Ráj went after him. Chandra Mani had just time to catch him by the lock of hair on the back of his head (*choti*) before he vanished. He then directed that every Khattri of the Khana Sub-division should offer up his *choti* in that place before marriage, and so should other tribes when making vows. He then disappeared. I mention the legend and the old name of the town, as they may have some bearing on the question who were the Oxudrakae (*Ancient Geography of India*, p. 214), but it is incredible that the Káthias should ever be allies of the Khattris. The present name of the town is said to be derived from Dípa, one of Raja Sálváhan's sons, who re-founded the town. Rasálu, another son, lived at Dhaular. The love adventures of his queen Kokilán and Rája Hodi are still sung by Mirásis. There are, however, several other stories regarding the name Dipálpur. The town is the chief seat of the Khattris. It has a very bad reputation as regards the honourableness of its inhabitants. The following verse expresses this:—

Shor Shorion, té kor Láhoron, Jhagrá Chinioton;
Peo putra te chughli karé, Dipálpur de Koton.

Which implies that Shorkot is the place for uproars; Lahore for falsehood; Chiniot for quarrelling, and the town of Dipálpur is the place where the father tells lies on his son.—*W. E. Purser: Settlement Report*, p. 41, *sq.*

[For the story of Rání Kokilán and Rája Hodi, *see* Major Temple's *Legends of the Panjab*, Vol. I.—ED.]

27. *Calcutta—A Folk Etymology.*

The first European who landed at what is now Calcutta, saw two Bengális sitting near a tree which had been cut down. He asked them the name of the place. They thought he was asking them when the tree was cut. They said it was cut yesterday (*kal kata*). He thought this was the name of the place, and wrote it down accordingly. Others say that there was a fort there erected in the name of Káli. This was known as *Káli kot*, and Calcutta got its name from this.—*M. Husen Ali: Mirzapur.*

28. *Gya—Chand Haji—The Saint.*

At the village of Duryápur Párbati is a small Musalmán shrine (*dargáh*). Tradition says that an old Hindu *faqír* once lived here, when a corpse came floating down the river Sakri, and the *faqír* dreamed that the corpse told him that its name was Chánd Háji, and that it wanted a decent burial in a grave, to be dug on the spot, near the south-east end of the hill which he described, and as a reward, he promised the sovereignty of the district to the *faqír*. The *faqír* did as directed, and became king afterwards. The shrine that now stands was the one built by him. Chánd Háji, or Chánd Saudágar, is a saint of wide celebrity in Bengal. Many are the spots where this benevolent saint is said to have put silver and gold vessels, etc., for the use of travellers. A traveller on an evening at one of these fortunate spots, which was generally either a well or the banks of a tank, had only to make known his wants, when Chánd Saudágar's vessel of gold and silver would float up and allow themselves to be used by the traveller, who had, however, scrupulously to return them when done with. But men are covetous, and at each of these places some unlucky man has been too weak to resist the temptation of appropriating them, and since then the miracle has ceased.—*G. A. Grierson: Geography of the Gya District, p. 15, sq.*

29. *The King's Son and his Fairy Bride.*—*A Folktale told by Abdulla, a Weaver of Mirzapur.*

Once upon a time there was a King who had seven sons, all of whom got married, except the youngest. So all his brothers and his sisters-in-law used to worry him to marry. At last he said:—"Well! if I marry, it will be one of King Indra's Fairies." So he rode off. On the road he saw a well, and as heavy rain was falling, he sat down under a tree close by. Soon after a Chamár's daughter came to the well for water, and the Prince saw that, though heavy rain was falling, she and her clothes remained dry. He said to himself:—"This must be one of Indra's Fairies." Then he went to her father and asked his daughter in marriage. But he said:—"How can a Chamár marry a King's son?" However, the Prince insisted, and at last the marriage was arranged. Then the Prince came and told his father that he was to marry a Fairy, so his father started with a grand equipage. They went a long distance, but they saw no grand house, and the King sent a camel-rider ahead to see where the bride's mansion was. The camel-man came back and said:—"I see no mansion, but there is a hamlet of Chamárs, where marriage preparations are going on, and they are saying:—'Hurry up! Hurry up!' the King will be here in a minute." Thus the King was wroth, and told his son to come home at once; but he would not obey, and married the Chamár's daughter.

After they were married the bride said:—"We are married, it is true, but I will not recognize you as my husband unless you cross the seven oceans and get my ring from the faqír who lives there." So the Prince crossed the seven oceans with the utmost difficulty and found the faqír. Now this faqír used to sleep half the year and wake the other half. This time he was asleep, and the earth had fallen on him, and grass was growing on his body. So the Prince cleaned him. When the faqír woke he was about to kill the Prince, but he was appeased, and gave him the ring; at the same time he warned him not to give the ring to his bride the day he returned. When he came home and his bride asked him about the ring, he put her off and went to sleep. But in his sleep she searched for the ring, and when she found it, disappeared.

In despair the Prince returned to this faqír who was again asleep. He cleaned him, and when he woke the faqír said:—"What brings you here again?" He said:—"I have been very careless. While I was asleep my bride secured the ring and now she has disappeared." The faqír answered:— "To find her now is very difficult. She is now among the Fairies in the Court of Indra." "Well," said the Prince, "unless you help me I shall never find her." The faqír said:—"Well! I will tell you a plan. There is a certain stream in which the Fairies come to bathe. Sit near the place, and when they are swimming in water, seize their clothes and run to me. They will come to me and complain, and I will say to them:—'Well! give him what is his.' And they will say:—'If he can recognize her thrice, let him have her.' Then the first time seize hold of the hand of the oldest of them all: and as you hold her they will all clap their hands and say 'he has forgotten! he has forgotten!' But do not let her go. The next time seize the smallest of them all, and they will again mock you. But do not let her go. The third time seize her who is a leper, and do not let her go. Then they will give you up your wife and go away."

And it all happened as the faqír predicted. So when the Prince had recovered his bride she said to him:—"If Rája Indra hears that you and I are married he will kill us both. Now I will give you a flute, and whenever you want me you have only to blow it and I will come to you." The Prince, with the advice of the faqír, took the flute, then the Fairy flew off, and the Prince went home. As he was on the road he came to a wrestling-ring (*akhára*) where a number of Gusáins were wrestling. The Prince sat down and blew his flute. Then his Fairy bride came and asked what he wanted. "I want to see a Fairy dance," said he. So she went away and soon come back with a number of other Fairies and musicians, and the Prince showed the dance to the Gusáins. When the Fairies went away the Gusáins said to the Prince:—"We thought that our stick had most excellent qualities, but your flute beats it." He asked:—"What are the qualities of your stick?" And they told him:—"You have only to tell this stick to strike any one, and it does so at once." The Prince said:—"Let us make an exchange:" so he gave them the flute and went off with the stick.

He then sent back his stick and told it to beat the Gusáins until they gave up his flute, which they did when the stick beat them within an inch of their lives. Going on further, he saw a crowd of people looking at a cooking-pot (*deghchi*) which used to produce any kind of food required. This he acquired in the same way as he had done with the stick: and similarly he obtained a goat whose dung was gold. So he went home with his treasures. One day as he was going out hunting he forgot to bring his flute with him. And while he was away his eldest sister-in-law saw it and blew it. On this the Fairy appeared, and seeing it in her hand, began to scratch and tear her, whereupon she dropped the flute which the Fairy carried off. When the Prince returned from hunting and missed his flute, and learnt what had happened, he began to lament. He went off again to the faqír who, when he saw him coming, knew for certain that the Prince had lost the flute. So he told the faqír the whole story, who said:—"Well! it is a very difficult business to recover it now, because the Fairies have given up bathing in this world, and I do not know where they do bathe now." But the Prince implored the faqír to help him once more. Then the faqír said:—"I will give you one more chance, and if you lose the flute now, you will never get it back. The plan is this:—"The Fairies' washerman (*dhobi*) comes here to wash their clothes and then carries them back in his carriage (*rath*): so when he is starting you cling on to the wheel, and when you get to Fairyland (*Paristán*) you will recover your bride. So next day the Prince hid near the washing-ghát and clung to the carriage wheel till he got to Fairyland. When the washerman saw him he was confounded: finally, the Prince induced him to take pity on him and keep him in his house.

One day while he was there he met his wife. Said she:—"You have not given up following me?" Then she took pity on him and said:—"Well! I will come with you. But you must do one thing. To-night there will be a great dance in Rája Indra's palace. You must come, and when a dance is over you must shout out:—"The dancing is good enough, but the drumming is atrocious. Then the drummer will go off in a huff, and you must take the drum and play, and we will all dance our best. Then the Rája will be delighted and give you anything you ask." And so it happened as she said. And the King said:—"Ask your guerdon." The Prince made him swear three times that he would give him anything he asked. Then he said:—"Marry me to this Fairy." The King agreed, and married them forthwith, and the Prince took his bride home, and they lived happily ever after.

[This is, of course, one of the "Swan Maiden "type of stories of which the best example is that of *Hasan of Bassora and the King's Daughter of the Jinn* (Payne's *Arabian Nights*, Vol. *VII*, p. 121 ff.) For numerous parallels, see Hartland: *Science of Fairy Tales*, p. 255, *sq.*—ED.]

30. *Changes in the Courses of Rivers—Salivahana and the Saint Farid-ud-din Shakkarganj.*

A tendency to change their course is to be observed in the case of most of the Panjab rivers. In the case of the Satlaj this is accounted for among the people by the following legend:—In the time of the great Rája Salwan (Sálíváhana), the Satludra (Satlaj) flowed southward from the Himálayas through this country now occupied by the Bikanír and Bháwalpur States and onwards through Sindh to the sea. Puran, the eldest son of Salwan, who had become a religious ascetic, for some reason invoked a curse upon the river, and ordered it to leave its bed and go to join the Rávi. The river obeyed, and began from that time to change its course more and more towards the west, till 650 years ago it entered the Biyás Valley. The western branch of the Naiwal, thus deserted by the stream, was the last of these channels connected with the Hákra, which, therefore, at this time (about A.D. 1220), finally ceased to flow. The land-holders, afraid that the river, in obedience to the command of Puran, would soon leave their lands, as it had already done further south, besought the intervention of the holy saint Shekh Faríd-ud-dín Shakkurganj. This great apostle of Islám, having prayed, commanded the wandering stream not to move 5 *kos* (7 miles) from the bed in which it was then flowing. Shekh Faríd died in 1261 A.D. at the age of 77, or according to another account in 1265, aged 95. His tomb at Ajudhan, now Pák Pattan (holy ferry), was ousted by Firoz Sháh and Timur, and is still a celebrated place of pilgrimage.—*Calcutta Review, Vol. LIX, p.* 9.

31. *The Tricks of Shekh Chilli (told by an Ayah).*

Once upon a time Shekh Chilli came to his mother and said:—"Mother! every day I go to the well when the women are drawing water, and none of them laugh at me." His mother said:—"If you throw stones at them they will laugh at you." He went next day to the well, but only one woman came, so he threw stones at her, but she did not laugh, so he pushed her in. Then he ran and told his mother what he had done. She bribed some people to help, and they took out the corpse, and in its stead threw a goat into the well. The next day the friends of the woman began to look for her, and Shekh Chilli told them that he had thrown her into the well. Some said:—"We will go and see." Others said:—"No! It is only Shekh Chilli. Don't listen to him." But they decided to go, and when they got there, they made Shekh Chilli go down into the well. He caught the goat and said:—" Oh! it has got two long ears!" The men above told him to bring her out and not to mind if her ears were long. He then called out:—"Oh! listen to me! She has four legs, long hair and two horns. Shall I bring her up?" They told him to do so at once, thinking he mistook her two hands for legs and jewelry for horns. So Shekh Chilli tied the goat to the rope, and when the animal arrived at the top they gave him a beating, and then at last he succeeded in getting the women to laugh at him.—*Una Briscoe: Bulandshahr.*

[Shekh Chilli is the regular type of the idiot humourist, and many tales are told of him.—ED.]

32. Jinns and Europeans.

No Jinn can stand a European. A place near Dera-Gházi Khán was so possessed with them that passers by were attacked. A European officer poured a bottle of brandy on the spot, and the Jinn disappeared.—*Calcutta Review, Vol. LX, p. 99.*

33. The Brahman's Sons and the Gusain (told by Lachhman Ahir, a cultivator of Mirzapur).

Once upon a time there was a Bráhman who had a wife and two sons. When the Bráhman went to beg, it was so with him that whether he begged for an hour or for the whole day, he never got more than a small basket of grain. So one day he consulted his wife and said:—"We are both starving. We had better make over our boys to some one to teach. When they are able to write and read, we will take one and leave the other with their teacher." This was agreed on, and the Bráhman went out to beg and got his basket of grain which he brought home and told his wife to cook at once, and give him the boys to dispose of. So he went off a long way with the children until night fell. Then they rested and ate their supper and went on again. At last they came to a forest, where they saw a Gusáin sitting in his hut. The Gusáin said:—"Maháráj! where are you going?" The Bráhman told him of his difficulties. Then the Gusáin said:—"Well! give me the boys. I will teach them. When they are educated you can have one and I will keep the other." The Bráhman agreed, and made over the children to him. Then the Gusáin taught the elder boy carefully, but gave him very little food, while he taught nothing to the younger boy, but fed and clothed him well, and used to take him about. His object was that the elder should remain thin, and when the time came for his father to select a boy he would chose the younger, and leave him the elder who was well versed in magic.

Meanwhile, when he came home after leaving the boys, the Bráhman attended a funeral of a rich man and got a cow as a gift. This cow had a calf, and the Bráhman and his wife lived well on milk and cream. After four years had gone his wife said:—"The boys must be educated by this time. You had better go and fetch one of them." He agreed, and told his wife to prepare some curds and milk to take with him for the boys. She did so, and he started next morning. When he reached the forest he saw his elder boy up a tree breaking wood, a piece of which fell in the curds. He called out, and the boy recognizing his father, said:—"O father! I am dying. The Gusáin gives me only half enough to eat." His father hearing this wept, and gave him the curds. When the boy had eaten it he told his father how the Gusáin had fattened up the younger boy. "If you choose him," said he, "six months will finish you off in supporting him. But if you take me I will support you all your life." Then the father said:—"All right! I will choose you." So the son said:—"You better stay here. If we come together the Gusáin will kill us both." The father stayed behind and the son went back. In the evening the Bráhman went to the Gusáin's hut, who received him kindly, and made him sleep near him for the night. In the morning the Bráhman said:" I am going to take one of the boys." Then the Gusáin made both of them stand before him and said:—"Take whichever you like." Then the Bráhman took his elder son by the hand, and the Gusáin said:—"You are wrong. This boy will cause you trouble and expense. You had better take the younger: at any rate you can live on the jewelry he is wearing for a whole year." But the Bráhman said:—"His mother told me to bring the elder boy." "All right," said the Gusáin, "but you will live to repent what you are doing." So the two went off together, and at last the boy said to his father:—"You must be tired. Look behind you." When he looked round he saw that his son was turned into a horse, which said:—"Mount on my back, and ride me into the town and sell me. Go away then, and when I get the chance I will turn into a man and come to you." So the father sold him for Rs. 100 and went away. When his owner tied him up and left him, the boy immediately took his former shape and came back to his father and said:—"It was well you took me, or you would not have made this money so easily." But as he looked round he saw the Gusáin, and warned his father to go home, and said:—"I am off, and will bring my brother with me. If I don't go you will never see my face again." So he turned round, and, seeing a tank there, turned himself into a fish and went into the water. When the Gusáin came up and saw the father alone he opened his book of spells to find out what had become of the boy. He discovered that he was in the tank in the form of a fish. So he turned himself into paddy-bird (*bagula*) and began to devour all the fish in the tank. Meanwhile an oilman brought his ox to water at the tank; and the Bráhman's boy at once went into the stomach of the ox. When the Gusáin had finished off all the fish in the tank and could not find the boy, he looked in his book again and found that he was in the stomach of the ox. Then he hastened to the oilman's house and offered him any price he liked for the animal. At first the oilman declined to sell the ox, but finally the Gusáin so worried him that he sold it. Then the Gusáin carried it off and killed it, and began to cut it in pieces and separate the bones. But the boy made the bone in which he was concealed jump away, and a kite seized it and carried it to the river bank where the Ráni was bathing. The kite dropped the bone on her clothes, and she called to her servants to pitch it away. But the boy from within the bone implored her to save his life. So the Ráni took the bone and shut it up in her box. Meanwhile the Gusáin worked his spells again, and traced the boy to the Ráni's box. Then he went to the Rája and said:—"Your Ráni has stolen my bone." The Rája was fiercely angry and struck the Gusáin, but he said:—"Beat me as much as you please, but I won't leave this." Then the Rája asked his Ráni about it. The Ráni said:—"It is not a bone at all, but a Bráhman's son," and told the Rája the whole story. Then the Rája said:—"It is a bad business. The bone must be given up to the Gusáin." "At any rate," urged the boy, "if you must give me up, sprinkle a little sesamum (*sarson*) about the place. But please break the bone first." Then the Ráni did, and immediately the Gusáin turned himself into a pigeon and began to eat up the sesamum. But the Bráhman's boy became a cat and ate up the Gusáin. Then he went off to the hut, recovered his brother, seized all the Gusáin's treasure, and the two boys lived happily with their father ever after.

34. The Black Partridge.

The planet Saturn, according to Hindú Astrology, is supposed to exercise a very malignant influence on human beings in certain conjunctions. The length of time for which such influence lasts is supposed to vary with the different conjunctions, the very longest period being seven-and-a-half years. Rája Nala, at one period of his life, it is stated, came under the adverse influence of Saturn. His good luck at gambling deserted him with the result that he lost all he possessed,—his treasure, his kingdom, and eventually his wife. Reduced to starvation, he one day managed to snare a few partridges and set about roasting them. The malignant influence of Saturn asserted itself, the dead partridges came to life and flew away. The black colour is said to be the result of the charring that the partridges got in the roasting. The cry of the black partridge is imagined to be "*Subhán, teré qudrat*:" equivalent to "great is Thy power," being a reference to God's power in bringing the dead birds back to life.—*Jwala Prasada.*

35. Lalitpur—A Tank which cured Dropsy.

Rája Sumer Singh had the disease called *jalandhar* or dropsy in his stomach, and as the case baffled the doctors, he started on a pilgrimage to Ajudhya. On the way he and his Ráni stopped at a port on the present site of Lalitpur. Here the Ráni dreamt that if the Rája would eat some of the *confervæ* (kái) on the pool he would be cured. He ate some accordingly, and was cured. Again, the Ráni had a dream that there was treasure buried under a tree on the embankment of the tank. A hole was dug under the tree and the treasure taken up. The Rája then called the tank Sumer Ságar or Tál, and founded a town which was named Lalitápura after his Ráni.—*Cunningham: Archæological Reports, Vol. XXI, p.* 175.

36. The Tricks of Shekh Chilli.

Next day, Shekh Chilli said "*amma! amma* (mother! mother) I am going to get a red wife (*lál bahu*), so make me some cake." When they were ready he set off, and on the road he saw a thorny tree, so he stuck half the cake on it, and sat a short distance off with the rest before him. An old woman and her daughter came by and said she was very hungry. He said "*amma!* I got these from that tree, yonder. Leave your daughter with me, and you go and get some too. What is the use of tiring her?" So she left the child with the Shekh, and when she was out of sight, he persuaded the girl to go home with him. So he brought his wife home and said "mother! did I not tell you I would bring home a wife." So this was how Shekh Chilli was married.—*Una Briscoe: Bulandshahr.*

37. Diamonds at Panna—Legend of.

Once upon a time a holy man came and settled at Panna, who had a diamond as big as a cart-wheel. The Rája hearing of this, attempted to seize it by force, but the saint buried the wheel in the ground to keep it out of the Rája's way. The Rája visited the saint, who told him that the diamond-wheel could not leave his dominions, but that no one would ever be able to find it. The Muhammadans say that all the diamonds found since are fragments of the wheel.—*Archæological Report, Vol. VII, p.* 50.

38. The Princess who got the gift of Patience—A Folktale told by an old Muhammadan Cookwoman, and recorded by E. David, Native Christian, Mirzapur.

There was once a king who had seven daughters. One day he called and asked:—"In whom have you confidence?" Six answered "in you," but the seventh said "in myself." The king was displeased with her and directed that she should be taken to a jungle and left there. This was done. She went wandering about and came on a house, but the door was locked. She rapped, but no one answered. Looking down she saw a key hanging on a nail in the corner: with this she opened the door and went in. She found the house full of furniture and food; so she stayed there. Some time after the king was going on a journey and asked his daughters what they wished him to bring them: one said a *dhoti,* another a doll, and so on. Then he remembered the little princess, and sent a servant to the jungle to see if she were alive, and if so, to ask her what she wished her father to bring for her. The servant came to the house and found her bathing. He gave her the king's message. She called out "I am bathing. Have patience (*sabar*)." He thought she wanted this, so he came and told the king that she wanted patience. As the king was returning from his travels he brought the presents for all the princesses, but forgot the little princess. When he went on board the ship it somehow or other would not move. The captain said to the passengers:—"Think, if you have not forgotten something." All of them began to think, and the king suddenly remembered that he had forgotten the present for the little princess. He went on shore and asked, a shopkeeper "do you sell patience?" Every one laughed at him. Then he met an old woman, and asked her if she knew where "Patience" was to be bought. She said "I have some. But, tell me who you are and who wants it." The king told his story to the old woman; she went into her house and brought out something wrapped in a dirty rag which the king took and went on board. When he embarked the ship started of its own accord. When the king reached home, he gave all the things to the princesses and sent her present to the little princess. When she saw the dirty rag, she said "the servant did not give me time to tell him what I wanted. Pitch this dirty rag away." They did so. Years after by chance her eye fell on the rag, and she thought "it is queer that this rag, which I threw away an age ago, has not decayed." She took it up and began to open it, and found in it a lovely fan. She was delighted, and, as it was hot, began to fan herself with it. Then she laid it upside down, and lo! a prince stood beside her, and said:—"Why did you call me?" She said:—"I don't know who you are, and I never called you." He replied:—"When you put the fan upside down I had to come to you; I am the king of a distant land." So they began to chat, and after a while, as they looked at each other, they fell violently in love; and soon after agreed to be married. They lived together many days, and whenever the prince wanted to go home the princess used to lay the fan straight, and whenever she wanted him she used to turn it upside down.

Long after the princesses said to the king:—"If you allow us, we will go and visit our little sister." He gave them leave, and just as they came to the house of the little princess the prince happened to come up. When they saw him her sisters were filled with envy. The prince used to stay all night with the princess and go home every day. Next day the princesses said to the little princess:—"Let us make the prince's bed to-day." She said:—"Do so." They took off all their glass bangles (*chúri*), and grinding them up, sprinkled it on his mattress and spread a fine sheet over it. When the prince got into bed the broken glass ran into his flesh. He called out:—"I am in horrible pain. Quick put the fan straight and let me go home." The princess wondered, but she put the fan straight and off he went. Next day the princesses went away, and in the evening the little princess put the fan upside down, but the prince never came. She went on turning the fan up and down, but to no purpose. She was in great grief, and suspected that her sisters had been up to some trick. Next day she put on man's clothes, shut up her house, and went off to the prince's palace. On the road night came on and she slept under a tree. On the tree sat a parrot and a *maina*. At midnight the parrot said to the *maina*:— "Tell me something which may make the night pass." The *maina* said:— "Well; there is a princess whose father turned her out into the jungle. There she fell in with a prince. When her sisters saw how happy she was, they put broken glass into the prince's bed. He was in such pain, he had to go home, and now though many physicians have treated him, he does not recover." The parrot asked:—"Well, and what is the way to cure him?" The *maina* replied:—"If any one were to take some of our dung, boil it well in oil and rub it on him, all the pieces of glass would come out." The princess heard all this and collected some dung and started off. When she came to the palace she shouted:—"Physician ho! "(*baid, baid*). The sentry announced her arrival. The king called her in and said:—"My son is very ill. If you can cure him I will give you a great reward." She said:—"Light a fire and give me some oil, and I will put him right at once." She followed the *maina*'s advice, and the prince recovered at once. But she took as her reward only the clothes the prince was wearing. These she took home, turned the fan upside down, and the prince appeared. The whole matter was cleared up, and they lived happily. Thus "Patience" stood the princess in good stead.

39. Jalandhar—Rural Superstitions.

On the 1st, 5th, 7th, 9th, 10th, 21st and 24th day of each month, the ground is supposed to be sleeping, according to the following couplet, of which there are more versions than one—

Sankránt mitti din pánchwen, nauwen, sátwen lé,
Das, iki, chaubíswen khat din prithivi suwé.

That is, on the six (*khát*) days detailed above the earth sleeps. On these days ploughing and sowing should not begin, though once begun, they may go on. Working a well or ploughing during eclipses is most unlucky. The cane-mill should be set up and started on a Sunday, but in case of absolute necessity, Thursday may be permitted. Tuesday is the day on which reaping should begin, and Wednesday that on which to commence sowing. Care must be taken never to commence work with a cart or well-bucket on Tuesday or Thursday. Before sowing, cane sugar and concrete sugar (*gur*) are often distributed in the field, and after the spring sowings are completed, the agriculturist prepares sweetmeats for home consumption and distribution. When the spring crop has been threshed out, if it cannot be immediately removed, the Chamár goes round the heap with a winnowing bucket, and makes an indented figure (*cháng*) in the grain close to the ground. The object of this is to protect the produce from goblins (*bhút*) and ghosts (*paret*), who would otherwise steal part of it, or at least diminish its usefulness. The grain must be weighed before sunrise, or at noon, or after sunset, as at other times these malevolent agents are wandering about the world. When weighing is going on, the weigher must face the north, and no woman, stranger or person with uncovered head, may approach. Water should be at hand: and a cake of cow-dung, prepared at the Díwáli festival, should be kept burning. Muhammadans are not particular when it has been prepared, and those among them who are enlightened, smile at these superstitious customs, and think a piece of cloth with *Bismillah*—"Glory to God"—written on it sufficient protection. If the grain cannot be at once removed, it is fumigated with bdellium (*gúgal*), or felt, and a piece of iron, or an iron tool, as a sickle or trowel, is placed in the heap. Sometimes a menial (*sepi*) taking a blanket, sickle and pitchfork with him, draws a line round the heap, and whence the circle meets, places his head on the ground.—*W. E. Purser: Settlement Report, p. 55.*

40. The Dahani Firang Stone.

It is believed by Muhammadans that the possession of a stone called *dahani firang* is a cure for pains in kidneys. The stone is of three kinds—golden, silver and copper, and is sold very dear, specially the golden one.—*Aziz-ud-din Ahmed.*

[What is the *dahani firang* stone?—Ed.]

41. Mirzapur—A Swinging Elephant.

I went the other day to see the Ráni of Barhar, and noticed near her gate an elephant swinging its body continually about. I remarked on the curious way the animal was moving its body, and was told that it was specially selected for this peculiarity, as it is very lucky to have an elephant that swings its body about tied up at one's gate.—*W. Crooke.*

42. Battle-field Ghosts.

With reference to the procession of the ghosts of the slain which is said to traverse the field of battle nightly, the people of Khánwa are not singular in their belief as the same superstitious fears prevail at Pánípat and also at Chillianwála. I heard of the ghosts of the latter battle as early as 1864, only fifteen years after the battle, and the ghosts of Pánípat are mentioned by Abdul Qádir during the reign of Akbar, about 40 years after that battle. I cannot find the passage now, but I remember that he records, being obliged to cross the plain at night, he felt awestruck, and hurried over the battlefield as quickly as possible. Shouts of rage and shrieks of agony are said still to be heard mingled with the groans of the wounded and dying. The same story is told at Chillianwála, where the field of battle is known as the *qatalgarh* or place of slaughter. Moans of pain and wild lamentations are said to be heard at night by persons passing near the graveyards which lie between the 30th and 31st milestones from Gujarát.—*Cunningham: Archæological Reports, Vol. XX, p.* 96.

[This is of course a common idea: for the case of Marathon, see Grote's *History of Greece*, Vol. IV, p. 285; and for Neville's Cross, Henderson's *Folklore of the Northern Countries*, p. 308.—ED.]

43. Garhwal—Shaving.

Hindús of Garhwal do not shave on the day of their birth in the week. Some men go so far that they do not shave for the whole month in which they were born.—*Aziz-ud-din Ahmed.*

44. Farrukhabad—A Fort supplied with Oil.

In Jiragaur are the remains of a fort said to have been built by Rája Bhoj. There is a tradition that it was supplied with oil from another ruined fort some miles away, and traces are found of what is supposed to be a masonry conduit.—*A. W. Trethewy.*

45. Gaya—The Legend of Kunwar Bijai Mall.

Párbati and Aphsaur are indissolubly connected with the legend of Kunwár Bijai Mall, which forms the theme of a long poem sung by men of the Teli caste all over South Bihár. The song has been printed in full and translated in the journal of the Asiatic Society, and the following is a condensed abstract of the version of the story given in the eighth volume of the Reports of the Archaeological Survey of India:—

Kunwar Bijai Mall used to live in Jhunjhunwa Garh, a place which I have not been able to identify. He came to Párbati to be married to Báwan Subáh's daughter, and was accompanied by his father and his elder brothers, being himself a child. Báwan Subáh treacherously seized his father and brothers, and put them into prison. Kunwar Bijai Mall's horse, however, fled with his rider and carried him safe back to Jhunjhunwa Garh. Here he grew up in ignorance of the fate of his father and brothers, and there being no male relations to avenge his wrongs, his female relations, of whom his sister-in-law was chief, kept him in this condition, lest he should rashly venture to fight and lose his life. This sister-in-law, named Sonmatí Ráni, took great care of him, had him taught all arts, and intended, when he should grow up, to live with him as his wife. When Bijai Mall did grow up, he wanted bows and arrows and a tipcat and stick (*guli danda*) to play with. Sonmatí Ráni gave him the ordinary wooden ones, but he broke them, and wanted stronger ones: finally, he had made for his special use an iron *danda* of 84 maunds weight, and an iron *guli* of 80 maunds. These he took and went to play with his companions, but on their refusing on the ground that they could not use his stick, it was agreed that each should use his own. When Bijai Mall's turn came to hit his iron tipcat he struck it with such force that it flew to Garh Párbati, and smashed a part of Báwan Subáh's palace. His companions searched for the tipcat for seven days, but not finding it, they came disgusted to Kunwar Bijai Mall, and asked him, why, when he was so strong, he did not go and release his father and brothers from confinement. Accordingly, he went to his sister-in-law, and demanded to be told the circumstances of their confinement. She long tried to evade his questions, but finding him persist, she went and adorned herself superbly, and, radiant with gems and beauty, came out. He asked her why she had adorned herself. She said:—"Your brothers and father went West to fight, and I expect them back to-night." This he would not believe, but drawing his sword, threatened to kill her: then she told him the whole truth. The groom of the horse, Jhengna Khawás, was called and confirmed her story, and Bijai Mall ordered the horse and arms to be brought and prepared to go. Sonmati Ráni begged him to eat before going. He sat down and finished his supper. She then besought him to lie down and rest for a while: he did so and fell asleep. She then went and laid herself beside him. On waking and seeing her he said:—"I consider you as my mother; be not uneasy. I will go and rescue your husband and my father in four days." She then left him and he went to Párbati—*G. A. Grierson: Geography of the Gaya District, p. 16, sq.*

(To be continued.)

46. Mirzapur—Threshing-floor superstition.

In the southern hilly country, I find that one way of protecting rice on the threshing-floor from the attacks of ghosts and demons is to form it into a circular sort of platform, carefully patted down all round with a stick, while in the middle a sort of cone is constructed. It thus assumes the forms of the platforms (*chabutra*) which are found in every village devoted to the worship of local deities like Gansám and Rája Lákhan.—*W. Crooke.*

47. How the Washerman's Ass became a Qazi—A Folktale told by Shekh Abdulla of Mirzapur.

There was a certain school master who had a very stupid pupil. One day, when he did not know his lesson, the master called him "Ass." A fool of a washerman who was passing by, on hearing this, said:—"Mr. teacher, was this boy once a donkey?" "Yes," said the master, "he was a donkey, and my teaching has made a man of him." The washerman said:—"I have nothing in the world but an ass, and if you can turn him into a man, I shall be delighted to bring him to you." "All right," said the teacher. "Go and bring him." So the washerman came up, thrashing his ass to make him come quickly; and asked the teacher:—"How long will it take to turn my ass into a man?" "A year's time," replied the teacher. A year after he returned and asked the master where his ass was. The master replied:— "Your ass has become the Qázi of So-and-So City," and draws a salary of Rs. 1,000 a month, and holds a Court." By chance, when the washerman first went to the teacher, the Qázi was in the school and knew all about the master. The washerman asked the way to the Qázi's Court and went on. The Qázi did not know him and paid no attention to him. The washerman came back and said to the master:—"In truth he has become a great man, and when I went into his Court he did not even look at me." The master replied:—"Of course, he won't notice you if you approach him in this way as he is a great officer on a high salary. But take a rope and hobble and go into his Court and shake them and say:—"Have you forgotten the rope and hobble with which you used to be tied?" He did as he was told, and then the Qázi remembered the circumstance, and he thought:—"If I don't get rid somehow of this fellow I shall become a laughing-stock." So the Qázi gave the washerman a thousand rupees and dismissed him. The washerman showed the master the money, and he took half of it as the feed of the ass. The washerman went home blessing his good luck, and in this way every year he used to receive a present from the Qázi and lived a happy man for the rest of his days.

48. *Another Version of the Fairy Gift Legend.*

At Pathári, in Bhopal, there lived a Muni or a Pír in a cave unknown to any one. His goat used to graze with the herdsman's flock. The shepherd one day followed the goat into the cave and found an old man seated intent in meditation. He made a noise to attract the saint's attention, who asked the object of his visit. The herdsman asked for wages, whereupon the saint gave him a handful of barley. He took it home, and in disgust threw it on the fire, where the wife soon afterwards found it turned into gold. The herdsman went back to thank the old man, but found the cave deserted, and its occupant was never heard of again. The shepherd devoted his wealth to building a temple.—*Archæological Reports, Vol. VII, p.* 71.

49. *Irich—Legend of.*

A form of the legend attributing the formation of the Vindhyun and Kaimúr ranges to the wars of the Rámáyana is found at Irich in Jhánsi. The monkey allies of Ráma were bringing loads of stones to form the bridge across the channel to Lanka. Ráma sounded his conch to announce that no more materials were required, whereupon a monkey, who had happened to be then passing over Irich, dropped his load which now forms the mass of rocks at the bend of the river.—*Archæological Reports, Vol. VII, p.* 35.

50. *The Excellent Qualities of the Plant Mundi.*

The *mundi* plant (*sphaeranthus indicus*) is a favourite medicine with hakíms. The following account of its properties is taken from a Persian MS. in the possession of a faqír at Chunár. It must be plucked in a particular way. After ablution offer a prayer of two *rakah* (prostrations), repeat the Fátiha and the Sura Ikhlás thrice, dig it up on a Sunday at a time when no shadow falls on the plant. Taking out the root put it in a cloth and not in earth: if dug before sunrise, its effects will be in every way superior. If eaten for a month with cow's milk and sugar it preserves the sight. If eaten for two months, fire will not burn one who falls into it; eaten for five months, it increases the strength; eaten for six months, a person's hair will never turn grey; eaten for seven months, it secures an interview with Khwája Khizr the prophet; eaten for two months it enables the eater to perform the miracles of the saints. If dried in the shade and eaten with milk and sugar, it wins the love of women. A lotion of the pounded root is a cure for sore eyes. If the leaf be pounded, dried in the shade, and one *tola* of the powder drunk in cow's milk the Jinn and Satan will appear before the user and await his orders. Eaten for a year with an equal quantity of wheat flower, the body turns the colour of the *mundi* flower. *Mundi* eaten with the weed *bhangra*, restores youth. Similarly eaten for forty days the invisible things of heaven and earth manifest themselves. Eaten with curds from cow's milk, it is an antidote to poison. Eaten with deer's milk, it makes the user a miraculous runner, and the user will surpass the speed of ten horses. Eaten with dates, it removes hunger and thirst. In short, used in various ways, it is considered by Muhammadan Hakíms to be a remedy for most of the diseases common to humanity.—*Bhán Pratáp Tiwári.*

51. The School of Love—A Folktale collected by Munshi Karam-ud-din of Mirzapur.

A merchant had educated his son in all branches of learning, except the art of love. He employed a clever Kathak singer to instruct his son in this department. The Kathak showed the world to the youth for some time, and finally pronounced him perfect. The son got a lakh of rupees from his father and went abroad to trade. When he reached a certain city, as he was walking about, he was fascinated by a lady, whom he saw on a house top. She marked him down as her prey, and sent her attendant to negotiate with him. He induced the young man to believe that she was a fairy, and came only occasionally from fairyland. She constructed an underground passage in her house, and her mysterious appearances caused the young man to believe her story. Finally, though he was allowed to approach no nearer the object of his desires, she and her friends swindled him out of all his money. He returned and told his father, who called the Kathak and remonstrated with him on the result of his instruction. The Kathak engaged to recover the money if the merchant would advance him another lakh of rupees. The merchant agreed, and the Kathak procured a monkey, whom he taught to keep a quantity of precious stones in his pouch, and to produce them when called on. The monkey was named Arzu Beg—"the lord of desire." When the monkey knew his business the Kathak and the young man proceeded with the monkey to the city where the lady lived. Number of persons visited the monkey, and to each, under the Kathak's orders, he presented a valuable jewel. This attracted the lady, who became exceedingly affable to the young merchant, and the monkey constantly made her valuable presents. Finally, she asked to get the monkey; but the young man referred her to the Kathak, who finally sold him to the lady for two lakhs of rupees. For some time he produced precious stones to order, but one day the lady's mother asked him for a couple of rupees to buy food, when, his supply of jewels being exhausted, he fell on her and her daughter and entreated them despitefully. By this time the Kathak and his pupil had left the place with the money, and the lady was left to lament the trick that had been played upon her.

52. Upturned City—Legend of a Human Sacrifice—Cannibalism.

There was once a king at Sunit, named Rája Manj Gend or Punwár, who treated his subjects with great violence and cruelty. The king was afflicted with an ulcer, and was told that human flesh would do it good. So an order went forth to bring him a human being as occasion required from each household. One day it so happened that it was the turn of a Bráhman widow who had an only child ten years of age. The myrmidons of the tyrant came to carry off the child, when the tears of its mother moved the sympathies of a holy man, Sháh Qutb by name. He, after a vain attempt to turn away the soldiers, swore that they should never see their homes again, and so it happened. They turned towards Sunit, but both Sunit and its Rája had disappeared off the face of the earth. Another story is that the Rája was in the habit of eating a goat every day, but the supply of goats having ceased, his cook served up the flesh of a young child. The Rája observed the difference, and the cook explained the difficulty. Sirkap, the Rája, was satisfied, and ordered the cook to serve up a young child daily. At last the child of a Bráhman widow was taken, when the mother at once went to Ludhiána and implored the great saint Qutb Sháh to assist her, which he did most effectually by killing Sirkap.—*Cunningham Archæological Reports, Vol. XIV, p. 67.*

53. *The Tricks of Shekh Chilli.*

Shekh Chilli said:—"*Amma! Amma!* (mother!) I am going to seek my fortune in another country." She said "all right my boy! Go! "So he started and stayed at a potter's house. After he had been there two or three days the potter and his wife went to a wedding and left their only child, a boy, with him. When they had gone the boy began to ask for food, but Shekh Chilli said:—"I won't give you any till you tell me where the money is kept." For a long time he would not tell, but when he got very hungry he said:—"It is under the flour-mill, in a pot in the opposite corner." Then Shekh Chilli went and dug it up and mixed it with some flour, and said to the boy:—"If you tell your father I will murder you." Next day the boy's father and mother came home, and Shekh Chilli said:—"*Amma!* I have been here a long time and I must go home, so give me leave and give me the one-eyed ass to carry my things on." Now Shekh Chilli had given this ass the money mixed up in the flour, and the one-eyed ass had eaten it. So she said:—"Pick a nicer one out of the drove." But he said:—"I only want it for my luggage." So thinking no evil she gave it to him. The Shekh started, and when he got home he said:—"*Amma!* I want to show the people my good fortune; you must clean the house." Then the chief people of the village came, and the Shekh brought out the donkey and beat it with his bludgeon when all the money fell out of its mouth. Then they said:—"Will you sell the ass?" At first he refused, but after a lot of persuasion he gave it for a tremendous sum of money. The buyers, to purchase the donkey, sold some of their lands, some their houses and cattle, and so on till they had collected the amount. Then they took the ass away, and all of them collected that night and beat the ass so that it died, but no more money came out of its mouth. So they returned in a rage to Shekh Chilli and said:—"Return our money." "Return my ass," he said. So they cried and beat their breasts and had to stand the loss.—*Una Briscoe: Bulandshahr.*

[Animals which drop money appear in many folktales.—ED.]

54. *King Akbar and the donkey—A folktale told by Baldeo Prasad, village accountant of Haliya, Mirzapur District.*

One day Akbar said to Bírbal:—"Show me something new. I have seen all the sights of the world." Bírbal was puzzled, and his daughter enquired the reason. When he told her, his daughter sent for a donkey and had it trained to the saddle. She then made it known that her father was on the point of death. When the news reached Akbar he hastened to visit his minister; but his daughter sent out word that if Bírbal saw the king in his last moments he would go to hell. Then she announced that Bírbal was dead, and after some time mounted her father on the donkey, and made him ride to the house of one of the ladies of the court. The lady was surprised to see Bírbal risen from the dead. He said:—"God has provided me with a divine conveyance, and I am going about collecting information for Him." She informed the king that Bírbal appeared, and he desired to see the divine conveyance. So Bírbal appeared to the king and told him the same story. The king said he wanted, too, to go to heaven; so Bírbal made him cover his eyes and mount on the donkey. He led the king on the donkey to the chief market-place and left him there. After a time the king removed the bandage from his eyes and saw where he was. "This is something you never saw before in your life," said Bírbal, and Akbar was much pleased.

[There is a great cycle of legend describing the cleverness of Bírbal and his daughter, of which this is one.—Ed.]

55. *Jalandhar—Superstitions about Cattle.*

It is very unlucky for a cow to calve in Bhádon (August–September), or a buffalo in Mágh (January–February), or for a mare to foal in Sáwan (July–August.) Such a cow is called *bhadwai*, and is sure to give little milk. One's only chance is to swim her in a pond or stream. If the offspring of either of the three cannot be sold to a Muhammadan neighbour who has no scruples, it should be given as a present to a Gujarátí Bráhman. A similar course should be followed if two young are produced at one birth. Kine, buffaloes and horses, male or female, that get on the roof of the house, should be summarily disposed of; they are unlucky. So, too, are cows and bullocks, whose colour is black with certain white points (*kaila*), or iron-grey with black spots on the whole body (*phangat*), or on the tail (*megat*). When cattle-disease breaks out a Jogí or Sunnyási or Muhammadan Faqír, who knows the proper incantations, is called in, and proceeds to exorcise the illness. Each practitioner may have his own method, but the broad lines are these. The cattle are first fumigated with bdellium (*gúgal*). Then a proclamation issues that grinding and churning are not to be done that night. A thick rope of cane fibre is tied over the gateway of the village, and to it are attached a couple of small earthen saucers, a little board of *siris* (acacia sirisa) or *dhák* (butea frondosa) wood, and sometimes a couple of parcels of seven kinds of grain (*satnaja*) and a piece of iron. The whole is called *tona*. The board and saucers are daubed with red paint with figures supposed to represent Ganesa or Hanumán or Saturn; or they may bear what are supposed to be texts from the Qurán. In the early morning the cattle are driven under this charm, and are sprinkled with water, and sometimes diluted butter-milk. The manure of the night should not be used, but thrown out on the road. Sometimes the charm is suspended to a post (*mani*) fixed outside the gateway. Another excellent remedy for cattle-disease is a wrestling match (*chhínj*) in honour of Sultán Sakhi Sarwar by professional athletes, and a third is a feast to Bráhmans' *jag* and poor people.—*W. E. Purser: Settlement Report, p. 55, sq.*

56. A Folktale told by Jumai, a village Julaha in South Mirzapur.

There was once a certain king. One day he was sitting in his court with all his officials. Then he fell asleep and saw in a dream a lovely woman whose breast was a full-yard wide and her waist narrow as a leopard's. She lay down beside him. When he woke the woman had disappeared. The king called his officials and said:—"Whoever recals this dream to me, to him will I give half my kingdom." And he placed a piece of betel in his court for whoever would undertake the enterprise. But no one succeeded. Soon after the king's son went out hunting. When he returned and came to his father he saw the piece of betel there and asked the meaning of it. The prime minister said:—"This is no concern of your's." The prince insisted on enquiring. Then the prime minister told him the whole story. The prince at once took up the piece of betel and ate it, and came to his mother and ate and drank. Then he asked his mother for some money as he had taken the betel on condition of undertaking the duty. Her mother gave him money. When the prince came out he met the Wazir's son. He offered to accompany the prince. At first he refused to take him with him. But he insisted on going with the prince. As they went on they came to a desolate forest. The prince was very hungry and thirsty. The Wazir's son replied:—"Where are we to get food and drink in this jungle." So the Wazir's son said "get up on this tree and I will go in search of water." As he went on he came to the foot of a mountain. There was a spring, so he filled a vessel with water and returned to the prince. The prince was delighted to see him. When he tested the water he found it was like rose water. The prince asked where he had got the water. The Wazir's son said:—"First drink the water and then I will tell you all about it." He refused, and said he would not drink till he heard the story. Then the Wazir's son said:—"Come with me and see for yourself." They went on together and came to the spring. Both ascended the mountain and saw a splendid tank full of pure water; and a washerman was washing clothes on it banks. The prince asked him to whom the tank belonged. The washerman said:—"This tank was made by the princess of this land." The prince asked him what she was like. The washerman said:— "Since she was born no lights have been lit in my land." The prince asked the washerman to show him the princess. He took them on, and made them halt in a flower-garden. The washerman went to the princess and told her the story. She said:—"Send them to me tonight by the secret door." The washerman returned to the prince, who gave him valuable presents. At midnight, dressed in his best clothes, the prince went to the princess. When he came in he found vessels of perfumes and dishes of betel placed before her in abundance. The room was full of pictures. He was delighted; and the princess made him sit down when they forthwith fell in love. After sometime the prince left her and was going again to see her the next day. But meantime the princess with her maidens came into the garden. She ordered her maidens to retire. She saw a man asleep in the garden. She thought how she could wake him, and knew not if he was a demon (*dano*) or a man. Finally, the prince woke, and asked her to go home with him. So she took the prince and the Wazir's son to her house. [The rest the narrator forgets.]

57. Jalandhar—Rural Medicinal Treatment— Unlucky Names.

When human beings get ill a Dakaut Bráhman is summoned. A fowl, or goat, or young buffalo is selected to carry the disease, and has its ear cut, its face smeared with red paint, and is taken round the village and out of it, and then made over as a present to the Dakaut. Pleurisy is charmed by a gram-parcher with a sickle, the iron of which is rubbed over the body where the pain is felt. Another plan is to get a piece of the stalk of the *saccharum munja* reed, and cut off a piece from it; as it diminishes, so does the pain. Other vows and the efficacy of bathing at certain places need not be mentioned in detail. There are some places which it is unlucky to call by their proper names before breaking one's fast in the morning. Such are the towns of Ráhon and Jadla. In villages the doors and walls are often marked with an open hand, usually in black; but sometimes in red or white, to keep off the evil eye. The *swástika* in black is also common. It is the mark of Ganesa, who is worshipped at the beginning of anything new.—*W. E. Purser: Settlement Report, p.* 56.

58. The Magic Ring of the Lord Solomon—A Folktale recorded by Maulavi Karamud-din Ahmad of Mirzapur.

There was a king who had an only son, who was worthless and did not obey his father. The king was much displeased with him. One day the prince asked his father for Rs. 300, and said he wished to travel. The king gave him the money, and the prince went to the stable and selected a horse. This he mounted and started on his travels. He came to the shore of the ocean and saw four boys diving in the water. Soon after they brought up a box out of the water. The prince offered to buy it. They asked Rs. 300 for it. He bought it and took it home. The king asked him what he had brought. He showed his father the box. The king ordered the box to be opened, and out of it came a dog. The king kept the box and the dog. Again the prince went on his travels, but before he started he gave his mother a cup of milk and said:—"Mother, as long as this milk does not become sour know that I am alive." Again he reached the same shore of the ocean, and again he saw some boys dive and bring out a box. He purchased this box also and brought it home. When he opened the box a cat came out of it. His mother said:—"You are a nice fellow! You never learn anything, and go about buying dogs and cats." Again the prince took Rs. 300 and went to the shore of the ocean. Again the boys brought out a box. He bought it and took it home. When it was opened a snake appeared. The king was afraid at the sight and told the prince to put the box in a jungle. He did so. The prince reflected that the wretched snake was shut up in the box and would die: so he opened the box and immediately a lad came out of it. The prince said:—"Who are you?" "I am the son of the Lord Solomon. A sorcerer turned me into a snake and put me on board his ship and shut me up in a box. He threw me into the ocean, and immediately he and his ship were submerged." Then he and the prince went to the Lord Solomon. When he saw them he was much pleased and began to distribute alms. One day the son of the Lord Solomon said to the prince:—"If my father offer you any present accept nothing but the ring he wears." Then the Lord Solomon called the prince and offered him many jewels, but he would accept none of them. The Lord Solomon asked him what he wanted, and thrice promised to give him anything he wished. Then the prince asked for the ring. The Lord Solomon with much regret was obliged to fulfil his promise. Then the prince asked the son of the Lord Solomon what were the virtues of the ring. He replied:—"Whatever you desire will be produced from the ring." As they went on they came to a certain city where a princess had made a proclamation that she would marry any one who in a single night would build a palace in the midst of the sea. The prince went to her and said he could fulfil the condition. The princess told her servants to take him to the shore of the ocean. They took him there, and having dismissed them near morning he drew out the ring and ordered it to build a palace in the sea. At once a splendid palace was built. So the prince and the princess were married and lived in the palace. One day the prince went out hunting: two or three hairs of the head of the princess, which were of gold and silver, got broken. She put the hairs on a leaf and threw them into the river. As they floated they came beneath the palace of the king of another land. The king had the hairs taken out and said:—"What must she be to whom these hairs belong!" So he called many wise women and said:—"I will give half my kingdom to any one who will bring this woman to me." One wise woman traced out the princess, and standing under her window, began to weep. The princess called her and said:—"Who are you!" She replied:—"I am your grandmother." The princess ordered her to be entertained. The old woman knew that the palace had been produced by magic. She noticed the ring with the prince, and knew that this was the magic ring. She asked the princess if the prince ever give her his ring. She said:—"He will give it to me if I ask for it:" so the prince gave the ring to the princess. The old woman got hold of the ring and worked the spirit of the ring and ordered him to carry the palace as it was to her country. This was done, and the old woman obtained half the king's kingdom, but did not give him the ring.

When the prince returned from hunting he found the palace and the princess gone. He was plunged into grief, but finally traced out the palace and went there. He wanted to go in, but the servants prevented him. On this there was a quarrel, and the king's servants killed him. When he died the cup of milk which he had given his mother became sour. She knew he was dead, and took out the cat and the dog which had come from the ocean. They went off to try and restore their master to life. The dog dived into the ocean, and taking the cat on his back, reached the palace where the prince had been slain. They found his corpse hung to a tree. Then the dog and cat brought their master to life and put him in a safe place. The prince said:—"Go and search for the ring." They went off and reached the palace of the princess. The dog sent the cat to get the ring from the princess. The princess told the cat that the old woman had the ring. The cat went into her house and found that she used to keep the ring in her mouth when she went to sleep so the cat made friends with a mouse, and told him to put his tail in the old woman's nostrils when she went to sleep. He did so: the old woman sneezed, and the ring falling from her mouth, was seized by the mouse, who took it to the cat. The cat took the ring to her master. He called the spirit of the ring, who carried the palace back to its original place: so the prince and the princess lived happily ever after.

59. The Pranks of Hop-o'-my-Thumb—A Folktale told by Karam-ud-din of Mirzapur.

A man had four sons. The youngest was only a span long, and was called Bittan or "Hop-o'-my-Thumb." The elder boys used to kill game and eat it, and leave only the bones for Bittan. One day Bittan in his anger went out hunting and hunted two hares, which he followed into their hole and drew them out. He gave them to his elder brother's wife. When he came to dinner she told him to go to the kitchen for his food, and then he found as usual that his brothers had eaten all the meat and left only the bones for him. Then he said:—"Give me my share of the inheritance and let me shift for myself." So they gave him his share of everything. He sold his share of the cattle and gave the money to his wife. He went off in search of service.

On the road he met an Ahír's son who had a lot of cattle. Bittan said:—"Come with me and I will marry you to a King's daughter." When Bittan got him on board a boat he pitched him into the river and took all his goods. He returned and gave the money to his wife. Then he bought a horse and burned his house down. He loaded the ashes on the horse and went off on his travels.

He met a merchant with a heap of money. The merchant's mother was very tired. The merchant said to Bittan:—"Give my mother a lift on your horse." Bittan said:—"If I put your mother on my horse all my money will turn into ashes." He said:—"If it does I will make it up for you." So he put the merchant's mother on his horse, and when he came to the house Bittan put the old woman down and said:—"There you see! All my money has turned into ashes. Pay me up." Then the merchant had to pay.

Bittan brought all the money home. When his brothers saw all the money they said:—"Where you did get all this?" He replied:—"I got it by selling ashes." So they all burnt down their houses, loaded the ashes on their horses, and went off to sell it. But every one laughed at them, and in the end they fell into poverty.

60. *Shekh Chilli and his Gram Field.*

Once upon a time Shekh Chilli thought of sowing gram. So he asked some Lodha cultivators:—"Do you sow it parched or raw?" They said:— "Raw, of course;" but he would not believe them, and said:—"Please tell me the truth." One out of mischief said:—"We sow it parched." So the Shekh got all his seed-gram parched and sowed it, and out of the lot only three plants, the seed of which had by chance escaped parching, came up. The Shekh was very pleased, and built a little hut near the place, and used to keep the plants under a blanket at night to guard them from the cold. By this arrangement two of them died, and he continued to watch the single plant as before. One night some thieves came to his hut and asked him to come with them. He said:—"How can I, when I must watch my gram?" "Where is it?" they asked. So he showed them the plant. "Put it in your turban and come along," said they. So he agreed. By and by they came to a village, and they sent the Shekh and one of the thieves to untie some cattle in a cow-house. One of the cows bit at the gram plant in his turban and caught some of his hair as well. He called out, and the people of the house woke and caught him, but as he was only Shekh Chilli, they let him off with a beating. Again the thieves took him with them, and when they got into a house he said:—"Hullo! here's a drum in the corner. Let us have some music." On this the owner woke and the thieves escaped with difficulty, while the Shekh was again let off with a beating. When he met the thieves again he wanted them to let him accompany them. At first they refused: at last they said:—"We will give you one more chance." So they went into a house where there was an old woman asleep with her hands over the fire boiling some pottage. They shared the contents of the pot, and Chilli seeing the old woman's hands still spread out, thought he would give her a share, so he poured some of the boiling pottage over her. She cried out in a fright. The Shekh got up into the roof, and the thieves crouched in the corners of the room. "What is the matter?" asked the neighbours. "The Lord above only knows," said she. So the Shekh from the cross-beam called out:—"Look in the corners of the house." Then the thieves were caught and hanged, and the Shekh escaped in safety.—*Una Briscoe: Bulandshahr.*

61. Phulmati Rani—A Folktale told by Ganesh Prasad, Kayasth, cultivator of Mirzapur District.

A King was returning home after marrying his son. In the bázár he saw an old woman selling a handkerchief, which he purchased for Rs. 500. One day the Rája's son saw the handkerchief, and suspecting it to be the work of a Rája's daughter, asked his mother where it came from. She referred him to the old woman whom he found selling a similar handkerchief in the bázár. She told him that it was embroidered by a Rája's daughter. He asked her to procure him an interview, and she advised him to wait at a temple, where the Princess used to go every night to worship Devi. There he met her, and they fell in love. The Princess advised him to secure one of her father's camels which could go 300 *kos* (600 miles) in the day. By mistake he selected a camel which could go only 200 *kos*. They started together, but the father of the Princess overtook them on the swift camel, and then she made a bow and arrow out of some reeds which grew near the road and killed her father. She then took the swift camel and went on. When they got to a city the Princess gave her lover a ring to sell. He took it to the shop of a one-eyed Banya, who knew at once that it was a Princess' ring, and telling the Prince to wait, went out by the back way, and inducing the Princess to believe that he was taking her to her lover, brought her to his house and locked her up. The Prince searched for her in vain, calling out, "O lady of the handkerchief" (*rumál-wálí*), all over the city. Then he, being in distress, took service with a ban-gle-maker (*chúrihár*), and went about selling bangles. One day he went to the Banya's house and recognized his sweetheart. She took two bags of the Banya's money and told him to go and buy two horses. He brought the horses and they went off: but the stupid Prince fell asleep and the Princess went ahead. Meanwhile the Banya came up, and suspecting that the Prince had taken the Princess, though he did not recognize him, began to beat him. But the Prince convinced him that he was innocent, and the Banya took him as his servant, and they went on in search of the Princess. As Princess Phúlmati went along five Thags met her and began to dispute who was to have her to wife. She said:—"Whoever can shoot an arrow ahead of mine shall marry me." But they all failed, and she took them all before the King of the land dressed as a youth. The King adopted her as his son, and when she took her seat on the throne, she sent for the seven men who were following her on the road, and among them she at once recognized the Prince, her lover. She dressed him in royal robes and married him.

62. *The Faqir and Sher Shah—A Folktale told by Baldeo Prasad, Village Accountant of Haliya, Mirzapur District.*

A certain King had no sons: he ordered his ministers to distribute alms and get the people to pray that the King might have a son. One day a Faqír entered the city, and when he learnt what was going on, promised the King two sons, on condition that he got one of them. The two sons were born and named Sher Sháh and Azim Sháh. When they grew up the Faqír appeared and called on the King to fulfil his promise. The King, unwilling to give up one of his sons, was about to present him instead with a low-caste boy: but the Faqír read the King's heart and was going to curse him, when the King, in fear, gave over Sher Sháh to him. Sher Sháh went to take leave of his mother and encouraged by saying he would fix an arrow in the palace wall: as long as it stuck there she might know he was alive. Then he went with the Faqír to his hermitage (*takiya*), and the Faqír leaving him there, took a large leathern vessel (*kuppa*) and went out to beg for oil. While he was away Sher Sháh saw a skull in the room which addressed him, and said:—"You will soon be like me." Sher Sháh asked why was this. The skull replied:—"The Faqír has a large iron boiler, and it is his custom to boil boys in oil in it as a sacrifice." "How can I escape," asked Sher Sháh. The skull answered:—"When the Faqír comes back with the oil, he will ask you to go five times round the boiler and bow to it. You must pretend not to know how to do it, and ask the Faqír to show you. Then, as he is bowing to the boiler, you must seize him by his legs from behind and pitch him in. Then you must take some of the oil and sprinkle it on all the bones which lie round the hut of the Faqír. These are the remains of boys whom he has sacrificed. When the oil touches them they will revive and be your servants." Sher Sháh carried out his instructions, threw the Faqír into the boiling oil, and revived the bones. They all became his servants and returned home. Then his mother told him that the arrow had shaken a little in the wall just about the time of his danger, but then became firmly fixed.

63. *The Man who fought with God—A Folktale told by Rahmat, a Weaver of Mirzapur.*

Once upon a time there was a Musalmán who was very poor, and used to earn four pice a day by wood-cutting. Now he heard that whoever gives charity gets double in return. So he used to give a pice daily in alms, one pice to his wife, kept a pice for his own food, and laid by one pice.

After some time he thought he would see if his store had doubled, but to his disgust, when he counted his savings, he found he had only just as much as he put by. So he said:—"I will go and fight[1] God, because He has not doubled my pice."

So he shut up his house and started off, and when his neighbours asked him where he was going, he said:—"God has written in His book that whatever a man gives in charity He doubles, but He has not done so; so now I am going to fight Him." So his friends advising him, said:—"You fool! has any one ever fought with God?" He said:—"No matter. I am going all the same."

On the road he met a man and the same conversation passed. So the man went to the King and said:—"There is a traveller here who says he is going to fight God." The King said:—"Bring him before me." Then the King asked him:—"Where are you going?" And he made the same answer.

Then the King said:—"You might as well, as you are going, ask God one question. My kingdom goes on all right during the day, but is burnt up at night. Why is this so?" At first he refused to do what the King wished, but finally, after great persuasion, agreed. As he went on he felt very thirsty, and seeing a well, approached it, and found that it was full of filth, in which a man and woman were submerged. When these people saw him they asked him who he was, and where he was going. He said:— "I am going to fight with God." Then they said:—"When you meet Him, ask Him either to kill us, or to take us out of this well." He agreed and went on.

When it became very hot he sat under a tree, but the tree was dry and did not keep off the glare. Then he said:—"What is the use of this tree? It is only cumbering the ground." Then the tree asked him who he was, and he replied:—"I am a Musalmán, and am going to fight with God." The tree said:—"You might ask Him either to make me green again, or cut me down because I am useless to weary travellers." So he agreed and went on.

Then he saw a great fire burning in the jungle. As he was considering how to avoid the fire, he found that the blaze proceeded from an Angel (*firishtah*). The Angel asked him where he was going, and he said:—"To fight with God." Then the Angel asked:—"Has any one ever fought with God?" "What matter," replied the traveller, "I will do it all the same." The Angel said:—"Well! stay here and I will inform God." Then God sent the Angel back to enquire what the man wanted to say. The man answered:—"In such and such a land there is a King, and his kingdom goes on well by day, but it is burnt up at night. What is the reason of this? Secondly, on a certain road there is a man and a woman in a well who want to be killed, or relieved of their trouble. Thirdly, there is a tree in a certain place—why has it withered. It wants either to be cut down, or made green again." But he forget to tell his own complaint to the Angel.

Then God answered his questions by the mouth of the Angel:—"The reason why the King's kingdom thrives by day and goes to ruin at night is that the King has a daughter. All day she amuses herself with her companions, but at night her breath becomes cool (*thandi sáns bharti hai*), and then everything goes wrong. When the King gets her married this will cease. And as regards the two persons in the well—they are great sinners, and are now receiving their punishment. So when you reach this well throw a pinch of clay into it, and it will gradually fill up, but when the earth rises to the top, place a large stone upon it. As to the tree—at its root there is a great snake in whose belly are two sapphires: near this tree is a smaller tree. Take the root of this, and dig a little near the foot of the large tree. The snake will then appear. Put the small root near his nose: he will vomit up the jewels and escape. Then the tree will become green again."

So the man did as he was directed. When the snake appeared he was insensible, but when he smelt the root he vomited up the sapphires. Then he came to his senses and disappeared, and the tree became green again. But the man touched not the sapphires. When he came to the well he said to the man and woman:—"You are being punished for your sins." Then he threw a pinch of clay into the well and it became filled with rupees. But he took none of them, and closed the well with the stone.

Then he came to the King and told him that if he got his daughter married, the trouble in his kingdom would cease. So the King said:—"Where can I find a better husband for my daughter than yourself?" So he had them married. And from that day the trouble in his kingdom ceased. The Musalmán went back, dug the treasure out of the well, and brought away the sapphires. And thus by the grace of the Almighty became exceedingly rich and the son-in-law of the King, and after his death reigned in his stead. So in this way his charity was rewarded.

64. Princess Pomegranate (Anar Sháhzadi)—A Folktale told by M. Karam-ud-din Ahmad of Mirzapur.

A certain King had four sons. Three were married and one was a bachelor. His sisters-in-law used to chaff him, and said:—"Are you waiting to marry the Pomegranate Princess?" (Anár Sháhzádi). He asked about her, and found it was hard to find her, as she lived in a pomegranate and was guarded by lakhs of Deos (Demons). At last the young Prince said:—"If I can't marry Princess Pomegranate, I will never show my face again."

So off he went and met a Deo in the jungle. The Prince addressed him as "Uncle" (*Mámu Sáhib, salám!*) The Deo said:— "Well! you have come at last." The Prince stayed some time with the Deo and told him his mission. One day the Deo wrote something on a bit of a tile (*thikri*) and gave it to the Prince. As he went on he met another Deo. He gave him the tile and said:—"*Mámu Sáhib, salám!*" The Deo read what was written on the tile, and asked the Prince what he wanted. "All right," said the Deo, "I will turn, you into a crow and you must break one pomegranate from the tree: but don't take more than one. The Deoni (Demoness) who is there will try to make you take more, but don't mind what she says, and come back." The Prince did so. As he was going the Deoni said:—"You may as well have another." The Prince gave way, and the Deoni wrung his neck at once, and took the pomegranate.

The Deo knew that he had been destroyed by his greediness, so he went and brought back his corpse and revived him. "You are a great fool," said he. "You did not take my advice, and this is the result." The Prince admitted his fault. "Well," said the Deo, "now it is hard to get the Pomegranate Princess: but I will give you another chance. I will turn you into a parrot, and you must obey my order." So the Prince, in the form of a parrot, brought the pomegranate. The Deoni tried to make him take a second, but he refused. She followed him to the Deo's house. When the Deo saw her he turned him into a fly. The Deoni came and said:— "Where is the parrot who brought the pomegranate?" "Search for him," said the Deo. Of course, she could not find him and went away. Then the Deo restored the Prince to his original form and sent him off with the pomegranate.

On the way he hid the pomegranate and went home to arrange his marriage procession. As he went along the pomegranate burst, and a lovely Princess came out of it. By chance a sweeper woman (mehtaráni) came up and saw the Princess. She said to the Princess:—"Give me your jewels which I will put on, and we can then look down a well to see by our reflections in the water who is the lovelier." So the mehtaráni pushed the Princess into the well, and sat down in place of the Princess.

When the Princess fell into the well she turned into a Lotus flower. When the Prince came he saw the mehtaráni and said:—"Why! you are not half so pretty as I thought you would be." However, he put her into a litter and brought her home. When her sisters-in-law saw her they said:—"This is not Princess Pomegranate at all." Some days after the Prince went to hunt, and one of his horsemen came to draw water from the well. As he put the *lota* into the well this flower used to come into the vessel and then jump out again. They called the Prince to see this wonder, and when he put in the *lota* the flower came into it and he pulled it out. He took the flower home with him.

When the mehtaráni saw it she knew it must be the Princess. So she pulled it into pieces while the Prince slept. He was much distressed when, where the pieces of the flower were thrown, a pomegranate tree grew and produced a single flower. The mehtaráni knew that this must be the Princess. She had the tree dug up and thrown away, and sent the flower to her gardener's wife (*málin*), and told her to keep it for seed. The málin put it into a pot, and when the pomegranate burst, out came a lovely Princess. She stayed with the málin as her daughter. One day one of the Prince's men saw her and told him. Then the Prince said:—"Marry me to the málin's daughter or I will die."

The mehtaráni knew that this must be the Princess. So she pretended to be ill, and said:—"I must have this girl's liver or I shall die." The King sent for the málin and told her to give up her daughter. She refused at first, but finally the girl was given to the executioner, and her liver was brought to the mehtaráni. She thought the Princess must be dead at last.

But by the will of the Almighty a house suddenly appeared where the Princess was killed. Two peacocks were there as sentries, and the Princess was inside. The Prince asked for an audience. The peacocks said:—"You have so worried the Princess that now you cannot see her." But finally he persuaded them to let him in. Finally they were persuaded, and the Prince came in to the Princess. He got her to forgive him and took her home as his bride. All his sisters-in-law said:—"This is Princess Pomegranate at last." So they were married, and the wicked mehtaráni was buried up to the waist in the ground, and the soldiers shot arrows at her till she died.

65. The Tasks of the Witch-Queen—A Folktale recorded by M. Karam-ud-din Ahmad of Mirzapur.

Once upon a time a Rája went to hunt. By chance he came into a desolate jungle. He sent his servants to search for game. They went off. They saw a light burning in a grove, near which an old woman was sitting. She asked them what they wanted. They said:—"We have come in search of game." The old woman gave them two or three deer. When they cooked the deer they found they were nothing but eyes. So they contented themselves with the broth.

When all of them started with the King the old woman turned herself into a lovely girl and pursued the King. As she pursued him the King's horse was tired. The woman caught the horse's tail. The King jumped off and got up a tree: just at that moment a second King came up, and seeing the woman, fell in love with her. She agreed to go with him. So he took her home and treated her as his Queen. Now her custom was at midnight to steal out and eat one of the best horses of the King. The King tried to detect the thief. The Queen heard this and took some of the horse's flesh and put it on the bed of the other Queen who was in child. In the morning she pointed to the young Queen as the thief. The king said:—"How are we to punish her?" The wicked Queen said:—"Put out her eyes and abandon her in the forest." This was done by the King's orders.

While the young Queen remained in the jungle a mysterious jar of milk used to come for her every day, and when her son was born the milk was increased two-fold. One day when the young Prince grew up he wandered away and met a horseman. He asked the horseman for some food which he got. He took the food to his mother. One day he wandered to his father's Court. The King gave him service, and put him to tend his most vicious horse. The Prince tamed the horse. The wicked Queen discovered who he was. She pretended to be sick, and no medicine would do her any good. The King said:—"Is there any medicine you would like?" She said:—"If I had tiger's milk I would get well." So the King ordered the Prince to bring tiger's milk.

He went off, having got a lakh of rupees from the King for his charges. He gave the money to his mother and went off to the jungle. There he met a tiger's cubs and made friends with them by feeding them on sweets. They became attached to him, and at his request brought him a little of their mother's milk. When the tigress heard of this she died of grief, and the Prince took the Cubs and the milk. He brought the milk to the wicked Queen. She said:—"Now I want the milk of a goat which belongs to a Demon (*Deo*)." Then she wrote a letter to a certain Demon, which she gave to the Prince, and said:—"When you show this letter you will get the milk." But she wrote in the letter:—"When this son of man (*adamzád*) comes to you kill him at once." He went off with the letter after taking a lakh of rupees for his road expenses, and coming to his mother, he gave her the money, and went off to search for the milk. But before he started he took the precaution of getting the letter read, and when he knew the contents, he threw it away and got another letter written to the Demon to the effect that when this man reached him he was to receive him with great courtesy and assist him in every way.

With this letter he went to the Demon. He was very civil to him, and said:—"I am going about some business. You stay here. But take care not to loose the goat which is tied to this tree, or a witch (*Dáin*) will appear and eat you up." As an experiment the Prince loosed the goat. The witch jumped out of the tree. The Prince said:—"There is a great storm coming. We had all better cling to this tree, which will not be broken, and for this reason I untied the goat." The witch was satisfied, and the Prince hung her and the goat to the tree, and then broke the witch's neck.

When the Demon came and saw what had happened to her he was sore afraid, and said:—"I make you a present of the goat. Take it away." The Prince came with the goat to the King's Court.

The Ráni said:—"I want the hair of the horse Shyám Karan." The Prince with a lakh of rupees went off at once in search of the horse. He came to the same Demon again. He asked his errand. He said:—"I want the Shyám Karan horse." The Demon said:—"This horse is in my charge and I will never tell you of it." Then the Prince threatened to serve the Demon as he had served the witch. Then the Demon said:—"Go and sit in a *pípal* tree near a certain tank. Many horses come to drink there. One horse stays apart from the others and is always jumping about: be sure that this is the horse Shyám Karan. Mount him, and no matter how much he plunges, never let him go, and make him agree to bear you." The Prince did so, and the horse said:—"All right: I will come to-morrow, and then you must recognize me." Next day this horse came in the form of a miserable worn-out animal. The Demon also appeared there in disguise and pointed this horse to the Prince. The Prince caught this miserable horse. The horse made many attempts to escape, but the Prince held on to him, and finally he brought the horse to his mother, and took the hair of it to the King. The King gave it to the Ráni.

She said:—"There is a kind of flower which grows in the ocean. This I must have." The Prince again started with a lakh of rupees, which he gave to his mother. Then mounting Shyám Karam he went again to the Demon. The Demon said:—"Ride to the shore of the ocean. But the peculiarity of this flower is that when any one comes near it, it turns into a woman and kills him." But the horse Shyám Karan said:—"Remain behind me. I will catch the flower for you." The Prince did so, and when the flower advanced to attack him, Shyám Karan caught it in his mouth.

The Prince brought the flower to the Demon. It turned into a woman, and said to the Prince:—"This Ráni, who is always imposing tasks on you, is a witch and sister of this Demon. It was she who had your mother blinded, and she is planning to take your life. There is a parrot here which you must take. The life of this witch remains in this parrot. When you kill it you will kill her at the same time." Then the Prince took the parrot with him and the flower-woman.

When he came to his mother he said to the flower-woman, "laugh"; and when she laughed a flower came out of her mouth, which he took to the Ráni. Then he said to the King:—"Come with me and I will show you a strange sight: but don't bring the Ráni." Then the Ráni took the form of a witch and came to kill the Prince. He at once wrung the parrot's neck. When it died the Ráni died too.

Then he told the King the whole story, married the flower-woman, and they passed their lives in happiness till the Separator of all things removed them from this world.

66. The Merchant, the Princess and the Grateful Animals— A folktale related by Altaf Husen, and literally translated by Mirza Mahmud Beg.

Once upon a time there was a merchant who died, leaving a widow and an only son. After his father's death, the young man squandered all the family property; at last, at the request of his mother, he agreed to go on a voyage to earn his living.

Now, in his will, his father directed him always, if he could, to save the life of an animal by buying it. On the way he met some boys trying to kill a rat. He purchased it from them and took it home. Next day he met a bird-catcher with a parrot, and this he also bought for a couple of gold-mohurs. The third day he saw a man beating a cat, and this he also bought and took home. The fourth day he met some people carrying two corpses and behind them a man was holding a jar (*ghara*). The young man asked what was in the jar.

They said:—"In this jar is a snake who has bitten these two people, and now we are going to kill it at their grave."

The young man bought the snake, and then and their determined to release it. When he opened the jar the snake flew out, kissed him on the face and disappeared. When he went a little further he met a man on horseback with his face concealed.

"Who are you?" said the young man.

"Don't you know me?" he replied. "I am your slave whom you purchased to-day for Rs. 500; and now I have come to invite you to a feast on behalf of my father."

"I will come," said the young merchant.

As they were going the horseman said:—"My father is deeply obliged to you for saving my life, and he will ask you to take any gift you please. If you follow my advice don't take anything but the ring he wears on his finger."

"I will follow your advice," replied the merchant.

Then they came to a big cave in the hill, and left their horses outside. When they entered they found themselves in a spendid palace in a lovely garden. The horseman introduced his friend to his father, who was an old man like a king. After dinner the old man thanked the merchant for saving the life of his son.

"Take any gift you like," said he.

"If you please, I would like to have the ring you wear."

The old man smiled. "My son must have told you this. But here, take it."

So saying he took off the ring and gave it to the merchant, who put it on his finger. The moment he put on the ring four demons (*deo*) appeared to him. They saluted him, and he asked "who are you?"

"We are at the command of him who wears the ring."

So he returned home and prepared to start on his voyage.

Now one of the demons was one-eyed (*kána*): he brought the merchant a plant, and the merchant said to his mother:—"Plant this in the house, and if ever you see the leaves wither, be sure I am in trouble, and when it dies, be sure I am dead."

So saying he left her, and ordered his four demons to assume human shape and accompany him. After a long voyage they reached a city. The king of the land had a daughter so lovely that the light of her countenance illuminated the city, and there was no need to light lamps there. She had vowed not to marry until she met a man who fulfilled certain conditions. The merchant desired to win her, and inquired of the Wazir what her conditions were.

"Appear as a suitor and you will be told," he answered.

So the merchant proclaimed his suit, and the Wazir took him to the palace and showed him a row of human heads. "That will be your fate if you fail," said he.

Then the Wazir took him to a garden outside the city, and showed him a mountain of mustard seed.

"The condition is that you spread the mustard all over the garden in a single watch (*pahar*): then you must collect it all together in a watch: then you must press all the oil out of it in a watch; and the fourth condition is, that with the first arrow you must shoot the white crane which sits on the roof of the palace of the princess."

When the Wazir departed the four demons appeared. First they blew at the heap of mustard and spread it all evenly over the garden. Then they ran and called the Wazir and said:—

"Come back and let our master out."

"I am glad," said the Wazir, "to hear that he has given up the competition."

But when he came in he was thunderstruck to see that the mustard was spread all over the garden.

"I merely called you," said the merchant, "to satisfy you that I had fulfilled the first condition."

So the Wazir had to admit the fact, and again he went away.

Then the demons at once blew the mustard into a heap again, and then called the Wazir again.

"I don't know what to think of it," he said, "but I must admit that the second condition is satisfied."

Then he showed the merchant an oil-press (*kolhú*) and departed. The demons commenced to grind the mustard, but were surprised to find that no oil came out of it. At last the one-eyed demon examined the press, and lo! he found a white demon concealed inside who was drinking all the oil. So he dragged him out and asked who he was.

"I am the white demon," he answered, "and am in love with the princess. It is I who imposed these conditions, and I wish no one to win her by accomplishing them. I am the white crane who sits watching her on her palace roof."

So the four demons thought it best to kill the white demon, and they did so and burned his body. Then they hurried off in search of the Wazir, who was confounded when he saw that the third condition was fulfilled.

"Now show me the white crane," said the merchant, "as I want to finish this business to-day."

Then the Wazir took him to the princess and told her the story. The princess said:—"Take him and show him where the white crane always sits."

But when they went there, lo! the white crane had disappeared. They searched for him in vain, and then the merchant told how he had disposed of him.

So the wedding day was fixed; the merchant married the princess, and they went to live in a palace of their own on the bank of the river. One day the princess was sitting near the water and one of her shoes fell in which a fish immediately swallowed. Some way down the river was the kingdom of another king. The fishermen were fishing and caught a big fish which they took to the king's steward. When the cook opened the fish he found in its stomach a beautiful shoe. Expecting a present, he took it to the king. The king said at once:—

"The wearer of the shoe must be my queen."

So he sent for all the old women of the city, and at last one of them undertook to find the lady. She prepared a boat and sailed up the river in the direction from which the fish had come. By and by she came to the palace of the merchant and anchored the boat close by, and going below the palace, began to weep. The princess was looking out of the window and called her in. When she saw the princess she began to weep even more violently than before. At last she said:—

"I had a lovely daughter, just like you, and she was drowned in this river the other day. I weep because you remind me of her."

So the princess entertained the wily old woman. She amused the princess in every way and soon gained her favour. At last the princess told her how her husband had fulfilled all the conditions by means of his magic ring. The old woman said:—

"You should keep such a precious ring very carefully, and never allow your husband to wear it when he goes abroad, lest he may lose it."

When the merchant again went to hunt, the princess warned him about the ring.

"Don't be anxious," he said, "I take the greatest care of it."

"You must leave it with me," she replied. "I will lock it up carefully and send the demons to guard you."

So the merchant left the ring with the princess, and when he had gone the old woman took her to walk on the river bank. The princess showed her the ring which she wore on her finger. The old woman asked to see it, and when she had got it she summoned the demons, put the princess into her boat and carried her off.

When the king got the ring he called the demons, and told them to go and throw the merchant into a well. They went to do so, and found the merchant lamenting his lost princess. As they were fond of the young man, all they did was to throw him into a dry well, and they returned and reported to the king that he was dead.

Then the king told the princess that she was in his power, that her husband was dead, and she must marry him. She at first refused, but finally was obliged to promise to marry him in six months.

Now at this time the leaves of the tree which the merchant's son had planted near his house began to wither. His mother began to feel anxious, and the parrot, the cat and the rat all decided to go and help him. It was settled that the parrot should go first and find out where their master was. The parrot flew night and day, and finally alighted on a tree over the dry well in which the merchant was dying of hunger and thirst. So the parrot flew all over the jungle and collected every kind of fruit which he gave his master, and then took his leave, promising to devise some means for his rescue. On reaching home he told everything to his companions, who started to the city of the wicked king. There they learnt that the king kept the ring on his finger during the day and in his mouth during the night, and that he had four ferocious dogs posted on watch near his bed. So the rat made a hole on the roof and the cat came into the room. The dogs pursued the cat and the rat put his tail up the king's nose, so that he sneezed violently, and blew the ring out of his month. The rat seized it and ran away, and going at once to his mistress gave it to her, at the same time explaining how he had succeeded in recovering it. So the demons at once appeared before the lady, who directed them to seize the old woman who had caused all the trouble, and transport the whole party home. Thus the princess recovered her husband, and they lived happily ever after, and the parrot, the cat, and the rat, were well cared for as long as they lived.

[Here we have a number of familiar incidents brought together in an ingenious way.

(1). For the aiding animals Mr. Jacob (*Folklore Congress Report*, 1891, p. 88) quotes numerous parallels. Also see *Grimm's Household Tales* I, 420.

(2). Metamorphosis of living beings into animals. See instances collected by Temple, *Wideawake Stories*, 421: and Jacob, *loc cit*, 93.

(3). The magic ring—Tawney, *Katha Sarit Sagara*, I, 59, 61, and the tale of Aladdin.

(4). The plant, a life index—Temple, *loc cit* 405.

(5). Tests for the hero—Grimm, *loc cit* II, 386, 414.

(6). The fish swallowing the ring is familiar in Herodotus.

(7). For the slipper token, see Cinderella and Jacob, *loc cit.*—ED.]

(15). The following is the curious old song which used to be recited by little school-boys to teach them Indian Geography:—

> *Piyá gaye pardesa; kawan sá desa bilhmé piyáré?*
> *Piyá ke káran, sakhi, main dhúnrhi phíri mulkán sáré.*
> *Chalí Sundari Ríwa, Jabalpur, Ságar, Búndi ko játi.*
> *Muluk Chaneri, Gualyár, Púna, Sitára nagicháti.*
> *Amráwati, Gujarát, Málwa, Burhánpur tak nahin pati.*
> *Jhánsi, Datiya dhúnrhke Jhanna Panna pachtáti.*
> *Nimach, Haidarábád, Nágpur, Súrat, Bambai, Gulzáré.*
> *Piyá ké káran, Sakhi, main dhúnhi mulkain sáré.*
> *Piyá gayé pardesa; kawan sá desa jahán bilmhé piyáré?*

My sweetheart is gone to foreign lands? which is the land where my beloved is enamoured? For the sake of my beloved, O companion! I have searched all lands. The damsel proceeded to Ríwa, Jabalpur, Ságar: thence she went to Búndi. She then arrived at Chaneri, Gwalior, Poona, Sitára. She could not find him at Amráwati, Gujarát, Málwa, and Burhánpur. Having searched for him at Jhánsi and Dattia, she regrets at Jhanna Panna. She then goes to Nimach, Hyderabad, Nagpur, Surat, Bombay and Gulzára.

Chorus as before.

II

Prayág, Bánda, aur Lakhnan, chalí Sundari Kampú
*   miyání.*
Kanauj, Koil, Farrukhábád, Kálpi—sab jánai.
Mírath, Murádábád, Bhágalpnr, Sadar Agra sun
*   sánai.*
Dihli, Ambála, Jalandhar, Baghnáré tak lag
*   jánai.*
Kashmír, Karnál, Láhaur, gai hai Kábul
*   Kandháré.*

The damsel goes to Prayág (Allahabad), Banda, Lucknow, and Cawnpore; thence to Kanauj, Koel, Farrukhabad, Kalpi which are known to all. She found no trace at Meerut, Moradabad, Bhagalpur and Agra, the head-quarters. She then went to Delhi, Lahore, Ambala, Jalandhar and Baghnári. She then went to Kashmir, Karnál, Lahore, Kábul and Kandahár.

III.

Takht Jaunpur, Tánra, Bangla, Ajudhya, pahunchi
*   nári*
Butául Betiya, Janakpur, Azámgarh ki tayyári.
Támsen, Népal, Gorakhpur, Chín, Atak, dhúrhai jári.

Thence to Jaunpur, seat of empire, Tánda, Bengal, and Ajudhya: then she started to Butwal, Bettiah, Janakpur and Azamgarh: thence to Thompson (?), Nepal, Gorakhpur, China, and Attock.

IV.

Rámnagar, Káshi, Nainagarh, Gházipur ko gai
*   abáta.*
Rasara, Chhappra, Dánapur, Patné tak na mila
*   páta:*
Munger, Murshidábád. Bharatpur, Rájmahal jahan
*   bana qila.*

Chali Bánkuri, Sayyadpur, Kalkatta púrubi
*   zilla.*
Dháka dhúnrha, Bangála dhúnrah Katakpuri men
*   piya piyári.*

Thence to Ramnagar, Benaresi, Chunar and to Gházipur. She did not find him at Rasra-Chapra, Dinapur and Patna. She then went to Monghyr, Murshedabad, Bharatpur and Rájmahal where a fort is built, and so on to Bankura, Saidpur and Calcutta in the eastern district. She searched Dacca and Bengal: the lovers met at Cuttack.

V.

Mihr hui us rab ki nári par, bahut dina par mílí
*   saján.*
Rasúl gir guru hain man piyári par sada
*   makán.*
Hanumán ka chela Durga zilla sháhr ka kiya
*   kai than.*
Benirámji nái nit banáké gáté hain chhand.
Mirzapur darmiyán khiyál kath Babaigir hé
*   lalkáré.*

God was merciful on that damsel that she found her sweetheart after many days. My teacher Rasúl Gir's mind is always devoted to his friends. Durga, pupil of Hanumán, resident of the city, has made this song. Benirám always sings new songs. At Mirzapur Babaigir sings this song loudly.—*Bhán Partáp Tewari.*

67. How the Jackal got the Weaver married— A Folktale told by Akbar Sháh, Manjhi of Manbasa, Dudhi, Mirzapur District, recorded by Pandit Ram Gharib Chaube.

A jackal used to come at night into a village and steal chickens. One day a Panka[2] said to him:—"Why do you risk your life coming here to steal fowls? Some day or other a dog will catch you. Marry me to a princess and I will feed you all your life."

The jackal agreed, and went to the Rája and said:—"Máharáj! I have arranged the marriage of your daughter with a Rája greater even than you are. Your daughter will be very happy with him."

"I agree," said the Rája, "and I will send my Bráhman and barber with you to perform the betrothal (*tilak*)."

"In my land," answered the jackal, "the ceremonies of betrothal and marriage are done at the same time; but we have a rule that no guns or dogs are allowed to accompany the marriage party."

The Rája agreed to this, and went to the Panka and told him to make his preparations, and he would invite the guests himself. The jackal invited as guests all the paddy birds and jackals and mainas, and they started to fetch the bride. When they came near the Rája's palace some one fired a gun, and all the birds flew away; then a dog ran up, and all the jackals disappeared except he that made the match, and he hid himself till the dog left the place.

"What a small marriage escort!" remarked the Rája. "No matter, bring the bridegroom and let us get over the marriage quick."

When the Panka came in and saw the bamboos of which the marriage shed was built, he said:—"What a fine loom these would make!"

"This seems a low fellow," grumbled the Rája, but the jackal said:—"It is only because he sees so few bamboos in his own country."

The marriage was performed, and the Rája sent an escort with the pair.

When they got near the Panka's village the jackal dismissed them, saying:—

"In our country it is not the custom for the bride's people to go to the bridegroom's house."

[A common custom: a survival of marriage by capture.—ED.]

When the princess saw the Panka's hut she wept bitterly, and she made her husband go to her father and confess the whole matter.

The Rája was wroth, but what could he do? He had to build a palace for his son-in-law and give him half his kingdom. But as for the jackal, he sent out his men and had him hunted to death.

68. How the Manjhi won his wife—A Folktale told by Akbar Sháh, Manjhi of Manbasa, Dudhi, Mirzapur District, recorded by Pandit Ram Gharib Chaube.

There was once a Mánjhí who was so niggardly that he would marry his daughter to no one who would not agree to be satisfied with as much food as a leaf could hold.

One day a suitor came, and the Mánjhí said:—"You must agree to live for a month on as much food as can be piled on a leaf. If you fail I am at liberty to cut off your nose and ears."

The suitor agreed and got on for a few days on as much food as could be piled on the leaf of a lime tree. But at last he had to give in, and the old Mánjhí cut off his nose and ears.

In this way twelve suitors lost their ears and noses. At last the thirteenth man came and agreed to the test. But he brought a plantain leaf, and the Mánjhí had to give as much food as could be piled on it. So he only got fatter and fatter every day, and at last the Mánjhí had to give him his daughter.

So when he brought her home all the villagers said:—"What a clever fellow you are!"

69. The Bráhman and Mother Ganges—A Folktale told by Akbar Sháh, Manjhi of Manbasa, Dudhi, Mirzapur District, recorded by Pandit Ram Gharib Chaube.

There was once a poor Bráhman who lived by begging, and all the alms he got in a day would hardly fill a lamp saucer. One day as he was going about begging, he came to the door of a Chamár (currier).

The Chamár seeing him, said:—"Máharáj! What has brought you here?"

"I am starving," said the Bráhman, "give me alms."

"If you will take an invitation for me I will pay you handsomely," said the Chamár.

The Bráhman agreed, and the Chamár gave him a betel-nut,[3] and said:—"Take this and present it to Mother Ganges."

The Bráhman went to Gangá Mái and gave her the betel-nut which she accepted and said:—"Tell the Chamár that I will come at the appointed time, and here! take this bracelet of gold, and give it to the Chamár, telling him that Gangá Mái has sent it as a present for his wife."

The Bráhman took the bracelet, and after saluting Gangá Mái, went back. On the road he was overcome by covetousness, and instead of giving the bracelet to the Chamár, he hid it in his loin cloth and merely said:—"Gangá Mái accepts your invitation. Now give me the present you promised."

The Chamár told his wife to give the Bráhman a ration (*sidhá*) of five *sers* of grain.

The Bráhman went home, well pleased at his good luck. His wife, too, was delighted, and gave him an excellent dinner. Then he made a plan and thought he would give the bracelet to the Rája, who would be sure to reward him handsomely. So he went to the Rája, and after giving him his blessing (*asírbád*), asked for alms. The Rája rose from his seat and asked the Bráhman to sit down.

The Bráhman said:—"Maháráj! I have been supported by you for many years. So I have brought you a present which I got from a charitable client (*jajmán*) of mine."

The Rája was much pleased, and took the bracelet into the inner room to the Ráni. She was very much delighted, and said to the Rája:—"It is very nice indeed, but I must have a pair to it."

The Rája thought to himself that if he rewarded the Bráhman he would never bring the second bracelet; so he said to the Bráhman:—"Go and bring a pair to this and I will give you a reward." The Bráhman went home very sorrowful, and at last told the whole story to his wife. She comforted him.

"Don't fret yourself. She who gave you one bracelet will give you another, if you ask her."

The Bráhman returned to the Chamár, and with great penitence told him what had happened. The Chamár said:—"You had better take my invitation again. But whatever Gangá Mái says to you, you must tell me."

The Bráhman went to Gangá Mái and gave her the Chamár's invitation. She accepted it, and said to the Bráhman:— "Go and pour a *ser*-and-a-quarter of *ghí* on the ground in my name."

The Bráhman promised to do so, and when he came to his house, told his wife that Gangá Mái had ordered her to pour a *ser*-and-a-quarter of water on the ground in her honour.

The Bráhman replied:—"Bad luck to you and Mother Ganges! You have spent the day wandering about and brought nothing home, and now you are telling me to pour water on the ground in the name of Gangá

Mái! Why should I pour water on the ground which I have been toiling all day to drag from the well?"

The Bráhman returned to the Chamár and told him what Gangá Mái had said. When she heard the message, the Chamár's wife bathed, put on clean clothes, and poured five jars of *ghí* on the ground in the name of Mother Ganges.

Then the Bráhman said to the Chamár:—"Brother! my life is at stake. Give me a bracelet. If you refuse the Rája will have me hanged."

"I have no bracelet to give you," answered the Chamár. "When Gangá Mái gave you a bracelet you never showed it to me."

The Bráhman was plunged in grief, and sat⁴ at the Chamár's door, saying he would die there.

At last, after a couple of days had passed in this way, the Chamár said:—"Come aside and I will tell you something."

The Chamár took him behind his house and said:—"You are a rogue, and your wife is such a fool that she cannot spare even a pot of water for the gods and goddesses. How can you expect ever to become rich? I and my wife are charitable, and see how we prosper. Take a lesson from us."

Then the Chamár took a wooden kneading dish (*kathwat*), filled it with water, and put it at his door, and told the Bráhman to say:—"When the heart is pure even the Ganges comes into a platter."

[A common proverb: *mán changá, kathautí Ganga.*—Ed.]

The Bráhman repeated this verse and then put his hand into the water and pulled out a pair to the golden bracelet. He took it to the Rája, who gave him five villages and much wealth, and the Bráhman changed his manner of life and lived happily ever after.

May Paramesar change us as he changed him!

70. *The Tiger, the Bráhman, and the covetous Goldsmith.*⁵

There was once upon a time a poor Bráhman who used to get his living by begging. One day in his wanderings he came to a stream in the jungle near which a tiger had his den, and it was guarded in turns by his four servants—the swan, the parrot, the jackal, and the crow. On that day the swan and parrot happened to be on duty. When they saw the Bráhman approach they called out:—"Miserable Bráhman! make your escape while you can. If the tiger knows you have come he will surely devour you."

"I throw myself on your protection," said the Bráhman. You can eat me or spare me as you will."

The swan and parrot, pitying him, went to the tiger and said:—

"Master! a beggar Bráhman is standing outside. What is thy pleasure regarding him?" The tiger answered:—"If he is really hungry, you can open my treasure-house and let him have as much as he pleases."

The Bráhman was taken into the treasure-chamber, where he loaded himself with as much wealth as he could carry. He took it home, thanking Bhágwán for his mercy, and lived in prosperity for a long time.

He had a friend, a jeweller, who went to him one day and said:—"Panditji! as we are friends let me have a share in your good luck."

The Bráhman agreed and offered to take the goldsmith with him when he next paid the tiger a visit.

They started, though the Bráhman's wife advised her husband not to go. By ill-luck the jackal and the crow were on guard that day. When they saw the pair approaching they said one to the other:—"Let us tell the tiger and he will kill these people, and then we can have a good feed."

Meanwhile the tiger called out to the Bráhman—

"The parrot has gone to the forest of Nanda, The swan to Mána Sarowar lake:

The crow and jackal are my ministers. For you the times are evil[6]

The goldsmith asked the Bráhman what this warning of the tiger meant.

The Bráhman replied:—"The times are changed and the guards are different. Escape at once if you value your life."

The goldsmith said:—"You can run away if you please. I will steal in through the back of the den and get hold of some of the treasure."

The Bráhman went away and the goldsmith crept into the back of the den. But the jackal and the crow saw him, and informed the tiger who jumped out and killed him. The Bráhman returned home, and that was the last visit he paid to the tiger.

71. Kumaon-Folklore.

Can any one say where a collection of folktales of Kumaon by Minaef can be obtained? The following abstract of the book is from the *Saturday Review* of 12th May, 1877:—

The tales which Mr. Minaef found in Kumaon are of the usual kind, dealing with themes which are tolerably familiar. But what he calls the legends are somewhat peculiar. They are intended to be sung to a kind of flute or drum accompaniment, their monotonous and protracted chant reminding the Russian traveller of the builinas or metrical romances of his native land—

"At their exact meaning it is somewhat difficult to arrive; for they are extremely verbose and obscure. The stories, on the other hand, are sufficiently simple, some of them being abridged versions of tales occurring in the *Panchatantra* and other collections. In No. 2, for instance, we find the ingenious jackal, which frightened away the lion by its braggart language; in No. 9, a Kumaon Alnaschar shakes his head when his imaginary children ask for food, and so breaks the pot on which his dream of success was based; No. 27 tells somewhat feebly the well-known tale of the Forty Thieves; and No. 45 is one of the numerous varieties of the Oriental history of King Lear and his youngest daughter. Magic implements play an important part in the stories. Fortunatus meets the supernaturally endowed beings who enable him to overcome all difficulties, and the dead are brought to life by means of the resuscitating fluid which so often figures in the tales of the East of Europe. More than once we meet with the story of 'the giant who had no heart in his body,' the Punchkin of *Old Deccan Days*, the Koschei the Deathless of Russian tales. One story—No. 10—tells how a Faqír carried off the wife of the youngest of a king's seven sons, and concealed her 'beyond the seventh sea.' Her husband and his six brothers went in search of her, but were turned by the Faqír into trees. The king's solitary grandson, when he grew up to man's estate, went in his turn to look for his father and his uncles, and came to the place where the magician lived. One day the youth, hiding in the sand by the seashore, saw the Faqír go down to the water-side. 'All the water dried up. The Faqír went away, leaving his sandals behind him. Now all the strength of his magic lay in those sandals. The youth donned them and went to his aunt, the abducted princess. Having consulted with him, she extracted from the Faqír the secret of his life. 'On the shore of the sixth sea,' he said, 'there is a palace; and under the palace there is a hall of justice; and underneath it, below the ground, there is an iron cage, and in the cage is a parrot. If any one kills that parrot, then I shall die.' And the youth laid his hands on the parrot, and by killing it put an end to the Faqír, who before dying breathed upon the seven trees and turned them back again into living men. In the other story—No. 46—a boy is handed over by his father in fulfilment of a vow to a Yogin who is a cannibal. The Yogin receives the boy kindly, and shows him all the rooms in his house but one. That 'Forbidden Chamber' the boy enters during the Yogin's absence, and finds it full of bones. From them he learns what he must do in order to save his own life and restore theirs. After a time the Yogin returns, places butter in a cauldron, and sets it on a fire, and then tells the boy to walk round it in a circle. The boy pleads ignorance, and induces the Yogin to show him how to do so. But while the Yogin is stepping round the boy kills him with a knife, and throws his body into the cauldron. Out fly two birds, the one red the other black. The boy kills the red bird, and flings the black one into the cauldron. Having thus put an end to the Yogin, the boy finds in his house a gourd containing life-giving nectar, with which he brings back the dead bones to life.

"Some of the tales are about the demons who, according to the natives, haunt every hill or tree. Thus in No. 4 a man goes into a wood and meets a bhút. At first it appears in the shape of a dog, and follows at his heels. Presently he hears a strange sound behind him, and becomes aware of a herd of swine chasing him. Having driven them off by throwing stones, he goes a little further and meets a lion. Having escaped from it by climbing a tree, he next meets a fair damsel. 'Rejoicing thereat, he began to talk to her. He said much, but she kept silence. Presently they came to a bridge. She pushed him off the bridge, and he fell into the water. The poor fellow was all but drowned.' According to Mr. Minaef, bhúts of Kumaon are frequently the souls of the dead, to whom worship is paid by the natives. The Rákshasa or demoniacal cannibal frequently occurs. Thus, in No. 42, a variant of the well-known 'Right and Wrong' story, four Rákshasas devour a harmless demon of the Pisácha class. In No. 43 a king marries a Rákshasí, or female demon, who induces him to fling his seven other wives into a cavern, where hunger compels them to eat six out of their seven children. The seventh escapes, and eventually destroys the Rákshasí, discovering her life in a bowl at the house of her family whither she has sent him with the intention of having him devoured there by her relations. Along with her six other lives are found, each in its own bowl; just as in a Samoyed tale told by Castrén, seven brothers are in the habit of taking out their hearts every night and sleeping without them, which hearts are found and destroyed by the hero of the tale, who thus puts an end to the seven brothers. In No. 44 seven brothers go abroad, and after long journeying arrive at a town which is 'all in ruins.' There they take up their quarters in a palace, sleeping by night in a huge bed which holds them all. Through that palace there all day wanders a goat, which at night becomes a Rákshasí, and from time to time eats one of the brothers. Their number gradually decreases till at length only two are left. These survivors tie themselves together at night. One of the two suddenly awakes and finds the other being devoured by the Rákshasí, who thereupon takes the form of a fair damsel, and says that next day she will become his wife. At earliest dawn he runs away from his proposed spouse, but she follows him. He climbs a tree, and she sits at the foot and weeps. Presently up come a Rája's servants, to whom the man hands over his would-be wife in return for two lakhs of rupees. So the Rákshasí is taken to the palace, where she proceeds to kill and eat all the birds and beasts in the neighbourhood. Perhaps the most eccentric of the stories of this class is No. 11. A Bráhman received one day from a bhút a feather which enabled its bearer to tell what people had been in a previous state of existence. Now the Bráhman was cursed with a quarrelsome wife. By the help of the feather he found out that he had previously been a tiger and she a dog. So he set aside his uncongenial wife, and chose another, in whom his feather enabled him to recognize an ex-tigress. After which his house became a happy home. The reason why the bhút gave the feather to the Bráhman was this:—The demon was in want of a human body to eat; and, being fastidious, it did not wish to eat the body of a man who in a previous state of existence had been a beast. So it commissioned the Bráhman to pick him out from among the heaps of corpses lying on a battle-field the body of a man. But, before sending him off on his quest, it gave him a feather to put on his head. The Bráhman arrived on the field of battle, 'and saw millions and millions of corpses, but only one or two of them were shaped like men. He took one of these human bodies and delivered it to the bhút. The bhút rejoiced greatly, and gave the Bráhman many rupees.' On one occasion, according to a legend related by Mr. Minaef, the English Commissioner 'Sahib Tiliar (*i. e.*, Trail)' referred a dispute between two natives of Kumaon to the decision of a judicial demon who was the ruler of fifty-two other bhúts. The demon caused blood to burst forth from the native who was in the wrong. 'This occurrence was made known to the Sahib. So he inflicted punishment on the wrong-doer.'"

72. *The Rival Queens.*[7]

There once was a Rája who had two Ránis, the younger of whom he loved exceedingly. She became in child and brought forth a beautiful son.

But the other Ráni put two stones in her bed, and sending the child into the jungle, told the Rája that the Ráni had been delivered of stones. The Rája was wroth and drove the Ráni out of his palace. She wandered into the jungle and found a child lying under a tree. When she saw it the milk rose in her breasts and she gave it suck. Then a Rája passed by and pitying her took her home with him and supported her and her child.

By and by the boy grew up. One night the Rája in a dream saw the most beautiful woman he had ever seen in his life. In the morning he called his courtiers and said:—

"Whoever finds this woman for me shall receive my kingdom." All the courtiers searched for the woman, but failed to find her. At last the prince went in search of her. He came to the city of a Rája who offered him service.

"What pay do you require?" the Rája asked.

"A lakh of pice daily," answered the prince.

"What work can you do?"

"I will do what no one else can do."

So he was appointed, and one night in the month of Bhádon the Rája heard a bitter cry outside his palace walls. The prince went out to see what was the matter. He came to a burning-ground south of the palace, where he saw a woman standing naked with a drawn sword in her hand. The prince asked the cause of her grief.

"I am a witch (*Dáin*)," she answered, "and I am weeping because your Rája will die to-morrow."

"Is there any means of escape?" the prince enquired.

"Yes; if any servant of his offer his head to me, the Rája will live for twenty years."

When he heard this the prince at once cut off his head with a sword. Then the witch ceased from her lamenting. Next morning when the Rája heard of the death of the prince he was much grieved. He went to the temple of the Devi to pray. The goddess was appeased, and offered him any boon he chose to ask. He asked for the life of the prince. When he revived he tried to cut off his head a second time, but the goddess held his hand and said:—

"I am pleased with thy devotion. Ask for anything thou choosest."

The prince asked for the woman of the dream. The goddess granted her to him. He took her to the Rája, who conferred his kingdom on the prince, and he reigned happily for many years.

[This is the wicked step-mother type who in Indian folklore is represented by the jealous co-wife. Their intrigues are a stock-subject in the folktales. (See, for instance, Tawney, *Katha Sarit Ságara* I., p. 356, see Temple: *Wideawake Stories*, p. 397).

[Instances of people falling in love in a dream are common: Tawney *loc cit,* I., 276, and Dunlop, *History of Fiction*, edited by H. Wilson, I., 258). The story also supplies an example of the nudity spells, of which I have given numerous examples in my "Introduction to the Popular Religion and Folklore of Northern India."—Ed.]

73. The Four Fools.[8]

Four men, one of whom was lame, the second blind of an eye, the third bald, and the fourth hump-backed, were sitting one day outside of the village, when a stranger came up and made a *salam* to them. They at once began to quarrel and disputed for which of them the salute was intended. The stranger smiled and said:—"For the biggest fool of you four." So they went to the Rája to decide who was the biggest fool.

The bald man said:—"I had a wife whom I deeply loved. One day I asked her for fire. She replied that she had just coloured her hands and feet with *lac* dye (*maháwar*) and could not dirty them. So I took her on my back and went to a neighbour's house, who gave me fire in an earthen pot (*borsi*). As I was taking it home the pot began to burn my head, but I could not take it down as I was holding my wife, and I was afraid to break it. So the end was that my crown was so burnt that all my hair fell off."

The humpback said:—"I was one day ploughing and a stranger came and told me that my wife was delivered of a son, and that I ought to go and give her the birth present (*lochana*). So I took some clothes and jewellery and went as he told me. A woman then showed me a baby and took the presents. As I was dandling the baby on the top of the house her real husband came in and knocked me down. So I have been hump-backed ever since."

Then the lame man said:—"I had two wives who loved me so much that they used to wash my feet daily and drink the foot ambrosia (*charnamrita*). One day only one wife was at home. She washed my feet and drank the water. When her co-wife returned she was so much enraged that, she cut off my leg with a knife."

The one-eyed man said:—"I also had two wives, who used to sleep each on one side of me on my extended hands. One night the lamp needed trimming, so I called a maid who let the burning wick fall into my eye. I could not release my hand except by waking one of my wives. So my eye was lost." Then the Rája said:—"The man who had neither wife nor child and still gave the birth offering was the greatest fool of all." So the others returned home in grief and mortification.

A second version runs as follows[9]:—

There were once four idiots who started in search of work. On the road a horseman met them. They all saluted him and he gave a salam in return. On this all four began to quarrel, each saying that the salute was meant for him. At last they referred to the horseman.

"I meant," said he, "the salam for the greatest fool among you."

Just then a Pandit passed by and they asked him to judge between them.

Said the first of them—

"I am the greatest fool and this will show it. After I was married I went to see my wife and when I approached her village her friends came out to welcome me. But I was ashamed to go with them. So I dressed myself as a mendicant and went to the house of my father-in-law to beg alms. My mother-in-law came out and said to me: "Sháhjí![10] here is some bread for you."

But when I saw her I covered my face as I was ashamed to look at my mother-in-law. She went on pressing me to take the bread, and as she advanced I retreated until I fell into the well. Then she cried out—

"Help! Help! neighbours! the beggar has fallen into the well."

They all ran up and hauled me out. Then up came my father-in-law who recognized me, but was too ashamed to own me. He took me into the house on pretence of giving me food. Then he said:—

"What do you mean by coming in this way?"

"I was very anxious to come," I answered, "but I was too shy to show myself."

"Well you are the biggest fool I ever saw," he said and turned me out.

"Now, am I not the greatest fool?" he asked. "I am a greater fool than you," cried the second. "Once I went to see my wife and she received me most affectionately, made me sit down and gave me a betel to chew and a pipe to smoke. Then she went off to arrange for my dinner. I was terribly hungry and looked about for something to eat. I saw some dry rice in a pot and filled my mouth with it. Then in came my mother-in-law and began to ask me of my household and friends. I could not answer as my mouth was filled, and when she saw my cheeks swelled she sent for the barber.

"This is a very bad case," he said, "and it was well you called me in."

So out with his knife and he slit open both my cheeks.

"That was a bad abscess," he said, and when he saw the grains of rice he added: "what a terrible lot of maggots were in it too!" But when my wife learned the truth she said:—"Clear off! who would live with such an idiot?"

"Now, am I not the greatest fool of all?"

Said the third:—"After I was married I was too shy ever to visit my wife. Soon after my wife's sister was about to be married and I was asked to the wedding; but I was ashamed to go. At last my father-in-law sent a servant with an ox cart (bahali) to fetch me. Even then I would not go, but when the day came I thought I would like to see the dancing and I went on foot. When I got near the village I halted at a shrine" where a faqír lived, and I changed clothes with him and sat down among the beggars. First all the relations and clansmen were fed, then the neighbours, and last of all the scraps were passed on to us. Then one of the beggars who knew I was an outsider, called out:—

"A little fresh meat is wanted to complete the feast."

And with this he knocked me into a pit full of water and mud. The others pulled me out, but my father-in-law saw me and said to my father:—

"Do my eyes deceive me? Can this be my son-in-law?"

Then I saluted my father, but he ran at me with evil language, and drove me out of the place. Now, am I not a bigger idiot than the others?

Then the fourth said:—

"I am a greater fool still. I am a Rájput by caste and a cultivator. When I came home one day from the field my wife put stale bread (basí rotí) before me. I told her to bake some more fresh, but she would not, and I ate nothing and went back to work. When I came home at nightfall I was very hungry, but she put the same bread before me and I would not eat. I lay down to sleep, and next morning I held my breath and lay in bed like a dead man. She came up and whispered to me:—

"Thákur Sáhib" You had better eat the bread, or I will call in the people and have you cremated."

But I paid no heed to her words; so by and by she began to wail.

"Alas my husband! Alas my husband!" and the clansmen assembled. They asked:—"How did he come to die? He was well yesterday."

"Yesterday," she said, "he fell ill of obstinacy and this caused his death."

So they made a bier, laid me on it, carried me to the river bank and prepared a pyre. They put me in it and were just lighting it when my wife whispered to me.

"Thákur Sáhib! the bread is still ready, and you had better eat it or be cremated."

"Bring it," I cried out, "and I will eat it perforce." So all the folk were amazed; but when my wife told them the story they jeered at me and said:—

"Fool! be off!" Am not I the greatest fool of all?

But the Pandit said:—

"No one can, judge between you, as you are all perfect in folly." So they went home.

74. The Tale of Four Fools—(para. 66).

The Panjábi version (Swynnerton, *Indian Nights' Entertainment*, 65 *sqq.*). "The four weavers" is more elaborate, but hardly reads like unadulterated rural folklore. The last episode is part of the cycle of the "Silent Couple" of which numerous parallels have been given by Mr. Clouston in the 2nd Volume of his *Popular Tales and Fictions*. It is the "Beggar and the five Muffins" of Pandit Natesa Sástri's "Folklore of Southern India."

The same idea appears in the story of the "Takka who submitted to be burnt alive rather than share his food with a guest" (*Katha Sarát Ságara*, II, 109), with which Mr. Tawney compares one of Ralston's Russian Tales of the Miser (p. 47), where Marko the Rich says to his wife in order to avoid the payment of a copeck:—"Hark ye wife! I'll strip myself naked and lie down under the holy pictures. Cover me up with a cloth and sit down and cry just as you would over a corpse. When the Moujik comes for his money tell him I died this morning."

In this connection the following is interesting:—

"The Barrin' o' the Door."—Students of the genealogy of popular fictions will be interested to learn that the humorous Scotch song "The Barrin' o' the Door," of which Herd discovered an old version entitled "Johnnie Blunt" in 1776, finds parallels in one of the tales in Mr. Swynnerton's *"Indian Nights' Entertainment* (noticed in the *Athenæum,* February 4th,

1893, p. 151), and in Pandit Natesa Sastri's "Tales of the Sun; or, Folklore of Southern India." In Mr. Swynnerton's Panjábí version, No. XI, a farmer and his wife are sitting together in their house, when a sudden gust of wind blows open the door, and they agree that the first to speak shall go and close it. They go to bed and remain silent; a dog comes in and eats up all the food he can find, but 'never a word they spak'. In the morning the wife goes with some grain to be ground by a neighbour, and while she is absent the village barber comes and asks the husband why he sits thus speechless, but receives no reply. Then he shaves the man's head, but cannot get him to speak; next he shaves off half his beard and moustache, and daubs him all over with lampblack. When the woman returns and sees the plight he is in she cries out, 'Ah, wretch! what have you been doing with yourself?' Quoth the man triumphantly, 'You've spoken first—go and shut the door!'

"The Pandit Natesa Sastri's Tamil version, entitled 'The Beggar and the Five Muffins,' is peculiarly interesting, as it presents a pretty close resemblance to a Venetian form of the story given in Professor Crane's 'Italian Popular Tales.' Here the agreement is that the first to speak should have the fifth muffin. 'Let us both close our eyes and lie down. Whoever first speaks shall get only two muffins, and the other shall have three.' One day, two days, three days pass, and the neighbours wonder that the house should remain closed. The beggar was missed in his usual rounds. At length the watchmen climb on the roof and jump down into the house, where they find the worthy couple stretched like two corpses. Neither of them would open eye or speak. At the public expense two litters of green bamboo and cocoanut leaves are prepared to remove the pair to the cremation ground, and old graybeards exclaim, 'How loving they were thus to die together!' The couple are placed on the pyre, and when the flames reach the man's legs he cries out, 'I'll be satisfied with two muffins!' upon which his wife screams, 'I have gained the day—let me have the three!' All the folk ran off, save one bold fellow, who questioned them as to the meaning of such extraordinary conduct. What was to be done with a couple who had braved death for an extra muffin? They couldn't be allowed to return to the village, so the elders built for them a small hut in a deserted meadow, where they were compelled to reside, and ever after they were called the 'muffin beggars,' and old women and young children used to bring them muffins morning and evening out of charity, since they loved muffins so well.

"Under the heading of 'The Silent Couple,' I have brought together several European versions of this diverting story, also Arabian, Turkish, and Hindu variants, in the second volume of my 'Popular Tales and Fictions.'"—*W. A. Clouston: Athenæum, 18th March, 1893.*

75. The Frog and the Snake.[13]

A frog and a snake were once quarrelling as to which of them could give the more poisonous bite. They agreed to test their powers.

When a man came to their tank the snake bit him beneath the water while the frog swam on the surface. The man called out to his friends:—"A frog has bitten me."

"What harm is that? Come along."

He went away and felt no effects from the bite.

A year after he came again and the frog bit him beneath the water while the snake swam on the surface.

"Alas!" he cried, "a snake has bitten me," and he died.

"Now," said the frog, "you will admit that my bite is more venomous than your's."

"I deny it altogether," said the snake.

So they agreed to refer the case to Vásuki Nága, the snake king, who, when he had heard the arguments of both sides, decided in favour of the snake, and said the man had died of fright.

"Of course the snake king sides with the snake," grumbled the frog.

So both of them bit him and that was the end of him.

76. Mr. Good and Mr. Evil.[14]

Once upon a time Mr. Good and Mr. Evil[15] made friends and went off in search of employment. They came to a stream. Mr. Evil drew water and Mr. Good went for firewood. Meanwhile Mr. Evil opened his companion's bag and stole his provisions.

When Mr. Good came back and found his bag empty he told Mr. Evil, who said:—"It must have been your wife stole your food. My wife often does the same when she does not want me to go out."

Mr. Good suspected his friend and said nothing.

Mr. Evil cooked his food, but gave none to his companion.

They went on till they came to the cross roads, and there Mr. Good said to Mr. Evil:—"Friend, we had better part, as we cannot get work if we stay together."

So they separated, and Mr. Good being hungry went on into the forest. At last he saw a hut, and going in—what does he see—four animals,—a tiger, a jackal, a snake, and a mouse,—were sitting, each in one corner of the hut. They took no notice of him, and he sat down in the middle.

Now, Mr. Good knew the speech of animals, and presently he heard them talking.

The tiger said to the jackal:—"What a lot of treasure the snake has in the house! If any one would come and dig it up while he is away looking for food what a good thing it would be; for we should then be no longer forced to guard it for him."

"Indeed, I do wish it were so. But, brother, do you know that there lives in the city of Ujjain a Rája who is stricken with leprosy, and he has promised to give his daughter and half his kingdom to the man who cures him?"

"Is it really so?" asked the tiger.

"It is so, indeed," answered the jackal.

"And how could he be cured?" was the next question.

"If any one," said the jackal, "were to get some of the dung of a swan (*hansa*), mix it with oil and rub it over him with a feather of the eagle Garuda, he would be cured of the disease."

Mr. Good heard all this and started for Ujjain. Then he walked through the market crying:— "A physician, ho! Does any one want a physician?"

The Rája sent for Mr. Good and he prescribed for him as the jackal had said, and he was cured. So Mr. Good married the princess and became lord of half the kingdom.

Then he went back to the hut and dug up the snake's treasure.

"Can I do anything more for you?" asked the tiger.

"Well, if you would devour the next person who comes here, I would feel obliged," said Mr. Good. Soon after Mr. Evil, wandering about in great poverty, came to the hut, and the tiger at once killed him.

So this was the end of Mr. Evil.

May Paramesar so reward right and punish wrong!

77. *The White Witch.*

There was once upon a time a white witch who ever tried to compass the ruin of human beings, so she one day sat by a roadside and transformed herself into Rs. 500. Now there was also a great sage who, when he found out what she had done, went to the end of the road to warn people away from the spot. He had not long to wait, however, for presently four sepoys rode past that way so he said to them:—"Do not go by this way, sirs, for a white witch is seated by this roadside who seeks to compass people's ruin."

But the four sepoys laughed. "What," cried they, "we, who have been in the heat of battle and are just returning from bloody warfare to fear a woman?" So they went on their way. As they rode on, they presently came to where the witch was lying in the shape of Rs. 500. "Oh!" they exclaimed, "the cunning old sage, did not wish us to pass this way because of this money, for he knew we would take it, and he no doubt wanted it all for himself." So they got off their horses to take it, but finding it too much to carry, they sat down beside it to watch it. But soon they began to feel hungry. "What good is the money to us if we starve by it?" said they. "Let two of us go to the bazar and buy some food for all of us while two of us still keep guard here." To this they all agreed. So two of them went to the market to purchase some food for all of them. But as they went on, one said to the other:—"Let us poison some sweets (*laddu*) and give them to those others, then they will die, and we shall have only two to divide the money between, and consequently will have more than we would if it was divided among four." To which the other agreed. So when they reached the market, after they had feasted themselves they poisoned some sweetmeats and went back to their companions who were watching by the Rs. 500. As they sat watching they saw their comrades returning from the bazar and coming towards them, so one said to the other:—"Let us shoot those fellows as they are coming along, and then there will be only two of us to divide the money, so we shall have more than we would were it divided among four." The other agreed, so they raised their guns and shot their friends as they were coming towards them. As they fell down dead the ones that were keeping guard by the rupees said:—"Let us now go and search their bodies, and what food we find on them we will eat, for we are very hungry." So they went and searched their bodies and found the poisoned *laddus* on them. Of these they had a good feed, and of course died too. They were not long dead when the sage passed by that road. When he saw their corpses he sadly shook his head. "Alas! said he, I warned them against their fate, but they would not listen, and the white witch (*dáin*) has compassed their ruin."—*Ida Casabon: Aligarh.*

86

78. *The Lament for Sobhan.*[16]

There was a certain washerman who was a servant in a king's house. He had a donkey which he called Sobhan (beautiful). One day that donkey died, the washerwoman wept for its loss. At that time the queen summoned the washerwoman. The washerwoman came weeping. The queen asked—"Why are you weeping?" She said:—"My Sobhan has died" and crying out—"alas! my Sobhan; alas! my Sobhan," began to weep. The queen, too, then began to cry out "alas! my Sobhan! and to weep." The queen's hand-maidens seeing the queen was crying, began to weep too. The king hearing the queen crying, began to weep and call out:—"Alas! my Sobhan!" and the king's servants also began to cry. When the king's wazir heard all this noise of weeping, he was struck with wonder as to what might be the cause of this noise. In fear and trembling he came to the king and said:—"If I may, I would speak a word." The king said:—"Speak on."

The wazir asked:—"Who was Sobhan?" The king said:—"I do not know, ask the queen; for when I saw her crying, I too began to weep." In short, the wazir inquired of the Rani. The queen said:—"I do not know, ask the washerwoman." In short, the washerwoman was asked, and she said:—"It is the name of my donkey which has just died." Then everybody felt ashamed.

79. *How silly a Woman can be.*[17]

Once upon a time a man began lecturing his wife on her duties. "A good wife," said he, "instead of wasting her time, spins cotton, makes thread, and gets cloth made." "Oh! all right," said she. "Get me a spinning wheel and some cotton, and see what wonders I will do." The husband bought a spinning wheel and some cotton for her. The wife began spinning, and when the thread was made, went out in search of a weaver. On enquiring from her neighbours, she learnt that a clever weaver lived near a certain tank. She went there, and seeing no one, called out "O weaver! ho!" A frog in the tank called out "*tar!*" She looked in, and being sure that the answer came from the water, she said:—"Ah! the weaver lives here," and she called out:—"Look here! I want some cloth woven. Here is the thread:" and throwing in the thread she said:—"Please weave it nicely. When shall I call for it?" The frog again happened to call out "*tar!*" so she answered "all right I will call to-morrow" (*kal*). So she went home well satisfied with what she had done.

When her husband came home she told him all about it, and next day she went to the tank and called out:—"Weaver! here I am. Please give me the cloth." The frog called out "*tar*" again. "What? to-morrow! (*kal*). This will never do. I will wait another day, but I must have my cloth to-morrow. If you don't give it I will punish you by carrying off the door of your house."

Next day she came again, but the frog called out "*tar*" again. "Do you think I am going to be fooled in this way?" But all the frog said was "*tar*."

So in her anger she plunged into the tank in search of the weaver's door. Presently her hands fell on two heavy pieces of something. She brought them up and they looked like bricks. "I have got the door of your house at any rate," said she. "I hope this will make you more careful in future." When she came home she told the whole story to her husband, "Let me see the bricks," said he, and when he saw them he said:—"These are bricks of gold. We are now rich: take care of them." "What will you do with them," she asked. "I will buy good clothes and ornaments and slave girls," replied her husband.

Next day she thought she would save her husband trouble by buying some slave-girls and other things. So she sat at her door and began asking every pedlar who passed if he had clothes and ornaments and slave-girls for sale. At last an old woman passed by, and when she heard her question, said to herself:—"What can this foolish creature want?" So she asked:—"My daughter! have you any money to buy these things?" "No," said the lady, "but I have two bricks of gold, and my husband said he would buy these things with them. You may take the gold bricks if you bring me what I want." "All right," answered the old woman. "I will bring the things to-morrow."

Next day the old woman came and said:— "Here, my dear! I have brought you all you want," and she showed her a lot of shining brass ornaments and some red and green dresses of common cloth. "Oh! how beautiful," said the lady, "and where are the slave-girls?" "Here they are," answered the old woman, and showed her half-a-dozen big dolls, all dressed up. The lady was delighted, and the old woman went away grumbling that she had been a loser by the bargain.

The lady then put on one of her new dresses and the ornaments and began to distribute work to her slave-girls. She put two of the dolls in the kitchen and said:—"Cook dinner for your master who will return soon."

Two she seated at the door and said:—"You must open the door when your master comes." Then she lay down for a nap, putting the two remaining dolls near the bed with orders to wake her when their master arrived.

The husband came and knocked at the door, but no one answered. He knocked again, saying "what on earth is up with this precious wife of mine?" and so he went on knocking until at last the lady woke, opened the door, and let the husband in.

"What happened to you, my dear?" he began, without noticing her new dress and ornaments. At last he said:—"Hullo! from where did you get these?" "I will tell you all presently," said she, "but why did not the slave-girls open the door? I put two of them there on the look-out for you." "Slave-girls! What on earth do you mean," he asked. She made no answer, but seizing a stick began to thrash the dolls. He looked on in amazement, and asked his wife to explain what these dolls were there for. "Come down and have your dinner first, and I will tell you all," she replied.

Then she went to the kitchen and said:—"I hope the girls have got ready dinner and have not been lazy." But when she saw no dinner ready her anger increased. "I thought," said she, "that like a good and faithful wife I would spare you the trouble of buying ornaments and dresses and slave-girls, so I found an old pedlar woman who got me all these things." "And the money?" asked her husband. "Oh! I paid her the money, and she was so obliging as to take the two golden bricks." Then her husband lost all patience. "Wretch!" said he, "you have ruined me," and he turned her out of the house in disgust.

So she wandered about in the jungle, and next morning a party of thieves arrived there, and began to examine and divide their plunder. She had been awake all night, and had just fallen asleep, and she dreamt that her husband had followed her, and was calling her to come back. She called out, "I am coming! I am coming!" and jumped up. The thieves thinking themselves pursued, took to their heels, leaving all their plunder behind them. She came up, and seeing a lot of money and jewels, she took possession of them, and tying them up in a bundle proceeded homewards. She showed all the wealth to her husband, who was delighted and took her back.

She had no idea, however, of the value of the property, and asked her husband what they should do with it. "We will spend it," said he, "when Shabrát, Ramzán, and 'Id come," meaning the feasts.

She thought these were people to whom her husband intended to give the things. She was curious to know who they were, so next day when her husband went out she asked every one who passed if his name were Shabrát, 'Id or Ramzán. One man happened to be called Ramzán, and when he told her, she asked him in, and told him to take what her husband had left for him. Then she brought out a third part of the property, and was giving it to him when he asked the reason. "I am sure I don't know," she replied, "but there is a lot of these things, and my husband said they were intended for Ramzán, Shabrádt, and 'Id. I was waiting for them. You are Ramzán, and this is your share. I wish the others would come and take their shares too." "O! I see," he answered, beginning to understand how the land lay. "I think I can help you by sending these men, for I know them both." "O! do please," she answered. So he went off and sent his brothers, instructing them to give the names of 'Id and Shabrát. When they came and gave their names, she said:—"I am glad you came. I have been bothered waiting for you. Wait till I bring your shares;" and so saying, she gave them what remained of the plunder. "I suppose you can divide it?" she asked. "That we can," they answered, and cleared off. "How pleased my husband will be at what I have done!" she thought to herself.

When her husband returned she told him all she had done. "I hope you are pleased now!" she asked in triumph. But he cursed the day when he had married such a fool, and again he turned her out.

She went again to the jungle, and it so happened that a camel, laden with the king's treasure, had lost its way. She found the camel, and seizing the nose-string, led it home and showed it to her husband. He killed the camel and buried the treasure in his house. But he was afraid his wife would blab out the whole story, so he made her go to bed, and going to the bazar bought a lot of parched rice (*khil*) and sugar sweets (*batásha*), and having scattered them in the courtyard, woke his wife and called out "run! run! see how it has been raining *khil* and *batásha*:" so she came out and began collecting them in great glee.

A few days after a cryer came round, proclaiming that one of the king's treasure camels had been lost, and that any one who knew anything about it should give information on pain of death if they failed to do so. So she went to the door and called out that she knew all about it. Then up came the Kotwál, and she told him that she had found the camel and brought it home. "And to whom did you give it?" he asked. "To my husband, of course," she answered. "Where is he?" "He is out." "Well I will wait for him."

When he came back the Kotwál asked him where was the camel and the treasure, "What do you mean?" the husband asked. "He means," said his wife, "the treasure on the camel I gave you a few days ago. "Please sir," said the husband, "don't believe a word of what my unfortunate wife is saying, To tell you the truth, she is a lunatic." "What!" screamed his wife, "I am mad, am I? I can point out the treasure this moment." "Ask her," said her husband, "what day did she bring the treasure?" "Yes! my good woman! tell me that." "Why that was the day it rained *khil* and *batásha.*" "There now," asked her husband, "can you doubt she is mad?"

So the Kotwál laughed and went away, pitying the poor woman.

But her husband thought it was not safe to keep her any longer, so, like an ungrateful wretch that he was, he turned her out, and never had anything to say to her as long as he lived.

[For the incident of deceiving the wife by scattering sweetmeats about, see Clouston, *Book of Sindibad*, 262. On surprising robbers, see the parallels collected by Jacob (*English Fairy Tales*, 231), and for keeping the door, "Mr. Vinegar" (*ibid.* 231).

80. *The Parrot, and the Maina.*[18]

Once upon a time a parrot and a maina were friends. At that time famine raged in the land. They went into a field to pick up food, and they found a grain of gram which they wanted to divide, but when they tried to break it with a stone it got stuck in a piece of wood, and do what they would they could not get it out. So they went to the Rája and said—

> "*Rája, ho Rája.*
> *Chana khunta khaya hai.*"

"O Rája, the post has eaten our gram."

The Rája told the carpenter to break the post and take out the gram; but the carpenter would not do it.

Then the birds went to the snake and said:—

> "*Sánp, ho sánp, khunta chana khaya hai. Barhai*
> *chirai urai nahin. Tuhare lage aye hain.*"

"O snake, O snake, the post has eaten the gram, and the carpenter will not split it, so we have come to you."

The snake did not heed them, so they went to the stick and said:—

> *"Lauri, ho lauri, chana khunta khaya hai.*
> *Barhaí chirai urai nahin. Rája dárain oke*
> *nahín. Sánp katai oke nahín. Aye tuhare lage*
> *hain. Máro sánp Rája ken."*

"The post has eaten up the gram. The carpenter will not split it. The Rája will not punish him. The snake will not bite him. We have come to you to kill the snake."

But the stick paid no heed to them.

Then they went to the fire and said:—

> *"Agi ho agi. Chana khunta khaya hai. Barhai*
> *chirai oke nahin. Rája dárain okai nahin. Sánp*
> *kátai oke nahin. Lauri marai sánp he nahin.*
> *Bhaiya kato laur kahin. Tuhare goren parat*
> *hain."*

"The post has eaten up the gram. The carpenter will not split it. The Rája will not punish him. The snake will not bite him. The stick will not kill him. Brother burn the stick. We throw ourselves at your feet." And so they went in turn to the ocean, to the elephant, to the creeper. At last the creeper took pity on the birds and the elephant feared the creeper, and the ocean feared the elephant, and the fire feared the ocean, and the stick feared the fire, and the snake feared the stick and the carpenter feared the snake, and split the post which gave up the gram to the birds who went away happy.

81. The Prince and the Sadhu.[19]

Once upon a time there was a Rája who had no children. One day a Sadhu, who had wandered in many lands, came to the Rája and promised to give him a son, on condition that he would give him one of the twins who would in due time be born. The Rája agreed to this, and the Sadhu blessed him and said:—

"I will return in a year and take one of your sons." Within the year two sons were born to the Rája, and at the same time a dhobi in the city also had twin sons. In a year the Sadhu returned and asked for one of the

Rája's sons. The Rája took by force one of the dhobi's sons and gave him to the Sadhu.

The Sadhu took leave of the Rája and took the child with him. On the way he said to the boy:—

"If I take the shortest way I shall reach my hermitage in six months, but I shall have to cross dangerous jungles. The longer way is easier, but it will be a year's journey. Now which way shall we choose?"

The boy chose the longer road, so the Sadhu knew that he was not a Kshatriya, because if he were he would never have feared the jungle. He took him back to his father and said:—

"This is some low caste boy. Give me your own son, or I will curse you."

The Rája was forced to give him his own son, and when the prince was going with the Sadhu he shot an arrow into a nim tree at the gate of the palace and said to his brother:—

"Whenever I am in trouble the arrow will fall. Then you must come and help me."

His brother gave him a sword and said:—

"Keep this sword always with you. Whenever I am in trouble it will break in pieces."

The prince set out with the Sadhu who, when they reached the same place in the jungle, put the same question to him which he had asked the son of the dhobi. The prince at once voted for the shorter road, and the Sadhu knew that he was a true Kshatriya. When they reached the hermitage the Sadhu said to the prince:—

"I am going to the bazar for food. Wait here, but do not attempt to open any of the four locked rooms."

When the Sadhu had gone the prince opened one of the rooms, and what did he see? There were two bitches identical in form. When he opened the second room he saw in it two mares of the same shape. In the third room he found several headless corpses, and when they saw him all the heads began to laugh. The prince asked them why they laughed.

"Because," said they, "you will soon be as we are."

When he enquired the meaning of their words, they said:—

"When the Sadhu comes back he will ask you to walk round the image of the goddess and then to bow before her. When you do so he will cut off your head with his sword. Your only chance of escape is this. When he asks you to bow, ask him to show you the way. Then cut off his head and open the fourth room. In it you will find a pitcher of nectar (*amrita*.) Drink some of it yourself and sprinkle some upon us. You will become immortal, and our heads will join on to our bodies again."

Then the prince shut up the room, and when the Sadhu returned he did as the heads had told him. When he had killed the Sadhu and restored his victims to life, he started for his own country and at night lay under a tree. In this tree lived a Shardul bird and his mate, whose eggs a snake used to eat daily. The prince killed the snake, and when the birds returned and found their eggs safe, they were very grateful to him and gave him one of their young ones.

Then he came on to a city where the Rája was performing the swayamvara of his daughter. She passed over all the Rájas and threw the garland of victory (*jaymal*) round the neck of the prince. So he married her and took her home.

The prince used to go out hunting every day, and one day he met a Rákshasí in the jungle who asked him to gamble with her. She had tamed a cat and taught it to put out the lamp whenever it saw its mistress being defeated. Then the Rákshasí said:—

"I will keep you in prison until you defeat me."

When the prince fell into this trouble the arrow fell out of the nim tree, and his brother at once set out to help him.

After travelling for many years he reached the palace of the Rákshasí, and she challenged him to play. When he played the first day and saw the trick of the cat, next day he took a dog with him, and when the cat ran away he defeated the Rákshasí and won all her goods. Then he brought his brother home. His father was delighted to see him, and having made over the kingdom to him, spent the rest of his life as a devotee.

82. The Manjhi Girl and the Bamboo.[20]

Once upon a time there was a Mánjhi who had seven sons and a daughter. One day the girl went into the field and brought home some vegetables, and as she was preparing them for dinner, she cut her finger with the sickle and a drop of blood fell among the greens. She said nothing about it; but when her brothers tasted the dish and found it more tasty than usual, they asked her about it, and when they learnt the reason they began to think how good human flesh must be. So they determined to kill their sister. All but the youngest agreed to this, and finally his brethren forced him to kill his sister, but he would not taste her flesh. When the others had eaten, they buried the bones of the girl under a clump of bamboos, and from them sprang such a bamboo as was not to be found in the jungle for beauty.

One day a Rája came into the jungle to hunt, and when he saw the bamboo he was so pleased with it that he had it dug up carefully and planted in his garden.

Every night the girl used to come out of the bamboo and walk about the city. At last the servants watched her and saw her going back into the bamboo. They went and told the Rája, who lay in wait for her next night, and when she came out of the bamboo he caught her by the band. Then he took her to his palace and married her. He summoned her brothers, and the youngest he rewarded with five villages, but the others he banished from his kingdom.

[This is on the lines of "Little ankle bone" in Temple's *Wide-awake Stories*. The tradition of cannibalism among the Manjhis is interesting. For cannibalism in folktales, see Lady Burton, *Arabian Nights*, IV, 496. The best parallel to this tale is the "Magic fiddle" of Campbell's "*Santal Folktales*," 52, *sqq.*, and Jacobs' Notes, "*Indian Fairy Tales*," 240, *sq.*—ED.].

83. *The Goat and the Tiger.*[21]

There was once a he-goat and his wife, and she was about to kid. So she said to her husband:—"Let us find some quiet place where I may lie in."

By chance the goats selected the den of the tiger, and there two kids were born. A day or two after the tiger came back, and when the he-goat saw him coming he asked his wife what had better be done. She said:—"Don't be nervous. When the tiger comes near I will squeeze the kids' legs and make them squeal." Then you say to me:—"Why are the children crying?" And I will say:—"They are crying because they want some fresh tiger-meat. I have some of it dried here, but they do not care for that."

When the tiger came they did as they had planned, and the tiger was so much frightened that he forthwith ran away. As he was still running he met the jackal, who said:—"Good morning, uncle, I have not seen you for a long time. Where are you running to?" The tiger replied:—"I am running away because some animals have occupied my den, who eat tigers, and when I went there just now I heard them planning to eat me." "What nonsense," said the jackal. "Come with me and I will soon drive them out." So the tiger and the jackal came together to the den, and the he-goat saw them and asked his wife what it were best to do. She said:—

"Leave it to me." So she began to squeeze the legs of the kids, and when she made them squeal she called out:—"I can't think what ails these children to-day. They want some tiger and jackal-meat for their breakfast, and I have plenty dry in the store-room, but they must have it fresh."

When they heard this the tiger and the jackal scampered off and never came near the place again. So the goats had the use of it as long as they pleased.

[A tiger is befooled in a similar way in a Kashmir tale in *Indian Antiquary*, 1882, quoted by Clouston: *Book of Sindibád*, 252.—ED.].

84. The Piety of the Bráhman.[22]

Mahádeva and Parameswar came down from heaven to see how the world was going on. When they reached the earth, Mahádeva asked Parameswar where they should go. Parameswar answered:—"Go wherever you please, I will follow you." Mahádeva replied:—"I have many votaries in this land. One of them is an Ahír, who is very rich. Let us go to him." Parameswar agreed: they went in search of the Ahír and found him in his fields looking after the ploughing. They sat down on the ground close beside him, but he paid no attention to them. After a while Mahádeva said:—"My son, is this your field, and is it being ploughed for you?" The Ahír replied:—"Yes; this is my field and it is being ploughed for me." Mahádeva said:—"I am your Guru, and the Bába who is sitting near me is my friend. Go and make arrangements for our food and drink." The Ahír replied:—"You are a pretty pair of Bábájís, to come asking for food and drink in this way. Go your ways and do not trouble me." Then Parameswar said:—"Come, Mahádeva, we had better be going. I have seen your votary, and I do not think much of him. Now let us go and see a poor Bráhman, who is a disciple of mine." So both the deities went to the house of the Bráhman. When the Bráhman saw, then he ran up and fell prostrate before them, and, bringing water in a dish, washed their feet. Now the poor man had nought in his house wherewith to entertain, his guests: but he spread a carpet in his portico, and respectfully asked them to take their seats upon it. Then he went into the village to try and beg something to lay before them. Meanwhile his wife bathed them with her own hands. The day passed, but the Bráhman failed to get any alms, and both host and guests had to lie down supperless.

That night the Bráhman and his son agreed that they must break into some one's house, in order to get the wherewithal to entertain the visitors. Accordingly they got up and broke into the house of a banker. There they tied up everything necessary for a feast, and the son gave the things to his father and told him to pass out first through the hole in the wall. He was following him, when he made a noise which woke the people of the house. They raised an alarm and lighted a lamp. Then the son of the Bráhman was arrested. The Bráhman, who was outside, reasoned within himself that if his son was arrested as a thief all his honour would be lost. So he cut off the head of his son which was sticking out of the hole in the wall. He buried the head in the ground and then ran away home. Next morning the news spread that the house of the banker had been robbed, but no one troubled himself to look at the thief who had been caught. When the Bráhman went home he gave all the things he had got to his wife and she prepared food. When the food was ready the Bráhman asked the deities to partake of it. The deities asked:—"Where is your son?"

The Bráhman was very much confused what answer to make. But he went outside and called out "Son, Son." Immediately his son stood before him, and said:—"I have been away and have returned with great difficulty." The Bráhman remained silent, and they all sat down to eat. When they had finished eating the Bráhman cried out:—

> *"Prán gáen jo pati rahai, rahai prán pati jáya:*
> *Dhik hai wah jíwan ko-kahain Akabar Ráe."*

"Better even at the cost of life to save one's honour.
Fie upon the man who saves his life at the expence of his honour."
So says the Lord Akbar.
The Bráhman then told the whole story to Parameswar, who was much pleased and conferred upon him much wealth and honour.

[The incident of cutting off the thief's head is part of the cycle of the "Robbery of the King's Treasury" (Herodotus, *Euterpe*, 121: Clouston, *Popular Tales and Fictions*, II., 115, *sqq.*

The Bráhman's exaggerated idea of the obligations of hospitality is something like the famous Falcon of Boccaccio (*Decameron*), VII, 9,—ED.].

85. The Bráhman and the Snake.[23]

In a hole in a hillock there lived a snake. One day a Bráhman was passing by with his religious books under his arm, when the snake called out to him:—"Panditjí, where are you going?" "I am going to give a religious recitation (*katha*) to one of my parishioners (*jajman*)." "Is there any harm in your reading the scriptures to me?" enquired the snake. "If you give me a recitation I will pay you a gold-mohur daily." The Pandit agreed, and the snake made a holy square (*chauk*) and put a stool inside it and spread the sacred *kusa* grass. The Pandit read the scriptures, and when he was done the snake gave him a gold-mohur as his remuneration (*dahshina*). So it went on for a year or two, and the Bráhman became so rich and lazy that one day he told his son to go and do the recitation. The snake gave him, as usual, a gold-mohur as his fee. But as he was going home the lad thought to himself "This snake must have an enormous treasure in his charge. Why should I not get it all?" So he went back and made a blow at him with his bludgeon. He missed the snake, who promptly leaped upon him and gave him so sore a bite that the lad fell on the ground senseless. When the lad did not return the old Pandit went in search of him, and seeing what had happened, said:—"O snake! my kind client! what a sin you have committed in killing my son!" "I gave him only what he deserved," replied the snake. "Don't you know the proverb: If any one strikes at you, strike at him first and don't think of the sin?" (*marante ko mariyé, dosh, páp na giniye*).

"You and your son have cheated me. Take care I don't bite you too."

Then the Pandit implored the snake to suck out the poison and restore his son to life. The snake, who was of a kindly disposition, did so, and the boy revived. Then the snake said:—"If you harm one who in confidence lays his head in your lap, the lord of the world is his guardian "(*Jáhi bharosé soiyé dei god men sir, soí anhit jo karé rakhwáro jagdis.*)"

86. The Faithful Mungoose.[24]

Once upon a time there was a man who was childless: he prayed to Mahádeva, who, after twelve years, took pity on him and blessed him with a son. The parents loved the child and put him in charge of a maid. She got a tame mungoose to play with the child. One day a snake got into the baby's cradle and the mungoose killed it. The maid came in and, seeing the mungoose covered with blood, cried out:—"The mungoose has killed the child!" The father hearing this rushed in and killed the mungoose with his club. But when he saw the dead snake under the cradle he was overcome with remorse for his hastiness.

[This is the well-known Bethgelert story, which appears in the *Katha Sarit*

Ságara as the "Story of the Bráhman and the Mungoose "(II, 90), on which Mr. Tawney notes:—"Benfey does not appear to have been aware that this story was to be found in Somadeva's work. It is found in his *Pancharantra*, Vol. II, 326. He refers to Wolf, II, 1; Knatchbull, 268; Symeon Seth, 76; John of Capua, K. 4. German Translation, (Ulm, 1483) R., 2; Spanish Translation XLV a: Doni, 66 Anvári-Suhaili, 404; Cabinet des Fées XVII, 22: Baldo fab. XVI (in Edele stand du Meril, p. 240: Hitopadesa IV, 13 (Johnson's Translation, p. 116). In Sandabar and Syntipas the animal is a dog. It appears that the word dog was also used in the Hebrew Translation. John of Capua has *canis* for ichneumon in another passage: so perhaps he has it here. Benfey traces the story in Calumnia Novercalis C. I. Historia Septum Sapientum Bl: Romans des Sept Sages, 1139: Dyocletian, Einleitung, 1212; Grasse Gesta Romanorum II, 176: Keller Romans, CLXXVIII: Le Grand d'Aussy, 1779, II: 303: Grimm's Marchen–48 (Benfey, Vol. I. PP. 479–483). To Englishmen the story suggests Llewellyn's faithful hound Gelert, from which the parish of Bethgelert, in North Wales, is named. This legend has been versified by Hon'ble William Robert Spencer. It is found in the English Gesta (see Bohn's Gesta Romanorum, Introduction, XLIII, p. 24. The story, as found in the Seven Wise Masters, is admirably told by Simrock, Deutsche Volksbucher, Vol. XII, p. 135: see also Baring-Gould, "Curious of the Middle Ages," 1st series, p. 126.]

Another version is localized at Mirzapur.

There was once a Kabuli who had a splendid dog called Motiya or "Pearl." He fell into difficulties, and was compelled to mortgage his dog to a banker for Rs. 1,000, which he promised to refund in a year, and meanwhile the dog was to remain in pledge with the merchant. Soon after dacoits attacked the merchant's house and robbed his treasure. He was in despair, when one day the dog came up to him and began to pull his loin-cloth. Gradually the dog led him to the lake on the top of the hill, and then, hidden in the water, was found nearly all the missing treasure. The merchant was so delighted that be wrote a quittance of the dog's mortgage, and tying it to the animal's neck, ordered him off to his master. The year had nearly expired, and his master, who was ignorant of all this, was coming with the money to redeem. On the way he met Motiya, and supposing that he had broken faith with the merchant, he plunged his sword into his heart. The matter was soon explained, and the merchant in grief at the dog's fatal end, made steps round the tank and built a temple, and called the place Motiya Talao or Motiya's Tank, which name it bears to the present day.

[In a similar form it appears as the "Snake and the Cat" of the book of

Sindibád. Mr. Clouston (*Book of Sindibad*, 56, 236, *sqq.*) has collected a number of parallels. Also see his *Group of Eastern Romances*, 211, 515.—ED.].

87. The Master-Thief.[25]

Once upon a time there was a king who was always magnifying himself, and he had an only son who was always hearing his father singing his own praises. One day as the king was eating his dinner, he said:—"On such and such a day I caught so many thieves, and another day I caught so many, and I will catch another tonight." His son wondered at this. "Why, he sleeps all night through and how can he catch thieves?" So he determined to try him, and that night he went quietly into his father's room and stole the bowl (*katora*) out of which he used to drink. When the king woke and wanted a drink of water he could not find his bowl and began to beat his servants. Then the prince came up and said:— "Father, you are always boasting. What a hand you are at catching thieves, and now some one has stolen your bowl from your very bed head. This indeed is strange." Then he produced the bowl from under his arm and gave it to his father. The king asked:—"Who stole my bowl?" "It was I," said the prince, "who stole it in order to try you." "I don't believe it," said the king. The prince replied:—"Let me try you again." The king said:—"If you can steal my tray from my bedside to-night, then I will be certain it was you who stole my bowl, and I will reward you and give you half my kingdom." The prince replied:—"All right. I will steal it." So when he went to bed the king hung his tray over his head and filled it with water, in order that if any one touched it the water might fall on his face, and he would wake and catch the thief. When the prince saw that his father had gone to sleep, he took some sand and, going into the room, poured a handful into the tray, and when the sand had soaked up all the water he carried off the tray. In the morning when the king opened his eyes, what did he see that his tray had been stolen. So he called his son, and the prince, coming with the tray, presented it to him. The king said:—"Well done, my son. In a certain land there is a king and he has a horse of the sea (*daryai ghora*). If you can steal this horse; I will admit you are a clever fellow, and will give you my whole kingdom." The prince replied "I will steal it." So the prince started to steal the horse. Now the king of that land had many astrologers (*failsuf*), who used day by day to inform him if any enemy or suspicious character came into his kingdom. That day, when they opened their books, they gave notice that a thief was coming to steal the horse of the sea. The king was in great anxiety, and every day would ask the astrologers:—"How far off is the thief now?" When they informed him that the thief was close by, the king ordered that the city gates should be closed, and a guard posted to see that no stranger was admitted, and that no person left the city. So a guard was posted on all four sides to prevent any one entering or leaving the city. It so happened that there was an old woman who used to go out of the city every day and collect fire-wood, by which she supported herself. When the guards prevented the old woman from going out as usual, she went forthwith to the king and began to weep and strike her head on the ground, and implored leave to go out, saying:—"I live by collecting wood, and this is my only means of support." She made so great a disturbance that the king had to give her permission to go out once and return once to the city during the day time. So she used to go out, as usual, every day, and meanwhile the prince arrived near the city. When he saw that the gates were closed and no one admitted he was in great perplexity. But next day, when he saw the old woman come to collect wood he approached her and said:—"Old lady, if you take me into the city I will give you many rupees." She said:—"How can I take you in; the guards will never admit you." The prince answered:—"Well, let me sit in your basket, put some wood over me and take me in; and if any one on the road asks you to sell the wood, don't sell it, but say:—'I wont sell my wood to-day." The old woman agreed, put the prince in her basket, put some wood over him, and brought him in. On the road many persons wished to buy her wood, but she answered:—"I wont sell my wood to-day." So she brought the basket into her house, and there the prince alighted. Then the astrologers said to the king:—"Your majesty, the thief has arrived in the city and will certainly steal your horse." The king was in great perplexity and issued a proclamation to this effect:—"If any one arrests the thief, who has come to steal my horse, I will give him half my kingdom."

Then the prince got himself up as a Pandit, went to the palace and asked for employment. The king said:—"I must try you first before I give you a place among my other astrologers. Come now, tell me what is going to happen." The prince pretended to open his books, and soon after replied:—"Your majesty has a horse of the sea, and a thief has arrived in your kingdom with intent to steal it, and it is quite certain he will succeed." So the king appointed him one of his astrologers. Now the king used daily to make proclamation that "whoever arrests the thief to him I will give half my kingdom; "but no one accepted the task. At last the kotwal went to the king and said: "I will arrest the thief."

The prince heard that the kotwal was preparing to arrest the thief, so he went to the house of a poor woman, and putting on a single cloth round his loins and some grain in a basket, began to grind it, and sat up grinding till midnight. Then he tied himself hand and foot with a rope, and just at that moment the kotwal approached on his rounds in search of the thief. When be heard the noise of the grindstone, he began to think who can be grinding at such an hour. So he looked in and saw a woman tied with a rope, going on twisting the grindstone. When the prince saw the kotwal he began to weep. The kotwal said:—"Why are you grinding at such an hour, and why are you weeping." He answered:— "A man tied me up here, gave me so much grain and went away, saying:— "I am coming back by-and-by, and if you haven't finished grinding it by the time I return, I will kill you."

The kotwal was quite certain that this person must be the thief: so he took off all his clothes and put on a loin-cloth and tied himself up with a rope, and said to himself:—"When the thief comes and unties the rope, I will arrest him." So he told the other to leave, and he went away. In the morning the king made search for the kotwal and found him tied up. So the kotwal went and said to the king:—"Your majesty, it is out of my power to catch the thief."

Now the king had in his employment three Pandits, who were brothers. They said:—"Your majesty, we will catch the thief." So the prince went to their house and said to their wives:—"Tonight a devil (*shaitán*) or an evil spirit (*bhút*) will come to your house; if you wish to escape, then light a good fire at night and sit beside it." The women believed him, and he went, and getting himself up as a barber, went to the Pandits, who were sitting on a river bank. When the Pandits saw him, they said:—"Who are you?" He said:—"I am a barber. I thought it was daybreak and came to shave you: now what may you be doing here?" They replied:—"We are sitting on the look-out for a thief." He said:—"If a sharp thief, like this, sees you, he will run away. Now I have a thing with me which, if you shave your heads and rub it on, you will be able to see everything yourselves, but will remain invisible to others." So they were much pleased and said:—"Come and shave us at once." As he was shaving them he cut their scalps in a number of places, and rubbed in hot lime well and said:—"Take a dip in the water." They all took a dip in the river, and as the lime was fresh, the moment the water touched it, it began to heat and burn their heads, so they ran home, screaming with pain. Their wives were quite certain that a devil had come into the house. So they took up sticks and commenced to thrash them. The Pandits kept on crying out:—"Stop, we are your husbands." But the more they cried out the more the women beat them, till at last the women lighted a lamp and saw what they had done and were filled with sorrow. Next morning the king sent for the Pandits, and when he saw them he was at first out of his mind with astonishment, and finally burst into laughter. After this no one would volunteer to catch the thief. At last the king said:—"I will catch the thief myself." So he mounted his horse of the sea, and started at night to catch the thief. The prince met him, and the king said:—"Who are you?" He replied:—"I am your majesty's Pandit, and without your orders I have come out to catch the thief, because it is written in my books that the thief will certainly come here to-night. Now, please tie up the horse here and sit at a little distance. I will watch by the horse, and when the thief comes I will straightway arrest him." The king believed his words and tethered the horse there and went and sat down a short way off. Without losing a moment the prince mounted the horse and rode off at full speed to his own land. The poor king remained wringing his hands.

When he got home his father was much pleased and seated him on the throne of his kingdom, which he ruled with the utmost wisdom and ability.

88. The Master-Thief.[26]

A certain Rája had four sons. When they grew up he sent them abroad to learn wisdom. After a time they returned, and when he examined them the Rája found that the three elder boys had learned various useful accomplishments, while the only knowledge the youngest had acquired was the art of robbery. The Rája was greatly grieved, but said to him:—"Let me see if you have learnt even to rob. Go and steal Syáma Karna[27], the black-eared horse of the Rája of Behár." At the same time he sent a warning to the Rája of Behár to watch his horse. The master-thief soon reached the boundary of the kingdom of Behár. He had great trouble in eluding the frontier guards; but at last he got past them, and put up in the house of an old woman. The moment he arrived the Court astrologer announced that the thief had come. The Rája sent for the kotwal (chief constable) of the city and sent him in pursuit. The master-thief got himself up as a lovely girl, and the kotwal carried her off to his office, where a stocks had been erected to hold the master-thief. "Let me see how it works," said the master-thief. So the kotwal got into the stocks and the master-thief fastened him up and left him there till next morning. Next morning they released the kotwal, and then four of the royal wrestlers volunteered to arrest the master-thief. Meanwhile the master-thief disguised himself as a Sádhu (ascetic) and took his station on the banks of a tank near the city. The wrestlers came to the tank and consulted the Sádhu how they could effect their object. He made a lump of mud and threw it into the tank and said:—"Take off all your clothes. Dive into the water, and whoever brings out the lump is the man to catch him." They dived in, and meanwhile the Sádhu disappeared with their clothes. Then he went to their wives and said:—"A horrible *bhut*, stark naked, will come to each of your doors to-night. Be ready to receive him." When the wrestlers came out of the tank they could not find their clothes and had to hide till it became dark, before they could return home. At nightfall they went to their houses, and the moment they knocked at the door their relations sallied out with bludgeons and beat them so severely that they had to take refuge in a sugar-cane field.

Next morning the master-thief dressed himself as a courtier and invited the Rája to come out and hunt. The royal hounds were put into the field, and at last the wrestlers had to run out naked and covered with blood. When the Rája discovered the trick he was in despair.

At last a wise woman promised to arrest the master-thief. She got a camel and loaded it with treasure and let it stray on the road. The master-thief found it, took the treasure home to the old woman's house, killed the camel and buried it, and took a pot full of its blood home with him. The wise woman went about the city asking every one for a little camel's blood as a remedy. At last the hostess of the master-thief gave her a little, and with this the wise woman made a mark on the door.[28]

When the master-thief came back he was very angry with his hostess. But he similarly marked several doors at each side, and when the Rája's officers appeared, they could not discover which was the house of the master-thief.

The master-thief returned to the court and said to the Rája:—"Go out mounted on your horse Syáma Karna and arrest the thief yourself."

The Rája agreed. The master-thief disguised himself as an old woman and sat by the roadside grinding flour. The Rája came up and asked her if she had seen the master-thief pass that way.

"He passed just now," she answered. "Change clothes with me and go on working the mill, and I will bring him to you in a moment."

The Rája changed clothes with the old woman and sat down at the mill. The old woman ran off, mounted Syáma Karna and galloped off to his own country. The Rája, his father, was delighted with the horse, and the Rája of Behár was so pleased with the cleverness of the master-thief that he gave him his daughter in marriage, with half his kingdom as her dowry.

[The Master-thief appears in European folklore. We have it in the *Royal Hibernian Tales* as the "Black Thief and Knight of the Glen." Mr. Jacobs quotes the following:—Grimm, *Household Tales*, I, 431, 464. Kohler in *Orien and Occident*, 305–13, 678: *Jahrbuch*, V, 4–8; VII, 138. Also see Herodotus, II, 121. He is the Ahmad Kamakim of the *Arabian Nights* (Lady Burton's Edition II, 475). For other folklore parallels, see Clouston, *Book of Sindibad*, 330, *sqq.* 370, *sqq.* Also see "The Day Thief and the Night Thief" in Knowles, *Folktales of Kashmir*, 279, *sqq.*, and Clouston, *Popular Tales and Fictions*, II, 47.]

89. The Valiant Weaver Bird.[29]

A *Podna*, or weaver bird, and his mate, the *Podni*, once lived happily in a tree, but one day the King came by and had the Podni caught and put in a cage. The Podna was greatly angered, and set about making preparations to release his wife. So he set about building a cart for himself, which he made out of thin stalks of reed (*sarkanda*), and he constructed a kettle-drum, which he placed in the cart to which he yoked a pair of frogs. Then he took his seat, armed with a piece of reed, with which he began to beat his drum and proclaimed war with the king.

On the way he met a cat. She asked:—

"Where are you going, Mr. Podna?" He answered—*Sarkandé ki to gári, domendak joté jáen, Rája mári Podni, ham bair bisáhne jáen:*—

"My carriage is of reed with two frogs yoked thereto.
The king has seized my Podni; I go to take revenge."

"Will you take me with you? I may be of some use."

Hus! hus! meré kán men ghus.

"Shish! shish! get into my ear," was the answer.

So the cat jumped into the ear of the Podna. Further on he met some ants, and when they asked him where he was going, he made the same reply, and when they offered to join him, he said:—"*Hus! hus! meré kán men ghus.*" Further on he met a rope and a club. They too got into the ear of the Podna. And so when he came to a river, the river too went into the ear of the Podna.

At last the Podna arrived at the King's palace and desired the servants to announce him. But they all laughed and told the King, who ordered that the Podna should be admitted into his presence. So the Podna drove his carriage into the courtyard and demanded that the Podni should be surrendered at once.

"I like the Podni," said the King, "and I refuse to surrender her." "Then, beware of the consequences," replied the Podna. "Seize this insolent bird," said the King, "and confine him in the fowl-house, where the chickens will kick him to death."

The servants seized the Podna and shut him up in the fowl-house. During the night the Podna said:—

> *Nikal billi, teri bári.*
> *Kán chhor, kanpati máré.*

"Come out, cat, it is your turn. Come out of my ear and hit them on the head."

So the cat came out of the Podna's ear and killed all the fowls in an instant.

Next morning the King said to his servants:—"Go down and bring up the carcass of this insolent Podna, who must have been killed by the fowls during the night." But when they went in they found the Podna safe and sound and all the fowls dead.

So they informed the King, who said:—"Confine him in the stable, where the horses will kick him to death."

So he was shut up in the stable, and during the night he called to the rope and stick in the same words:—

> *Niklo rassi aur sonte tumhári bári,*
> *Kán chhor, kanpati máré.*

Out came the rope and club: the rope tied up all the horses and the club beat them till they died.

Next morning the King again sent for the remains of the Podna, but the servants found him safe and well and all the horses dead.

Then the King fell into a terrible rage and ordered the Podna to be confined in the elephant-house, thinking that the elephants would trample him to death. But in the night the Podna called the ants as before:—

Níklo chiúnti tumhári bári,
Kán chhor, kanpati máré.

The ants went out and entered the trunks of the elephants, and getting into their brains, killed them all.

In the morning the King said:—"The Podna must be dead. Go and see if any part of his body or cart can be found." The servants went and found the Podna safe and well and all the elephants dead.

When he heard this the King was greatly grieved. "Well," said he, "I want to know how he manages to do this. Tie him to-night to the leg of my bed and I will see what happens."

So the Podna was tied to the King's bed, and during the night the Podna ordered out the river:—

Niklo darya teri bári,
Kán chhor, kanpati máré.

Out came the river, and the King and his bed began to float in the water. "For God's sake, Mr. Podna," said the King, "take your Podni and depart in peace." So the Podni was restored to the Podna, and they went home and lived happily ever after.

[We have here the faithful animal again, for whom see Temple: *Wideawake Stories*, p. 412: and see the instances collected by Clouston: *Popular Tales and Fictions*, Vol. I, p. 223, *sqq.*—ED.]

90. *The Sepoy's Son.*[30]

In the vicinity of Delhi there was a small village, and in this village a Maulvi kept a school, which was largely attended by the village boys. Every day the Maulvi used to go home at twelve for his mid-day meal, but in his absence he always told the boys to keep guard over the school by turns while he was away lest anything should be stolen.

One day when he returned from his breakfast he found one of his pupils, a sepoy's son, whose turn it was to keep guard, sleeping. "You fellow!" he exclaimed, beating him, "supposing while you slept some one had crept in and stolen the school property? You would not have known anything about it."

The boy woke with a smile. This annoyed the Maulvi very much, and he struck him again. But the more he struck the boy the more he laughed.

"You are a strange boy to laugh when you are beaten," said the Maulvi. "Why do you laugh?" "I do not know why I laugh," replied the boy, and all his teachers questioning him on the subject could elicit from him no other answer. It became noised abroad that there was a sepoy's son in a certain village who laughed when beaten instead of crying, and when questioned about it he always said he did not know why he laughed. At length it came to the ears of the Bádsháh of Delhi, who at once sent for the lad and said to him:—"Why did you laugh when beaten by your master? Is a beating a thing to laugh over or cry over?"

"I do not know, your Majesty, why I laughed," answered the boy.

"If you do not tell me I shall have you put into prison," said the Bádsháh.

But even this threat was not effective. The lad persisted in saying that he did not know why he laughed when struck. So the Bádsháh had him consigned to jail without food or water.

A few days after this the Bádsháh of Rum sent the Bádsháh of Delhi two dolls, asking in a letter to tell him which was the prettier and which the heavier, and which the better of the two. So the Delhi Bádsháh sent for the wisest men in the land, but none could tell which was the better one, though they weighed them both and tried in every way to find out the superiority of the one over the other. So the news spread everywhere that the Bádsháh of Rum had sent two dolls to the Bádsháh of Delhi, asking him to find out the superiority of one over the other, and though the Delhi Bádsháh had sent for the wisest men in the land, none were able to tell. At last it reached the ears of the sepoy's son in prison, who, when he heard it, said he thought he might be able to tell. So his jailors told the Delhi Bádsháh that the boy who was imprisoned for not telling why he laughed when beaten, said he could tell which doll was better than the other that were sent by the Bádsháh of Rum. So the Delhi Bádsháh sent for the lad. When he came before His Majesty he sent for the dolls and two bits of straw. When they were brought he put one bit of straw into the ear of one of the dolls and it went down its stomach, then he put the other bit of straw into the ear of the other doll and it came out of its mouth.

"Your Majesty," said he, "the doll into whose stomach the straw went is the better one, the prettier one, and the heavier one; for whatever you say in her ear she will never repeat; but as for the other doll, whatever is whispered in her ear comes out of her mouth." The Bádsháh of Delhi was very much pleased when he heard this, and at once had him released from prison and gave him a grand mansion to live in with a beautiful garden attached to it, and also wrote to the Bádsháh of Rum, saying, he had a boy in his court who had been able to answer his question. When the Bádsháh of Rum read this he sent several questions to be answered by the boy. But the lad said:—"What is he sending such childish questions to be replied to, which any boy in my village could answer: let him ask something worth answering." When the Bádsháh of Rum got this message he sent to ask the lad what his god was like, and if he ate and drank like human beings. When the sepoy's son heard this he said to his own Bádsháh that this question he would only answer at Rum in the presence of the Emperor of that country; so his Bádsháh sent him to Rum. When he came into the presence of the Bádsháh of Rum, that monarch said to him:—"Who is your god, and does he eat and sleep like people do?"

"I will answer your question," said the boy, "if you get off your throne and place me on it, and take your crown off your head and place it on mine." "Well," thought the Bádsháh of Rum, "it is not much he is asking me, I might as well do as he wishes." So he got off his throne and placed the boy on it, and took off his crown and placed it on the boy's head.

Then the boy said: "My god is so great that he has taken you off your throne and placed me on it, and has taken your crown off your head and placed it on mine."

The Bádsháh of Rum was so struck with the lad's reply that he at once embraced him and went to his queen's apartments and told her all about him, at the same time asking her what reward he should give him.

"Marry him to our daughter," said the queen "for though low in birth he is high in intellect; you will never find a boy like him." The Bádsháh of Rum took his queen's advice and married the lad to their daughter.

After a few days the boy returned to Delhi with his bride, and a letter from his father-in-law to the Delhi Bádsháh, telling him what a wise boy he was. When the Bádsháh of Delhi read the letter he went at once to his queen, and asked her what should he do for this boy who had saved the honour of his court by answering all the questions put to him by the Bádsháh of Rum.

"Marry him to our daughter," also said his queen; "for he fully deserves that reward." So the Bádsháh of Delhi also married him to his daughter.

One day, some time after this, the fortunate youth was lying on his cot in the beautiful garden attached to his mansion, when his two wives came towards him,—the Bádsháh of Delhi's daughter with something for him to eat and the Bádsháh of Rum's daughter with something for him to drink. When he saw them he sent for one of his servants and said to him: "Go, tell the Bádsháh of Delhi that when I was a school-boy and was beaten by my Maulvi for going to sleep when I should have kept guard, I laughed because I dreamt that I was lying on a cot in a beautiful garden attached to a mansion, and that the Bádsháh of Delhi's daughter was bringing me some food to eat and the Bádsháh of Rum's daughter was bringing me some water to drink, and it seemed so absurd to me that I laughed in spite of the beating I got; but when asked about it I was afraid to tell, for your Majesty would surely have had me beheaded if I had, angry at the impudence of a poor village-boy and a sepoy's son dreaming of marrying your daughter; but now that my dream has come true, I tell your Majesty what I feared to tell you then why I laughed though beaten."—*Ida Casabon: Aligarh.*

91. The Wit of the Four Brothers.[31]

There was once a man who had four sons. When he was dying he called them and said:—"I have buried my wealth in four pots, under each of the four legs of my cot. When I am dead you can dig it up, and each one is to have the pot he happens to find."

When their father died the sons dug up each a copper pot, and when they opened them they found that the pot of the eldest contained earth; that of the second, bones; that of the third, rice husks; that of the youngest, rupees. So then the three eldest wanted him to share, but he refused, and challenged them to go to Rája Daksha, the ruler of the land, to decide the matter.

When they came to his palace they met his daughter at the door, and she asked their business. Then she said:—"My father has been absent from home for twelve years."

So they were going home when they met the Rání. She asked their business, and said:—"The Rája is asleep. He will wake in an hour and settle your business."

They answered:—"The Princess just now told us that he had left the country."

The Ráni answered:—"The reason she said this was that though she is grown up, she is not yet married. Had her father been at home he must have found a husband for her."

They waited for an hour and came back to the palace door again. There the Rája's son met them and asked their business.

"Go away," he said; "my father is dead."

As they were going away a man spoke to them and said:—"The Rája is not dead, but his son says he is dead because his father has not got him married yet."

The brothers sat down to wait. Meanwhile the younger Ráni came out and said:—"What is the use of your waiting? The Rája is blind for the last twelve years."

But as they were leaving the place a maid-servant said:—

"The Rája is not blind, but the Ráni says he has lost his sight because he has not sent for her for twelve years."

Just then a Pandit passed by, and they asked him about the Rája.

"The Rája is certainly at home," he said, "but he is deaf."

Again they started to go, when the Pandit's son met them.

"The Rája is not deaf," he said but my father calls him deaf because he will not listen to the advice of his ministers. "This Rája will never do for us," the brothers concluded, "let us go to Rája Bhoj."

So they started for the kingdom of Rája Bhoj. That day it so happened that a washerman of the city had given his wife a beating, and she started off on his donkey to escape him. The four brothers were on the road at the time, and the washerman was running up from behind in search of his wife. The brothers hid behind some bushes, and as he passed they went on talking to each other.

One said:—"An ass must have passed by." "But it had only one eye," said the second.

"Yes! It was blind," said the third, "and a woman was riding it."

"Quite right," said the fourth, "and she was pregnant." When he heard this talk the washerman made sure that these men had run away with his wife. So he followed them, and when he met them near the city, he said:—"You appear to be strangers here. If you like I will give you a lodging."

They gladly agreed, and the washerman gave them a place to stay in: and when he had got them safe he went and complained to the Rája that his wife, who had a quarrel with him, had been enticed away by the brothers who were Thags. He told the Rája how he had heard their conversation. Hearing this, the Rája had a watch put over them.

In the night the guard heard them talking. One said:—"The rice we have eaten was stale." "Yes," said the second, "and the *ghi* was some one's leavings."

"So it was," said the third, "and the meat we got was dog-flesh."

"True," said the fourth, "and the Rája of this city is base-born "(*dogla*).

The watchmen heard this and reported it to the Rája. Next morning he called them and asked:—"What did you mean by saying that the rice was stale?"

One said:—"Ask the man who grew it." The peasant was brought and examined about the rice.

"Well! O king! the rice was stale in this way. When we were sowing it night came on and some of the seed remained unsown. This was sown next morning. So its produce was stale."

"Well! and what did you mean by saying that the *ghi* was some one's leavings?"

"Ask the cowherds," they said.

The cowherd was called and examined. "Yes! O King!" he answered. "It was so. As I was boiling it the pot overflowed and I blew on it. Hence it was my leavings." "What did you mean," next asked the Rája, "by saying that the meat was dog-flesh?"

"Ask the shepherd," they answered. The shepherd was called and examined.

"Yes! O King! it was dog-flesh. It was so in this way. After her kid was born a leopard killed my goat, and we suckled it on a bitch we had."

"And why do you call me base-born?" asked the Rája.

"Ask your mother," they answered.

The Rája rushed off to his mother with a sword in his hand, and said:—"Tell the truth, am I base-born or not. If you refuse to tell me I will kill you and myself afterwards."

The Ráni trembled and said:—"When I was bathing on the sixth day after your birth, a washerman passed by and his shadow fell on me. This affected me, and in this way you are base-born."

[The influence of the mother over the child remains until she is purified on the sixth day. A shadow of any one falling on a woman in this state is believed to affect the child.—ED.].

The Rája came back and asked the washerman how he knew these men had taken his wife away. He told the Rája what they had said.

The Rája asked:—"How did you know an ass had passed?"

"By his foot-prints."

"And how did you know he was blind of an eye?"

"Because he ate the grass on only one side of the road."

"And how did you know the woman was in child?"

"Because the ass went on very slowly and had she not been in this state she would have galloped away from her husband."

The Rája said:—"You are clever fellows. I will try you again." So he got a gourd (*lauki*), and put it in an earthen jar, and asked them to tell what was inside.

One said:—"It is green."

Another said:—"It is round."

The third said:—"It is a fruit."

The fourth said:—"It is a gourd" (*kohara*).

[Something is wanting here to exploit the grounds of their answer.—ED.].

The Rája rewarded them and sent them home. On the road they met a lot of boys, one of whom pretended to be a Rája and the others his ministers.

"Let us refer our case to him," said one, and all agreed.

The boy-Rája, when he heard their story, said:—"The man who got the earth in his pot is to have the land, he that got the bones is to have the cattle; he that got the rice husks, the grain; and the youngest is to keep the money."

They said:—"How did you learn this wisdom?"

"Under where I am sitting," he answered, "is buried the throne studded with jewels, which belonged to Maharája Vikramaditya."

So the four brothers dug up the throne and lived in luxury ever after.

Parameswar do to us as he did to them!

[On the riddle test, see Grimm: *Household Stories*, Vol. I, p. 368: their identification of the woman and the ass is like the "Story of the Lost Camel" (Clouston: "A Group of Eastern Romances," p. 194, and other parallels, p. 511). The same idea is found in one of the Cento Novelle Antiche (Dunlop: *History of Fiction*, Vol. II, p. 45).—ED.]

92. *The Cunning of the Lala.*[32]

There was once a Lála who was very poor, and used to wander about the country in search of work. At last he took service with a Rája, who gave him an anna a day, and put him in charge of his horses. He used to collect the stable manure and sell it to a grain-parcher for an anna a day. He lived on half his earnings and saved half, until he had enough to buy respectable clothes, and then he attended the Darbar.

The Rája was surprised to see him so well dressed on his wretched pay; so when he caught his eye he held up one finger and smiled, meaning that his pay was one anna daily. The Lala smiled, and in reply held up two fingers, meaning that he made another anna beyond his salary.

The courtiers saw this interchange of signs going on between the Rája and the Lála, and when the Darbar broke up they went to him very civilly and began to ask what the signs meant. "Well, "said the Lála, "the Rája meant to ask if I could look after his affairs myself or not. And I signed back that I should want one assistant." On hearing this they came to him that night, each with a bag of rupees, and asked him for his recommendation as his assistant. By this means the Lála collected a considerable sum, which he brought next morning to the Rája. "How my present officials must be robbing me!" thought the Rája, "and I cannot do better than make over my affairs to this honest fellow." So the Lála became Wazír and prospered exceedingly.

[The original of this is perhaps "the rogue who managed to acquire wealth by speaking to the King (*Katha Sait Ságara*, Vol. II, p. 120) with which Professor Tawney compares one of Morlini's stories. Other parallels are given by Mr. Clouston: *Popular Tales and Fictions*, Vol. II, p. 360, *ff.*—Ed.].

93. *Shekh Chilli in love.*[33]

One time Shekh Chilli was hotly in love with a girl, and he said to his mother:—"What is the best way of making a girl fond of one?" Said his mother:—"The best plan is to sit by the well, and when she comes to draw water, just throw a pebble at her and smile."

The Shekh went to the well, and when the girl appeared, he flung a big stone at her and broke her head. All the people turned out and were going to murder him, but when he explained matters, they agreed that he was the biggest fool in the world.

94. *The Raja and the Sadhu.*[34]

Once upon a time a Sádhu was sitting by the road side, and a Rája passed by, who gave him a shawl. Just as the Sádhu got the shawl and was blessing the Rája, a thief came up and ran away with it. Him, too, the Sádhu blessed as he had blessed the Rája. At this the Rája was wroth, and said to the Sádhu:—"Bábaji, why didst thou bless him even as thou didst bless me?"

The Sádhu answered:—"I blessed you both that the works of each of you may prosper. Thy piety will receive its reward. He will progress in evil doing, and he, too, shall have his reward."

The Rája was convinced, and bowing before, the Sádhu went his way.

95. The Judgment of the Jackal.[35]

A merchant was once returning home from abroad. On his way he was belated, and put up at the house of an oilman. He gave his horse to his host, and said:—"Brother, tie him up carefully." The oilman tied him to his mill. In the morning, very early, the merchant awoke, and was waiting for the oilman to come out. When he appeared he said:—"Friend, your horse got loose during the night, and I know not where it has gone." Just then the merchant came out, and seeing his horse tied to the mill, said:—"Why, here is my horse." "That is not yours," said the oilman. "My mill gave birth to it last night."

The merchant was very much enraged, and said:—"If you wont give up the horse let us go and get Siyár Pánre the jackal to judge between us." So they went to Siyár Pánre and explained the case to him. He said: "Go back to the house of the oilman and I will come in a couple of hours."

He went off to a tank, and after wallowing in the mud for some time, came out and sat on the bank. When he did not come at the appointed time the merchant and the oilman went to look for him, and found him sitting there. They asked him why he had not come at the appointed time. He replied: "I have been so busy that I could not come." "What were you so busy about?" asked the oilman. "The tank took fire," he answered, "and I was hard at work in putting it out." "Are you mad?" said the oilman. "Did any one ever hear of a tank taking fire?" "Did any one ever hear," asked the jackal, "of a mill giving birth to a horse?"

The oilman was confounded and restored the horse to its owner.

[This is pretty much the same as the "Traveller and the Oilman "in Swynnerton, *Indian Nights' Entertainments*, p. 142.—ED.].

96. Ganga Ram the Parrot.[36]

There was once a fowler who used to go every day to snare birds in the jungle. One day he wandered about till the evening and caught nothing, so he lay down under a tree. On the branches he saw perched a number of parrots, and he began to think within himself that if he could catch one of them he would be able to support himself comfortably. So he went and told his wife, and she went with him next morning, and they laid a set of snares. Meanwhile they heard the parrots talking among themselves, and the leader of them, whose name was Gangá Rám, said to the others: "Brethren, we ought not to stay here any longer. Let us go to some other jungle." The others said:—"O Gangá Rám! whenever we find a comfortable place you are always advising us to go elsewhere. Why should we mind your words? We intend to stay here." Gangá Rám answered:—"If you do not mind my advice you will rue it." "We intend to stay here all the same," they said.

The fowler heard what they were saying, and he climbed up the tree and laid bird-lime on the branches. When the parrots flew back in the evening they were all snared. Then they said to one another:—"Brother! what Gangá Rám predicted has now come to pass." "Yes," said Gangá Rám. "By and by the fowler will come and kill us all. They cried:—"Pardon us, O Gangá Rám! you are our leader. Now plan some device whereby we may escape from this misfortune." "Brethren," said Gangá Rám, "there is only one means of safety. When the fowler climbs up the tree we must all pretend to be dead; then he will throw us down one by one. There are seventy-four of us. You must listen carefully and count seventy-four thuds on the ground, and when you are sure that we have all come down, we can fly away in safety."

They agreed to his plan, and they did as he advised. But they counted wrong, and when only seventy-three parrots had been thrown down they all flew away, and Gangá Rám, who was the last, was caught by the fowler. When he found that he was a captive, he said to the fowler:— "Friend! I am now at your mercy. If you kill me it will be no advantage to you. But if you save my life I will bring you large profit." The fowler spared his life, and shutting him up in a basket brought him home. When his wife saw the bird she said:—"You must take him to the King." The fowler said:—"O Gangá Rám! may I sell you to the King?" Gangá Rám answered:—"You may sell me, but you must take my proper price." "And what is your price?" the fowler asked. "My price," said Gangá Rám, "is a lakh of rupees."

So the fowler took Gangá Rám to the bazar, and as he went along he called out:—"Who will buy my parrot for a lakh of rupees?" At last a merchant bought the bird for the price he asked and put him in a cage. His wife was always talking to the parrot, and one day he said:—"I am lonely; get me a *mainá* to talk to me." So she got a *mainá*, and it was hung in a cage close to Gangá Rám's, and they became great friends.

Soon after the merchant had to go abroad on business, and he told Gangá Rám to watch his affairs. One day the merchant's wife went to see a dance at a neighbour's house and by accident she took away a young man's shoes and left her own there. When the young man saw the shoes in the morning, he was seized with love for the owner of them. So he employed two old women to search for them. One of them went about with the shoes, crying out:—"Who has lost a pair of shoes?" The banker's wife came out and recognized her shoes, and the old woman, pretending to be her aunt, got into her confidence, and by and by tried to induce her to pay the young man a visit. But as she was going Gangá Rám asked her what she was about. When she told him, he explained to her the old woman's wiles, and taught her what her duty was to her husband. So her honour was saved, and when, her husband returned she told him what had happened, and he was so pleased at the fidelity of Gangá Rám that he asked him to choose any boon he pleased. Gangá Rám said:—"The only boon I crave for is my liberty." So the banker let him go, and he went back to the jungle and ruled the parrots as before with wisdom and justice.

97. The Disguised Princess.[37]

There was once a king who had three daughters—one by his first wife who was dead, and the others by his second queen. The king arranged the marriage of his eldest daughter with a very young and handsome prince, and this raised the envy of her step-sisters; so they were on the watch to do her evil. When the litter arrived in which she was to go to her husband's house they scattered some sugar inside, and such a number of flies collected that the prince was disgusted with her and told the bearers to take the bride and abandon her in the jungle. They did as he ordered them, and he rewarded them, and gave out that, the bride had died on the road. Her step-sisters thought that he would then marry one of them; but he did not care for either of them, and never visited their city again.

When the bearers put down the bride's litter she kept quiet for some time, thinking that she had arrived at her husband's house, and that some of the women would soon come to escort into the house; but when she had waited a long time and nobody came, she looked out and found herself in the middle of a lonely jungle. She was in great fear; but at last she came out of the litter and tying up her rich clothes and jewels in a bundle, she smeared herself with dust and wandered on. After some time she came to the house of a carpenter and he gave her shelter. After some days she gave the carpenter one of her jewels, and asked him to make her a covering of wood, which would conceal her and enable her to go about unobserved. The carpenter did as she asked him, and putting on her wooden covering she went her way.

After a long journey she reached the kingdom of her husband, and there she pretended to be a man and called herself Sháh Tangar. She heard that her husband's first wife was dead, and that he was about to marry a second time. She waited on him, and he was surprised at her appearance. She said that her name was Sháh Tangar, and that she was ready to enter his service. So she was appointed a servant in the palace. The prince was pleased with her, and made over to her three duties in connection with his coming marriage. One was to clean the city, the second to prepare the dishes, and the third to have the wheat ground for the wedding feast. Sháh Tangar went to the Kotwál and ordered him to have all the sweepings collected on the road where there was a low place. He instructed the dish-makers that every dish was to have a hole in the bottom; and to the wheat-grinders he gave an order that every grain was to be ground into no more than ten pieces. Every one was surprised at these extraordinary orders, but the instructions of the king were that Sháh Tangar was to be obeyed in everything, so they had to do as he told them.

When the flour was brought to the palace the bakers could make none but the coarsest loaves, and when the cooks poured the stew into the dishes, all the soup ran out through the holes in the bottom and nothing remained but the bones. The prince was very angry when he heard of this; but when he called for Sháh Tangar and asked him to explain matters, all he could say was that he was hard of hearing and had misunderstood the orders of the prince.

Sháh Tangar went with the marriage procession, and when they reached the house of the bride they were all surprised at his appearance. He was taken in to see the bride, and there he began to move his wooden hands clumsily about and as if by chance knocked out one of her eyes, The women were afraid to say anything lest the marriage should be put off. But when the prince started for home with the bride and found that she had only one eye he was much disgusted. But there was no help for it. Soon after one day the washerman brought the prince very dirty clothes, and when he asked the reason of this he said:—"Your servant, the man of wood, comes every day and bathes near where we wash, and he is so beautiful that we cannot keep our eyes off him, and we cannot wash the clothes."

So the prince sent for Sháh Tangar and asked him to take off his wooden covering and show his beauty; but he said he would not do so until a separate house was furnished for him. When this was done and the prince saw him without his wooden covering he was amazed at his beauty, and when he ran and seized him he found that Sháh Tangar was a girl. Then the whole story was told, and the prince took her as his wife, and they lived ever after in the greatest happiness.

[This is one of the Indian variants of the Cinderella or Cap O'Rushes cycle. I cannot find any exact parallel to the wooden covering in Miss Cox's exhaustive analysis.—ED.]

98. The King and the Fairy.[38]

There was once a king who had no son. Many plans he tried, but none was of any avail. Now Raja Indra had a fairy with whom a Deo was enamoured; he wished to marry her, but she would have nothing to say to him. Then the Deo went to Raja Indra, told lies about her, and had her turned out off Indrasan.

The fairy then came and was re-born in the family of this king. When she grew up she was one day sitting in her bower (*mahal*) when an enormous monkey appeared and ran at her. She screamed and escaped into the palace; but she did not tell her father and mother what had happened. Now this monkey was the same Deo who wished to marry her, and had got her turned out of Indrásan, and he had become a monkey intending to find her and kill her. When he found out where she was, he put up near the palace, and was always looking out for a chance of catching her and devouring her. She was so much afraid of him that she never left her room, and day by day she got so weak and thin that her father and mother were very anxious about her. Finally they agreed that if they could get her married she would perhaps recover; so they married her to the prince of a neighbouring land.

When she started for home with her husband the Deo followed her, and when they reached a jungle he rushed up and began to devour the retinue of the prince. When she saw him eating her men she was afraid and ran away. At length in the jungle she saw a house, and in it was a room with a single door. Into this she ran and bolted the door so tight that she could not open it again. She heard people talking at the other side of the wall, but they did not hear her cries: at last she found a nail, and with this she scraped a hole in the wall, and the people of the house heard her voice and took her out. The man who lived there was a Chamár, and as she was very hungry he gave her food to eat. When she had eaten she said to the Chamár:—"Make me such a robe that my whole body may be hidden. If you do this for me I will give you my golden bangle." So the Chamár made her a leathern dress, which she put on and rubbed all over with treacle and covered herself with a dirty sheet and went her way. On account of the treacle multitudes of flies settled upon her, and wherever she went on account of the flies no one would allow her to stay. At last an old woman, who lived by parching grain, took pity on her and gave her shelter. She used to make the girl do all her work, and gave her a cake or two at night. One day the old woman said to her "Go to the river and bathe." So she went to a retired place, and there she took off her leathern dress, and when she had bathed she put it on again. As she was bathing one of the golden hairs fell from her head, and she laid it on a leaf and let it float down the stream.

By chance the hair floated down past the palace of a king, and the king's son took it out, and when he saw it he went to his father and mother and said:—"Marry me to the girl whose hair this is." The king was much grieved, and next day he made a feast to all the people of the land, hoping that the girl whose hair this was would come to the feast. Great crowds assembled and the girl came too, but as she was covered with flies she had to sit apart.

Now in this land it was the custom that whenever kings were about to be married a trained elephant was let loose, and whatever girl it raised three times she was married to the king. When the elephant was loosed it went searching all round the company, and finally raised this girl three times. When the king and queen saw that the elephant had selected such a dirty girl, they supposed that there was some mistake; so they sent for a second elephant, but the result was the same. And with a third elephant the same thing happened. So they had to marry her to the prince.

When he went home that night, and it was time for him to retire with his bride, he went to his mother and told her with tears that he could never live with such a person; that he wished to marry the owner of the golden hair, and would never touch a creature who was so foul that no one would let her sit near them. "Well," said his mother, "I will have her put to sleep to-night in the elephant shed, and one of them is sure to trample her to death." So she was sent there, but in the night four other fairies came to her, took off her robe of leather, bathed and perfumed her, and when the watchmen saw her they were surprised at her beauty. They went and told the prince, and he ran there, and when he saw her he was delighted. He sat there, on the watch, and when the four fairies left her and she was about to put on her leathern-robe again, he ran and seized her. But she cried—"If I do not put this on I shall die." "Who is there who can harm you?" he asked. Then she told him her whole story, and when he asked her if she could think of any plan for killing the Deo she said:—"There is only one way to kill him. Take this leathern robe of mine, fill it with honey and place it on a finely-decorated couch on the roof of the palace. When the Deo comes he will seize it and think that he is sucking my blood. Then you can lay in wait and kill him."

He did as she advised, and when the Deo came in the form of a monkey and began to suck the honey the prince cut off his head with his sword. Then he went and told his wife that the Deo would trouble her no more, and they two lived together for many years in the greatest happiness.

[This is also of the Cinderella or Cap O'Rushes type.—ED.]

99. The King and his secret.[39]

There was once a Rája on whose head two horns grew. He kept them always concealed by his turban, and the only one who knew the secret was his barber; but the Rája warned him to disclose the matter to no one. But as the proverb runs:—*"Adh ser ke patra men kaise ser samát?"* "How can a half-ser cup hold a ser." The barber could not keep the matter concealed: he had to tell it, so he went and whispered it to a tamarind tree.

It so happened that the tree was blown down by a storm, and the Rája gave it to his musicians to make a drum. When the drum was beaten it said:—*"Rája ke kapáre per sing bayá"* "There are horns on the Rája's head." The Rája at once dismissed the musicians and the same sound came from the drum when he played it himself. He thought to himself "if I dash the drum to the ground and smash it some greater trouble may come upon me. It is better that I should become a faqír."

So he left his kingdom and wandered in the forest. One day he sat under a tree and two thieves came up and began to quarrel over some plunder they had gained. When they went away a number of servants appeared and spread carpets, when a party of fairies came and began to dance while the Rája beat his drum for them. When the fairies were done dancing they asked the Rája who he was, and when they heard his storey they took off his horns and fixed one on the head of each of the thieves. No sooner was this done than the two thieves were turned into

Rákshasas, and one was named Kála Deo or the "Black Demon" and the
other Lal Deo or the "Red Demon."

Then the Rája asked the fairies why the drum gave out that sound, and
they answered

Bhed apno jo kahai kahuson bhar máya,
Bhediya ho jo jiwa biná tan nij kaj nasai.

"He who discloses a secret to one who gains his confidence by flattery
will come to ruin even if his confidante be an inanimate object."

O Rája you disclosed your secret to a man of low birth, and he not
being able to keep it, told it to the tamarind tree, whence the wood of the
drum spake."

The Rája returned home a wiser man.

[This is the Eastern version of the Greek legend of King Midas.—ED.]

100. *The Fate of the Raja of Chandrapur.*[40]

The Rája of Chandrapur was once sitting in his palace when he heard a
noise outside; he called the guards and asked them the cause of the noise,
but no one dared to go and enquire. Just then a man named Bírbal came
to the palace and was brought before the Rája who asked him his business. He said:—"I want to serve your Majesty." "What pay do you
require?" asked the Rája. "My pay," said Bírbal, "is a thousand *tolas* of
gold a day." "And how many men are in your force?" enquired the Rája.
"My force," said Bírbal, "consists of myself for one, my wife for two, my
son for three, and my daughter for four." "Your pay is large," said the
Rája. "But I will appoint you, and I shall need service from you to correspond with it."

Next night the cry was heard again outside the palace walls, and the
Rája sent for Bírbal and sent him to investigate the matter. Bírbal took
his sword and went out, and there he saw a woman lamenting bitterly.
He asked her the cause of her grief, and meanwhile the Rája, who was
desirous of testing the fidelity of his servant, came from the palace and
hid himself close by. The woman said:—"I am weeping because the Rája
of this land, who is famed for his deeds of piety, will die within a month."
Bírbal asked her "is there any means whereby his life could be saved?"
The woman answered:—"The Rája can live for a hundred years more if
any one will sacrifice his only son to the goddess Jyotí Bará."

Bírbal went at once to his wife and told her what the woman had said. She replied:—"Act as you please in this matter. I will make no objection to whatever you do." Then he went to his child's bed and woke him, and told him what the woman had said. The boy answered:—"I am ready to give my life for this virtuous king, and I shall give my life before no mean godling but before the mighty Jyotí Bará."

So the whole family went to the temple of the goddess. There Bírbal laid his son before the altar and severed his head with a single blow. Seeing this the mother cut off her own head with a single blow of the sword. And immediately her daughter did the same. Then Bírbal thought "what is the use of life? It were well for me to join my family in Heaven." So he too cut off his head.

The Rája saw all this and was so grieved that he too determined to die. As he raised the sword the goddess appeared and said:—"O Rája! I am pleased with thy devotion. Ask what boon you desire." "If thou art appeased," he said, "I desire that all these may be restored to life." The goddess granted his prayer, and they all revived. Then the Rája took Bírbal home and rewarded him with half his dominions.

[This is the famous story of Viravara in the *Katha Sarit Ságara* (Tawney, II., p. 251, *sqq*). It is also found in the Hitopadesa, and is the oriental type of Grimm's "Faithful John." The "Rama and Luxman" of Miss Frere's "Old Deccan Days" is of the same class.

In the original form the deity to whom the sacrifice is made is Chandí Durgá. Jyotí Bará seems to be some Sánsya deity. The tradition of human sacrifice among these Gipsy people is interesting.—ED.]

101. How the Qazi's wife became a widow.[41]

The king once sent the Qázi to a distant village to make an investigation. While he was away his wife happened to take off her nose-ring when she went to bathe. The barber's wife who came to the house at the time saw her and told her husband. He rushed off to where the Qázi was, and when he saw him, began to weep violently:—"What on earth is the matter?" asked the Qázi. "I am very sorry to tell you," replied the barber, "that your worthy wife has become a widow." When the Qázi heard this he was overwhelmed with grief and prepared at once to return home. The people came to him and said:—"Qázi Sahib, why are you going away, leaving the enquiry unfinished?" "I am very sorry," he answered, "but it cannot be helped. My poor wife has become a widow." "How can that be when your

Honour is still alive?" they asked in surprise. But the Qázi paid no heed to their words and came home.

When he arrived at his house he began to weep and bewail his misfortune. His wife heard him, and coming out asked him what had happened. "Everything is well," he answered, "but I have heard that you have become a widow." "Are you mad?" she shouted. "Don't you see that I am alive and so are you? How can I be a widow?" "I cannot help believing this most respectable barber, who has served my family most faithfully for many years," he said. She sent for the barber and asked him how he came to know that she was a widow. "I heard it from my wife," he answered. When she was called and asked, she said that she knew the Qázi's wife was a widow because she had seen her without her nose-ring.

"What fools you all are," said the Qázi's wife.

> *Nak men nahín básar.*
> *Ránr bhái mehar.*

"The married woman became a widow as soon as she took the ring out of her nose."

102. *How the Soldier's Wife foiled her Lovers.*[42]

There was once a soldier who had a very handsome wife, whom he was obliged to leave at home when he went abroad on service. He used to send her money through a banker, whose son took it to her one day, and when he saw her fell in love with her. He spoke about her to his friend the Kotwal's son, and he told the Wazir's son, and he told the Prince. So all the four youths fell in love with her, and she was at her wits' ends how to save her husband's honour. At last she said to a go-between who persecuted her:—"I have no place to stow away my clothes, and I want some big boxes very badly. Let your friend send me a large box and a bag of rupees, and then I will fix a time for our meeting." This same message she sent to each of her lovers, and each of them did as she desired. So she fixed a time for them to come, each an hour after the other on the same night.

The banker's son came first and was brought in by the maid. The lady conversed with him for sometime and then said:—"I am just going out to eat; wait here and I will be back very soon." Meantime the Kotwal's son arrived and the first lover was very much frightened. She said:—"It is only the son of the Kotwal; he will soon go away." But the banker's son was afraid that he would tell his father of his doings, so he implored her to hide him away somwhere. She put him into one of the boxes and locked it.

Hardly had the Kotwal's son sat down than the son of the Wazir arrived, and the Kotwal's son entreated her to hide him some where; so she locked him up in another box.

When the Prince arrived she in the same way locked up the Wazir's son. After the Prince sat down, as had been previously arranged, her maid dressed up as a soldier, knocked at the door:—"My husband has returned. What is to be done?" she whispered; so she locked the Prince up in the fourth box.

Next morning she loaded the four boxes on an ass, and in the guise of a merchant drove them off to the bazar. Now it was the custom of the King to go round and inspect his markets, and when he saw a new merchant there, he asked her what she had for sale. "Whoever buys these boxes," said she, "must buy them on chance, and the price of them is a lakh of rupees apiece." The King paid the price she asked, and then had the boxes opened, when the four youths appeared. Then he enquired into the case, and the woman said:—" This is the way these young rascals pursue unprotected women. How can any one be safe from them?" The King was wroth, and delivered the four to the executioners. Then she sent for her husband, and they lived happily on the money she had made.

[The oriental original of this famous story is probably the tale of Devasmita (*Tawney: Katha Sarit Ságara*, I., 85. The parallels are discussed by Clouston: *Popular Tales and Fictions*, II, 289 ff.) and in the *Book of Sindibad*, 311 *ff.*—ED.]

103. Lal Bahu, the Red Wife.

Once upon a time there lived a jackal, and he had eaten all the fruit this side of the river, and wanted to get across, and did not know how to. At last he thought of the alligator, and went to the river side and called out to him, and when he came the jackal said:—"If you take me across I will bring you a Lál Bahu." The alligator agreed and carried the jackal across, where he stayed till all the fruit was done, when the same difficulty arose, and he knew he must get the alligator the Lál Bahu, or there was no hope of getting across; so this cunning little jackal stole some red cloth, and propped up some bones like a figure in the distance, and draped the red cloth on it to look like a sheet and petticoat, and then called the alligator and said:—"See, I have brought you the Lál Bahu, but she is shy of me, so carry me across, and she will come to you." The alligator did so at once. And when the jackal was out of the way the alligator called to Lál Bahu as he thought, but of course it could not answer because it was only bones. The alligator got angry and went up to it and gave it a slap: all the bones hurt his hand, and he discovered the jackal's trick. When he saw the jackal again he said:—"See, if I don't pay you off for this!" One day after a little time had elapsed the jackal came back and was getting up a fig ties on the bank of the river, when the alligator, who always laid in wait for him; caught his leg. The jackal thought "now I am done for," when a thought struck him, and he called out:—"You think you have caught my leg, but all the same you have caught the root of the tree." The alligator hearing this let go his leg and caught the root, thinking he had made the mistake. The jackal then jumped down and ran away laughing, which left the alligator more angry than ever. The alligator then consulted his friends, and they said "Try and get into his house when he is out, and then he cannot escape you." The alligator then watched for the jackal to go out and crept into his house. When the jackal came home he saw the track the alligator had left behind him on the sand and guessed at once who it was, so he called out:—"House, house, is all well;" but the alligator kept very quiet. The jackal then said:—"Something must be wrong. My house always answers me when all is well." The alligator at once said:—"All is well." The jackal laughed to himself and ran off, but soon returned, dragging a dry prickly bush, and placing it at the door, set fire to it, and called out in delight:—"I knew you were in there, Mr. Alligator. Have you ever heard of a house that spoke? You will plague me no more." The smoke smothered the alligator inside the house, and the jackal lived in peace the rest of his days.—*Irene Briscoe: Bulandshahr.*

104. *The Sparrow and the Shell.*[43]

There was once a hen-sparrow who found a cowrie (shell) with an eye in it. She sat on the top of a tree and began to boast:—"I have that which the King has not." When the King heard this he was wroth and sent his men to catch the sparrow. They caught her, and when they searched her nest they found only the cowrie (shell), which they took to the King.

Then the sparrow sat at the gate of the palace and began to cry:—"I was the King's banker, and he has borrowed all the money I had." The King was still more angry when he heard this, and told his men to catch the bird and bury her in the ground. They did as he ordered: and it so happened that soon after a dog came up, and smelling the bird, began to scratch the place, and taking her out alive, was just about to eat her when she said:—"Friend, if you intend to eat me, please wash me first." The dog washed the mud off her, and was going to eat her when she said:—"Please dry me first." So the dog put her out in the sun to dry, and when she was dry he opened his mouth to devour her; but she said:—"Let me flap my wings and shake out the dust; if you don't, perhaps you may find me gritty." When the dog gave her time to shake her wings she flew off and sat on a tree, and the dog had to go off hungry.

105. *The Raja and the Musahar Girl.*[44]

A Rája once went hunting in the jungle. He was very thirsty, and wandering about could find no water till he came to the hut of a Musahar. The Musahar was not at home, but his daughter, who was a very handsome girl, was there. The Rája asked her for water, but she said:—"How can you drink from my hands?" He answered:—"I am dying of thirst; give me to drink." He sat there for some time to rest, and when her father came back the Rája said:—"Give me your daughter to wife." He replied:—"I am a low caste man and you are a Rája. How can this be?" But the Rája would not heed, and said:—"I will come shortly to take my bride; see that she is ready."

In a few days the Rája came with a large party, and the Musahar was obliged to marry his daughter to him. When the Rája brought his bride home, and it became known that he had married a Musahar girl, all the people were very angry, and his father, the old Rája, called the executioners and ordered them to take the young Ráni into the jungle and bury her there. They had no sooner carried out these orders than in the place where she had been buried a golden tank and a golden temple of Mahádeva were formed. The Rája, who was mourning for his Ráni, went to see her grave, and when he saw the tank and the temple he was astonished, and commenced to sit there and mourn.

After many days a pair of birds, named Bahengwa and Bahengiya, came and sat on the roof of the temple beneath which the Rája lay. One said to the other:—"Husband, this Rája has been long mourning here. Is there any means whereby he may recover the Musahar girl for whom he is mourning?" The other said:—"She is not the daughter of a Musahar. She is a Fairy. If he wishes to get her he must watch till she comes to bathe at this tank, and then he must steal her garment." The Rája understood these words and did as the birds said. When he took her robe he said to her:—"I have been long awaiting you. Now take pity and come home with me." But she said:—"Why should I return with you when my father-in-law had me buried? Give me my robe, else I will curse you." The Rája feared her words and gave back the robe and she disappeared from his sight.

He went on mourning at the temple as before, and again he heard the birds talking. One asked:—"Husband, did the Rája recover the Fairy?" "He got her back, but he did not know the right words to say to her, and so she went away." "What should he do when she comes again, so that she may never leave him?" "He should swear to her that he will never leave her, and that when she dies he will have himself buried with her."

When the Fairy came again the Rája followed the advice of the birds, and as she was bathing he seized her clothes and ran into the temple. The Fairy came to him and said:—"I cannot live with you now because your father had me buried." He answered:—"Pardon me this once. I swear that I will never leave you, and when you die I will be buried with you." She was appeased and came into the temple. Then he said: "I will never return to my father. Have a palace built here and we will live together." From the fold of her robe she took out the picture of a demon (*deo*) and ordered him instantly to perform the wishes of the Rája. Within a single night he built a palace of gold. When it was done the demon immediately became a picture again. The Rája and the Fairy lived there many years in happiness.

[Here again we have the talking birds and the swan maiden incident.—Ed.]

106. The Tale of Princess Phulande.[45]

There was once a Rája who had a daughter named Phulande, and when her mother died he took another Ráni. This Ráni hated the Princess, and one day while her father was away, she had her exposed in the jungle. When she felt hungry she planted there the *ber* tree of delusion (*máya-ka-ber*) and lived on its fruits. When the Ráni heard of the *ber* tree she would not eat or drink and lay on her bed. She said to the Rája:—"I shall never get better until you have this *ber* tree cut down." The Rája did as she wished, and then the Ráni got up and took her food. Then Princess Phulande planted the fig tree of delusion (*máya-ka-gúlar*) and ate its fruit.

One day it so happened that a snake ran to her and said:—"Save me from my enemy and I will give you to eat." The Princess hid the snake in her robe, and soon after up came Garuda, and said:—"Surrender my thief." The Princess said:—"Your thief is not here." Then Garuda went away and the snake gave Phulande his jewel (*mani*) and said:—"Whenever you want anything you need only plaster a piece of ground and lay the jewel inside it. Whatever you require it will provide you."

Meanwhile the Ráni had heard that Phulande had planted a fig tree and was living on its fruit, so she again asked the Rája to have the tree cut down, and he did so. Then he remembered his daughter, and had all the preparations made for her wedding, and had men sent to search for his daughter. When the Ráni heard of this she had all the marriage supplies sent away to her father's house.

When the Rája found his daughter in the jungle and was about to get her married, he found that all the marriage supplies had disappeared, and he was almost broken-hearted on account of the disgrace which would fall upon him. But the Princess plastered a holy square, and placing the snake's jewel inside, asked it to provide all that was required. At once all that was necessary was provided, and the guests were well entertained.

One day a Jogi came to the palace of the old Ráni, and she got him to transform Princess Phulande into a bird. She flew away to the village where her husband lived and perched on a tree in the courtyard of a Kori. She asked the Kori:—"Is the Rája asleep or awake?" The Kori said that he was sleeping. Then the bird wept, and the tears which fell from her eyes were turned into pearls. Again she asked the Kori:—"Is the Rája asleep or awake?" "He is awake," he answered. Then the bird laughed, and immediately flowers fell from her lips, so that the ground was covered with them. When the day dawned the bird flew away and the Kori went and told the Rája, who was the husband of the Princess Phulande. The next night the young Rája came himself to the Kori's house and lay on watch. At midnight the bird came again and said to the Kori:—"Is the Rája asleep or awake?" The Kori said:—"He is awake." Then from the lips of the bird flowers began to fall, so that the ground was strewn with them. The Rája succeeded in catching the bird, and putting it into a cage, went home. One day the Jogi, who had transformed the Princess, came to beg alms at the palace. The bird cried out to the Rája:—"This is the

Jogi! This is the Jogi!" The Rája said to the Jogi:—"Explain this mystery." "I will do so," said the Jogi, "if you promise to spare my life." The Rája gave the promise, and then the Jogi told him the whole story. The Rája ordered him to restore Princess Phulande to her former shape, and he did so. The Rája accepted her as his Ráni, and dismissed the Jogi with a lordly present.

[This combines a number of familiar incidents—the wicked step-mother, the faithful animals and animal transformation.—ED.]

107. *The Princess and the Cat.*[46]

There was once a King who had an only daughter, whom he loved exceedingly. One day she went into the bazar and saw a man selling a kitten, which she bought and took home. She was very fond of it, and took such care of it that it became an enormous cat. When the time came for the Princess to be married the cat was very angry and jealous. He asked her if it was true that she was going to be married. She said nothing, and hung down her head for shame. When the procession arrived the cat again asked her if she was going away. Again she made no answer. When the bridegroom's people came the cat jumped upon them and began to scratch and tear them until they were obliged to run away to save their lives. When the King heard this he was astonished; but what could they do because the cat threatened to kill them all. The Princess was so afraid of him that she was obliged to be kind to him.

One day the cat said to her:—"I am going out hunting." While he was away the Princess took the chance of escaping and went off to the house of a Chamár. She got the Chamár to, make her a covering of skin so that the cat should not know her, and when her skin-coat was ready she put it on and started on her travels. On her way she met the cat, and when she saw him coming she sprinkled some barley on the ground and began to pick it up. The cat asked her who she was, and she answered:—"I am Chamni (the skin-woman), and I live by picking up the grains that fall on the ground." The cat went back to the palace and searched everywhere for her, but he could not find her.

At last the Princess reached the land of the Prince, her husband, and came begging at the palace door. Her mother-in-law saw her, and taking pity on her, gave her service in the kitchen. But as her skin-coat gave a foul smell no one would let her sit near them, and she had to remain apart. One day the man who grazed the elephants fell sick and there was no one to tend them; so Chamni was sent out with them. When she was alone in the jungle she used to take off her coat of skin, and she made a swing in which she used to lie and sing while the Fairies from Indrasan came and sang, and sported with her. This so pleased the elephants that they stood round her and listened to the music. As they would not graze they became so lean that the Prince could not understand the reason, and one day the Prince went himself to inspect them, and when he saw Chamni in her real form he was fascinated with her beauty. When she came back he sent for her, and when he had made her take off her coat of skin and heard her story, lie accepted her as his wife. She told him about the cat, but he said:—"Do not fear. When he comes I will kill him."

Meanwhile the cat had traced out the Princess, and taking the form of bangle-seller (*Chúrihárin*) arrived at the palace. She stood outside crying:—"Bangles to sell. Who wants bangles?" The Princess called her in and was having a set of bangles fitted on, when the bangle-seller suddenly sprang upon the Prince, and would have torn him to pieces had not the servants come to his aid. The cat escaped, but some days later as the Prince and Princess were in their room, he made a hole in the roof and was just about to spring upon them when the Princess, who was awake, saw him and called to her husband. He seized his sword and cut off the cat's head; after which they lived in the utmost happiness.

[This is another version of the Cinderella, Cap-o-Rushes Cycle.—ED.]

108. *What's in a Name?*

There was once a Mahájan, whose name was Thanthpál or "the protector of the decrepit." His wife thought this a name of evil omen, so she told him to change it. Finally he said:—"As you persist in asking me to change my name I will take a journey and look out for a better one."

When he had gone some distance he saw a dead body being carried to the burning-ground. "What was the name of the deceased?" he asked some of the mourners. "His name," said one of them, "was Amar Sinh" (Immortal!).

He went on a little farther and met a poor man carrying a bundle of wood to sell in the bazar. "What is your name?" he asked. "Sundar Sáhu" (Lovely Banker) he answered.

Going on further he met a poor old woman begging and limping on with the help of a stick. "What is your name?" he asked. "My name is Lakshmi "(the Goddess of Prosperity) she replied.

Next he came to a village, and being anxious to bathe, he asked them if there was a tank there. "There is a tank and its name is Ságar" (the Ocean) they answered. But when he went there he found it quite dry.

Going on again he saw a miserable lean ox which a man was driving along with the greatest difficulty. "What do you call your ox?" the Mahájan asked. "His name is Sonait "(the Golden One) he replied.

Then the Mahájan laughed and said:—

> *Maral dekha Amar Sinh;*
> *Sir per lakri Sundar Sáhu;*
> *Sabai mangat Lakshmi dekha;*
> *Jhúra pokhar Ságar nám;*
> *Gariyar bail Sonait nám;*
> *Ník mor Thanthpál nám.*

"Immortal I saw dead; wood on the head of the Beautiful One; the Goddess of Prosperity begging alms; an empty tank was called the Great Ocean; the broken-down ox the Golden One. My own name, the Protector of the decrepit, is not so bad after all." So he went home, and when he told the whole story to his wife, she never bothered him again to change his name.

109. The Cow and the Tigress.[47]

There was once a Bráhman who lived in a village with his wife, and so unlucky was he that whenever he went out to beg he never got more than enough flour to make a single cake, and if he walked through half-a-dozen villages he never got more than this. One day his wife said to him:—"Why do you not go, to the Rája? I am sure if you asked him he would make you a handsome present, which would relieve us from this wretched poverty."

He took his wife's advice and went to the Rája, and the Rája gave him a cow. He brought the cow home, and from that time his circumstances began to improve, and he became quite comfortable. But his wife was a very silly woman, and one day, while she was eating her food, she saw the cow chewing the cud. She said to the cow:—"You, insolent brute! You feed at my expense, and still you make faces at me. Wait till my husband comes home, and I will have you turned out of the house." The cow did not understand what she said and went on chewing the cud. The Bráhman's wife got still more angry, and when her husband came home she said to him:—"Maháráj, this cow is as bad to me as a second wife in the house. She makes faces at me when I am eating. Either she or I must leave the house." The Bráhman answered:—"My dear, why should I turn you out of the house? I will drive this wretch into the jungle."

So he took the cow to the jungle and left her there. After some time she made friends with a tigress, who ruled that part of the forest, and both of them were in young. In due course the cow gave birth to a calf and the tigress to a cub. The calf and the young tiger became great friends. One day the cow was drinking at a stream and the tigress below her. Some of the cow's spittle floated down the stream, and when the tigress tasted it she thought to herself:—"If her spittle tastes so sweet, how sweet must her flesh be!" And then she determined to eat the cow the next day. The cow knew what she was planning and despaired of her life. That night when she was suckling her calf she said to him:—"My son, this is the last time I shall be able to give you suck. To-morrow the tigress will take my life." In the morning she put a little milk in a cup and said to her calf:—"I am now going out with the tigress. I shall die to-day: as long as this milk keeps its natural colour be sure that I am alive; but when it turns red, you may be certain that I am dead." The tigress and the cow remained some time together, and when the noon had passed the tigress killed her friend. Immediately the milk in the cup was changed into blood. When the calf saw this he fell on the ground in an agony of grief, and soon after the tiger cub appeared and asked him the cause of his sorrow. The calf was in too great grief to speak, and in the evening when the tigress came home the cub told her that the calf was very sick, and asked why the cow did not return. The tigress answered:—"How do I know what has become of her?"

When the calf told the cub the fate of his mother he was very wroth, and immediately fell upon his mother, saying:—"Wretch, you have killed and eaten the mother of my friend." After this the calf and the tiger cub lived together. One day the tiger said to the calf:—"Brother, you are not happy here. Let us go into another jungle, where there is plenty of pasture." So they went into another jungle, and the tiger tied a bell round the calf's neck and said:—"My friend, whenever you find yourself in trouble ring this bell and I will come to your assistance immediately." One day the calf thought to himself:—"I will try how far the cub is telling the truth." So he rang the bell and the tiger ran up at once. He asked him into what trouble he had fallen, and he said:—"I only did it to try you." Soon after a marriage party of butchers passed that way, and seeing the calf they determined to seize him. So they fell upon him and killed him. The tiger heard the sound of the bell and rushed up. When he saw the butchers cutting up his friend he sprang and killed several of them. Then he collected the bones and flesh of his companion, and erecting a pyre, set fire to them, and when the fire was well alight, he in his grief jumped in and was burned with him.

In course of time two bamboos grew from the ashes, and one day some of the Rája's men came and saw them. They were so straight and without a flaw that they tried to cut them down, but when they laid their axes to the roots, out of one came milk and from the other blood. They were awe-stricken, and went and told the Rája, who sent his Wazir to enquire into the matter. He found it to be as the men had said; so he informed the Rája, who came himself to the place. He had the ground excavated from beneath, and lo! from below appeared two boys of exquisite grace and beauty. The Rája took them home, married them to his daughters, and after his death they ruled the land.

[For the magic tree growing from the ashes, see numerous parallels collected by Miss Cox: *Cinderella*, 477: for the kindly tiger-cub, *ibid*, 526.—ED.]

110. *The best thing in the world.*[48]

There was once a King who used to walk about the city at night, and listen to what his subjects were saying. One night he heard four girls talking at a well. One said:—"The most enjoyable thing in the world is wine." "No;" said the second. "Lying is the best." "Meat is best," said the third. "A man is the best thing in the world," said the fourth.

Next day as he sat in Darbar the King sent for the girls and asked them what they meant. The first said:—"Behind our house is a grog-shop. People are always coming there and spending all their money on drink. Then they fall into the ditch, and their relations abuse them and turn them out. Wine must be the best thing in the world, or no one would undergo so much for its sake."

Then he asked the second why she praised lying. "I see," said she, "what goes on in your Majesty's court. One calls you "Protector of the Poor;" another, "The Incarnation of all the Virtues," and so on. "You know, of course, that they lie to you; but if they did not say so you would be displeased."

Then the King asked the third why she praised meat. "Men eat meat," she said, "and cast away the bones; the dogs chew them; the birds pick them; the hyaenas crush them, and the ants eat the fragments. Nothing can be better than meat."

The turn of the fourth came, and the King asked her why a man was the best thing in the world. "When my sister's baby was born I saw what trouble she was in, and how she cursed the day she was married. But when her husband died she was scarce a year before she took another mate, and a new baby was on the way to be born. A man is surely the best thing in the world."

The King was pleased with their answers, and dismissed them with a present.

III. The Mischievous Boy—A Folktale from Kumaun.

Some women were once carrying some large vessels of milk on their heads when they met a boy and said:—"Tell us something which will cool our ears," i. e., relieve the tedium of the road. "I will cool your ears for you," said he, and he at once broke the vessels and the milk poured over them. Then he went to the bazar and bought a pice worth of oil. As he was taking it up the vessel overturned and the oil was spilt. "No matter," said the Banya. "Your ill-luck (*ála-bála*) for the day is gone through this trifling loss." "Is that so?" asked the boy. Then he upset one of the Banya's oil jars. "There goes your ill-luck," said he. Then he upset another. "There goes your father's ill-luck." He upset a third. "There goes your grandfather's ill-luck." And he would have wrecked the whole shop if the Banya had not caught him by the ear and turned him out.

Then he went to the confectioner and asked:—"What sweet is that?" The answer was "*Khájá*." The boy ate it up, and when he was asked for the price, he said:—"You told me to eat it (*kha ja*), and I did what you told me."

All the people went to the Rája and complained. When he heard the case the Rája said:—"If you will do foolish things you must bear the loss," and he let the boy go.—*Pandit Janardan Joshi.*

112. [49] Mr. Knowall—A Folktale from Kumaun.

There was once a man who used to give his wife a ser of flour every day, out of which, as every one knows, she should have made a dozen cakes; but she never produced more than five, and used to keep the remaining seven for a friend of hers. At last the husband smelt a rat, and one day he made a hole in the roof and looked on while she was cooking. When the meal was served, and only five cakes were produced as usual, he asked where were the remaining seven. She was confounded and asked him how on earth he managed to find it out. "It is hard to deceive a man like me who am skilled in astrology," he answered. After this the fame of his knowledge of astrology spread through the land; and when the King's pearl necklace was lost he was sent for, and told that if he did not trace it his life would be the forfeit. He was in sore distress and lay down at night in the palace. Then he cried:—"*A ninúri, a, bhor tu mara jaoge,*" which means:—"Come sweet sleep, for to-morrow thou shalt die." Now it so happened that one of the King's slave-girls named Ninúri had stolen the necklace, and she was on the watch to see what the astrologer would do. When she heard him mention her name as she thought, she was stricken with fear, and told where she had hidden it. Next morning he took the King and his people to the place, and the jewel was found.

From that time his reputation was established, and soon after when a rival monarch came to attack the kingdom of his master he was sent to lead the army. He had never mounted a horse before, and his wife had to tie him with ropes to prevent him from falling. As he rode on in advance of the army his horse bolted, and to save himself he caught at the branch of a tree by the side of the road which came off in his hand. When the enemy saw this terrible demon approaching, tearing up trees as he advanced, they were stricken with panic and immediately retreated. When he returned his grateful master gave him half his kingdom.—*Pandit Janardan Joshi.*

113. The Lady who became a Cat.

A king was once sleeping in his inner apartments and the queen was sitting by his side. He was half asleep, and, looking round, he saw the wife of his Wazír coming into the room in the form of a beautiful white cat. When she came near his bed she rolled on the ground and at once turned into a lovely woman. She then said to the queen: "To-day is the marriage of the king of Fulána country, which is fifteen hundred miles from here. The king is a friend of mine and I must be present." The king was much surprised at this, but he remained silent and pretended to be asleep. Then the Wazír's wife said again "Your friend will be there too, and you also should go." When the two women found that the king was sleeping soundly they turned themselves into cats and set out. The king followed them unseen, and when they came to the outskirts of the city they climbed up a banyan tree, which, the moment they sat on it, was torn from its roots and flew through the air. The king also took hold of a branch and was carried off in an instant to the place where the marriage was going on.

When he entered the assembly he found that the bridegroom had only one eye. When the people saw that the king was a handsome man they made him the bridegroom and escorted him to the bride, who was in the inner apartments. There he saw the wife of his Wazír sitting among the other women and his own queen with her paramour. Seeing this he was overcome with grief and shame, and began to consider how he should punish his queen. When he came out of the bride's chamber he put off all his wedding robes and kept only his marriage bracelet (*kangan*); then he took his seat in the hollow of the banyan tree, and shortly after the Wazír's wife and his queen turned themselves again into cats, and came and sat on the tree, which flew back with them to the palace.

He got to his room before the women could return and lay down on his bed as before. As he was tired, he slept till a late hour, and when he woke the queen came to him with a washing ewer full of water and said with a laugh: "You got through the marriage well last night." "And you," said he, "had a pleasant time with your lover." When she heard this the queen threw some sesamum (*sarson*) over him, repeated some *mantras,* and he was immediately turned into a peacock. She shut him up in a basket, and when the Wazír came to the Darbar she sent to tell him that the king was sick. The Wazír, when the king did not appear for some days, consulted his wife and proposed to go to the palace and find out, what was the matter with the king. "There is no use in your going," she said; "I know that the queen has turned him into a peacock." Her husband asked her if there was any way of getting possession of the king. "Bring me another peacock and I will manage it," she answered. So her husband brought her a peacock, which she took to the palace and contrived to change it for the basket in which the king was kept. She returned to the Wazír with the king in the form of a peacock, and he requested her to bring him back to his original form. So she threw some sesamurn over him, repeated some *mantras* and he was restored to his real form.

The Wazír said to his master: "It is dangerous for us to remain here with this wretched woman. Let us go to some other land." So they wandered far away, and came at last to a kingdom, where the king recognised them as men of worth and good breeding, and took them into his service. He gave the king his daughter to wife and ordered his Wazír to marry his daughter to the strange Wazír. One day the king and his new queen were sitting on the roof of the palace and they saw a great bird flying in the air above them. The king asked the queen what this bird was, and she said: "This is not a kite, as you suppose; it is your first wife." He answered: "Then we are in great danger." "Do not be anxious," she answerd. "She, is a white kite, and I will turn myself into a black kite. I will fight with her and we will both fall to the ground together. Then you must kill her."

Meanwhile the Wazír came up, and the king asked him which of the birds he should kill. "They are both evil witches," he replied, "and we should kill them both." So when the kites came down on the ground and were struggling together, the king and the Wazír fell upon them with their swords and put them both to death. Then the king went back to Fulána country, claimed the bride he had married by mistake and went back with her to his own land, where he ruled for many years in the utmost happiness and prosperity.[50]

114. *The Opium-eater and the Demons.*

There was once an opium-eater, who was so addicted to the vice that he fell into extreme poverty. One day he said to his wife: "Bake two cakes for me and I will go and seek for some employment." She borrowed some flour from a neighbour and made the cakes for him. He started off, and after he had walked thirty miles he came upon a well, where he washed and ate his dinner and took his usual dose of opium. When he was at the height of his intoxication he saw a one-eyed Deo, who was known as Kanua, or the "one-eyed demon," approaching him. As he came along he was dancing and singing, and when the opium-eater saw him he began to do the same. When the Deo came near he said: "Why were you laughing at me?" "Why did you dance before me?" said the opium-eater.

"I," said the Deo, "have travelled four and twenty miles this morning in search of food, and when I saw you I could not help thinking what a good dinner I am going to make off you." When he heard this all the trance of the opium passed off at once and he knew that he was in evil case. So he said to the Deo: "If you really want to know why I was laughing, the real reason is this that the left tower of the palace of the Lord Solomon (on whom be peace!) has fallen down and he has sent me to catch twelve thousand demons to rebuild it. I have now got you for one of them; but I regret to say that even this one has only one eye." When he heard this Kanua Deo was sore afraid. "How can I alone do the work of twelve thousand demons?" he asked. "Please take a little present from me and let me go this time." The opium-eater, who was now getting a little more confident, answered "I can let you go only on one condition, that you give me a good present and tell me where I can find the twelve thousand Deos of whom I am in search." Kanua Deo gave him a purse of twelve thousand rupees and said: "To the west of this well, at a distance of five hundred paces, there is a grove, in which twelve thousand Deos of my brotherhood assemble. These you may catch if you please."

The opium-eater took the money, let Kanua Deo loose and went his way. When he got home he said to his wife: "Hasten to the bazar and purchase all the delicacies you can find. Here is as much money as you want." When his friends and neighbours saw the sudden change in the fortunes of the opium-eater they wondered, and at last they asked him how he came by all this wealth. He answered: "I have found out a way to get wealth when I please, and the next time I go out in search of it you can come too." So when he had spent all the money he determined to go and get some more. But when he asked his friends to go with him they began to suspect that he had made his money by robbery or some other improper way; so no one would go with him except one grey-bearded old fellow, who was near the end of his life and had little to risk. The pair went off together and reached the grove where Kanua Deo had said that the Deos lived. They both climbed up into a thick tree and the opium-eater got the old man to tie him to the tree with his turban. The old man hid himself, and when it was near midnight a multitude of Deos appeared. Some of them swept the ground while others spread carpets in several rows. By this time twelve thousand Deos had assembled, and then four flying thrones full of fairies came down from Indrasan, and they began to dance before them. Kanua Deo was also among them, and while the dance was going on his friends noticed that he got up several times and looked round him anxiously. They said "Why are you continually getting up and looking round?" He answered: "None of you have ever come across Kalsira (black-head: the Deos' name for man). If you had you would have been as anxious as I am." Meanwhile the old man from sheer terror fell out of his tree, and when Kanua Deo saw him he said: "Here is Kalsira: fly for your lives." At this all the Deos ran away, and when they had left the place the opium-eater came down too and found the old man unharmed. So they both packed up all the vessels, ornaments and other valuables which the Deos had abandoned in their flight. These they took home and lived on them in great magnificence till the end of their days.[51]

115. The Wisdom of Bírbal.

Akbar once said to Bírbal:—"Is there a man in the world wiser than yourself?" Bírbal replied: "Great king, there is no man wiser than myself." So Akbar made a proclamation throughout his dominions that whoever would exceed Bírbal in wisdom should be richly rewarded. When the brother of Bírbal heard of this he went to Akbar and said: "Oh, great king, I am wiser than Bírbal." The king said: "Very well. Prove it." So he went to his brother and said: "I desire to live apart from you. Divide the ancestral property equally between us." Bírbal said: "I have no objection. We will divide the property; you can live in half the house and I will live in the other." But his brother said: "This plan will not answer at all; you must pull down the house and cut every brick in two." Bírbal was surprised when he heard this foolish proposal; but he said to himself: "How am I to answer this fool? And if I do not answer him Akbar will think that my brother is wiser than I am."

On the whole he thought it best to leave the land: so he went off to the king of Ríwa and asked for employment. The king asked him who he was and he answered: "Men call me Bírbal." The king then received him very kindly and asked him why he had left the court of the Emperor. He said: "I had some private reasons for going away. If you give me employment here I will stay; if not I will go away." The king said: "My kingdom is yours; you may stay as long as you please." So he got honourable service and stayed there.

When the buffoons of Akbar's court heard that Bírbal had gone away they came to the Emperor and performed before him. When they were done Akbar was so pleased that he said: "Choose what boon you please." They answered: "All we want is, leave to bathe in the royal chambers." Akbar was perplexed at this demand and thought "If I had only Bírbal here to baffle these scoundrels. If I consent I am disgraced before my subjects for ever." So he said: "Give me six months' time and then I will give you an answer." Meanwhile he made great search for Bírbal, but could find no trace of him. Then he sent a circular letter to all the subject Rájas saying: "I have exacavated a well and a tank, and I wish to get them married. Send me all the wells and tanks in your dominions so that suitable matches may be selected." This he did, thinking that the Rájas would be perplexed to find an answer, and that only the Rája who had the benefit of Bírbal's advice could get out of the difficulty.

As he expected, all the Rájas were perplexed how to give an answer to such an extraordinary letter. But when the Ríwa Rája consulted Bírbal he said: "Write to the Emperor and say 'My tanks and wells are all ladies, and it is the custom of my land for the bridegroom to fetch the bride; if you send your well and tank I have no objection to the alliance.'" When the Emperor read the letter of the Ríwa Rája he was quite certain that it must have been written by the advice of Bírbal; so he came himself to Ríwa and brought Bírbal back with him with the greatest honour to Delhi.

When Akbar got back to Delhi he sent for the buffoons and said: "Do you still desire to bathe in my private chamber?" They said that such was their desire. He said: "You can do so." But when they came in they found Bírbal standing there with a drawn sword in his hand. "Come and bathe here my friends; but if any one lets a drop of water fall on the floor, off goes his head." They were afraid to attempt the task, and going to the Emperor they said: "Great king! we have received our reward. We merely wished to know if you had found in your court any man wiser than Bírbal."[52]

116. The Kingdom of the Mice.

There was once a kingdom of mice, of which a mouse was king, and he had a fox for his Wazír. All the animals of the forest did homage to him and did nothing without his permission. One day it so happened that a caravan passed through the forest, and one of the camels was so tired that it could go no further. The owner waited a day or two to see if it would recover, but it was too weak to move, and he was obliged to leave it there. After a while however the camel began to graze about and got so strong that it used to devour the gardens of the mouse king. When Mr. Fox, the Wazír, heard of this he went and told the king, who ordered his Wazír to produce the camel before him. Next morning the Wazír brought the camel before the king. When the camel saw that the king was only a mouse and his Wazír only a fox he showed great disdain for both of them, and began to grunt and gurgle and said: "What can these miserable creatures do to me?" So saying he went back to the forest and began to graze as usual where he pleased. The mouse king was very angry and said to his Wazír: "See that this ruffian meets the due punishment he deserves." "Your Majesty!" answered the fox, "you will soon see that he reaps the reward of his action."

So the fox was always on the look-out to wreak his revenge on the camel, and one day it so happened that the camel's nose-string got entangled in a creeper, and as he could not release himself he was in a fair way to starve. When the fox heard of this he was much pleased and took his master to the place. "O, foolish camel!" said the mouse king, "you would not heed my words and you are now reaping the fruit of your misconduct." The camel answered: "Mahárája! I confess my fault and pray for your forgiveness. If you save me this time I swear that I shall be ever your faithful servant and obey you in everything." The mouse king took pity upon him and climbing up the creeper cut the cord with his teeth. The camel was so grateful that he used to attend the mouse king every morning and take his orders.

One day it so happened that some wood-cutters came into the forest, and as they were cutting fire wood they found this stray camel, which they seized and carried to their king. When the fox heard of this he told his master, who was sore wroth. Next day, when the wood-cutters came again into the forest, he had them arrested and brought into his presence; he reprimanded them for their insolence and said: "If your master will not restore my camel he must be prepared for war." The wood-cutters returned and told their king, but he despised the threat of the king of the mice and sent no favourable reply. The mouse king collected his armies of mice and sent them to the capital of the king of the wood-cutters with orders to dig in his treasury and each to bring in his mouth as many rupees as he could carry. They carried out his orders and soon made an enormous pile of treasure in the forest. One day a wise man came into the forest in search of employment and chanced to come upon the place where this great treasure was in charge of a detachment of mice. He began to think to himself: "How can I gain this great riches?" But an old mouse, who knew his thoughts, said: "Why are you envying this treasure? Go to our king and he will give you service." So the mouse king took the wise man into his service, and the king said: "Go and call more of your brethren and I will employ them." The man went to his village and returned with a very large force. When the army of the mouse king was thus made complete he started off to invade the dominions of the king of the wood-cutters. He sent his army of mice ahead with orders during the night to undermine the walls of the enemy's fort. They did so and creeping in tore up the walls and destroyed all the enemy's property. Then all the army of the wood-cutter king fled and he was obliged to throw himself on the mercy of the mouse king, who, after he had got back his camel, made the wood-cutter king his vassal, and returned in great triumph to his dominions.[53]

117. The Perfumer and the Rustics.

A perfumer once went into a remote village, where the people had never so much as heard of a perfumer. He offered some rose water for sale, but no one could tell whether it was good or bad. At last a lout who prided himself on his cunning took some on his hand and licking it up said: "This is bad because it does not taste sweet." The Gandhi laughed and went on. Another lout came running after him and said: "My brother says that this is not sweet enough, but I don't mind buying a little as a condiment for my curry."[54]

118. The Advice of the Rajput.

There was once a Rájput, whose son was great friends with the son of a Banya. His father was always warning him, but he paid no heed to his advice. At last he said to him one day: "Kill an animal and smear your sword with blood and see what your friend will say." The boy did so and, going to the Banya's son, said to him: "I have killed a man; help me." The Banyas drove him off at once saying: "Be off; do you want to get us ruined by harbouring you?" The boy came and told his father, who said "Now go to a Pathán who lives in the village. and tell him the same story." The boy did so, and the Pathán at once said: "Come in, my friend. No one shall harm you as long as I am here."

119. The Height of Laziness.[55]

Two lazy fellows were once sleeping under a jamun tree, when a fruit fell on the nose of one of them; but he was too lazy to pick it up himself, and waited till his companion would do it for him. But, his friend was as lazy as himself, and would not help him. So he lay there waiting till a traveller should pass that way and come to his assistance. Meanwhile a dog came up, and he began to slobber the face of his friend. He was too lazy to drive him off and asked his companion to help him. But his friend lay quiet and did nothing. By and by a horseman passed, and one of the pair asked him to dismount from his horse. When he got down one idler said:

"Would you be kind enough to put this jamun into my mouth?"

The horseman was so angry that he gave the fellow half a dozen lashes with his whip.

"You have done quite right," he said. "Just before you came a dog was beslobbering my face and I asked my friend to drive him off, but he was too lazy to help me."

"O! Bhagwán, are there two such people in the world?" he cried, and went his way.

[This is the "Three Sluggards" of Grimm's *Household Tales,* No. 151: and the *Gesta Romanorum,* No. 91.]

120. *The Gallant Young Buffalo.*[56]

An Ahírin used to take out her father's buffaloes every day to graze in the jungle. One evening she fed and watered them and took them to the pen (*arár*), and they lay down and began to chew the cud. As they moved their jaws about she thought they were jeering at her, so she said:

"If you don't stop making faces at me I will leave you here and go home."

But they paid no heed to her, so she went home and left the two of them in the jungle. Now they were both in calf, and one of them gave birth to a bull and the other to a heifer. The old ones used to go out every day to graze and left the calves in the pen. One day the bull said to the heifer:

"I am very thirsty. You hold my legs and let me down into the well for a drink and then I will do the same for you." The heifer held the bull while he drank, but when the turn of the heifer came he let go her legs and she fell into the well and was drowned. When her mother came home in the evening she could not find her calf, and asked the bull what had become of her.

"Let me suck you," he said, "and I will tell you." So he used to suck the other buffalo as well as his own mother and kept putting her off with one excuse or another day after day until he became fat and lusty.

Then he went off and used to eat the field of melons which the tiger and the jackal had sown in partnership. The jackal saw him and said:

"Who on earth has the impudence to eat the field of my uncle? (*mámú*)."

The buffalo cried

> *"Ath chunchillá main plún*
> *Khuriyán búren dúdh*
> *Tere mámú ke aise taise.*
> *"Ek thokar ek thokar men janya."*

"I drink from eight teats and am up to my fetlocks in milk. Who cares a hang for your uncle! A single kick would make him flee."

Every day this sort of chaff went on between the jackal and the buffalo. Finally the jackal went and complained to the tiger, and they both went to the field. The tiger went and lay down behind some bushes and the jackal began as usual to argue with the buffalo. He gave the same answer as before; then the tiger got up, sprang upon him and gave him a slap with his paw in the face. The buffalo got angry and crushed him to death with his horns. Then the jackal collected the flesh of his friend and taking it to the tigress told her that it was the flesh of a deer which her husband had killed and had sent her a piece. She cooked and ate it. Then the jackal sat outside the den and taunted her

> *"Baghe kí meharí, siyárin ká kám;*
> *Marde ká másu khailu, hai Rám."*

"The tigress is but a she-jackal after all!
Alas Rama! She ate the flesh of her husband!"

121. The Advice of the Sadhu.[57]

Once upon a time a Sádhu wandered about the streets of a city and called out:

"I will sell four pieces of good advice for four lakhs of rupees."

No one except a merchant would accept his offer. When he paid the money the Sádhu said

> *"Bina sang na chaliye bát:*
> *Thonk thánkke baitho khát:*
> *Jagat ko pucche na koi:*
> *Krodh mari pácche phal hoe."*

"Do not travel without a companion.
Do not sit on a bed without touching it first.
No one interferes with a man as long as he is awake.

He who restrains his anger reaps the fruit of it."

Soon after, when he went on a journey, the merchant remembered the advice of the Sádhu and went in search of a companion.

The only one he could find was a khenkra or crab. They started together and came to a city, where the merchant made much wealth by trade. On their way back they came to a jungle, and the merchant lay down under a tree in which lived a crow and a snake who were sworn friends. When the merchant fell asleep the crow said to the snake:

"Go down, brother, and bite this man to death, and then I can make a meal of his eyes."

The snake crawled down at once and bit the merchant, so that he died, and the crow flew down and was just about to peck out his eyes, when the khenkra caught the crow with six of his claws and held on to the merchant's turban with the other six. The crow was afraid lest the man should revive and kill him: so he asked the khenkra to let him go. But the khenkra said:

"I will not spare you until you bring my master to life."

So the crow had to ask the snake to come down and suck out the venom, and the merchant came to life again. He said:

"What a sleep I have had!"

"May no one sleep such a sleep as your's," said the khenkra. He asked the khenkra to explain, but the khenkra said:

"First shoot the crow which is sitting on that tree."

The merchant killed the crow with his bow and arrow. When the khenkra told him the story he said:

"I have got back one lakh of my rupees."

He went on further and came to the house of a thag. His daughter sat outside, and near her was a seat hung over a concealed well on which she used to entice travellers to sit, and then pitch them in headlong. She offered the merchant water and invited him to sit down: but he remembered the advice of the Sádhu and touched the seat with his stick, when it toppled into the well. When he saw this he cried:

"I have got back my second lakh of rupees."

He went on further and came to an inn where there were seven thags, who planned to rob him, but he again remembered the advice of the Sádhu and kept awake. In the morning the thags said:

"You are the disciple of a great teacher, otherwise you would certainly have lost your wealth."

On hearing this, the merchant said: "I have got back my third lakh of rupees."

At last the merchant came home, and as he went into his house he saw a young man sitting with his wife. He suspected evil and was about to kill him when he remembered the last precept of the Sadhu and restrained his hand. Then he asked his wife who the young man was and she said:

"This is your own son born after you left home, and of course you do not recognise him."

The merchant cried:

"I have got back my four lakhs of rupees."

[We have the trap and concealed pit in the Decameron of Boccaccio (II. 5). For these tales of advice compare "The lakh of rupees "(Knowles' Folk Tales of Kashmir, 32 *sq.*) and Jacob's Notes (Indian Fairy Tales, 246)].

122. The Prince who became a Kol.[58]

There was once a Rája, who had an only son, whom he loved very dearly. The Prince was in the habit of going out hunting, and his father warned him never to go towards the south. For a long time he obeyed the orders of his father, but one day he determined to go in the prohibited direction. When he had gone some distance he felt thirsty, but could find no water. At last he saw a Kol felling a tree, and called to him. The Kol replied: "I was in search of you." The Prince asked him to point out where water was to be found. The Kol showed him a tank close by and said: "You can bathe here and refresh yourself."

The Prince took off his clothes and dived into the water, and no sooner had he done so then he was turned into the Kol. But he retained his senses as before. Then the Kol dived into the water and he was turned into the Prince. He put on the clothes of the Prince and went his way.

The Prince could do nothing but put on the clothes of the Kol, and just as he had done so up came the wife of the Kol. She gave him a box on the ear and said: "Why are you sitting here, you lazy rascal?" The Prince asked her who she was.

"Are you out of your wits that you don't know your own wife, you fool?" she answered. The Prince said: "You are not my wife. Go away; don't trouble me." When he said this she called out "Justice, O brethren! justice!" And at this all this all the other Kols came up and asked what was the matter. When they heard the case they said: "What, are you mad to-day? Don't you know your own wife?"

So the Prince had to put the wood which the Kol had cut on his shoulder and go home with the woman. When they got home the Kolin said:

"Take off this wood and sell it in the bázár." The Prince took the wood to the town, and a man asked him what price he wanted for it. He said: "Give what you think fair." The man gave the Prince four pice, and he took it home with him. When he showed the money to the Kolin she said: "What did you mean by taking so little for such a lot of wood? Take me at once to the man to whom you sold it." So the Prince took the Kolin to the man to whom he had sold the wood, and the Kolin said: "Why did you give my husband only four pice for such a lot of wood?" "I gave him," he answered, "what he asked for it." "Well, you must give me the proper price now," she said, and the man had to give her two pice more.

They went home and the Kolin prepared food. When it was ready the Prince, who could not break his caste, said: "I will not eat bread and pulse. Give me some parched grain." "What on earth is the matter with you to-day?" she asked. "Other days you eat bread and pulse and to-day you are calling for parched grain." However, in the end she had to give him the parched grain, and in this way he lived there many days.

One day as he went to the bázár to sell his wood it so happened that a Kabuli merchant had brought some horses to the Rája for sale, and one of them was so spirited that no one dared to mount it. At last the Rája offered a reward to any one who would ride the horse. The Kol threw down his bundle and said he would try. Every one laughed and said: "What can a Kol wood-cutter know of riding?" However, he mounted the horse and rode it all over the place. Then he took the horse to the Rája, who said "Who are you?" The Prince said: "Just now I am a Kol, but when the time comes I will tell you my story." Then the Rája appointed him to watch the horse and gave him a hundred rupees a month, out of which he made an allowance to the Kolin and lived in the stables of the Rája.

Meanwhile the real Kol mounted the Prince's horse and rode off; but the horse knew the rider to be a stranger, and soon threw him off. The Rája, his father, had already sent men in search of the Prince, and they found him lying on the ground, and taking him up brought him to the palace. The Rája was surprised to find his son so rude and ignorant; but he thought that the reason was that he had spent so much time in the jungles; so he sent for Maulavis and Pandits, and ordered them to educate him.

One day the sham Prince went into the bázár and met a carpenter who was selling a very beautiful bed. The Kol Prince bought it for a lakh of rupees and made a present of it to the Rája. Now the quality of the bed was this that at night the legs used to talk to each other and tell all that was going on in the four quarters of the world. When the Rája lay down that night on his new bed he heard the legs talking. One said: "This is a very wonderful Ráj. The Prince is really a common Kol and the proper Prince is working as a groom in his father's stable." "That is quite true," said the second leg, "and the curious thing is that the Rája does not suspect the trick which this rascally Kol has played on him." "It is certainly remarkable," said the third leg. "But how is this wrong to be set right?" "If the Rája," said the fourth leg, "would only make them both bathe again in the same tank they would each recover his real form."

The Rája had suspicions already in the matter, and when he heard what the legs of his bed were saying he was much pleased. Next morning he sent for the Kol and the Prince, and sent his Wazír with them to the tank. When they entered the water the Prince and Kol recovered their original shapes. The Kol was beaten and driven back to his hovel in the jungle and the Prince returned to the palace, where he lived many years in happiness.

[These magical tanks which cause transformation are common in these tales. We have also the "direction taboo" and the speaking bed in other tales.—ED.]

123. How the Sadhu went Athieving.[59]

There was once a Sádhu who was believed to be a very pious man. He never begged for alms, but took what the benevolent chose to give him. One day four thieves came to him and said "Bábájí! you have had nothing to eat to-day, we think." "That is so," he answered. They gave him some sweetmeats, with which he was much pleased, and asked them what they wanted. They said: "We are going to rob a rich Banya to-night and we want you to give us your blessing." "Go on and prosper," he said. "If we succeed," said they, "we will give you half our booty." "I do not want your plunder," he said; "all I want is plenty of *balbhog*" (food offered to a Hindu god before the votary partakes of it).

The thieves went off and broke into the house, whence they carried off five thousand rupees. They returned to the Sádhu and gave him five rupees. He asked them if they had got a good haul and they replied: "Oh, we got fifty rupees or so, out of which we gave you five."

When they had gone away the Banya who had been robbed came to the Sádhu and told him that he had been robbed of five thousand rupees. "Tell me whether I shall succeed in recovering my money or not." The Bábá now saw how the thieves had swindled him, so he said: "Don't be anxious. You will recover your money."

Two or three days after the thieves again came to the Bábá and said: "Bábájí! give us your blessing again. We are going on another expedition." He answered: "Begone, I do not wish to associate with such wretches. You stole five thousand rupees the last time and made me believe that you had only got fifty, and you gave me only five." They knelt before him and begged his pardon. He said: "I forgive you this time, but I can never trust you again, and the next time I will go with you myself." They said: "All right, you can go with us if you like."

So the Bábá took his idol of Thákurjí and his conch shell, and they started. They came to the house of a very rich Ahír, and the thieves said to the Sádhu: "Bábájí! you must go inside." But he said: "You know more about it than I do. You had better go in first." When they went in he followed them, and as they began to tie up the goods he asked: "What am I to do now?" "Keep quiet," they said. So they went on collecting all the valuables, and meanwhile the Bábájí was looking about the place. In a corner he saw a pot of milk and he said to himself "I was near forgetting that Thákurjí is starving. It would be a good thing to offer this milk to him." So he made the offering in due form, and as he did so he blew his conch shell with all his might. At this the people of the house woke and cried: "Thief! thief!" The thieves all bolted leaving the goods behind them, and the Bábájí stayed behind. The people of the house began to beat him. He said: "Why do you beat me?" They said: "You have broken into our house." Finally however they let him go because he was a Sádhu, and he went back to his hermitage.

There the thieves attacked him and said: "You are a rascal and have spoiled our business." He said: "I made a mistake and thought I was in my hermitage. Next time I promise to be more careful." "We will never take you again," they said. "Next time I go I won't take my shell and Thákurjí," he promised.

So they agreed to give him another trial, and then they broke into the house of a very rich man. As the Bábá was wandering about the house he saw a Narsingha trumpet lying in a corner, and thinking it would be of use to him in his worship he took it, and being, anxious to see if it was in good order or not he just put his lips to it, when it made such a row that the household awoke. The thieves ran away, and when he was caught the Bábá still went on blowing the trumpet. "I am just seeing whether it is all right or not," he remarked.

When they met him next time all the thieves said was *"Ko na kusangati pái nasái."*

"Who is not ruined by keeping bad company?"

124. The Tale of Tismar Khan.[60]

Once upon a time an old woman came to a weaver's door selling treacle; he bought half a pice worth and applied it to his beard. Immediately a number of flies settled on it, and with one stroke of his hand he killed thirty. Then he said within himself: "I will weave cloth no longer. I am Tismár Khán, the slayer of thirty." I will go and take service with the king."

So he went to the king and asked for employment. The king asked him what his name was and what pay per month he would accept. He said: "My name is Tismár Khán and my pay is one hundred rupees a month. I can do work that no one else can do."

He was appointed in the king's service, and one day it so happened that a tiger missed his way and came into the city, and killed many people. The king sent for Tismár Khán and ordered him to kill the tiger. He was sore afraid, and thinking that it was high time for him to leave the place he drew his arrears of pay from the treasury and started. He went to a washerman to borrow an ass to carry his baggage. Just then a shower of rain came on and he went into the shed of the washerman for shelter, and found them all half dead through fear of the tiger. But Tismár Khán said: "I don't fear the tiger. But Tapakua (the dripping) has come, and I am much more afraid of Tapakua than any thing else." The tiger just then had crept into the ass shed to escape the rain, and when he heard these words he was afraid. "Who can this terrible Tapakua be of whom they are all so frightened?" he thought to himself, and he lay down quietly among the asses.

When the rain was over the washerman said to Tismár Khán: "I don't care to go out myself. But you can go and take any of the asses you please." Tismár Khán went out into the shed, and thinking the tiger to be an ass laid hands on him. He tied him up with a rope and fastened him to a post near his house. Next morning when he got up and found the tiger tied up he was much surprised and delighted, and when the king came and saw the tiger he was so much pleased with the bravey of Tismár Khán that he gave him a handsome reward.

Soon after a foreign sovereign with a great army invaded the kingdom, and the king appointed Tismár Khán Commander-in-Chief and sent him out with all his force. At first he marched in the rear of the army, but the soldiers shouted "Khán Sáhib, come on." Unaccustomed as he was to riding he suddenly spurred his charger, which carried him under a tree.

He held on to a branch, but the tree come out by the roots, and he rode on dragging it after him. When the enemy saw him advancing in this terrible fashion they were seized with sudden panic and immediately dispersed. Tismár Khán returned in triumph. The king was so pleased that he made him his Wazír and gave him his daughter in marriage.

[There is a tale with the same *motif* in Temple's "Wide-awake Stories."—ED.]

125. The Pandit and the Daughter of the Wazir. [61]

There was once a Pandit who devoted his time to the study of divine knowledge (*tatwa gyán*). One day as he was returning from bathing in the Ganges he happened to wander into the garden of the Wazír, where that official's daughter was walking at the time. She asked him who he was, and he told her how he spent his life. She said: "I desire to be instructed in divine knowledge." "This cannot be," said the Pandit, "because if we are seen together our characters will be lost." "No matter," said the girl. "Come to my house at night and I will arrange it." So the Pandit used to visit the daughter of the Wazír and instruct her.

One night the Rája was making his secret rounds at night and he heard talking going on in the house of the Wazír. He listened and heard some one reciting to a woman the love story of Krishna. He was wrath, and when the Pandit came out he seized him and asked him what business he had at night in the Wazír's house. The Pandit said: "I have been doing no harm. You can do with me as you choose." "You must be hanged to-morrow morning," said the Rája. "Is there any one who will stand security for you in the meantime?" "Who can stand bail for me but my parents?" said the Pandit.

The Rája took him to his father and said "Your son is to be hanged to-morrow; will you stand bail for him?" His father said: "He is always wandering about; I cannot stand bail for him." "Is there any one else who will aid you?" asked the Rája. "I have a friend," said the Pandit, "who may perhaps assist me." The Rája took the Pandit to his friend, who at once agreed to be his security. When the Pandit went into the house of his friend the Rája stood outside to hear what they would say. His friend asked him why he had been caught, and the Pandit explained the whole matter. "I do not care," he said, "if I am hanged, but I wish to finish reciting the story of Krishna to the girl before I die."

The Pandit went back to the Wazír's daughter, and when she heard his story she was much distressed. "Had there been more time," she said, "I might have interceded with the Rája for you. But I shall be at the place of execution in the red dress of a boy." Next morning after bathing the Pandit and his friend appeared before the Rája, who sentenced the Pandit to death; but he told the executioners not to hang him until they received further orders from him. Meanwhile the Wazír's daughter rode up to the place of execution in male attire. The Rája said to the Wazír: "Go and enquire who that horseman is." The Wazír returned and told the Rája that it was his own daughter. The Rája said: "As I have no son I adopt this virtuous Pandit as my son. He shall rule the kingdom in my stead, and you must give him your daughter in marriage."

So the Pandit married the daughter of the Wazír and became Rája; and few have ever ruled as virtuously as he ruled.

May Parameswar change our fate as he changed his!

126. The Amir and the Singer.[62]

An Amír was lame, and one day he sent for some singers to perform before him. One of them was blind and pleased him greatly. The Amír asked his name. "My name is Daulat" (wealth), he answered. "Can Daulat be blind?" asked the Amír. "Daulat must have been blind to come and perform before a cripple." The Amír was abashed and hastened to dismiss him with a suitable present.

127. The Amir and the Kathak.[63]

A Kathak once came and sang before an Amír and pleased him greatly. "I have no money about me just now," he said. "But if you care to send carts I could let you have some grain." A few days after the Kathak appeared at the Amír's house with a string of carts. When the Amír saw him he said: "Drive the rascal out. He charmed me with his sweet words and I gave him sweet words in return."

128. The Physician and his Son.[64]

There was once a physician who wished to train up his son to follow his own calling, so he used to take him with him when he went to visit his patients. One day he went to visit a sick man, and noticed some husks of gram under his bed. "Our friend has been eating gram to-day," he remarked. "Yes; that is so," they said. When they came out the boy asked:

"Father, how on earth did you know that the man had been eating gram?" "I saw the husks under his bed, my boy," was his reply.

Next day the boy thought he would go and visit a patient himself. When he went into the room he saw a stick lying under the sick man's bed. "I see," said he, "that our patient has been eating a stick this morning." They asked him how he knew this, and when he told them they made such fun of him that he went home abashed.

129. The Half-married Daughter of the Gardener.[65]

There was once a Rája who had only one son. One day the Prince went into the jungle to hunt and became very thirsty. He came to a well, where he found a Malin drawing water. He asked her for some, but she said:—"I cannot give you this, because it is intended for worship." "Very well," he said. "As sure as I am a Rája's son I will leave you half-married." "And," said she, "as sure as I am a Máli's daughter I will make you pound *kodo*."

When the Prince came home he lay down and covered his face. "I will take no food," said he, "unless you bring my father to me." When the Rája came, the Prince said: "I will neither eat nor drink until I marry the Málin." So the Rája sent for the Máli and proposed that the Prince should marry his daughter. The Máli said that he must first consult his clansmen. "If the Rája," they answered, "will eat and drink with us and promise that the son of the Málin shall be his heir, we have no objection."

The Rája agreed to these terms, and started with his procession. As the bride and bridegroom were moving round the fire, the Prince said: "I must pass the stool in front." On this pretence he got ahead of the bride and ran away, leaving her only half-married, as he had threatened to do. They waited for him for some time, but the girl said: "He will not return. His object has been accomplished." The Rája was much ashamed, and took pity on her and, bringing her to the palace, treated her as if she was his daughter-in-law. She sent out messengers with money to search for her husband.

Meanwhile the Prince had gone to the city of another Rája. The land was then beset by a very fierce tiger, and so much was it dreaded that they used to close the city gates at sunset. The Prince came late and was locked out. The gate-keepers would not admit him. Just then the tiger came up and, after a terrible fight, the Prince killed him with his sword. The gate-keepers were so pleased with his valour that they let him in. It so happened that the Rája of that land died that night, and the people of the land were so pleased with the bravery of the Prince that they made him Rája in his room. For it was the custom that when a Rája of that land died they used to release a hawk and on whosesoever's head he alighted, he was selected Rája. By chance he sat on the head of the Prince, and he was made Rája.

After some time the spies of the Málin traced the Prince, and came back and told her where he was. She was much pleased and rewarded them. Then she collected all the famous dancing-girls of the kingdom and went to the city where her husband was Rája. She gave notice that the Ráni of Singaldíp had come and would give an audience to no one who would not give her a karor of rupees. The Rája's Wazír went to him and said: "It will not be consistent with your Majesty's reputation that you should not visit this Ráni." When he went the Ráni knew him, and smiling said to him "You must visit me daily." She stayed there a month and became in child by him. She started for home, but first she asked for a sign, and he and she exchanged rings.

In due time a son was born to her, and she called the Pandits and asked them what his fortune would be. They said: "The boy will be fortunate, but he will be a thief;" and it was as they said. When he grew up his mother called him and said:—"Your father deserted me after half-marrying me, and I swore that I would make him grind *kodo*. If you succeed in this I shall consider you my son."

The boy went to the city of his father and stayed in the house of an old woman. As he was sitting near a tank four camel-men came up and he heard them say among themselves: "What lovely hair that boy has got." "If you like," he said, "I can make your hair like mine." "If you do," they said, "we will give you a camel as a reward." So he called a barber and told him to shave their heads till he drew blood. Then he told them to put their heads under water and keep them there. "What is your name?" they asked. "My name," said he, "is Fop and-a-half" (Derh Chhail). While they kept their heads underwater he walked off with their camels. They complained to the Rája, who offered a reward for any one who would catch Derh Chhail.

Some of the city Thags agreed to catch him. He put on a splendid dress and rode past their house. They sent out one of their daughters to ask him who he was. He seized her, put her on his horse, rode away with her, and let her go after robbing her of all her jewels.

The Rája then sent the Kotwál to catch him. Derh Chhail got himself up as a woman and went past the Kotwáli. The Kotwál called him in and asked him to sit down. On the wall were hanging handcuffs and fetters. "What are these?" the supposed girl asked. "Show me how you put them on." He did so, and Derh Chhail distributed drugged sweetmeats among the guards. He then tied the Kotwál to the roof of the Kotwáli and went his way.

The Rája himself determined to catch the thief. He rode along the road where Derh Chhail was posted in the disguise of an old woman grinding *kodo*. The Rája asked her if she had seen the thief. She said: "He was here just now and went down that lane. You put on my clothes and grind this *kodo* for me and I will catch him for you." He rode off and the Rája remained pounding *kodo* till the morning, when he returned home.

When the Rája's plans to catch the thief all failed, he made proclamation that if he would give himself up, he would pardon him and reward him richly. Then the thief appeared and showed the Rája the ring which he had given his mother the Málin. "You left my mother half-married," he said, "and she has had a son by you and made you pound *kodo*."

The Rája was ashamed, accepted the boy as his son, and sending for the Málin made her his chief Ráni.

[To gratify the revenge of the Málin the tale diverges into the Master Thief cycle (Clouston: *Book of Sindbad*, 370: *Popular Tales and Fictions*, II, 43). For the ring of recognition see Gubernatis *Zoological Mythology*, I, 55. The most familiar parallel is in *Sakuntala*.]

130. The Elixir of Youth. [66]

A poor old man, who was journeying along by himself, happened to over-take three other travellers who were going in the same direction; so they went along together, and after the usual questions as to where they had come from, and where they were going, and what was their respective business, they walked along. Their way lay through some forest when one of them proposed they should rest awhile in the shade, have a smoke and some refreshment, as he had a little rice with him. The old man was asked to join, to which he readily assented, as he was very hungry. He soon collected some dry sticks by way of making himself useful, and a fire was in a few minutes ready for cooking, the rice was duly boiled, but what was the surprise of every one when they saw that the rice instead of being nice and white was quite black.

The three travellers were much frightened and said they would not partake of black rice, thinking that the old man had brought some kind of poisonous wood from some tree in the jungle; so they resumed their journey, and said they would wait at the first village they came to. The old man said that, as he was very hungry and that he had lived a long life till his hair and beard were white, he would rather die from eating than from hunger: so little by little he finished the rice and then lay down for a short sleep. When he awoke he became aware that his beard, which was before snow-white, had now become quite black, and he felt such renewed energy that he started off at a quick pace and soon came up with his former companions. They did not at first recognise him as his long beard was now as black as a raven and his general appearance was that of a youth, and it was some time before he could convince them that he was the same person. Then they agreed that this change must have taken place through eating the rice, and they at once started off to the spot where they cooked the rice, to see if they could find any of it left; but they were disappointed, as the old man had eaten it all. They went on their way sad to think they had refused the rice.

131. The Two Liars.[67]

Once upon a time a liar set out in search of employment. He came to a city, and put up at a Banya's house. The liar and the Banya began to talk, and the Banya said: "My father was a very rich man and kept pack-bullocks. One day one of the bullocks got galled, so my father left it in the forest to take care of itself. As my father was returning with the laden bullocks he saw this bullock and a pipal tree was growing out of its back. So he at once determined to keep this bullock and sell all the others, which he did: and now he carries all his merchandise, no matter how much it weighs, hanging from the branches of the *pipal* tree, growing on the bullock's back." The liar replied: "I have seen this bullock of yours that has a *pipal* tree growing on his back. My father rented 200 acres of land from a Rája, and my father and I cultivated the land, and in October we sowed wheat in the fields. When the wheat began to grow my father said that there would not be any grain in the ears unless the fields were watered, and how were two men to do it? we must have help; so my father jumped into a tank, and went by a subterranean passage to where the clouds live, and began to beat the clouds. The clouds said: 'Why do you beat us?' My father replied: 'I have sown 200 acres of land in wheat, which wants to be watered: so go and rain in my fields.' The clouds said:

'Very well; we will go.' My father said. ' To ensure a good crop the fields must be watered three times.' The clouds replied: 'All right; we shall rain thrice.' They kept their word, and the crop was better than my father expected.

"Then my father went to your father and sold him all the wheat, which your father took away in sacks hung on the branches of the *pipal* tree that was growing out of the bullock's back. But your father did not pay all the money for the wheat, and he still owes my father 200 rupees, which I have come to recover." The Banya said: "Brother, forgive me, I cannot surpass you in lying."

132. The Virtuous Daughter of the Merchant.[68]

There was once a great merchant who had shops in many cities. One day news came to him that the affairs of one of his shops had fallen into confusion and that if he did not go there in person the whole capital would be lost. So he left his wife and family in charge of the Qázi of the city, who was known to be a man of integrity, and started on his travels. The Qázi used to visit the house of the merchant daily, and one day happening to see the daughter of the merchant, who was a most beautiful girl, he fell in love with her. When she went away, the Qázi said: "To-day there is a feast going on at my house and many girls will be present; I desire that your daughter also will come." "My daughter is as your daughter, and you can take her if you please," replied the merchant's wife.

When the Qázi got the girl quietly to his house, he took her into an inner room and spake to her words of love. "I cannot meet your wishes." she answered, "until you bathe." The Qázi asked her to heat water for his bath, and she did so. Now the Qázi was a physician as well, and in the room were some phials of acid. These the girl poured into his bath water; when he stepped into it he was burnt all over and lost his sight in the bargain. The girl escaped and told all to her mother, who advised her to tell no one.

Some time after when the Qázi recovered from his injuries, he wrote to the merchant and told him that he regretted to inform him that his daughter had lost her character. When the merchant heard this he was sore wroth and sent his son home with orders to take his sister to the jungle and kill her. When her brother took her to the jungle the girl said: "Do not let my innocent blood fall on your head. Leave me here; perchance a wild beast may devour me." He took pity on her and leaving her there went and told his father that he had carried out his orders. She sat down by the bank of a stream, and soon after it so happened that a Prince, who was hunting in the jungle, came there to drink. He asked her why she was sitting there. "I have been left here to die," she answered. "Will you marry me?" he asked; and she agreed and married him on the spot. He put her on his horse, and in due course a son was born to her.

Some time after she wished to visit her father, and her husband sent her off in charge of the Wazír. On the way he fell in love with her, and to avoid his love she was obliged to leave her child and escape by night from her tent. She stayed in a village and worked for her living for some time. She used to go about in maid attire, and one day as she was bathing she began to sing. A Kathak musician, who was passing by, heard her, and said: "A son has been born to the King. If you will join me and sing before him he will give us a great reward." She agreed and went with him before the King, and there she sang her own sad story till the King recognised her, and embracing her recognised her as his wife. Then she told him of the doings of the Qázi and the Wazír, and the King ordered them both to be put to death.

133. *The Foolish Ahír.*

There was once an Ahír, who was a very stupid fellow. One day an invitation came for him from the house of his father-in-law, and his mother was ashamed to allow him to accept it, because he was such a very stupid fellow, and was sure to disgrace the family. But all the neighbours said that he must go; so off he started. On the way he began to think: "What shall I sing when I come to my father-in-law's house?" While he was thus thinking he saw a fox. "Ah! I have learnt one song (*birha*) from him." Next he saw a harrow in a field and said: "I have learnt another from it." And some way on he saw some paddy-birds at a tank, and said: "I have learnt another from them."

When he reached the house where the wedding was going on, his father-in-law received him very kindly, and in the evening, when the procession was about to start, his father-in-law said to him: "We are all going to fetch the bride and there are none but women left in the house. You had better remain behind and see that nothing goes wrong." So the foolish Ahír remained behind to watch the house and the womenfolk.

Now a Chamár had plotted with some other rogues to rob the house that very night, and he came with his drum and began to play for the wedding guests, so that they should not hear his companions cutting the house wall. Then the women get hold of the foolish Ahír, and said: "You must sing us something."

So he began, and sang the song he had learnt from the fox.—

Khat khut kas kihale re!

"Why are you making a sound like *khat khut?*"

By this he meant the noise made by the fox as he scratches the ground, but the thieves thought he heard them cutting the wall. So they stopped their work for a while.

Then he began another song.—

Rendariya tar senhariya.

"Your little hole is under the little castor oil tree."

He was thinking again of the fox, but the thieves thought he saw them digging under the tree which stood behind the house; so they lay quiet.

Then he looked round and saw a box under a bed, and as he could think of nothing else to sing, he sang.—

Khatariya tar pitariya.

"There is a little box under the little bed."

Now it was this very box the thieves were after; so, thinking themselves discovered, they lay quite quiet.

Then he remembered the harrow, and sang:

Henga sa paral báte re.

"You are lying like a harrow."

The thieves were sure he saw them, so they ran away. In the morning the Chamár came to get a share of the booty, but when the thieves saw him they beat him well as the cause of their failure. When the people of the house went out in the morning and saw the hole in the wall, they said: "This fool has been the saving of us after all." And when his father-in-law came back, he said: "You are a very smart fellow," and when he was going home he gave him a fine cow as a present.

134. The Rája and the Snake.[69]

(Should anyone be unlucky enough to sneeze at the commencement of a journey or business undertaking, if the following story is related, it will do away with the evil effects of the sneeze.)

Once upon a time a Rája went out into the forest to shoot. He saw there a Cobra's wife crawling about in company with a little snake called a *Kaurila*. He said: "Why is the wife of so great a snake wandering about in such a manner with a *Kaurila*?"

The Cobra's wife heard this remark and was very angry and ashamed, and went home looking very sad. Her husband asked her what was the matter, and why she was so sad. Then she told him what the Rája had said, saying, "Why should I not be sad when the Rája said such things about me! I would rather die than hear such unbecoming remarks from a man!"

The Cobra could not brook such an insult to his wife, so he went at once to the palace and concealed himself in the Rája's shoe.

The Rája at the time was sitting in Court; and when he had finished he rose to go to the palace. At that moment a man sneezed. The Rája waited for a short time and again rose to go, and as he did so another man sneezed.

The Ráni then asked the Rája if he had been oppressing any poor person that day. The Rája considering the events of the day, said "I have done no harm to anybody; but when I was in the forest this morning I saw a Cobra's wife crawling about with a *Kaurila*, and I said: 'Why is the wife of so great a snake wandering about in such a manner with *Kaurila*.' This is the only unkind act I have committed to-day."

The Cobra on hearing the Rája thus speak, lifted up his head out of the shoe, and said: "Oh, Rája, you have committed a serious offence, no doubt, but as you confess it I will forgive you and return to my house. But don't insult our wives again.' As the snake departed, he added if anyone relates this story at the time it will do away with the evil effects of sneezing.

135. The Prodigal Son.[70]

There was once an Ahír lad whose father died when he was a boy. He had some friends who were employed in other countries, and he too was seized with a fancy for travel. His mother advised him not to go. "My son," said she, "you have plenty at home. Why should you go abroad and serve others, as your father never did?" But he would not attend to her words, and one night he took some of her jewels and went off. He searched in many places for work and found none. At last he had to make a gourd pot and go about begging. As he begged he used to sing this song:

> Khát rahé dúdh bhát,
> Charáwat rahé gaiyya;
> Naukarí kí sádh lagí
> Bhíkh dé maiyya.

"I used in the good old times to eat milk and boiled rice, and feed the cattle, but I longed for service, and now, mother, give me alms."

At last in his travels he came to his own house, and it was so long since he had seen it that he did not recognise it. He saw his wife cleaning the cooking pots at the door, but he did not know her and began to sing:—

> Ghar gaiyya dúi chár lagatu hain; gharhin
>   sundar nárí;
> Chakrí kí sádh lagí; barjat hai mahtárí.

"Two or three cows are milked at home. In the house is a pretty wife. I longed for service and my mother checked me."

When she heard the song she knew her husband and told his mother. She ran out; took the gourd from his hand and smashed it to pieces on the ground. "Now," said she, "you know the fruit of not listening to my words." The Ahír was abashed. He stayed at home for the future and never disobeyed his womenfolk.

136. How the Miserly Banya was Punished.[71]

A respectable Muhammadan gentleman (miyán) had once occasion to make a journey, and was obliged to stop for the night at the house of a miserly Banya, who entertained him in the most wretched way. The Banya and his wife were alone in the house, and when they lay down near the Miyán on the upper story, he began to think how he could pay them off. After a while the Banyáin said to him: "Cannot you tell us a story to make the night go quickly?" "I do know a tale," answered the Miyán; "but it is certain to make you and your husband quarrel." "Never mind," said she, "you must tell it." The Miyán pretended to be sleepy, and said nothing for a while. The Banyáin called out again: "Miyán Sáhib! won't you tell us the story?" He said: "I was very busy thinking of something." "What was it?" she asked. "Well," said he, "I was in the service of a Rája for ten years, and when I was leaving him I got from him two bricks of gold. As I was coming home with them I had to cross the river which runs just behind your house, and I dropped my golden bricks. Now I am thinking that I must get some boatmen to drag the place tomorrow."

The Banya was listening to all this talk, and when he heard of the bricks of gold he thought he would have a try for them himself; so he slipped quietly out of bed and went down to the river to grope about for them. Soon after, the Banyáin got up, too, on the same errand, and when she groped about to wake her husband to come with her, she found he was not in his bed; she asked the Miyán if he knew what had become of him. "Well," said he, "a woman came to him not long ago, and no doubt he went with her." When she heard this, the Banyáin was fiercely enraged and rushed out in search of her husband, abusing him at the top of her voice, so that all the neighbours awoke and heard about his misconduct.

Meanwhile having searched in vain for the golden bricks, the Banya came home wet and miserable. When he came he missed his wife, and asked the Miyán if he knew what had become of her. He said: "Well, not long ago a man came and called her out, and I suppose she has gone away with him." When the Banya heard this terrible news, he too, rushed out of the house, swearing and abusing her until he came to the end of the street, where he met her. There each fell on the other and they half-killed each other before matters could be explained. But before the time for explanation came the Miyán took good care to make himself scarce.

137. The Judgment of Solomon.[72]

Once upon a time there was a woman who had a very beautiful boy. Another woman envied her, and said: "The child is mine." They began to quarrel, and at last came before the King. He called on them to produce witnesses in support of their claims. Both parties produced witnesses in support of their story. The King was at a loss how to decide the matter. Finally, he called a soldier, and said: "Cut the child in two pieces and let each of them take half." On this the woman who was the real mother cried out: "Do not kill the child. Rather let the other woman have it." "The child is yours," said the King. Take it away with you."

[This famous tale (1st Book of Kings, III. 16 *sqq.*) forms the subject of one of the *Jatakas*, or Buddhist Birth Stories (Rhys David's Translation, I, XIV, XVI: XLIV, XLVII). Mr. Jacobs' (Folklore Congress Report, 1891, p. 96) quotes a parallel from Crane; *Italian Popular Tales*, 382.

138. The Thief and the Confectioner.[73]

A thief went one day to the shop of a rich confectioner, and said: "Are these all the sweets you have? I want some specially good ones to-day." "I have some better inside," he said. While he went into the inner room to fetch them the thief carried off his money box. When the confectioner found that he had been robbed, he followed the thief and demanded his money. The thief admitted having the money, but said that it was his own. At last they were both brought before King Akbar.

He said: "Bring some hot water and I will settle the matter." When the water was brought he had the money placed in it, and when some *ghi* rose to the surface, the King at once gave the case against the thief and ordered him to be hanged.

139. The Princess of Karnalpur.

Once upon a time a ship came sailing over the ocean, and the mariners cast anchor close to a city. The son of the Rája of that city happened to be close by, and seeing a princess on the ship fell in love with her. She made a sign to him by rubbing her ears and eyes, and immediately the sailors weighed anchor and departed.

The prince went home, and calling all his father's courtiers asked them to explain the meaning of the signs of the princess. No one could interpret them except a poor shepherd, who said:

"When she rubbed her ears it meant that she comes from the city of Karnálpur, and by rubbing her eyes she meant that the Rája of that city is named Sunetra Sinha[74]." Then the prince asked the shepherd to lead him there; they started and after many days reached Karnálpur. There they put up with a gardener's wife. The old woman asked their business, and when they told her said: "You must conceal yourselves, and represent yourselves as my son-in-law and the shepherd as your servant. If you do this I think you will meet the princess some day or other."

The gardener's wife used daily to take garlands to the princess. One day the prince asked her to allow him to twine a garland. He made a lovely wreath and put a letter inside for the princess.

The princess when she saw the wreath asked who had made it. The gardener's wife said that it was made by her daughter, who had come to pay her a visit.

The princess gave her a present, and as she was going away struck her with an orange branch. When the prince heard this he asked the shepherd what it meant. He said:

"It means that you are to meet her to-night in the garden of oranges."

The prince went there, but fell asleep, and do all she could the princess could not wake him. When she had gone away and he woke in the morning he cursed his folly and consulted the gardener's wife what he should do. She said:

"Make another wreath." The prince made another wreath, which so pleased the princess that she gave the gardener's wife a gold coin, and as she was going away struck her with a lime branch.

When the prince heard this he asked the shepherd what it meant.

"It means that you will meet her in the lime garden."

The prince went there and fell asleep, and again the princess failed to wake him, and went away.

When he told the gardener's wife, she said: "There is no helping you. But you shall have another chance."

The prince made a third wreath, and the princess was so pleased that she gave a gold coin to the old woman and said:

"Bring your daughter to see me tomorrow and you will be well rewarded."

The old woman dressed the prince in woman's clothes and took him to the princess. The princess asked him to sit with her, but he was afraid and sat on the ground. The princess gave him betel and asked the old woman to go home and leave her daughter with her. The prince then stayed with the princess and none of the people of the palace suspected what was going on.

But the Rája, the father of the princess, used to weigh her daily against a flower, and this day she weighed down the flower, and he knew she had a lover.

He proclaimed a reward for any one who would catch him; but no one attempted the task but a wise old woman.

She made a hole in the floor of the princess's room and put some red dye in it, so that the prince when he paid his usual visit fell into it, and his clothes were stained. He went off at once to the old woman's house, and she called a washerman and made him promise to wash the clothes before the morning but he went off next day dressed in the clothes of the prince to a marriage, and the wise old woman recognised him and had him arrested.

He was taken to the Rája and explained how he got the clothes. He was released and the old woman made a mark on the door of the gardener's house so that she might recognize it again.[75] But when the prince noticed the marks he made similar signs on all the houses near, and so the wise woman could not identify the house. Soon after the prince and princess met again in the palace garden, where there was a shrine of Mahádeva. One of the watchmen saw them, and locked them up in the temple, intending to betray them next day to the Rája.

The shepherd missed the prince, and learning where he was determined to save him. So he dressed himself up as a Banya woman and taking an offering of flowers, cakes, and sweetmeats went to the temple and said to the watchmen: "Kindly open the temple, as I desire to worship in pursuance of a vow I made that I would worship if my husband returned safe and sound."

The watchmen with some difficulty let the shepherd in, when he at once changed clothes with the princess, and she escaped in the guise of the Banya's wife. When the Rája came in the morning and saw only two men inside he was wroth and threatened to hang the watchmen.

But they protested that the princess had been in the temple and had escaped in the disguise of the Banya woman, and said to the Rája:

"Let all the men and women of the city pass through the fire and prove their innocence."

The King agreed and all the people assembled. The prince and the shepherd were also present in the guise of ascetics. The Rája ordered that the princess should first undergo the ordeal. Just as she was going into the fire the prince came up to her and caught her hand and said:

"Princess, before you pass into the fire give me an alms."

She did so and called out:

"If I have touched any man but this ascetic may the fire consume me!"

Then she passed through the fire unharmed.

The Rája said: "My daughter is pure and has been falsely accused."

Next day the Rája weighed his daughter again, and again she was heavier than the flower. He knew that something was wrong, so he gave notice that if his daughter's lover would appear of his own accord he would marry him to the princess and give them half his kingdom.

166

The prince then came forward and told him the whole story and explained how he owed it all to the cleverness of the shepherd. The Rája rewarded the shepherd. The lovers were married, and after some time the prince took his bride home, and they lived happily.

May Paramesar do to all of us as He did to them!

[A folktale told by Akbar Sháh Mánjhí of Manbása, Dudhi, Mirzapur District.]

140. *The King and the Evil Spirit.*

Once upon a time a king went into the jungle to hunt. He saw a deer grazing there which had silver ornaments (*ghungrú*) on its feet. The king said: "This must be some one's tame deer which has escaped." Now the deer was really an evil spirit (*khabís*). The King knew not that this was so. He pursued the deer, and it ran into a temple (*mandar*), and then turned into a woman, covered with jewels. She began to weep. The King forgot about the deer, and when he saw the woman asked her why she was weeping. She said that her husband had deserted her. Forthwith they fell in love with each other, and the King asked her if she would go with him. She agreed, and the King stayed all day with her, and in the evening put her on his horse and took her to his palace. When the King used to visit her at night she used to suck out the King's blood, and he became weaker day by day. One day he consulted a noted Faqír, and he advised the King not to keep even a drop of water in the house, and not let the woman know of this. "Ask for water in the night." The King obeyed these instructions. Near morning he asked the woman for water, and she put her hand out of the bed and searched in all the water pots and could find no water. Then she stretched out her hand so that it reached the ocean and brought water from there, which she gave to the King to drink. From that time the King feared her greatly and longed for the dawn. When day broke he called the Faqír and told him what had happened. The Faqír said: "She is not a woman, but an evil spirit (*khabís*); save yourself from her or she will kill you." The King inquired what he was to do. "Make," said the Faqír, "an enormous oven and a cover for it, and heat it well, and then by some trick push her in and fix the cover tight. Thus and thus alone will you save your life." The King did as the Faqír advised, and heated the oven so that it became red, and pushed the woman in. He put on the cover, and she was burnt to ashes, and thus the life of the King was saved.

[A folktale told by Maulvi Karím-ud-dín Ahmad of Mirzapur.]

141. The Faithful Son of the Wazir.

There was once upon a time a Rája, who had an only son, who had as his sworn companion the son of the Wazír. Both of them were married, but for a long time had not visited their wives. So they set off together for this purpose.

When the Prince arrived at his wife's house she received him with much affection, and when it was night he went to the inner room, but he wanted that the Wazír's son should sleep close by behind a curtain. It was the custom of the land when a bride approached her husband that she put on her finest dress and brought in various things as an offering to wave over the head of her lord.[76]

But before she went to him she remembered that she had not given food to the Bábájí.[77] So she took some meat in a dish and with a lamp in her hand went behind the palace where Bábájí lay. When he saw her he cursed her and said:

"Why are you so late in coming?"

"I was attending a guest who has come today."

"Dost thou love him more than me?"

"No, of course you are first of all, and how can I convince you of my love?"

"Bring me his head, and I will be satisfied."

The Wazír's son heard all this. Then she went in, seized her husband's sword, cut off his head and brought it to Bábájí. When he saw her he struck her on the leg with his red-hot pincers and said:

"Evil one: when you are faithless to your husband how can you be true to me?"

She ran back out of her senses with remorse and cried: "The Wazír's son has killed my lord."

He was seized and delivered by the Rája to the hangman. As he was being led away he said:

"The Rája is a wise ruler, but he has no justice in his heart?"

"How so?" asked the Rája.

"Send for the Bábájí and inspect the mark on the leg of the Princess," he said.

So the case was proved against them and both were put to death, and at the request of the Wazír's son he was allowed to take away with him the corpse of the Prince. So he took it to the house of his own wife. There he was received with great honour, and that night, when his wife dressed in her best clothes and taking an offering was about to visit her husband, a jackal howled. The girl put down the dish, blew out the lamp and went into the jungle.

"Why did you interrupt my love?" she asked. The jackal answered:

"Thy husband is grieved to death at the loss of his friend, and if he cannot be restored to life, your husband must die also."

She went back, and coming to her husband asked the cause of his grief. When he told her, she said:

"Cease your grief. I will find a remedy. Bring the corpse of your friend to the tank at the back of the house, and I will give him medicine which will restore his life." The Wazír's son next night brought the corpse to his wife at the tank. She told him to join on the head close to the trunk as it was in life. Then she covered it with a sheet and began to pray to Deví, but she told her husband to go and hide himself in the temple close by. Immediately Deví appeared and said to the girl:

"Why didst thou summon me hither?" She answered: "Mother! I have troubled thee because a servant of thine has died, that thou mayest restore him to life."

Párbatí Deví went at once and stood over the corpse. She cut her little finger and let some of her nectar-like blood fall upon it. She immediately disappeared and the Prince came to life. He embraced the Wazír's son and learnt what had happened. So they returned with the girl to her house, and the Prince offered to marry her sister. When the marriage was over, the Prince and the Wazír's son started for home with their wives.

On the way they rested for the night under a *pípal* tree. The Wazír's son was awake and heard a pair of parrots talking. Now, he was learned in the language of birds. The parrot said to his mate:

"All these people who are resting here will die soon."

"How?" inquired his mate.

"This tree will fall on them and they will be crushed, unless they move away at once. But they will undergo more danger later on. The flood will overtake them, and unless they hasten they will be drowned. And then when they reach the palace the iron lintel of the gate will fall and crush them."

"How can this be avoided?" she asked. "They should make a gateway of flowers and enter the palace beneath that." "And how can they learn this?" she asked. "If any one knows our language he can tell them. But if he disclose the secret he will be turned into stone."

Next morning the Wazír's son selected two horses, fleet of foot, and he and the Prince with their wives mounted them. He made them ride swiftly over the dangerous ground, and just as they passed the flood rose over it. The Prince asked:

"How did you know this?"

But he gave no answer. When they got some distance further the Wazír's son asked the Prince to wait, and he went on ahead and replaced the iron frame of the gate with an arch of flowers. As the Prince entered this fell upon him. He entreated the Wazír's son to disclose the secret of these events. For a longtime he refused to speak. At last he was obliged to disclose the talk of the parrots. Then he was immediately turned into stone.

The Prince paid no need to this and spent his time in idle amusements. At last a daughter was born to him. On this occasion, as the family gods were being worshipped, the Wazír's son in the form of a stone came rolling into the temple. The Prince asked what it was, and the servants told him that it was the son of the Wazír. So he sent for his wife and asked her how her husband could be restored.

"Kill your daughter and drop her blood on him," she said. "Then he will regain his human form, and I promise to restore your daughter's life." This was done. The Wazír's son regained his original form, and his wife by worship of Párvatí restored the child to life. And then they all lived happily.

[A folktale told by Bhawáni Prasád, village accountant of Mirzapur: recorded by Pandit Rám Gharíb Chaubé.

This is the oriental version of the European story of Faithful John. (No. 6. of Grimm's *Household Tales*, who gives numerous European parallels—II., 348, *sq.*) In its Indian form we have it as "the story of the Prince and the merchant's son who saved his life" in Somadeva (Tawney *Katha Sarit Sagara*, I, 253, who compares the story of Víravara in the Hitopadesa and in the Vetálapanchavinsati (chapter 78). This is "Rama and Laxman, or the learned owl" of Miss Frere's *Old Deccan Days*, p. 66, *sq.*]

142. The Princess who would not speak.[78]

There was once a Rája who had a daughter, who would not speak to anybody. Her father was in great trouble about her, and tried many physicians, but no one could do her any good. Then he made proclamation that if anyone could cure her, he should have her hand and half his kingdom. But he added this condition that whoever failed should forfeit his life and goods. No one for a long time would accept the Rája's terms, until at last a young Prince agreed to try. So he had to give a bond accepting the terms of the Rája, and then he was taken into the presence of the Princess.

Now the Prince was a great magician, and without the Princess seeing him, he managed to throw some of his magic powder on the bed on which she lay. Forthwith the bed began to pinch her horribly, and she could restrain herself no longer, and cried out:—

"Why does this bed pinch me so horribly?" "What is the use," said the Prince, "of your trying to keep yourself from speaking, when you cannot even control your own bed?" "I only wish I could burn it," she said.

When the watchmen at the door heard her they struck the big drum once and called out:—"The Princess has spoken." But she would not speak again. Then the Prince said "Whether you speak to anyone else or not, you must speak to me because you have spoken once." But still she said nothing. Then the Prince threw some of his magical powder on the lamp which hung on the wall, and the lamp called out:—"What is the use of troubling about such a fool? She has just spoken to you and now she won't speak again." "I will get you smashed, you lamp," she cried, "If you dare to say another word to me."

The watchmen heard her and gave another blow to the drum, and called out:—

"The Princess has spoken a second time." Then the Prince threw some of his powder on the door, and the door called out:—"She is a fool. Do not trouble about her. She spoke just now and still she won't speak again." "If you dare to address me again," she cried, "I will have you burnt to ashes."

The watchmen beat the drum again, and called out:—"Listen, oh people, the Princess has spoken again." But she would speak no more, and the Prince threw some powder on the window, and the window said:—"Prince, why are you troubling to make her speak? She is surely dumb." "If you say that again," she cried, "I will have you flung upon the dung-hill."

The watchmen struck the drum again, and called out:—"Listen, oh people, the Princess is certainly speaking." Then the old Rája, who was outside all the time, came in and said to the Prince:—"There is no doubt about it. Take her away and marry her straight off, and half my kingdom is yours." So the Princess had to give in, and the Prince married her. And ever after she spoke like anyone else, and they were as happy as their friends could wish them to be.

[In the original the name of the Princess is Anbolí Ráni.—ED.]

143. *The Wise Raja of Harbangpur.*[79]

Once upon a time there was a Rája in the city of Harbangpur, who gained the name of Chaupat or Topsy-turvy.

One day a Guru and his disciple came to the city and, after they had bathed, the Guru sent his disciple to the bazar to buy food. The disciple replied:—"I will go. If the people of the city believe in God (*Thákur*) and religion (*dharm*), I shall soon obtain sufficient alms to support us. Meanwhile, Bábájí! light a fire and smoke your hemp (*gánjá*)."

The disciple went to the bazar and there he saw a green-grocer woman (*kunjrin*) who was calling out:—"Buy vegetables! buy vegetables! only two pice a *ser*!"

When he went on a little further he heard a grain-seller shouting out:—"Who will buy flour, pulse, *ghí*, rice and spices? All two pice a *ser*!"

He was amazed at this, but when he went on a little further he heard a confectioner cry, "Sweets! sweets! every kind of sweets! only two pice a *ser*!"

The disciple asked the merchants:—"Is there not some mistake that everything is offered at the same price?" "No," they answered. "In this city, under the great King Topsy-turvy, everything sells at one price, two pice a *ser*."

The disciple was delighted to hear this, and returned and told the Guru. The Guru answered:—

"My son! you should leave this place. Do you not know the proverb: 'When everything white, be it camphor or cotton, is the same, never stay in such a country.'"[80]

The disciple answered:—"This seems a good city and I will not leave it." "Well, I am going," answered the Guru, "but I will stay in the neighbourhood and watch over your welfare."

So the Guru departed, and the disciple remained in the city, where he rapidly grew fat on the cheap food which he was able to procure in abundance. One day, one of the city watchmen reported to Rája Topsy-turvy that a thief had died owing to the wall of a house in which he was committing a burglary having fallen in upon him.

The Rája ordered the owner of the house to be fetched before him.

"Why," demanded the King. "Did you build the wall of your house so badly, that it fell in and killed the thief?"

"The fault was not mine," he pleaded, "but that of the mason who built the wall." "You can go," said the Rája, "but let the mason be called before me."

When the mason was produced, the Rája asked: "Why did you build the wall so badly, that it fell and crushed the thief?" "Your Majesty!" pleaded the mason, "the fault does not rest with me but with your daughter, who passed by as I was building it, and the tinkling of her anklets so distracted me that I was unable to build the wall properly."

"You can go," said the Rája, "but let my daughter be called before me."

"Why did you distract the attention of the mason and make him build the wall badly, which fell on the thief and crushed him to death?"

"I am not to blame," said the Princess. "The goldsmith is to blame in making such pretty anklets that their jingling distracted the mason."

"You can go," said the Rája, "but let the goldsmith be called before me."

When the goldsmith appeared, the Rája demanded: "Why did you make such pretty anklets for my daughter that their jingling distracted the mason and caused him to build the wall so badly, that it fell on the thief and caused his death?"

The goldsmith answered:—"I am a very thin, weak man. What will you gain by having such a scarecrow as I am executed?"

"All right!" said the Rája, "we must have a fat man hanged. So bring me the fattest man you can find."

The watchman went out and came on the disciple, who by this time had become the fattest man in the city.

"Come along," said the watchman, "to the King and be hanged."

The disciple asked:—"What fault have I committed?" "Bábájí," he said, "you are the fattest man in the city, and for this you are to be executed."

So the disciple, loudly appealing to Thákur (God) for protection, was hauled off to the Rája.

Just then the Guru arrived, and seeing him in this plight, said:— "Why? What is the matter?" "I am about to be hanged simply for being fat. What sort of justice is this?"

"This is the justice of Harbangpur," answered the ascetic. "Did I not tell you that evil would come when everything was sold at two pice a *ser*? Now you must look after yourself."

The disciple said:—"This is the result of neglecting thy words. Now save me!"

"I cannot go with you before the Rája," said the Guru, "but when you are being taken to execution, I will say that they may hang me in your stead. For whoever is hanged to-day will go straight to Swarga (Paradise)."

So as the disciple was being taken to the gallows, the Guru met him and began to dispute with him, saying, "You must hang me." "No," said the disciple, "I am the man to be hanged."

The news of this quarrel reached the ears, of the Rája, and at last he said:—"If this is the lucky hour for being hanged, I will be hanged myself."

And hanged he was in due course, and no one lamented for him.

[The Rája of Harbangpur or Harbongpur is a well known character in Folklore. The word means "the City of Confusion." It has been located on the Ganges at Jhúsi near Allahabad. Sir H. M. Elliot (*Supplemental Glossary, p.* 466, *sq.*) gives various stories of this Rája, and quotes the proverb:—

Andher nagarí, be bújh Rája.
Taka ser bhájl, taka ser khája.
[A blind city, a foolish Rája.
Vegetables and sweets, both a ser for a pice.]

144. The Prince and the Thugs.[81]

There was once a Rája who became tired of the world, and became a Faqír: but this life did not suit him, and at last he took service with a grain-parcher,[82] and used to stoke his oven. There the maid-servants of the Rája of that city came to get their grain parched, and, admiring his beauty, they told the Princess. She asked them to bring him before her, but they said:—"Mahádeví,[83] how can a grain-parcher come into thy presence?" So she went herself in disguise, and when she saw him, fell in love with him: and she used every day to pray to Deví to give her the grain-parcher as her husband. After a year or so the Rája determined to hold the Svayamvara, so that the Princess might make her own selection. When the Princes were assembled, she threw the garland of victory[84] over the Bharbhúnja, and though the Rája was astonished and disgusted, he was obliged to accept him as his son-in-law.

After a time the Princess became in child, and just then her husband received a letter from home, saying, that if he wished to save his kingdom he must hasten there. So he gave the Princess a ruby, a sword, a rupee and a handkerchief, and said: "If your coming child is a son, give him these things, and he will be able to find me, wherever I am, by means of these."

By-and-bye the Princess had a son, and as he grew up, the boys used to taunt him as he had no father. At last he went to his mother, and after much pressing she gave him the things and he started off in search of his father.

On the way he met a man, who asked him where he was going. But the Prince deceived him, and then the man gave him a leaf and half a leaf, and said:—"Make these over to my comrades, who are behind."

The Prince suspected that the leaf meant his ruby and the half his rupee; so when he met the man's comrades he said to them: "Brothers! a man met me on the road and gave me half a leaf for you."

Then these Thugs began to discuss whether they should murder him or not for the sake of a rupee. At last by the advice of a cunning, one-eyed member of the gang, they released the Prince. By-and-bye the Thug who had given the Prince the leaf and the half leaf came up, and when he heard how the boy had deceived him by his cunning, he and his comrades followed in pursuit. The Prince, hearing them coming, buried his property and hung himself from the branch of a tree. The Thugs came up, and believing him dead slashed him with their swords and went away. When they departed, the Prince loosed the rope and came down from the tree. He went on to a city, where an old woman gave him shelter. She went off to search for a *Baid* to attend to him. The Thugs, hearing her enquiry for a physician, said they would treat him and would come at midnight. The Prince heard them and made his escape. The Thugs saw him, but just then the Rája's equipage passed by and the Prince shouted,—"Thug! Thug!" and they ceased to pursue him.

Then the Prince put up in a house opposite to that of the Wazír. The Wazír's daughter used to sit on the roof reading, and she and the Prince soon fell in love, and he used to visit her. Some one told the Wazír, who had the Prince arrested and brought before the Rája, when he was condemned to death. Just as he was going to the scaffold, he remembered the things his mother had given him, which it was useless to conceal any longer, so he made them over to the Rája, who was his father. He was reprieved and acknowledged as son of the Rája, married the Wazír's daughter, and succeeded to the kingdom when the Rája died.

May Parmesar restore our affairs as he restored his!

[This tale combines many familiar incidents:—

(1) That of the forgotten bride and son cycle, of which we have an example in "Núr-al-din Ali and his son, Badr-al-din Hasan (Lady Burton: *Arabian Nights*, Vol. I, p. 172, *sq.*).

(2) The Svayamvara or public choice of a husband, of which numerous instances are quoted by Temple.—*Wideawake Stories*, *p.* 430.

(3) Pretended death. We have this in another of this series "The Four Fools," and compare Tawney (*Katha Sarif Ságara*, Vol. II, p. 109).

(4) Marks of recognition of hero: see reference collected by Temple, *loc cit*, p. 416.

145. The Tale of the Four Foolish Pandits.[84]

There were four Pandits in a village. One was a physician, the second a grammarian, the third a logician, and the fourth an astronomer. The four went to seek employment at the Court of a Rája. When they arrived at his capital, they thought it wise to eat their dinner before they attended on the Rája. They decided to make arrangements for their food, and said to the grammarian: "If you will act as cook, your knowledge of grammar will come of use."

As the physician was skilled in botany, he was asked to purchase the vegetables.

To the logician was entrusted the purchase of the *ghí*, as his skill in argument would aid him in making a good bargain.

The astronomer was asked to select an auspicious time for the meal.

All four accepted the tasks assigned them, and set about doing them.

When the rice began to boil, a sound came out of the pot like *bhad-bhad.*

The grammarian called out "This is not the correct word. It should be *bad-bad.*"[85] So he threw a handful of dust into the pot.

The physician said: "I do not like the vegetables in the market. But there is nothing so good for a man as *nim* leaves."[86] So he bought a lot of them.

The logician purchased some *ghí* in a leaf saucer,[87] and as he was going home he began to think: "Does the *ghí* protect the saucer, or the saucer the *ghí*?"

To remove his doubts he upset the saucer and spilt the *ghí.* So, regretting his folly, he came back empty handed.

The astronomer by his calculations found that the only lucky time for eating was midnight. At midnight the four Pandits sat down to dinner, and finding the food spoilt had to go to bed hungry.

Then the astronomer said:—"This is the only lucky hour to call on the Rája."

They went to the palace, and finding the gates closed made their way in through a drain. By this they dirtied their clothes, so they determined to have a bath. They could find no water, and one said: "The Rája's wife is as pure as mother Ganges. Let us touch her and we shall be cleansed." So they went into the room where the Ráni was asleep with the Rája. The four of them jumped on her, and her screams woke her husband. He had them put under guard. Next morning he heard them, and finding that they were only fools, laughed and dismissed them with a present.

They hired a bullock cart to take home what they had got. On the way the cart began to creak, and the physician said: "I am sure that the wheels are sick." So he felt the axle-box, and finding it hot, said: "This is in strong fever. I must cauterise it."

He applied a hot iron, and the cart and its contents were burnt to ashes. The Rája heard of this, and admiring the skill of the physician, gave them more presents and sent the four fools home in charge of his servants.

146. How Shekh Chilli went to market.[88]

Once upon a time Shekh Chilli said to his mother:

"I have not eaten meat for many days. Give me money, and I will go to the market for meat, onions and turmeric."

When he got the money, he went off to the butcher's shop and bought some meat. As he was carrying it along, a kite swooped down and carried off a piece. When he saw this, Shekh Chilli threw the rest on the road and said:—"O kite! sister of my mother![89] take the rest of the meat to my mother. Tell her to wash it, and say I will be back in a moment with the onions and spice." In a moment the kite carried it all off.

Shekh Chilli came home, and his mother asked to see what he had bought.

"Here are the onions and spice all right. The meat I gave your sister, the kite, to take home."

His mother said:—"You are a fool."

And this was the last time the Shekh was trusted to go marketing.

147. The Fool and the Jamun Fruit.[90]

A man once gave a foolish friend of his some *jamun* fruits,[91] which pleased him much. Next day he thought he would look for some for himself, as his friend told him that they were found under a tree. He searched long in vain, and at last he came across a lot of dung beetles.[92] He began to crunch them, and when they crackled in his mouth, he said:—"You may say *chen* or *men*, but I shall eat you all the same." And eat them he did.

148. The tale of the four drunkards.

There were once four drunkards, one of whom was addicted to spirits, the second to *bhang*, the third to *charas*, and the fourth to opium. They were reduced to great poverty and at last determined to go abroad in search of employment. As they were going along they came across a horse. One of them got up on the neck, the second on the shoulders, the third on the back, while the fourth clung on to the tail. They came to a city and stopped at an inn, but their lamp had no oil; so the first said to the second, "Go and bring oil," and the second passed the message to the third, and the third to the fourth. At last they agreed that they should all lie down and that he that woke first should go and fetch the oil. As opium eaters do not sleep, he lay awake and in the night a dog came and tried to carry away their food. The opium eater who was awake, struck, at the dog with a stick and this made him howl and run away. Hearing the noise, the others woke, and said to the opium eater, "Why don't you go for the oil?" When the lamp was lit they said, "Let us he down again; but we must tie up the horse lest, it be stolen." One said, "What is the use of tying the horse? Let us each hold on to one of his legs while we sleep." So they lay down and the horse, who was hungry, soon managed to get loose. When they woke and missed the horse they made sure it had been stolen. So they said, "Let us take the omens and find out who is the thief." They filled, a *chilam* and one took a pull, and said, "I am sure the thief is black." The second took a smoke, and said, "Yes, he is black and he has only one eye." "That is true," said the third, "and he has a long beard." "Yes." said the fourth, "and his name is Kále Khán."

When they had settled this, they went along the road and by and by they met a man in a palanquin. They stopped him and asked him what his name was. He said that he was a Mahajan and that iris name was Kále Khán. When they looked at him more closely they found that he was black and had a long beard. Then they made sure that he was thief; so they hauled him before the Rája and made complaint against him. The Rája enquired how they came to know that the Mahajan had stolen the horse. Said they, "We discovered it by taking the omens." "Well," said the Rája, "let me see how you take omens." So he got a pomegranate and put it in a box and said, "Now take the omens and tell me what is in this box." They were perplexed, and said, "Great king! Have a *chilam* prepared for us." When the *chilam* was brought, one of them looked at it and said, "It looks to me rather round." "Yes," said the second, "and it is red." "That is true," said the third, "and there are grains (*dana*) in it." "True" said the fourth "and it is a *kali*."[93] When the Rája heard this he was convinced that they had taken the omens aright and he gave judgment against the Mahajan and made him pay for the horse.

[Told by Lalman, Bráhman., and recorded by Amar Nath, Master of the Kas-gunj School, Etah District.]

149. Seeing the world.

There was once a Mahájan who loved the Princess of the land and he used to visit her daily through an underground passage between her house and his. One day the Princess said, "Let us go to foreign lands and see the world." So she dressed herself in male attire and they rode off together. They came to a jungle and found a house where they halted for shelter. There was an old woman in the house and she made some sherbet for them; but she put poison in it. As they were about to drink it, a voice came from the wall which said, "Do not drink it. There is poison in the cup."

As they were going away the old woman tied a bag of gram to the back of the horse on which the Princess was riding and she made a hole in the bag so that the grain fell on the road as they went on. When the nine sons of the old woman, who were Thags, came back, their mother told them and they went in pursuit of the Mahájan and the Princess. The Princess knew that they were being followed; so she kept on the watch, and when they came to a narrow place in the road, as they came up she killed eight of them with her sword. She was going to kill the ninth, but the Mahájan asked her to spare his life. "I will do as you ask," she said, "but you will live to repent it."

They rode on: but the one remaining Thag followed them and put up in the same inn. The Princess feared danger and kept on the watch. When he woke in the night, the Mahájan saw the Thag and challenged him to play at dice. They played for some time, and then the Thag asked his companion for a drink of water. As the Mahájan was stooping over the well, the Thag, pushed him in. Then he went and stood over the Princess with his drawn sword. "My time is come for taking my revenge," he said. "What is the good of killing me?" she asked. "Let me be your wife and servant." So they rode off together and they had not gone far when the Princess from behind cut him down with her sword. Then she went back to the inn and fastening the horse ropes together she pulled the Mahajan out of the well. "I think you and I have seen enough of the world now," said she. So they went home, were married, and lived happily for many years.

[Told by Sukhdeo, Gaur Bráhman, of Ramaipatti, Mirzapur.]

150. *The Virtue of Raja Rupa Angad.*

Of all the Rajas of the world the most virtuous was Raja Rupa Angad. One day a Vimána, or magic chariot of the gods, came down into his garden, and after collecting flowers went back to heaven again. The Vimána distributed the flowers among all the fairies of the court of Raja Indra and came down again next day and began to collect flowers. But the gardener of Raja Rupa Angad was displeased at this, and lighted a fire so that the smoke touched the heavenly chariot, and when the fairies with their flowers tried to ascend to heaven, it could not rise because it was defiled.

Then the fairies who came with it went to the Raja and complained that they used daily to come to his garden to collect flowers, but that now their chariot would not move. The Raja asked the fairies if they could explain why their chariot did not move as usual. They answered that they believed it was because his gardeners had lighted a fire and defiled it with the smoke. The Raja asked how it could be made to move. The fairies said: "If any man in your Majesty's city has kept the fast of the Eleventh regularly month by month he can make our chariot move."

The Raja had search made throughout the city, but none could be found who had kept the fast save one Dhobi. The Dhobi was brought before the Raja, who asked him how he came to keep the fast. The Dhobi replied: "On that day I had a quarrel with my wife and therefore I abstained from food."

Then the Raja took the Dhobi to the fairies and said that this was a man who had fasted on the eleventh day. The fairies told the Dhobi to bathe and then to touch the chariot: when he did so the chariot moved and ascended to heaven. The Raja was astounded to witness the virtue of the eleventh day fast. So he made proclamation throughout the kingdom that all his subjects on pain of death were to keep the fast. All his subjects then obeyed his order, and when their lives were ended they were caught up to heaven in a Vimána: but the end was that Hell the pit of worms (kiragar) was empty. Then Raja Indra, the Lord of Heaven, was sore afraid lest Raja Rupa Angad through the virtue of the piety should take possession of his kingdom; so he sent down a fairy from heaven to divert him from his works of piety. The fairy came down to earth and seated herself in a swing in the jungle where the Raja used to go a hunting every day. One day the Raja saw her and fell in love with her. He went up to her and asked her whose daughter she was and why she had come into the jungle. She replied: "I know not who my parents are, and I live alone in this jungle, but if any one would protect me I would live with him." The Raja said: "Will you come with me, if I take you with me?"

So the fairy went with the Raja, and then she said to him: "On one condition only will I live with you, and that is, you must either cutoff your son's head, or give up fasting on the eleventh day." The Raja agreed to her conditions and the fairy went home with him. When they arrived near the Raja's palace, the Raja happened to crush a lizard under his feet on the road, and the lizard was at once turned into a beautiful maiden. The fairy asked her: "For what sin were you turned into a lizard?" The maiden answered: "In my former life I had seven co-wives, and I was most beloved by my husband. Sometime after my husband insulted me and I poisoned him. For this sin I was born in this life as a lizard. As Raja Rupa Angad is the most pious of mankind, his touch has restored me to my human shape again."

When she heard this the fairy was still more desirous of turning him from the path of virtue. So she went with him to his palace, and he said to his elder Rani:

"I have brought home a very beautiful fairy. She will live with me only on condition that you give her the head of our son, or give up the eleventh day fast."

The Ráni replied:

"Take the head of our son if you will and put an end to your race, but I will not give up the eleventh day fast."

The Rája then called his son and said:

"You must either give your head, or surrender the eleventh day fast." The boy replied:

"Father, give my head to the fairy. Do not give up fasting on the eleventh day. If you maintain your virtue (*dharma*) you will have sons and daughters, but if you lose your virtue you can never recover it again."

The Rája then told the Rani to plaster a sacred square (*chauka*) on the ground and made his son to stand within it. With his own hand he cut off the head of his son by a single stroke of his sword. The Rani received the head of her son in her garment. When this was done, the fairy consented to live with the Raja, but she said:

"I can never truly love you until you eat the flesh of your son." So the Rája had some of the flesh prepared and as he was about to taste it, Bhagwán appeared from heaven and seizing his hand said: "My son, you have done well, ask for any boon you desire." Then the Rája said:

"Restore my son to life and maintain my virtue."

Then his son stood at once before the Rája, and Bhagwán disappeared. The fairy was put to shame and returned to the king of the gods without effecting her purpose.

[A folk-tale told by Akbar Sháh, Mánjhi, of Manbasa, Dudhi, Mirzapur.]

[We have here again as in others of these tales, traditions of cannibalism among the Mánjhis.]

151. How the banya baffled the robbers.

Once upon a time a Banya was going about on business and fell among thieves. When he found out who his companions were, he began to think how he could get out of their clutches. So he climbed up a tree and began to break some of the dry branches. They asked him what he was doing. "In my town," he said, "wood is so scarce that every scrap sells for two annas." The thieves, knowing that the Banya had very little money about him, thought that they would do better by selling wood than by robbing him; so they all fell to and collected a large bundle.

When they got to the town the Banya said, "Brethren, I am very sorry to hear that since I went away wood has fallen to two pice a bundle." "You rascal," said they, "we will pay you off before long." The Banya knew that they would come soon and rob him; so one night he was awake and he heard them outside. Then he whispered to his wife so that the thieves could hear him, "Did you bring in the bag of gold which I tied on the *nim* tree in the yard?" "No," said she, "it must be there still." "Then we are ruined," was his reply. When the thieves heard this, they at once climbed up the tree, when they touched a large wasp's nest, which they did not see in the dark. The wasps came out and stung them, so that they were hard put to make their escape.

(Told by Pyare Lal, a teacher in the High School, Mainpuri.)

152. Kali Das and his Parrot.

There was once a foolish Rája who kept fourteen Pandits in his court. It so happened that the celebrated Kali Das came to the Rája's court and the other Pandits were jealous of him. The Rája, in order to try his powers, put to him this question:— "My favourite cow and mare are both about to be delivered. State when their offspring will be born and what they will be." Kali Das naming the time said:—"The cow will have a calf and the mare a foal." In due time the animals were delivered; but in order to disgrace Kali Das the Pandits had them blindfolded at the time of birth and they put the foal beside the cow and the calf beside the mare and each animal adopted the young of the other as its own.

When the foolish Rája was convinced that the prediction of Kali Das was false he had him put in prison as an impostor. Now Kali Das had a favourite parrot which he loved exceedingly. When his master did not return, the parrot spoke to the wife of Kali Das and asked her what had become of her husband. She answered: "He has gone to the Rája's court and has not returned." The parrot replied, "I suspect that some evil may have befallen him. Take some charcoal, mix it in water and blacken my wings." The lady did so and the parrot flew off and sat upon the roof of the palace and went on calling "*Radha Krishna! Radha Krishna.*" When the Rája saw the bird he said to his Pandits: "I see a bird of the shape and voice of a parrot, but his feathers are as black as those of a crow. What is the explanation of this?" The Pandits were nonplussed; at last they said "Maharája! You had better ask the parrot." So the Rája asked the parrot to explain his case and the parrot said: "When the ocean took fire I was flying about near it and I so pitied the miserable fish that I tried to put out the fire and my wings got blackened by the smoke." "When did anyone hear of the ocean getting on fire?" asked the Pandits. "That was the same time," answered the parrot "when the cow was delivered of the foal and the mare of the calf."

When the Rája understood the parrot's meaning, he became conscious of his folly and, after disgracing his Pandits he released Kali Das from prison and dismissed him with a handsome present.

(Told by Shiu Sahai, Teacher of the Village School of Dagarhi Chakeri, Etah District.)

153. The Boy and the Monkey.

There was once a poor cultivator who died leaving an only son and he and his mother fell into poverty. One day the boy said to his mother, "Give me five rupees and I will buy a cow and then we can live comfortably." His mother gave him the money and he went to the bazar and there he saw a man selling a monkey. He bought it for five rupees and when he brought it home he called out to his mother: "Mother fix a peg in the yard." She thought he had brought the cow and was very angry when she saw the monkey. She was about to wring its neck, but the monkey said: "Spare my life and I will do you good service." She let the monkey loose and he ran off to the jungle and soon came back with a lot of fruits and in this way he used to bring them food every day.

One day he went out and sat on a tree near a tank and just then a jeweller came to bathe. He put down his bundle on the bank and, when he was in the water, the monkey came down and seizing it, brought it home. The bag was full of valuable jewels and the boy and his mother became rich and the monkey supported them for many years.

(Told by Iqbal Husen, Weaver of Bhuili, Mirzapur.)

154. The Metamorphosis of Raja Vikramaditya.

Once upon a time Rája Vikramaditya was reading with a Pandit the *Pinda Pravesha Vidya,* or the science by which a man acquires the power of entering the body of another person or beast. His servant, who was sitting outside the door, was listening and heard as much as the Rája. When the Rája was returning home the servant asked the Rája what he had been learning from the Pandit. The Rája answered: "If you bring me the body of an animal I will show you." The servant killed a parrot and brought the body to the Rája who immediately repeated the *mantras* and entered into it. When the servant saw this he cut his own body into pieces and tried to kill the parrot too, but it flew away. Then he went to the capital and giving himself out to be the Rája sat upon his throne. He issued orders that every parrot in the kingdom should be killed and offered a large reward for every one that was brought to him. One day it so happened that the parrot whose body the real Rája was occupying was caught in a snare and he at once asked the fowler what he intended to do with him. The fowler said that he was going to take him to the Rája and claim the reward. The parrot answered: "If you take me to the Rája you will get only a small reward. If you take me to the father-in-law of Rája Vikramaditya I will get you five hundred rupees." The fowler agreed and took the Rája in his parrot form to Rája Vikramaditya's father in-law. The old Rája asked him what he had brought and he showed the parrot. The old Rája asked the price and he said: "Ask the parrot and he will fix the price." The parrot when he was asked, said: "My price is five hundred rupees." "What can you do that you fix your price at so large a sum?" he enquired. The parrot answered: "O Maharaja! I can decide disputes and interpret the Shastras." So the old Rája bought the parrot and hung it up in a cage in his court and the parrot used to read Sanskrit and help the old Rája in deciding cases that came before him. The old Rája was much pleased with him and thought that he had got him very cheap.

Meanwhile the servant in the form of Vikramaditya went into the royal apartments and talked with the Ráni. She was surprised to hear his rude and unpolished conversation. She thought he was out of his senses and sending for the jailer had him shut up as a madman. It so happened that there lived in that kingdom a Bráhman and his wife. They lived by begging, but they got so little that they were almost starving and one day the Bráhman said to his wife: "We cannot live in this way. I am going into the Tarai on a begging excursion." His wife agreed and he started. No sooner had he left the village than a *Deo* who lived in a grove close by assumed the form of the Bráhman and went into his house. His wife was very much surprised to see a man whom she believed to be her husband returning so soon and he said: "What is written in my fate for me to get I shall get here as well as baroad. I am not going to the Tarai after all." She answered: "You have done well. Stay at home." So the *Deo* lived in the Bráhman's house and after some time when the Bráhman came home he was astonished to see a man just like himself sitting there. When the *Deo* saw the Bráhman he rushed at him with a club and the Bráhman began to fight him. The woman could not make out what was the matter when she saw two men of exactly similar appearance fighting about her. The villagers came up and asked what the quarrel was about. The *Deo* said "Help me brethren! Do you not see that this shameless ruffian has forced his way into my house?" The Bráhman said: "Don't you recognise me, neighbours?" The villagers said: "In appearance you are both exactly the same. We cannot judge between you." The parties then went to thirty-five villages, but they could find no one to decide their case. At last they went to the father-in-law of Vikramaditya. He asked the woman which of the men was her husband. She pointed to the *Deo* and said that he was her husband, that the other man was some impostor or other. The Rája then gave her over to the *Deo*. As he was going away the Bráhman called out: "O Bhágwan! Are you asleep and has justice perished out of the earth?" Then Vikramaditya in the form of the parrot called out: "You have decided the case wrongly. Call them back and I will decide the matter myself." The Rája did so, and then the parrot called for an earthenware vessel with a spout (*karua*) and a piece of yellow cloth and a thread. He put these things in the middle of the court, and said: "Whichever of you two will enter this vessel by the spout and come back the same way he shall be deemed the owner of the woman." The Bráhman said: "I would rather lose her altogether than undergo this ordeal." But the *Deo* agreed to make the attempt and when he entered the vessel the parrot shouted to the Rája's men to cover the vessel with the yellow cloth and to tie round it a thread of raw cotton. Then he said: "This is an evil-minded *Deo;* bury him in the earth that he may never arise again to trouble the land."

All were amazed at the wisdom of the parrot; and a few days after the wife of Vikramaditya heard of the case and sent for the Bráhman to find out how it was decided. When she heard the story, as she was learned in the sciences, she at once came to the conclusion that the parrot could be no other than her husband Vikramaditya. So she determined to go to her father's house, and when she met him he told her to ask any boon she pleased. She asked for the parrot, but he was too fond of him to give him away and he refused her request. But she sat *dharna* at the palace gates, and when he found that her life was in danger he sent for her. She asked him to whom he had married her. "To Vikramaditya, of course," he answered. "And where is Vikramaditya?" she asked. "In his kingdom, of course," he replied. "You had better ask your parrot," she said. When the cage was brought down the parrot said: "I am Rája Vikramaditya." Then he told them the whole story and the old Rája gave the parrot to his daughter and she took him back to the palace.

She asked him what he had been studying for so long a time with the Pandit and he told her what he had learnt. She sent for the false Rája and addresing him affectionately, said: "What did your Majesty learn from the Pandit?" He said: "Bring me the body of a lamb and I will show you." When the lamb was brought, the false Rája at once transferred his soul into it. The Ráni opened the cage at once and Vikramaditya came out, dropped his parrot form and entered his own body. Immediately he cut the lamb in pieces and the false servant died too. After this Vikramaditya and his Ráni lived for many years in the utmost happiness.

(Told by Devi Datt Dubé Bráhman, of Hariya, Basti District, and recorded by the Head Master, High School, Aligarh.)

[These animal transformations are, of course, common. We have an instance in the myth of Circe. In the Golden Ass of Apuleius Pamphile becomes an owl and Apuleius who wants to follow her is changed by mistake by Fotis into an ass. The demon shut up in a vessel appears in the "Fisherman and the Genii" of the *Arabian Nights* (Lady Burton's Edition I, 33 sqq.) Even now-a-days it is firmly believed that demons can be enclosed with a yellow cloth and a piece of raw cotton string.—ED.]

155. *The Greedy Bráhman.*

There was once a Bráhman who was so greedy that whenever he was going out to a dinner at the house of one of his clients he used to tell his wife to make his bed ready and when he came home surfeited he used to throw himself upon it and lie there for a couple of days till he worked off his indigestion. One day as he was going off to a dinner he did not as usual give his wife instructions about his bed and she began to laugh. When he noticed this he asked her why she was laughing. She said that she was laughing because he had given no orders about his bed. "To-day," said he, "I am going to have an extra good dinner and in any case I shall have to be brought home on a bed, so there is no need of arranging one for me."

He went to the dinner and there he ate so many sweetmeats that he became senseless and the people seeing him in this condition put him on a bed and brought him home to his wife. When she saw him, she went off to the grocer and bought two seeds of the myrobalan (*harra*) and asked her husband to take them. "What a fool you must think me," said he. "If I had room for two myrabolan seeds don't you think I would not have eaten two more sweetmeats?" And with that he died and no one lamented him.

[Told by Abul Hasan Khan, Teacher, Karaili Village School, Pilibhit.]

156. *The Lesson of the Sadhu.*

There was once a Rája whose habit was whenever a Sadhu came to him for alms he used to put to him this question: "Which is better, the life of the householder or that of the ascetic?" If he answered "The ascetic's life is better," he would say: "Then why do you come to the house of a house-holder?" But if he said "The life of the house holder is the better," he would answer: "Then why have you become an ascetic?" In this way he confounded all the Sadhus who came to him for alms.

After many days a Sadhu came to the Rája. The Rája put the usual questions to him and he said: "First give food and then I will give an answer." When he had eaten, he was again brought before the Rája, who called on him to solve the difficulty. The Sadhu answered: "Maharaj! You need not seek an answer from me. To-morrow early ride towards the south and go on riding up to noon; then your question will be answered."

The Rája was so anxious to test the words of the Sadhu that he lay awake all night and longed for the dawn. Then he mounted his horse and rode steadily on towards the south until noon; but he met no man who could answer his question. When it was noon he angrily turned back thinking that the Sadhu had deceived him. As he was returning he lost his way and came into a very thick forest. He tied his horse to a tree and sat down and there he remained the whole day and night without food or water. He feared an attack from wild beasts; so he collected some dry leaves and with his sword and a bit of flint he managed to strike a light and made a fire. Just then a pair of birds came and perched on the tree beneath which the Rája lay. The male bird said to the female: "You see that this man, who is a worthy prince, is dying of hunger. You know that we are all mortal and this body of our's will soon be reduced to ashes and be of no use to any one. If you agree I will throw myself into this fire and this man who is an eater of flesh will be saved." The female replied: "As a virtuous wife I cannot prevent you from doing an act of piety. You can do as seems fit to you." The male bird then threw himself into the fire and was roasted and the Rája ate his flesh. Then the female bird thought within herself: "My husband has devoted his life to perform an act of the greatest piety. I am left a widow and for me life is now unendurable. I had better follow the example of my husband and help to save this man's life." With these words she too threw herself into the fire and was roasted and the Rája ate her flesh.

By this food the Rája's strength revived and he managed to ascend the tree, from the top of which he saw a city which he reached in a few hours. There he saw a number of men assembled round a cauldron by which a woman was sitting. The Rája asked the cause of this assemblage and they said: "This woman has vowed that she will be his who passes through a cauldron of boiling oil for her sake." When the Rája saw her he was enamoured of her beauty and he told her that he was a Rája and that if she would agree to go with him he would keep her in the greatest comfort. But she said "I care not whether you are prince or peasant, I will go only with that man who passes through the ordeal for my sake." The Rája feared to undergo the terrible test; but he was so fascinated that he could not leave the place. Meanwhile a Sadhu appeared and when he heard the conditions he at once plunged into the cauldron and passed through. The woman immediately started with him.

As the Sadhu was taking her away with him, the Rája followed him. The Sadhu asked him why he did so. The Rája replied: "I am a Rája; you are a Sadhu; what use have you for this woman? Give her to me." The Sadhu asked the woman if she was ready to go with him." She answered: "I am your property, you can dispose of me as you please." The Sadhu gave the woman to the Rája and he took her home with him.

When he returned he sent for the Sadhu to whom he had originally propounded the question and called on him for the answer. Then the Sadhu made him describe all that had happened to him. Then the Sadhu said: "The pair of birds which gave their lives for you represent the house-holders among men and the Sadhu, who gave you this woman, notwithstanding all she had cost him, was an ascetic of the highest type. If a house-holder is charitable as these birds were, he need not covet the life of the ascetic; and the true ascetic is as free from covetousness as was that man. If all house-holders and ascetics are like these examples they are both equal." The Rája was satisfied and laid his forehead at the feet of the Sadhu. The Sadhu dismissed him with a blessing.

(A folktale told by Ram Lal, Banya, of Mirzapur.)

157. Banke Chhail and his Wife.

There was once a Musalman whose wife was such a shrew that every morning she used to give him a sound beating with her slipper. She had a daughter and when she grew up her parents were on the lookout for a husband for her; but the temper of her mother was so well known that no one would dare to marry into such a family. Finally one day a notorious character, who was known as Banke Chhail, or "the cunning rascal," came and proposed for the girl, and her father was so glad to settle her in life that he agreed to the match at once and they were married.

Before the ceremony took place Banke Chhail bought a parrot, a cat and a dog, and when he was taking his bride home he brought his animals with him. On the way the pair sat down at a well to rest and a number of village curs came out and began to bark at Banke Chhail's dog. His dog barked at them in return and his master, drawing his sword, cut off his head at a single stroke. "You rascal," said he, "do you dare to bark without my leave?" This astonished his wife; but they went on a little farther and as the morning broke the birds in the trees began to sing and when the parrot heard them it too commenced to chatter. Banke Chhail at once pulled it out of the cage and wrung its neck. "You fool," said he, "you did not remember that you belonged to Banke Chhail and you dared to open your mouth without his orders."

His wife was still more surprised, but she said nothing and they went on. They sat down to rest in a garden and soon a rat appeared. Banke Chhail called to his cat and said: "Catch me that rat." The cat at once obeyed his orders and killed it. When his wife saw this she began to think to herself "What a terrible husband I have got. It would be well for me to obey him." And when they reached home she found it to be her interest to obey him in all things and became a very loving and obedient wife; so much so that when some time after her father came to pay him a visit, she looked out through a chink in the door and was afraid to admit him without the leave of her husband. By and by Banke Chhail came home and said to her: "Your respected father his waiting at the door. Why did you not let him in?" "How could I do so without your leave?" she answered.

Then Banke Chhail went out and brought the old man in. When he saw how changed his daughter, was, he said to his son-in-law: "You know what a life my wife leads me. I wish you would tell me how you have succeeded in reducing your wife to order. Perhaps I may be able to deal with my wife in the same way." Said Banke Chhail: "Good, Sir, bring a brick and some moist clay and make me a lamp saucer out of each." "It is easy quoth the old man to mould the soft clay, but when the clay gets hard no power on earth would mould it."

"In short," said Banke Chhail, "your wife's character is fixed and cannot be mended. I dealt with my wife in season and you see the result." The old man went home sorrowful.

[Told by Madho Prashad, Khattri, of Mirzapur.]

158. The Magic Boat.

Once upon a time a rich man fell into poverty, and, leaving his wife and children at home, went into a foreign land to make his living. One day his wife was sitting at her door, lamenting the hardness of her fate, when a Sádhu passed by and asked her the cause of her trouble. She told him all her circumstances, and he then gave her a boat, and said: "The virtue of this boat is this. It will give you all you ask of it; but when it gives you one rupee it will give your neighbours two." She was much pleased, and when the Sádhu went away, she began to ask the boat for large sums of money, which it always gave her; but as much as she got, her neighbours always got double.

After a time her husband came back with a considerable sum of money which he had made. When he found all the neighbours, whom he had left in poverty, much richer than himself, he was amazed, and asked his wife how they had managed to get rich without ever leaving the village in which they were born. She then told him about the magic boat which always gave her neighbours double what it gave to her. When he heard this he was overcome by envy, and said "This was an evil gift you received from the Sádhu." So he took the boat, plastered a piece of ground, and placed the boat within it. He then implored the boat to burn one of his houses. It did so, and at the same time burned down two houses of each of his neighbours. Then he asked the boat to make a well in his court-yard. This was done: and there were two wells in each of the courtyards of his neighbours. Then he implored the boat to deprive him of one of his eyes, and if he became one-eyed all his neighbours became totally blind and began to fall into their wells.

Then they all came and begged him to restore their sight. But he said: "All the time you were making heaps of money out of my boat, you never gave me a share. Now I have made you blind and I will not restore your sight until you promise to give me half of all you make by me." So they had to agree, and then he asked the boat to restore him his eye, where-upon all his neighbours recovered their sight.

(A folktale told by Mukund Lál, Káyasth; of Mirzapur.)

159. The Brahman and the Sadhu.

There was once a Bráhman who had two sons, and as he was very poor he went with them into another land in search of a living. One evening he reached the hut of a Sádhu and halted there. The Bráhman told him all his troubles, and, as he had no disciple, the Sádhu offered to adopt one of the boys. So he gave the Bráhman a considerable sum of money and told him to go home leaving the boys with him; that he would educate the boys and, selecting one as his disciple, would return him the other. The Bráhman agreed, and, leaving the boys with the Sádhu, went home.

One day the Bába called the boys and ordered them each to bring him a *lota* full of hoar-frost. One of them, who was very industrious, some-how or other collected a *lota* full of hoar-frost from the grass and leaves.

The other, who was an idle fellow, went to the tank and filled his *lota* full of water. The Bába put both the *lotas* out in the sun, and soon discovered, which held the hoar-frost and which the water. So he dressed the idle boy in fine clothes and began to educate his diligent brother. After a time this boy became deeply skilled in magic.

Some years passed and the Bráhman returned to the Sádhu, who was away at the time. The magician boy told his father that he had better ask the Bába for him rather than for his ignorant brother. When the Bába came back he told the Bráhman to choose one of the boys; he chose the boy who knew magic. The Bába was bound by his promise, and though he tried to induce the Bráhman to take the other boy, he was obliged at last to give him up.

The Bráhman and his son started for home, and on the way the boy said: "Father, I am about to transform myself into a lamb. You can sell me; but mind do not give any one, who buys me, the halter." When he said this the boy was changed into a lamb, which a man bought from the Bráhman for a large sum of money. The Bráhman went his way and very soon his son stood before him in his original form. The Bráhman was delighted to see him, and the boy said "Father, I will now turn myself into a horse. You can sell me for two thousand rupees; but mind you do not give away the halter with me." As the Bráhman was trying to sell the horse the Bába came up in disguise and asked him what the price of the animal was. The Bráhman asked two thousand rupees, which the Bába at once gave, but the Bráhman forgot his son's warning and let him have the halter in the bargain. The Bába rode off to his hermitage on the horse and tied it to a post; but he took care never to take off the rein. He knew that if he did so the horse would die.

One day it so happened that the Bába was away and the other boy took the horse to water at the tank, and in his ignorance took off the rein. Then the horse instantly died. When the Bába returned and found out what had happened, he consulted his books and learned that the boy had been transformed, and was a fish in the tank. So he turned himself into a heron and began to search for him. The boy immediately became a parrot and flew away. The Bába turned himself into a hawk and pursued him. The boy then became a diamond necklace and hung himself round the neck of a Ráni. The Bába turned himself into a dancer and appeared before the Ráni. The Ráni was so pleased that she gave him the necklace. 'The boy then became a pile of mustard and the Bába became a pigeon and began to pick it up. The boy turned himself into a cat and devoured the pigeon.

Then he went back to his father and they lived happily ever after.

(A folktale told by Muníswar Prasád Tiwári, Bráhman of Gajádharpur, Gházipur.)

160. *How the Raja went to the Heaven of Bhagwán.*

There was once a Rája who thought himself the lord of the whole world. One day his son, who was blessed with great wisdom, asked him what he was always thinking about. The Rája said that he was always thinking of conquering the whole world. His son said: "That is well, but there are four duties of a King—devotion, protection of his subjects, justice, and the increase of his kingdom. Out of the four you practise only one." The Rája said: "You are right. I have done the first three, but I have never thought of the last. I am now an old man and I intend to pass the remainder of my days in devotion." So saying the Rája seated his son on his throne and began to wander about the world as a Sádhu.

Wandering through many lands, at length he came to a forest; and when any one asked him where he was going, he used to say: "I am going in search of Bhagwán." They laughed at him, and said: "You cannot find Bhagwán unless you keep tlhe company of ascetics." So he set out in search of ascetics, and at last he came to the Himálaya, where he found a Sannyási sitting absorbed in devotion. The Rája sat long before him, but the Saint paid no heed to him. He used daily to clean the place where the Sannyási lay. After many days the Saint opened his eyes and asked the Rája what he desired. The Rája said; "I am seeking for Bhagwán." The Sannyási answered: "For many years I have been concentrating my thoughts on the Creator (*Karta*) of all things, and have failed to find Him. How can you find Him in a single day? But I will give you a *mantra* which you must repeat morn and evening, and, if possible, at all times. Perchance some day you may find Him."

After he recited the *mantra* the Sannyási again became absorbed in his meditations, and the Rája went on repeating the *mantra* constantly. Many days passed, and the Sannyási again came to his senses and, finding the Rája still there, was much pleased. Then the Sannyási said: "I give you this cup. Whenever you ask it for anything it will give it. Now go away, repeat the *mantra* for twelve years and then return to me."

The Rája taking the cup went to a city and sat beside a well. He went on constantly repeating the *mantra* and earned his living by sewing. But he never asked the cup for anything. One day it so happened that the Rája when returning from hunting came to the place where his father lay. When he knew him he fell on his face before him and said: "Father, return with me to your palace. The life of an ascetic is very hard. How can you, who have always been giving orders to others, beg your bread?" The Rája answered: "My son, I am more happy than you are. You may give an order which is not obeyed, but even the fish of the, water and the birds of the air are ready to do my bidding. If you do not believe me, follow me to the bank of this tank." Then he led his son to the water's edge and throwing his needle in asked his son to bring it out. The Prince searched for it, but in vain. Then the Rája called a fish and ordered it to bring it out. The fish at once obeyed his order and laid the needle before him. Seeing this the Prince said: "Father, I will accompany you." The Rája reasoned long with him, and induced him to return home.

The Rája went into a forest and met another Sannyási. He was then absorbed in devotion, and the Rája remained standing before him. When the Sannyási opened his eyes he asked the Rája what he wished. The Rája said: "I wish to see Bhagwán." The Sannyási said: "Go and sit under that tree. Perchance you may see Him there sooner than elsewhere." The Rája went and sat under the tree and began to recite the *mantra*, which the first Sannyási had taught him. One day he saw an enormous tiger running towards the tree. The Rája went to the Sannyási and told him what he had seen. The Sannyási said: "You fool! the tiger from which you foolishly tried to escape was Bhagwán whom you were seeking."

When twelve years passed the Rája and the Sannyási went to the Saint whose dwelling was on the Himálaya. He was glad to see them, and said: "Let us now ascend to heaven." Then a heavenly chariot appeared, and the three took their seats on it. When they had gone some distance the Rája saw his own palace and thought to himself: "Why did I not enjoy the pleasure of living there some time longer?" No sooner did this thought come into his mind than he fell down from the chariot and was reborn in the family of a boatman (*Mallah*). When he came to be fourteen years of age he thought of the *mantra* which he used to recite, and he began to repeat it. When he had repeated it for twelve years a voice came from heaven: "Fool! thou didst all but gain thy desires and lost it again through love of this world. You have won it again by your devotion. The chariot will again appear. Beware! lest you lose the fruit of your piety by low desires." The chariot appeared and on it the Rája ascended to heaven.

(A folktale told by Mukund Lal, Káyasth, of Mirzapur).

161. The Parrot and the Guru.

There was once a banker who taught his parrot the speech of men. One day it so happened that a Sadhu passed by where the cage of the parrot was hanging and as he came near the parrot said: "Salám Maháráj!" The Sadhu looked round in every direction and tried to see who had saluted him. The parrot said: "It was I saluted you. Maháráj: you point out to all men the way which leads from this world of sorrow to the region of eternal peace. May it please you to explain to me the means whereby I may escape from this cage." The Sadhu answered: "Let me consult my Guru and then I will reply to your question."

The Sadhu went to his Guru and explained the case of the parrot. To his utmost surprise and terror the Guru, the moment he heard the case, spread out his limbs and lay in a swoon. The Sadhu poured water over him and revived him with great difficulty.

Next day as the Sadhu was passing by the place where the parrot's cage was hanging, the bird asked him if he had consulted the Guru about his case. The Sadhu told him the condition into which the Guru had fallen when the matter was laid before him. The parrot answered. "You did not perhaps understand the Guru's meaning; but I have understood it and I am greatly obliged both to him and to you. Salám Maháráj. Now go your way."

When the Sadhu had gone the parrot spread out his feet and wings and lay in a dead swoon in the bottom of his cage. When his master came to feed him and saw his state he cried: "Alas my parrot! He is dead!" So he opened the door of the cage and threw the bird on the ground. Immediately he got up and flew away.

(A folktale told by Bachau Kasera of Mirzapur.)

162. The piety of Raja Raghu.

Of all the the Rájas of the world none was so pious as Rája Raghu; for to every Bráhman whoever he might be that came to his gate he used to give a ration of grain and a piece of gold. One day he was out hunting and a Bráhman came to the palace gate and begged an alms. The Rání put a ration of food and five gold coins in a dish and sent it to him by one of her maids. He asked her who had sent it and she said that the Rája was absent and that the Rání had sent this for his acceptance. "I will not take it from your hands," he answered. "Let the Rání herself come and present it to me." When she heard this the Rání added to the gift and coming herself to the gate passed it out to the Bráhman by her maid. The Bráhman saw her and was amazed at her beauty. He asked her whence she got this loveliness. She replied: "In my former life I killed myself at Benares and hence in this life I have become so beautiful." The Bráhman said "I too will go to Benares and do as you have done."

So he left the food and money and went his way. When he had gone the Rání began to think that she had incurred the sin of allowing a Bráhman to leave her door without provision, and when her husband returned she told him what had happened. He armed himself with his sword and shield and started for Benares. On the way he was tired and lay down under a tree. On this tree a pair of birds had made their nest and were rearing their young. The parents were away at the time searching for food and as the Rája lay there he saw a snake climbing up the tree. Fearing the sin of seeing life taken in his presence he killed the snake with his sword. When the mother bird returned she began to bless the Rája and giving him a fruit said: "Whoever eats this fruit even if he be old will become young."

As the Rája was sitting there the Bráhman came up and the Rája asked him where he was going. He said that he had seen the beauty of the Rání and was going to Benares to end his life. The Rája answered: "If you were to get the kingdom and Rání of this Rája would you give up your intention?" "How can that be?" enquired the Bráhman. The Rája said: "I own that Rání and that kingdom and I will make both over to you."

The Rája brought him home with him and fulfilled his promise; he himself became a mendicant. As he was about to go into the forest he gave the fruit of youth to the Bráhman and told him what its qualities were. The Bráhman thought that the Rája had given him the fruit to work his ruin so he gave it to an old dog and no sooner had the dog eaten it than it became young again. Then the Bráhman felt remorse and following the Rája into the forest asked for another fruit like it. He took the Bráhman to the bird and asked her for the fruit. She said that the fruit had been given to her by Mahádeva and that they should go to him. They went to Mahádeva and asked him, but he told them that he had got the fruit from Indra. They went to Indra and he sent them to Bhagwán.

They went to Bhagwán and asked him for the fruit." It is in the garden of Rája Raghu," he answered. "I am Rája Raghu said the Rája." Then Bhagwán embraced him and said: "Thy piety is so great that there is a heavenly mansion and garden prepared for thee. Live here for ever in happiness." So the Rája gave the Bráhman as many of the fruits of youth as he desired. He returned to earth, and the Rání died and was carried to the heaven of Bhagwán where she and her husband lived for ever in happiness.

(Told by Bachau Kasera of Mirzapur.)

163. The Sádhu and the Princess.

Once upon a time a Sádhu was on his travels and saw on a pipal tree the following words written:—

> *Himmat karaí tain;*
> *Lai pahuncháun main;*
> *Ji ke na darai;*
> *Jo chahai so karai.*
> "Keep a stout heart;
> I will provide;
> Fear not for life;
> And you may do as you please."

When he came to the next city he went and stood in the court of the king. At that time the princess was sitting on the balcony, with her head uncovered. The Sádhu fell in love with her and remained there with his eyes fixed upon her. This was told to the king who came out and thus addressed him: "O Sháhjí what do you want?" He answered: "O Bába, I have fallen in love with your daughter." When he heard this the King had him driven out of the place. Next day the Sádhu came again and as before fixed his eyes on the princess. When the king heard of it he went to his daughter and said: "Do something to kill this man." His daughter said: "I will use some stratagem to destroy him."

When he came next day as usual, the princess called out to him: "If you want me you must bring me unpierced pearls." The Sádhu started off at once for the banks of the ocean and began to throw handfuls of water over his shoulders. In the evening the ocean (*samundar*) was moved by his devotion and assuming the form of a Bráhman came and asked him what he wanted. He said that he wanted same unpierced pearls. The ocean said: "Stand out of the water and you shall receive them." Then a great wave came up and a pile of pearls lay on the shore. The Sádhu tied up as many as he could in his blanket and took them to the princess. When the king saw the pearls he was amazed and remained silent. Then the princess said to the Sádhu: "If you want me you must cut off your hands and give them to me." The Sádhu at once cut off his hands and laid them before her. Next day she called him again and said: "If you want me you must cut off your head." He answered: "As I have no hands I cannot cut off my head but if you wish you may cut it off yourself." She did so and when the king heard of it he was pleased and had the corpse thrown away. A butcher who used to supply meat to the king saw it and took it home. That day he was short of meat; so he sent some of the flesh of the Sádhu to the palace. When the dish was laid before the king he complained that the supply was short, when immediately the meat spoke and said: "O foolish man, why do you say so? Can the flesh of a man in love ever run short?" When the king heard these words he was much astonished and said: "Is it possible for you to be restored to human shape?" The flesh replied: "Lay me on a couch and let the princess come and say 'If you love me, arise.' Then I shall revive." It all happened as he said, and the king gave him his daughter in marriage and made over the kingdom to him as her dowry.

[A folktale told by Bachau Kasera, of Mirzapur.]

164. The Prince and his animal friends.

There was once a king who had an only son, who never attended to his duties and was careless and wayward. For this his father was displeased with him. One day the prince went into the bázár and saw a snake being sold; he purchased it for a thousand rupees and brought it home. When the king saw how he had spent his money, he was still more angry. The next day the prince again went to the bázár and bought a dog for a thousand rupees, and after that he bought in the same way a cat and a rat. The king, his father, was so angry that he told him to go and make his living as best he could.

He took the animals with him and started on his travels. He came to a great jungle and the snake said to him: "My home is here and here the Madári snake tamer caught me. Will you kindly allow me to visit my parents, and my father will give you anything you ask in return for saving my life." As he was going away, the snake said: "If you are asked by my father to choose a gift, take nothing but the ring he wears on his finger. "When the snake went to his father he praised the prince and then his father came out of the hole and asked the prince to choose a boon; he asked for the snake's ring, which the old snake gave him.

When he had gone some distance he plastered a piece of ground and putting the ring in the middle said: "If you are a true ring build me a mansion here." No sooner had he uttered these words, than a palace appeared before him. There the prince began to live with his animals. One day a Bráhman and a barber passed by that way and when the prince enquired their business they told him that they were going in search of a husband for the princess of that land. When they saw the glory of the prince and found him to be a beautiful youth, they asked him if he would marry the princess, and he agreed.

On the day fixed for the marriage the prince spoke to the ring and ordered it to provide all that was needed for the occasion. The ring obeyed his orders and the marriage was duly solemnised. The prince brought his bride home and all he wanted was provided by the ring. One day as he was leaving home the princess said to him: "There is nothing, in the larder; leave the ring with me and I will order what is needed." He gave her the ring and went away. While her husband was absent, a Bráhman came and asked for alms; the princess asked him what he wanted. He said: "If you give me the ring you are wearing, I will say many prayers for you." So she gave him the ring and when he got to the other side of the river, he plastered a piece of ground and placing the ring on it, he said: "O ring, if you are true, bring the palace with the princess here." Immediately the palace with the princess was brought there.

Two days after, when the Prince returned home, he found that the princess and the palace had disappeared. He was very sad and began to weep. Then his wife's brother came and asked him where she was and when he could not answer his brother-in-law had him shut up a room. When they saw the state of their master the faithful animals were much grieved and the mouse and the dog said to the cat: "You are the wisest of us all and have a knowledge of magic; think and discover what has become of the princess." The cat sat down and began to consider and at last she said: "The princess and her palace are on the bank of Fulána river." They then agreed to go in search of the ring; they came to the palace, but the Bráhman had closed it in on all sides and there was no way of going in. Finally, the mouse crept in through the drain and saw the princess sitting on her bed. He creft up to her and began to lick her foot. She recognised the mouse and told him all her troubles. He asked her where the Bráhman used to keep the ring. She said: "When he lies down he puts it into his mouth and then he makes me fan him." The mouse said: "To-night when he goes to sleep you must put out the light with your fan." So saying, he hid himself in a corner of the room where the Bráhman used to sleep. At night the Bráhman lay down and the princess was fanning him. When she put out the lamp the mouse put his tail up the Bráhman's nose and he gave a great sneeze and the ring fell on the ground. The mouse took it in his mouth and ran away with it. He gave it to the dog and told him to run and give it to the Prince. But as the dog was crossing a river the ring fell into the water and though he did his best, he could not find it. He sat on the bank and wept and meanwhile the cat and the mouse arrived. The dog told them what had happened to the ring. The cat began to consider where the ring was and by her wisdom she discovered that it was in the belly of a fish. The animals waited there that night and in the morning some Malláhs came and were fishing in the river. They caught many fish and laid them on the bank. When the Malláhs saw the animals sitting there they wondered and said to each other: "The dog has a natural enmity to the cat and the cat to the mouse. How comes it that they are sitting together?" The animals said: "We are so hungry that we cannot move a step. Give us a fish out of your great store and we shall be grateful to you." The Malláhs said: "Come and choose which fish you please." So the cat chose that in which the ring was and brought it to the dog, who tore its belly and took out the ring.

They started with it and came to the room where the prince was confined and the mouse crept in through a hole and gave it to him. Then he called to the ring to bring back the princess and the palace, and this was done immediately. The princess and the prince, with their faithful animals, lived happily ever after.

[Told by Rám Govind Pánré, Bráhman, of Ghurhúpattí, Mirzapur.]

[This is the usual faithful animal cycle.]

165. The Fool and the Alphabet.

A stupid boy was once sent to school and though he was a long time under instruction he learnt nothing. When he came home his father gave him a book to read and as he turned over the leaves he burst into tears. "What a clever boy this is! "every one said. "See how he has already begun to realise the misery of human life." But whenever he was given a book to read, he always wept. At last some one asked him why he did this, and he answered: "When I was at school the letters looked big and fat on the black board and I now weep to think how thin they have become since they got into this confounded book."—*Pandit Janardan Joshi.*

[A Folktale from Kumaun.]

166. The Weaver and the Jackal.

A weaver was once going along the road with his cotton carding bow on his shoulder. A jackal came across him unexpectedly and was much surprised to see an instrument which was quite novel to him. "I have seen a gun," he said, "and I am used to bludgeons; but these men are always inventing some new plan for our destruction. It were well for me to be cautious. But I must stand whatever fate pleases to send. To run away is useless because even a gun would destroy me at this distance." So he came up to the weaver, who was even more frightened than the jackal was, because he had never seen such an animal in all his life. The jackal made a profound bow and said:

> *Háth bán sir men dhana;*
> *Kahán chale Díllipaty Rána?*

"With an arrow in your hand and a mighty bow on your head where are you going Lord of Delhi?"

The weaver was pleased and answered—

> *Ban ke Ráo, ban hi men rahana,*
> *Akhir bare ne bare ko pahchana.*

"Lord of the jungle, the jungle is thy fitting abode. At all events it is only the high-born who could recognise one of equal rank with himself."—*Pandit Janardan Joshi.*

[A Folktale from Kumaun.]

167. The Raja and the Hansas.

Once upon a time a famine raged at Mána Sarowar for fourteen years and a pair of Hansas who lived there had to go elsewhere to find sustenance.

When they had gone a long distance they came to a beautiful tank full of fresh water and inhabited by all kinds of birds. The female Hansa said to her mate: "Let us stay here till the famine ends." Her mate answered: "The tank is good but we cannot stay there until we obtain the owner's leave." When the Hansas heard that the tank belonged to the Rája of the place, they went to him and asked his leave to stay there until times improved. He gave them leave and they settled there.

They had lived there only a few months when one day the Ráni came to bathe in the tank and when she saw the Hansa's young ones she longed to have them. So she told the Rája and he sent a man to summon the Hansas to his Durbar. When he delivered the message they asked him why they were called and he told them what the Ráni had said. They answered: "My friend, to-day all the birds will meet at our house and we cannot attend the Rája to-day; but to-morrow, if Parameshwar spares our lives, we will be there."

Next morning the Hansas appeared before the Rája and saluted him. He invited them to sit down and then he asked: "It is true that birds hold meetings like men?" They answered "Máhárája, it is true that we have our disputes and quarrels like men have and yesterday we had a meeting to decide a matter in dispute between us." "What was the question?" he asked. "The question was, whether there were more men or women in the world." "And what decision did you come to?" "The number of women is greater than that of men, because we count those men and women who do not keep their word." The Rája was ashamed, and said: "I called you only to see you as I had not seen you for a long time." As they were going away they said: "Maharájá, listed to the words of the poet.—

> Bhánu uday udayáchal ten chalí ke puni purab pánv
>   dharai nahín;
> Jyon sar neh satí chharhi ke puni dhám ki or nigah karai
>   nahin;
> Háril ki prán hái lakri kadalí puní dajo bar pharai
>   nahin;
> Taise Zaban bare jan ki mukh ten níkali puní
>   pichhun tarai nahín.

"The sun rises from behind Udaychal and then sets out on his course, but he does not turn his feet again towards the east.

So when Sati puts the arrow to her bow she looks not back again to home.

The green pigeon sits on wood and the plantain does not fruit a second time.

So when a great man makes a promise he does not break it."

The Rájah was ashamed and thenceforth he protected the Hansas.

[Told by Rám Govind Pánré, Bráhman of Ghurhupatti, Mirzapur.]

168. The Thakur and the Goldsmith.

There was once a Thákur who was a very clever fellow; but his wife was unfaithful to him and loved a goldsmith. The Thákur knew this, but said nothing. One day the goldsmith paid her a visit while her husband was supposed to be asleep, but he was listening to what they said: "My dear," said the woman, "if the Thákur would only get blind, what a good time we should have." "I will tell you what to do," he replied. "Fast for the whole month of Kártik and then pray to Bhagwán to make your husband blind, and he will certainly perform your desires."

When the month of Kártik came the woman began a regular fast and planted a Tulasi tree on the bank of the river. When she went away the Thákur dug a deep pit just under the tree and hid himself there. When she came to say her prayers, she began to pray: "O Mother Tulasi! Make my husband blind." From beneath the ground he answered in a feigned voice: "My faithful devotee, give your husband the best of food and then he will surely get blind." So the wife began to feed her husband on every delicacy she could think of and after some time he said to her: "My dear, I really think my sight is not as good as it used to be." She was sure that the charm was working, so she went on feeding him on all kinds of excellent food. Until at last he said: "My dear, I really can hardly see at all."

Then she sent for her lover and told him the joyful news. But as he came in, her husband, who was behind the door, cut off his nose with his sword. The goldsmith was ashamed to tell any one what had happened to him and this was the last visit he paid the lady.

[Told by Bachan Kasera, of Mirzapur.]

169. The Discarded Princess.

There was once a Rája to whom a daughter was born, and when he heard of it he sent for the astrologers and asked them if the girl would bring him luck or not. Though all the omens were favourable, they told him that if he kept her in his house the family would be ruined. So he had her shut up in a box and putting some pieces of gold in it, ordered his people to throw her into the river. The box floated down to a *ghát* where a dhobi was washing clothes. He took the money himself and gave the child to a potter. One day when the girl grew up, the potter was going to fire his kiln, when she said: "Father, let me fire it this time." She did so and some time after when he opened it he found that all his bricks had turned into ingots of gold.

One day the potter asked her what kind of robe she would like to wear. She said: "Let me have a sheet of bright chintz (*chira*)." He gave her what she asked and when she had worn it for some time she gave it to a dhobi to wash. He washed it at the *ghát* and laid it out to dry, when just then the Rája, her father, happened to pass by. He stopped to smoke and seeing the bright robe and thinking it to be fire he sent his servant to get a light from it. The dhobi said: "This is not fire, but cloth." The Rája was surprised and asked to whom the robe belonged. When he learnt who the owner was, he went to the potter's house and finding the girl to be beautiful, he proposed at once to marry her. The potter agreed and made her over to the Rája. He took her home and called for the Pandits to perform the marriage ceremony. When the pair began to walk round the fire, the girl said:

> *Pahli bhanwari phirun; Rája pújai man kí ás.*
> *Janam ki pothí bicháro Pandit; pújai man ki ás.*

"I am making the first round; your desire is being realised; but beware; let the Pandit again consult his books." Hearing this the Rája stopped, but the Pandits again urged him to go on. Thus he performed the seven rounds; but as he was about to complete the ceremony by putting vermilion on the parting of her hair, the girl told him the whole story. The Rája expelled the Pandits from his kingdom and taking the girl to his palace, recognised her as his daughter.

(Told by Rám Ganesh Dúbé, Bráhman of Aksauli, Mirzapur.)

170. *The tale of Rani Kamlapati.*

There was once a Rája who had two sons and when they came to be twelve years of age their father was attacked by leprosy. He was in despair regarding his condition and the Ráni in her grief sent for the most noted astrologers of the court and consulted them regarding his case. They gave their opinion that unless Kamlapatí Ráni came and touched him he would not recover. So the Ráni had some packets of betel and a drum placed at the gate of the palace and announced that whoever wished to gain the favour of the Rája should accept the task of finding Kamlapatí Ráni. But no one dared to strike the drum and undertake the duty. Finally the Princes went to to their father and offered to undertake the duty. He tried to dissuade them, but without avail. They mounted their horses and started on the search.

After many days they reached the city where Kamlapatí Ráni lived. They found her sitting in her bower (*bárahdari*) near the river bank and as they rode past they recited the following verse:

> *Harit manin ke mál hain, motiyán máng*
> *guháya*
> *Suraj sam tawa chír duti, bin piya kachchu na*
> *soháya.*

"Thy garlands are of green gems; the parting of thy hair is decorated with pearls; thy garment is brilliant like the sun; but what avail these ornaments without a husband?"

To this the Ráni replied—

> *Uncha bhit talab ka; chalen musáfir dháya.*
> *Bhágu musáfir bát se; nahin márún nain*
> *ghumáya*

"High is the bank of the pond; the travellers ride rapidly by; hasten from the path lest I slay you with a glance of my eye."

The Princes hearing this stepped back and fell into the water and there was none to take them out.

When some time elapsed the Rája told the Ráni that the Princes must be dead, so she gave notice that whoever would bring them back should receive half the kingdom. The only person who would undertake the task was a Bráhman. He set out and soon reached the city of Kamlapatí Ráni. He searched for the Princes and at last found them in the ditch, whence he took them out. Then he went to the Ráni, whom he found sitting in her bower, and addressed her in these lines:

A fimchi posti doú jané, wah bhí mast díwán,
Langré hoya khandaq giré, abhín ghabrú
jawán.

"Eaters of opium are they and nothing short of mad; they were lamed falling into the ditch and still they are only youths."

Then the Rání signed to the Bráhman to meet her that night at the shop of a sweetmeat-seller. The Ráni came at midnight and the Bráhman spoke:

"Yah nagarí men bahut bastu hain; chatur base
na koi.
Bhúkha musáfir par raha; nínd kahán se hoe?"

"There are many things in this city, but no clever man; a traveller lay down can he feel sleepy."

The Ráni answered—

Hándí le Kumhár se; Modi átá dál;
Lakri le godám se; roti kar gawwar.

"Get a pot from the potter; flour and pulse from the grocer; take wood from the store and cook your food, you boor."

To this he answered:

Hándí liya Kumhar se; Modi átá dál;
Lakri liya godam se; Ráni káh tera ihsán?

"I got the vessel from the potter; flour and pulse from the grocer; wood from the store; now Ráni what kindness will you show me?"

The Ráni then making the Bráhman out to be her brother took him home and lived with him. She asked him what he would have to eat and he called for kodo, boiled with sugar and butter. When she brought it, he said:

Kodo aisa chhail chikaniya; tis par shakkar
ghiwá;
Ráni dáya ati bhai; kushal karen Sadasiva.

"Fine is the kodo and with it is mixed sugar and butter; Ráni you have been kind to me; may Sadasiva bless you."

The old Rání, the mother of the young Rání, was displeased, because of her intimacy with the Bráhman while her husband was absent; so she ordered her to swear before the Nág, and challenge it to bite her if she was unchaste. Rání Kamlapatí was dismayed at having to take this oath. But as she came before the Nág, the Bráhman, in the disguise of a Sannyási, appeared and asked an alms. Then the Rání touched him and swore: "May the Nág bite me if I have ever touched anyone save my husband and this Sannyási." So she escaped taking a false oath and saved her honour.

Meanwhile the Rání's husband returned and was wroth when he heard of his Rání's doings with the Bráhman. So he plotted against the Bráhman's life and one day challenged him to play dice, on condition that the winner should kill the loser. The Bráhman was defeated and the Rája killed him; when the Rání heard of his death, she too took her life. All the people were lamenting her, when Siva and Párvati happened to be flying through the air and coming down asked the Rája what had happened. When he told them the story, Siva said to him: "Close your eyes." Then the god revived Rání Kamlapatí and the Bráhman and killed the Rája.

The Bráhman returned home with Rání Kamlapatí and the Princes. She touched the old Rája and he was cured of his leprosy. The Rája gave the Bráhman half his dominions and he and Rání Kamlapatí lived for many years in happiness.

(Told by Saladat Khán, a Musalmán tobacco seller, of Wellesleyganj, Mirzapur.)

171. Entertaining angels unawares.

Once upon a time Mahádeva and Bhagwán were making a visit to the world and in the evening they came to the. house of a poor Bráhman and asked for shelter. He asked them to sit down and as he had nothing wherewith to entertain them, he sent his son to pledge his lota, and with the money thus obtained he supplied them with food. The gods were much pleased with his devotion and Mahádeva said: "My friend, I wish to have our son married." The Bráhman answered: "O good guests, I am so poor that I can hardly support myself. How can I provide for a daughter-in-law?" Mahádeva did not heed his words and sent a Bráhman and a barber to find a bride for the son of the Bráhman. They arranged the match in the family of a very rich and respectable man. They returned and informed Mahádeva that the marriage had been settled and a day fixed for the ceremony.

On the fixed date the Bráhman, accompanied by Mahádeva, and the planets Shukra (Venus) and Sanischara (Saturn) went with the bride groom to the house of the bride. When her father saw how small their number was, he asked Mahádeva why the marriage procession was so mean. Mahádeva said: "The others are coming behind." And when he looked he saw thousands of men and a splendid equipage approaching. When all was ready, the ceremony was duly performed and the party sat down to the marriage feast. Mahádeva said: "Let these two men, named Shukra and Sanischara, be first fed." The house master took them first inside and they at once devoured all the provisions. The Bráhman returned to Mahádeva and said: "There is no more food for the other guests and my honour is lost." Mahádeva said: "Shut the door of your food closet and open it again"; and when he did so, lo, he found it full of the most delicious food! So all the guests were fed, and when the bride-groom brought home his bride he found that his poor hut was changed into a palace of gold, with a lovely garden, and gems lay about it like the sand on the river bank. When his neighbours asked the cause of his pros-perity, he answered:

> *"Tulasi yá jag aike sab se miliye dháya,*
> *Kya jáneu kehi bhes men Náráyan mili jáya?"*

"Tulasi says: "When you come into this world be kind to every one. Who knows in what guise Náráyan may appear?"

(Told by Rám Ganesh Dúbé, Bráhman, of Aksauli, Mirzapur.)

172. The Prince and the daughter of the Gandhi.

There was once a Prince who was very fond of hunting. One day he went to the river bank and saw a dhobi blindfolded washing clothes. The Prince asked him whose clothes he was washing, but he replied: "What matter is it of yours? If you want anything washed I can do it." The Prince gave him his handkerchief to wash and when it was ready he gave the dhobi five pieces of gold. "That is not half what I get," said the dhobi, "for washing the clothes of the Gandhi's (perfumer's) daughter, and fur-ther she is so particular that I am not allowed to look at anything I wash; so I have to keep myself blindfolded." When the Prince heard this, he went to his father and said: "I will marry no one else in the world but the Gandhi's daughter."

The King sent for the Gandhi and proposed marriage between his daughter and the Prince. He replied that he must consult his daughter. She said: "I will marry him only on this condition, that for the first six months I am only to come for an hour or two and sit in my husband's house. After that he may do with me as he pleases." The Prince agreed to these conditions, and they were married. His wife used to come and see him for an hour every day and would then go home.

Now the son of the Wazír was a great friend of the Prince and one day when his wife was sitting with the Prince his friend came to see him. "Why does not your wife remain with you?" he asked. "I do not know," said the Prince. "Well," said his friend, "I will give you some magic lampblack and when you rub it on your eyes you will become invisible. Then you can follow her and see what happens."

So when his wife went away, the next time he rubbed the lampblack on his eyes and followed her unseen. At midnight she seated herself on a flying chariot (*bimán*) and was going to the Darbar of Rája Indra, when the Prince, without her seeing him, mounted the chariot and arrived at Indrasan with her. It so happened that the drummer of Rája Indra was asleep and the Prince, who was a skilled performer on the drum, took his place, and performed so well that Rája Indra was pleased and gave him as a reward a shawl, a ring and a diamond necklace. When his wife was going back he took his gifts and mounting the flying chariot descended with her to earth.

Next morning, as he had been awake all night, he was tired and was sleeping when his wife came. When she came in she drew off the cloth from over his face and he woke and said: "Why are you so attentive to me to-day?" She made no answer, but asked "Where were you last night." "I went up to Indrasan with a fairy," he answered. At this she was much displeased and settled in her mind that she would complain about that fairy to Rája Indra.

Soon after the Wazír's son came and the Prince told him all that had happened. Then his friend had a house built in the exact pattern of the Darbar of Rája Indra and there he hung up the presents he had received. When it was ready, the Prince asked his wife to see it and when she saw it she was certain that some fairy of the Heavenly Court used to visit her husband. By this time the six months had passed and his wife came to live with the Prince. Then a fairy went to Rája Indra and told him that the Prince was aping him, had built a palace like his. and was living with one of his fairies. Hearing this, Rája Indra was sore wroth and sent his demons to bring away the Prince's house and join it to his own, to fling his wife into the fort of Qáf, where a fire burns continually, and that the Prince should know nought of this. The demons performed the orders of Rája Indra and when the Prince lost his wife he would not be comforted and wandered into the jungle, where he found a Sannyási asleep. He attended to the wants of the holy man, who, when he woke was much pleased with the Prince and when he heard his story, he said: "Fear not, I will arrange your business." He then gave the Prince a magic sandal wand and powder, and said; "Go, sprinkle this powder on the fort of Qáf and the fire will be extinguished; then collect your wife's bones and strike then with the wand and she will revive. The powder will make you invisible on your journey." The Prince did as he was ordered; he recovered his wife and brought her home, where they lived many years in happiness.

(Told by Padárath Pánre, Bráhman, of Mirzapur.)

173. The Bráhman's Luck.

There was once a Bráhman who lived in a forest; his wants were small and as he possessed all he desired he was quite happy. One day the Rája went into the forest to hunt and being hungry he halted at the house of the Bráhman, who entertained him with fruits and water. As he was going away the Rája wrote down his name and said: "If you are ever in want and it is in my power to relieve you, I shall gladly do so."

Time passed and the Bráhman became so poor that he had nothing left but his *lota*. At last his wife asked him why he did not go to the Rája who had promised to help him in his need. The Bráhman answered: "I do not wish to come as a supplicant to a man whom I once obliged." But his wife told him of many great men who had gone to Rájas in their hour of need, and at last the Bráhman went to the Rája's palace and craved an audience. The Rája received him with honour and seated him beside him. When he learnt his case, he loaded a cart with money and goods and gave it to the Bráhman to take home to his wife. As he was driving home with the cart, he halted at a tank to bathe and left the cart and bullocks on the bank. When he had done bathing and returned, he found that they had disappeared. He went home to his wife lamenting his bad luck, and as his troubles increased, his wife induced him to go to the Rája a second time. The Rája was as kind as before and this time gave him a horse laden with gold. As he was going home he came to the same tank as before and went to bathe. When he came out of the water the horse and money were nowhere to be seen.

His wife forced him to go to the Rája a third time, very much against his will. The Rája said: "My friend, these are your evil days. I will now give you four thousand rupees and you can trade with them." The Bráhman started a business with the money and at the end of a year he had made a profit of one pice. When he told the Rája, he laughed, and said: "Now your luck is changing. Trade with this one pice and see what is the result." He put the pice into his business and made two pice; and so he by degrees made a large fortune. Then he started for his home and on his way he came to the same tank and there he found his cart and horse and all his money safe. Thus his bad luck left him and he lived for many years in great prosperity.

(Told by Iqbal Husen, a Muhammadan weaver of Bhuil, Mirzapur.)

174. The Devoted Wife.

There was once a woman who was such a good wife that she was known as Pativratá, or "the devoted spouse." One day she was pounding rice and her husband came in and asked for a drink of water. She dropped the pounder in the middle of a stroke and as the blessing of the gods was upon her, it remained hanging suspended in the air as it was. A woman of the neighbourhood who happened to be there saw the miracle and was astonished. "How can this be?" she asked. "This comes from my devotion to my husband," she answered.

Her friend came home and said to her husband: "The next time I am pounding rice you ask me for a drink of water arid I will prove to you what a devoted spouse I am." He did so, but the pounder fell on his head and broke his skull. All the neighbours ran up and beat and abused her, and one man made this verse:

> *Pativratá jo nári hoé,*
> *Músal akáse tange soé;*
> *Kulatá chalé pativratá chál;*
> *Apné pati ke phoré bhál.*

"A devoted wife can keep the grain pounder suspended in the sky, but if a vicious woman tries to imitate her, she breaks her husband's crown."

(Told by Hira Lál, village accountant, Haliya, Mirzapur)

175. The Boy and the Merchant.

There lived in the city of Kanauj a merchant who had four sons, three of whom were grown up, while the youngest was a boy. Once it happened that the merchant was about to undertake a long journey and his youngest son asked him to take him with him. His father objected that the road was too difficult and he too young for such a long journey; but the boy persisted in making the request and at last his father gave him two thousand rupees and allowed him to accompany him.

When they had gone a long way, the boy, somehow or other, became separated from his father and as he wandered on he came to a jungle infested by beasts of prey. He was in great terror and repeated the verse:

Faiza ja ajal kum la ista kharun;
Sa ataun yastak de mun.

"When the predestined time of death comes, it arrives neither a moment too early nor a moment too late."

Meanwhile, he saw an old man with sandals on his feet and a stick in his hand approaching him; the boy was in great fear, but when the old man came up and asked him who he was and where he was going, he told him his story. The old man pointed in a certain direction and said: "If you follow this way you will come to the city of Labútbáj and when you arrive there you can easily find your way wherever you please."

The old man disappeared and the boy followed his directions and after going some way he came to the gate of a city. He asked the people what the name of the city was and they said it was Labútbáj. He wandered about and at last came to the shop of a merchant, whose servant gave him a seat with others who were at tire shop at the time. The owner of the shop, whose name was Munír, asked the boy who he was. The boy told him his adventures and as he was speaking a pair of cats jumped down fighting from the roof on to the spot where the boy was sitting and the moment one of the cats touched him, he disappeared.

When the merchant Munír saw this he was grieved, and said to his servants: "I will not eat food until I find him." So he started with a number of men, horses and elephants and set out in search of the boy. When he had gone a long way he lost all his people and his means were exhausted; and he went on alone. Finally he was reduced to want and came to the house of a peasant. The peasant entertained him and Munír told his case.

The peasant promised to support him and he remained there. In this way five months passed, and one day the peasant lead occasion to go to a wedding in a neighbouring village and as he was going he said to him: "My friend, I am going away, please attend to one matter in my absence. To the south of the village is a pípal tree and in the morning smoke rises from it and after the smoke a hand shows itself from the branches. You must take daily a plate of cakes and a vessel of water and offer them to the hand when it appears. But take care, do not touch the hand, otherwise evil consequences will arise."

Next morning Munír took the offering to the tree and when the hand came out he offered them to it, but he forgot the warning of his friend and allowed the hand to touch him. No sooner had he done so than he was seized, carried through the air and dropped on the top of a mosque in a distant land. He rolled off the roof of the mosque, and dropped into a well which was close beside it. He began to grope about to find a means of escape; at last he saw a ray of light through a crevice and he made his way into the city.

Now it was the law in that city that when the king died they used to choose the first stranger who arrived to rule over them; so they chose the merchant Munír, and made him king. He reigned for many years and though he made constant search nothing was ever heard of the boy.

(Told by Iqbal Husen, a Muhammadan, weaver of Bhuili, Mirzapur.)

176. The height of Virtue.

Once upon a time famine raged in the land and the Rája sent for the astrologers and asked them how it could be removed. They said that the only way to stop it was for a truly devoted wife to bathe at the Amka Tírath. They searched for a long time and could find none who answered the conditions. At last they learned that the daughter of Bhagwán Das, the Mahájan, was a truly devoted wife; so they went to him and asked him to allow his daughter to bathe in the Amka Tírath and save the country from ruin.

Bhagwán Das went to his daughter and explained the case. She answered: "O Father, I do not come up to the conditions; one day a Faqír came to the house and asked for alms; as I was giving him something my hand by accident touched his and my virtue was thus stained. Go to my sister who is more pure than I am."

The Mahájan went to his second daughter and explained what was wanted. She answered: "The work cannot be done by me, for my purity has been stained. One day I was bathing in the Ganges and my garment blew aside and the water touched my person. You know that by the Shástras water is considered to be male; hence I do not answer the conditions. You had better go to my younger sister."

The banker went to his third daughter, and when he explained the case she said:—"I do not answer the conditions. One night, at midnight, my husband said to me: "The wind is blowing from the east." I replied: "No; it is from the west." "Thus I contradicted my husband and cannot be considered a truly devoted wife. You had better go to my younger sister."

The Mahájan went to his fourth daughter and told her the case. She said: "Father, since you gave me to my husband I am in his hands and do only what he tells me." The Mahájan took her to the Rája and he explained to her the case. She went with the Pandits and bathed in the Amka Tírath and immediately the famine was removed from the land.

(Told by Ganesh Dúbe, Bráhman of Aksauli,. Mirzapur.)

177. *The virtue of Faith.*

There once lived a Sannyási in the jungle and his disciple lived with him. Now the Sannyási had promised his. disciple to teach him a *mantra* by means of which he could do anything he pleased. He served him for twelve years but he was never taught the *mantra;* at last one day when the holy man was washing, the disciple came and said: "I have served you now for twelve years and you have not taught me the *mantra* as you promised; kindly teach it to me now."

The saint was wroth at being addressed on such a subject at such a time and said: "*Tanain jána na jaghai jána, na junai jána,*" that is to say, "You paid no heed to my state of ceremonial impurity, nor to place nor time." The disciple did not understand what his master was saying and thought that this was the *mantra* which he had promised to teach him. So he went away quite contented.

One day soon after while the saint and his disciple were sitting together, a party of men passed by carrying a corpse and when they saw the saint they asked for fire to burn the body. When the disciple heard this he asked them where the corpse was; they said that it was under yonder tree. He told them to bring it. When the saint heard this he was angry because he feared lest they might ask him to revive the body and if he failed his reputation would suffer. So he told his disciple not to allow the men to approach; but he paid no attention to his words. When the men brought the body the disciple muttered over it the supposed *mantra* which he believed the saint had given him and the dead man rose immediately. Every one was surprised and none more so than the saint himself. When they had all gone away, after thanking him profusely, he asked his disciple what *mantra* he had used and when he heard it he smiled and said *Vishwá am phal dayakam*. "It is faith that gives the fruit."

(Told by Akbar Sháh, Manjhi of Manbasa, Dudhi, Mirzapur.)

178. How Bhagwan gave a lesson to Narad Muni.

Once upon a time Bhagwán and Nárad Muni were walking in the jungle and came upon a wild pig with twelve young ones. Nárad asked Bhagwán: "Does the pig love all her offspring equally or not?" "She loves them all alike," answered Bhagwán. "Then," objected Nárad, "if that is so, you must love all human beings alike, the just and the unjust." Bhagwán said nothing and they went on.

Then Bhagwán created a tank and asked Nárad to bathe in it. As Nárad was diving under the water Bhagwán turned him into a lovely woman and he himself took the shape of a Kewat and sat on the bank. In a short time Nárad, in the form of a woman, came out of the tank and asked Bhagwán who he was. Bhagwán answered that he was a Kewat, and he asked her if she would marry him. She agreed, and they settled down in a village where they lived as husband and wife for a hundred years, and Nárad in that time bore to Bhagwnn sixty sons.

Then Bhagwán turned himself into a Sannyási and created another Kewat in his original shape and put him to live with Nárad. Next day Bhagwán in the shape of a Sannyási came to beg at Nárad's house. Nárad offered him some rice which he refused. Then Nárad asked: "What then will you take?" "I want one of your sons," said Bhagwán. Nárad answered: "Be off, you scoundrel. I have seen many rogues like you! Will any one give his son as alms? You have twenty fingers and toes which you got without any trouble to yourself. Will you give one of them in alms? And yet you have the impudence to ask for my son." Bhagwán answered: "Why then did you deny that the wild pig loved all her offspring equally? If you love all your sons equally, the pig does the same, because she has feelings like your own." Nárad was silent through shame, and Bhagwán, having taught him this lesson, transformed her and himself into their original shapes.

[A folktale told by Akbar Sháh, Mánjhi, of Manbasa, Dudhi, Mirzapur.]

179. *The Wise and the Foolish Brothers.*

There were once two brothers, one of whom was wise and the other foolish. They fell into poverty, and finally they agreed to go in different ways in search of employment, and whichever of them succeeded should support the other.

The fool went to a Rája and asked for service. "What can you do?" asked the Rája. The fool was puzzled what to say. At last he said: "I can make verses and work the fan." So the Rája took him into his service on sixty rupees a month. One day the Rája said: "It is quite time we heard some of these verses of yours." The fool did not know what to do, so he went out and stood reflecting under a tree. He stood without moving, and some pigs, thinking he was a tree, came up and began to rub themselves against him. When he could stand this no longer he said,

"Tum kitno ragaro ghiso main jánun tor chaláki."

"You may rub as much as you please, but know your cunning."

This was the only verse he could think of and so he went and stood before the Rája. Just then the barber came in and prepared to shave him, and as he was getting ready the fool recited this verse. When he heard it the barber turned pale, and falling at the Rája's feet begged his forgiveness. "What have you done?" asked the Rája. The barber said: "My razor is steeped in such deadly poison that had it touched your Majesty's beard you were dead in a moment. This is the work of the treasurer, who has induced me to attempt your life." So the Rája ordered the treasurer to be executed and appointed the fool in his room.

Some time after the Rája said to the new treasurer: "It is time we saw how you can use the fan." The fool was displeased at this order, because he thought it beneath his dignity to fan the Rája. But he had to go and when he began to fan him he knocked off the Rája's crown. The Rája was wroth, and called for the executioner; but just then a poisonous snake came out of the crown and bit the Wazír so that he died. The Rája was so pleased that he made the preserver of his life Wazír. Then the new Wazír sent for his wise brother, who was in extreme poverty. When he came he said: "Fate rules the world, and a nun's wisdom and exertions avail nothing."

(Told by Iqbál Husen, weaver of Bhuili, Mirzapur.)

180. The Jealous Stepbrothers; a folktale from Kumaun.

Shankar and Bhawáni were stepbrothers, and were left by their father considerable wealth in land and cattle. Bhawáni was hardworking, and Shankar, who was a lazy fellow, could not bear his brother. One day Shankar killed the oxen of Bhawáni so that he could not plough. Bhawáni skinned the oxen and, filling the skins with sand, went into the jungle and got up a tree. By chance some robbers came there to divide their booty, and he, taking heart, let the hides fall down on them. They ran away and he filled the hides with money and jewels and came home.

Shankar asked him how he had come by all this wealth. He said: "You killed my oxen and I made bags out of the hides. I filled them with mud and they fetched a high price." So Shankar killed his own oxen and filling the hides with mud went to the bázár shouting: "Who will buy mud in ox-hides for its weight in gold?" The people thought he was cracked and shoe-beat him out of the market. In his anger he came home and killed Bhawáni's mother and burned his house.

Bhawáni pretended to be cheerful, and put his dead mother and some bags of ashes in a cart and started off. On the way he met a rich man, and they halted at the same *sarai*. The rich man asked Bhawáni to have some food with him and he agreed. "But," said he, "first give some to my poor old mother, who is sitting over there in a corner." The man took her some food and asked her to eat. She made no answer, and in his rage he threw the dish at the corpse and it fell over. "Now see what you have done," said Bhawáni. "You have killed my mother, and I am going to the police." The man was frightened and gave him a lot of money to settle the matter.

Bhawáni came home, and Shankar asked him where he had got all the money. He said: "You did me a good turn by burning my house and killing my mother, because the corpse and ashes sold for a heap of money." Shankar answered: "You played me a scurvy trick once and I will not be taken in again." Bhawáni replied: "Did you ask the Pandit to fix a lucky time before you started?" "No, I did not," said Shankar. "There," said his brother, "you see the result of being niggardly." So Shankar got the Pandit to fix a lucky time and burned down his house. Then he killed his mother and went to the bázár crying: "Who will buy ashes and the corpse of my mother?" But all the merchants fell on him and beat him till he was half dead.

He went home swearing he would have his revenge, and the next day he caught his brother and put him in a sack, intending to pitch him into the river. When he came to the bank, he put the sack down, intending to have a smoke. Meanwhile a shepherd came up and Bhawáni whispered from inside the sack: "For God's sake do not touch me or open the sack. This is no common sack, but the magic bag of the Lord Siva. I am doing wonders here; do not interrupt me." Notwithstanding Bhawáni's remonstrances the shepherd opened the sack and got inside. Then Shankar came up and pitched the bag with the shepherd inside it into the river.

He went home triumphant, and soon after Bhawáni appeared driving with him all the shepherd's sheep and goats. "Where did you get these?" asked Shankar. "It was very good of you to throw me into the river. Such a sight I saw there! I met all my ancestors, and they gave me all these cattle and wanted to give me any amount of gold too, but I would not have it, and told them that I would come another time and fetch it. When Shankar made more enquiries, he said: "Your mother sent you her best wishes, and I am going again next Sunday morning." "I would like to come too," said Shankar. "Well, I do not care to take you," said Bhawáni, "because you will be making mischief, between me and my ancestors." "Nothing of the kind," said Shankar. "You and I are now one." And he was so anxious to go that he gave Bhawáni all his cattle in return for taking him with him. When they came to the river, Shankar got into the bag and Bhawáni pitched him into the deepest place he could find saying: "Go and join your ancestors, you scoundrel. I hope this is the last I shall ever see of you."

[This is another and a good version from the lower Himalayas of the "Little Fairy" Cycle. See Clouston: *Popular Tales and Fictions*, II, 229, *sqq.*—ED.]

181. The Kali Yuga.

There was once a banker who from great wealth was reduced to poverty and was left with a single ruby. This he was afraid to keep: so he made it over to a rich banker, his friend, and made his living by begging. At last he died, and his son went and claimed the deposit: but the banker denied the claim, and the case came before the Rája, who summoned the poor man's witnesses. But none would give witness for him, and he lost his suit and was driven from the Court.

The banker then complained against him and he was summoned to appear. The poor man took the oath, and, laying his hand on the head of his firstborn son, said: "O Parameswar! if I have spoken falsely against the banker, may my son die."

Immediately his son fell down dead and he took the corpse on his shoulders and was driven out of the Court. When he went outside he saw a man on horseback who had tied his old father by the hair to the hind legs of his horse and his old mother to the neck. The beggar asked him who he was.

"Tell me who you are," he answered, "and by and by you will learn who I am."

The beggar told his story, and then the man said, "You are a fool. Do you not know that this is the Iron Age? In it a man gains by lying. Why do you speak the truth? Go and tell the Rája that the banker has taken two rubies. And take the body of your son also with you."

Then the beggar went to the Rája and said "When I was here before I told a lie in saying that the banker had taken only one ruby, whereas he really took two." The Rája sent for the banker and called on him to give up the rubies. The banker answered: "Let the beggar say over the corpse of his son, 'If I have given two rubies to the banker, may the body of my son be restored to life:' then I have no objection to give him the two rubies."

The beggar took the false oath, and at once his son stood up. So the banker had to restore the original ruby, and was obliged to sell all his goods to purchase a pair to it. The beggar went back to the horseman and told him how successful he had been.

"I," said the horseman, "am the incarnation of the Iron Age. I govern the world. I am the deadly enemy of truth and righteousness. Whoever obeys me flourishes, while those who follow my rival, the Golden Age, come to misfortune."

With these words the incarnation of the Iron Age disappeared out of his sight.

(A folktale told by Akbar Sháh, Mánjhi, of Manbasa, Dudhi, Mirzapur.)

182. The Legend of Pipa the Rajput.

Pipa, the Rája of Gangrawangarh, was a worshipper of Durga, to whom he used to sacrifice forty goats daily. One day a party of Vaishnava ascetics came to him, and when they saw the bones of the goats, they refused to accept cooked food from his house. So he ordered his servants to give them supplies, and to point them out a garden where they could cook for themselves. When the food was ready the Sádhus offered it to the sacred Salagrama stone, and prayed that in future the name of the king should be changed from Pipa to Papi (sinner). That night, about midnight, Vishnu appeared to him in the form of a Deo (demon), and pulling him from his bed was about to kill him. Pipa asked what fault he had committed, and was told that his sin consisted in killing goats in honour of Durga. Pipa then meditated on Durga, who appeared to him in the form of a woman and said that she could not save him, because Vishnu in his form as the Salagrama was her superior and that his orders must be obeyed. Pipa asked if there were no means of escaping the anger of Vishnu. Durga advised him to proceed to Benares and to be initiated by Ramanand. Saying this Durga implored the Deo to have mercy on Pipa, and immediately both disappeared from his sight.

Pipa then, taking a large number of horses, elephants, and followers, went to Benares and sent a message to Ramanand that he wished to kiss his feet. Ramanand returned answer that his door was open to faqirs and not to Rájas.

Hearing this Pipa gave away all lips wealth in charity and became a faqir and awaited the orders of Ramanand. To test the firmness of Pipa Ramanand ordered him to jump into a well, and when he saw that he was ready to obey his orders he brought him to his house and whispered into his ear the Dwadas Achhar mantra or names of Vasudeva Bhagawati. When Pipa was thus initiated he was directed to return to his kingdom, to engage in devotion for twelve months and to abolish the goat sacrifice.

Ramanand also promised to go after a year to Dwarika and on his way to visit Pipa at Gangrawangarh. Pipa obeyed these orders, and on his return to his kingdom forced all his subjects to accept the Vaishnava faith. He fed a large number of Vaishnavas daily, but allowed no meat to be brought within his dominions. When a year had expired he sent a letter to his Guru reminding him of his promise.

So Ramanand, accompanied by his disciples, Kabir and Raedas, left Benares, and on his arrival in the dominions of Pipa sent him word. Pipa went to receive his Guru and brought him with his followers to his palace. He seated his Guru on a golden seat, worshipped him, and made handsome presents to him and to his disciples. They were his guests for some days, and were much pleased with their reception.

As Ramanand was starting for Dwarika Pipa proposed to accompany him, and his Guru, being now convinced of his sincerity, allowed him to abandon his Raj and adopt a life of poverty. Pipa had twelve Ránis, all of whom wished to accompany him on his pilgrimage. Kabir was directed to offer each of them a country blanket, and to warn them that they must discard all their jewels and rich clothes. Only one of them, Sita, accepted the sacrifice.

Then the family priest of the Raj objected to Ramanand that, according to the laws of Manu, it was not lawful for a Rája to abandon his Raj and become a faqir. When his remonstrances were unheeded he poisoned himself, saying that his ghost would obstruct Ramanand in his devotion, because he persisted in taking Pipa from his country. When Ramanand heard of the death of the priest, he washed his Salagrama with some Ganges water, poured it on the mouth of the dead man and restored him to life. The priest was ashamed of his folly and returned hone.

When the party arrived at Dwarika they spent some days in devotion, and when Ramanand returned to Benares Pipa gained permission to remain some time longer at Dwarika. One day Pipa learnt that the original Dwarika had been overwhelmed, in the sea: so being anxious to see it he took his wife, Sita, in his arms and jumped into the water. Krishna, the lord of Dwarika, thought it would bring disgrace on him if their desires were not accomplished, so he ran to meet them, and holding their hands led them to the original Dwarika. Pipa and Sita were received kindly by Krishna and his queen Rukmini. Before they returned to the upper world Krishna gave Pipa a seal (*chhap*) which he directed him to give to the Panda priests at Dwarika, by whom it was to be known as the "seal of Pipa" and every pilgrim to Dwarika was to have this mark branded on his arms. Whoever bore this mark would not be subject to burning after death.

During the night Pipa and his wife were thrown out of the sea by the Divine Hand, and all were surprised at the sight. Pipa made over the seal to the Pandas, and it is used, as Krishna directed, to the present day.

On his return from Dwarika some Pathans met Pipa and tried to dishonour his wife, but Vishnu saved her: and in the same way delivered them from a terrible tiger which beset the road. They then visited the temple of Shrisha Sai, and there a man refused to give Pipa a bludgeon which he wanted, whereupon Pipa recited a spell and turned all his sticks into green bamboos.

When one Chidhar Bhagat heard of the merits of Pipa he brought Pipa to his house and, not possessing the means of purchasing a meal for his guests he sold his wife's only garment for food. When the meal was ready Pipa asked him why his wife did not join them. Hearing the cause Sita tore her robe in two and gave her half. Next morning when Pipa went to bathe in the tank he noticed a hole where a quantity of gold coins were buried. On his return he told his wife Sita what he had seen. She warned him not to go near the place again as gold was of no use to a faqir. A servant was listening to their words and overcome by covetousness he went to the place, and lo! the hole was full of snakes. The thieves determined to be revenged on Pipa, so they filled several jars full of the snakes and poured them down on Pipa through a hole in the roof, when lo! they were turned into gold coins. From this originated the well-known saying, "When God wishes to bless a man he even breaks the roof to do it" (*Bhagwan chappar pharkar deta hai*). Pipa presented the gold to Chidhar and his wife.

Another day some merchants came to Pipa to purchase oxen. They left the money with Pipa, who spent it on feeding holy men. When the merchants returned, Pipa explained to them that these holy men would carry them to Paradise. The merchants were convinced and became initiated.

In Sambat 1556 (1634 A.D.) he went again to Dwarika, and there was carried to heaven in the chariot of the Almighty.—*Pándit Bhan Pratap Tiwari.*

183. Hari Raja and Moti Rani.

Hari Rája loved his wife, Moti Ráni, very dearly. One day she died, and he determined to abdicate his throne and commit suicide. So he took the corpse of his dead queen and, laying it on a boat, set sail into the ocean. He did not eat or sleep for seven days, and on the eighth day, when he was on the point of death, Siva and Párvati who were flying through the air, saw him, and Parvati remonstrated with Siva for his cruelty to the king. Siva said: "I will restore the Rání to life on one condition, that her husband gives half his life for her." The Rája, agreed and she was restored to life. Then the Rája who was worn out with fatigue, lay down to rest, and as he slept some fairies of the sea came up to the surface of the sea and induced the Rání to join their company. When the Rája awoke he found himself alone and in great trouble took service with the king of that land. One day a merchant was selling false pearls to the king, and Rája Hari detected the fraud; so the king made him his steward.

Now the fairies of the sea used to come out always and dance before the king on his birthday. So when they came, and Rája Hari saw Moti Ráni among them, he trod on the train of her robe. "Give me what was mine and I will let you go," he said. "What have I got of yours?" she asked. "You have what I gave you on the ocean," he answered. No sooner had he said this than, to the horror of the assembly, she fell dead at his feet. When the king heard the story he gave him his daughter to wife and made him heir to his kingdom.—*Pándit Janardan Joshi.*

184. Eating and the Evil Eye; the Introduction of Turmeric.

Once, they say, Rávana, king of Lanka, fell ill. He sent one of the Rákshasas in search of a physician. He went in the form of a bird and sat on a pípal tree beneath which a celebrated physician was sleeping. The bird called out "*korúk, korúk?*" i.e., "who is healthy? who is healthy?" The physician replied in a Sanskrit verse which means, "He who takes long walks in spring, who takes a short nap in summer, who eats very little in autumn and stays at home in winter: he alone is healthy."

The Rákshasa returned and put Rávana on this regimen, when he completely recovered. Then he sent to the physician, asking him what he desired as a reward, and the physician asked him to send whatever was rarest in Lanka. Now, as Lanka was all built of gold there was nothing so rare as iron, and Rávana ordered the Rákshasas to take the physician seven loads of iron. This he received with great discontent, but he was somewhat consoled when with the iron he found a root of the turmeric, which is indigenous to Lanka, and was thus for the first time introduced into India. To this day a careful housewife will never spread the whole dinner at once in the dish of her son or husband, but will give it to him by degrees lest the influence of the evil-eye cause it to disagree, with him.—*Pándit Janardan Joski.*

185. The good old times.

In the good old times the soil was not tilled and there was no ploughing. People used to take a single grain of rice in their hands in the morning, and after walking three times round an ox would ask him, "Will this suffice for the day?" And the ox used to nod, and the grain was sufficient for the family for the day. One day when a guest came to the house an over-careful housekeeper brought two grains of rice to the ox and he got angry and cursed the human race. Since then men have had to work for their living and the ox suffered too for his curses, for he has had to work in the plough ever since.—*Pándit Janardan Joshi.*

186. How the Raja got his deserts.

There lived once a Rája and a Rání: the Rání was so pious that she never left her bed in the morning without feeding five Bráhmans. But the Rája was an enemy of Bráhmans and insulted them when he got the chance. One day Bhagwán, in the guise of a Brahman, came to the Rája's palace and asked for alms. The Rája was in his stable, and when he saw Bhagwán he, as was his wont, said: "Here is dung in plenty: eat this if you will." By and by the Rája and the Rání died and their souls went to Swarga. There the Rání received all she needed, but the Rája began to starve. At last he went to the Rání and said: "You are my wife. You are enjoying all the comforts of life while I am starving. Out of your abundance give me to eat." The Rání answered: "I disown you, sinner. Why should I give you food. Go to Bhagwán and ask him for what you need." So the Rája in his distress went to Bhagwán and begged for food. Bhagwán took him to a storehouse where was collected all the dung the Rája had offered in his life to Bráhmans multiplied tenfold. Then Bhagwán said "In Swarga everybody lives on the alms he has given on earth, and all he gives is multiplied tenfold." The Rája wept bitterly, and just then Rája Indra was passing by and heard him. When he heard his trouble Rája Indra said: "Take all this filth and burn it into lime: then you may bring some pan leaves from my garden: prepare them and give them to the gods to chew. Perchance Bhagwán will pardon you and give you food."

The Rája did so, and Bhagwán took pity upon him and gave him food as long as he remained in Swarga.

(A folktale told by Akbár Sháh, Manjhi of Manbaaa, Dudhi, Mirzapur.)

[This native story admirably illustrates the Manjhi's idea of what a future life will be.—ED.]

187. The Soldier and his virtuous Wife.

There was once upon a time a soldier who had a beautiful wife, but he was very poor. At last his wife said: "My dear husband, our wealth is gone. What is the use of our living like this any longer? You had better go abroad and earn money for our support."

"How can I go abroad without money for the journey?" he asked.

"It is bad," she said, "to eat the bread of charity in the house of your father-in-law. I will get some money from there, and then you can go abroad and seek your fortune." As he was going away she asked him, "How shall either of us know if the other has ceased to love?"

"How can I provide for this?" he asked. So she went into the garden, and picking two buds of *chameli* came to him and said: "Let each of us keep one of these buds, and whichever of us loves another his or her bud will blossom."

When he was starting, she put on her finest clothes and was taking leave of him, but he turned away from her. She fancied that he did not like her dress, so she went and changed it for another. But even then he turned away his face from her. She was grieved and said:

"My dear husband, what have I done that you have lost your love for me?"

"Fine dress," he answered, "does not befit the wife of a soldier." He said: "Take my sword and shield. Now give me the shield and cut at me as hardly as you can with the sword." She did as he told her, but he parried all her blows. Then he said: "Keep these arms, and in time of need with them protect your virtue."

With this advice he left her and went to a distant city, where he took service with a Rája and guarded the gate of his palace. Every day he used to look at the *chameli* bud which he kept tied up in his turban. One morning the Rája was sitting at his gate and saw the soldier looking at the bud. He was curious, and sent one of his servants to see what the soldier was looking at. The soldier said: "I do my duty honestly. What concern has the Rája with my private affairs?"

The Rája was more curious still, and going himself to the soldier asked him about it, and the soldier told about the buds. Soon after the Rája went on his travels and came to the city in which the soldier lived. He was a man of dissolute habits, so he sent for an old woman and told her to bring the most beautiful woman in the city to see him. She went to the wife of the soldier and proposed to her that she should visit the Rája. She agreed to go for four lakhs of rupees, but the Rája gave her five lakhs, of which she kept one lakh for herself and gave four to the soldier's wife. When the Rája came she kept him in conversation for some time, and when he tried to approach her she drew her sword, fell upon him and wounded him sorely.

When he was recovered from his wounds he came back to his own city and told the soldier what had happened to him. The soldier told him that this was the work of his wife. The Rája approved of her fidelity to her husband and advanced him to honour.

(A folktale told by Ahmad Husen, Constable, Dhudi, Mirzapre.)

[The chastity test by a flower is common. See instance collected by Jacob, Folklore Congress Report, p. 89.]

188. The Raja and the Hansa.

Once upon a time a Rája went out hunting and saw a large flock of hansas flying in the sky. One of them broke its leg and had to stay behind on a tree near a tank. In the morning a heron came and began to catch fish in the tank, and the hansa being hungry followed his example. Then a baheliya appeared and the heron flew away, but the hansa was trapped. The baheliya seeing the Rája climbed up the tree and the Rája sat down below. The hansa was weeping in her sorrow, and her tears kept dropping on the Rája's head. At last he saw the baheliya in the tree and asked him what he meant by throwing water on him. The baheliya showed him the weeping hansa, and the Rája had pity and bought her for a thousand rupees. He loosed her and she flew away, but as he continued his journey he found that she was flying over him and shading him with her wings from the heat of the sun. The Rája called to her and said: "Why do you take such pains about me?"

She answered: "As you have done good to me, I will not return until I have done some good to you."

The Rája was obliged to bring her home with him, and one day he called his astrologers and enquired: "Where and when shall I be married?"

They answered: "There is no greater astrologer than the hansa. Enquire from her."

The hansa said: "Maháráj! If you wish to be married, put on the wedding dress and come with me."

When the Rája was ready he was going to mount his horse and take servants and equipage with him. The hansa said: "Mount upon my wing, and put all your goods on the other."

The Rája did so, and the hansa flew away with him. She flew for three months, night and day, and still the place was five day's journey distant. She told the Rája to dismount and take food. When he had eaten she flew on again and reached the place where the princess was imprisoned under seven troops of guards. She was so delicate that she lived only on the perfume of flowers. The hansa flew up on the roof of her palace and looked at the guards. At the first gate was a fox; at the second a dog; at the third a jackal; at the fourth a tiger; at the fifth a shardul; at the sixth a snake, and at the seventh armed men. The hansa brought the Rája past all the guards and made him sit outside the room in which the princess was. Then she made a hole in the wall and began to sing most sweetly. The princess opened the door and, letting the hansa in, asked her who she was, and offered her anything she chose to ask. The hansa answered: "If you are pleased with me, marry the Rája whom I have brought with me."

The princess said: "Bring in your Rája and I will play dice with him. If he wins I will marry him. If I win he will have to be my slave."

The hansa brought in the Rája to the princess and the game began. The Rája was very much afraid lest he should he beaten, but the hansa encouraged him and repeated such a powerful charm that the Rája won the game. Then the hansa made a hole in the roof of the palace, and mounting him on one of her wings and the princess on the other flew away with them.

The heat of the sun parched the delicate skin of the princess: so when they came to the shore of the ocean the hansa put her down and prepared for them food and drink. But as she was lighting the fire one wing of the hansa was burnt, and the Rája and Ráni began to wonder how they would ever reach their home. The hansa then made a raft of wood and seated them upon it and said: "Mount on this raft; but take care; if you let any other creature sit on it you will be seperated. In three months I will rejoin you."

The Rája and Ráni went floating across the ocean, and after many days they saw a rat drowning in the water.

The Ráni said: "This rat is drowning. Let us take him on the raft."

The Rája reminded her of what the hansa had said, but she would not heed, and when she took the rat on the raft it broke into three parts, and the three of them floated in different directions. The Rája floated a long way and at last came to the shore of the ocean, and his part of the raft stuck under a tree. A grain parcher happened to come there who took the Rája to his house and made him help in stoking his oven. The Ráni landed at the kingdom of a Mahárája and was taken to his court. The Mahárája was pleased and ordered her to be taken into his zanana. But the Ráni said: "I will not marry you at once. For six months I must worship Mahádeva and give alms to the poor. Then I will be your wife."

So the Mahárája built a separate house for her, and all the six months she lived on the perfume of the flowers. When the six months were about to expire the hansa came to the Rája and found him in a miserable state stoking the oven of the grain parcher. She seated the Rája on her wing and brought him to the Ráni and took him to her through a hole in the roof. They embraced each other and wept, and each told the other what had befallen them. The hansa went to the *dhobi* and stole garments for them both. She took them home on her wings and they lived happily.

227

Then the hansa saluted them, and, taking leave of them, flew back to the jungle where she spent the rest of her days in peace.

(A folktale told by Ramnandan Lal, village accountant of Kon Mirzapur.)

[This belongs to the Thankful Beasts Cycle, for which see Clouston, *Popular Tales and Fictions*, I, 223, *Sqq.* For the delicate skin of the heroine see Lady Burton, *Arabian Nights*, VI., 123. We have the deferred marriage in Tawney, *Katha Sarit Ságara*, I, 501. The prohibition of taking the rat on board the raft is one of the common folklore taboos, like the forbidden room, etc. (Clouston: *Popular Tales and Fictions*, I, 198.)]

189. Shekh Chilli and the Camel Man.

Shekh Chilli once asked his mother to tell him how to get to his father-in-law's house, where his wife was staying. She said: "My son, you have only to follow your nose." So he went on quite straight, and at last ran his head against a tree. He was sure that he ought not to turn, so he climbed up the tree. Then he did not know how to get down, but at last a camel man passed that way and the Shekh asked him to help him. The camel man agreed, and brought up his camel close under the tree and told the Shekh to hang down so that he might catch him by the waist. Suddenly the camel moved away and left them both dangling. Then the Shekh called out: "Friend, sing something."

The camel man said: "All right, if you will clap your hands." So the camel man sang and the Shekh clapped his hand, and then both of them fell down from the tree, and the Shekh broke his arm and the camel man broke his leg. The camel man asked the Shekh to bring some oil to rub his leg. The *banya* gave him the oil, and then the Shekh asked for the handsel. But the cup would hold no more, so the Shekh upset the oil out of the cup, and turning up the hollow bottom said, "Well, give it to me in this."

But when he came back and showed the camel man what a good bargain he had made the camel man said: "You are certainly the biggest fool I ever saw in my life."

[The vessel was the native *katorá*, which has a hollow bottom used as a stand like our tea cups.]

(A folktale told by Farzand Ali of Barcilly.)

190. *Akbar and his Son-in-law.*

One day Akbar and Birbal went out hunting, and Akbar saw a crooked tree: so he said to Birbal: "Why is that tree crooked?" Birbal answered: "This tree is crooked because it is the son-in-law of all the trees of the forest." "And what else is always crooked?" asked Akbar. Birbal answered: "The tail of a dog and a son-in-law are always crooked." (*Tircha*— cunning or cranky.) Akbar asked: "Is my son-in-law also crooked?" "Yes, O King," replied Birbal. "Then have him crucified," said Akbar.

A few days after Birbal had three crosses made—one of gold, one of silver, and one of iron. When Akbar saw them he asked for whom they were intended, and Birbal answered: "Your Majesty! One of them is for your Majesty, one is for me, and one is for your Majesty's son-in-law."

"And why are we to be executed," asked Akbar.

"Because," said Birbal, "We are all the sons-in-law of some one." Akbar laughed and said: "Well, you may let my son-in-law alone for the present."

(A folktale told by Akbar Sháh, Manjhi, of Manbasa, Dudhi, Mirzapur.)

191. *The Reading of Hearts.*

Akbar once asked Bírbal: "What is your opinion of me?" Birbal, replied: "I have the same opinion of you which you have of me; because hearts read hearts." Akbar said: "This is impossible." But Birbal said, "Come for a walk in the city and I will prove it to you." As they were going along they saw a miserable old woman begging. Akbar said: "I *do* pity this poor creature. Cannot you, in so great a kingdom as this, make some provision for her by which she may pass her last days in comfort?" Birbal asked Akbar to stop, and going up to the old woman said: "Old woman, do you not know that Akbar Bádsháh is dead?" When she heard this she began to weep and said: "Alas! alas! how shall I now pass my days? It was by his virtue that I gained my daily bread, and now that he is gone I must starve." Birbal came back to Akbar and said: "Now your Majesty sees that the old woman loves you because you feel for her." They went on a little further in the bázár and saw a Sewara faqír begging, and as he beat on his stick he was abusing a banker and extorting alms. When Akbar saw him he said: "Birbal, these wretches are the curse of the land. Why do you not make a law to repress them?" Birbal asked Akbar to stop, and going up to the faqír said: "O Bábá! Do you not know that Alibar Bádsháh is dead?" The faqír cursed him and said: "May his soul rest in the lowest hell! Did he ever give me a pice?" Now said Bírbal, "Your Majesty sees that this man hates you because you do not feel for him. Do not hearts read hearts?" Akbar said: "I am convinced."

(A folktale told by Shyám Lal, Orderly of Etah.)

192. *The Wise Son of the Weaver.*

Once upon a time while a weaver boy was asleep, he saw in a dream that the daughter of the King of Rúm was sleeping beside him and on the other side the daughter of the King of Delhi. At this he laughed in his sleep, and when his mother heard him she asked him why he was laughing. He could not tell, so they took him to the Kotwál and when he, too, could not find out the cause of his laughter, he was brought before the King of Delhi, in which city he was living. The king asked him why he laughed, and when he gave no answer the king ordered that he should be buried up to his neck where the three roads meet, and the sentence was carried out at once. just at the time the princess happened to be passing by, and when she saw him she said: "Why are you bringing all this trouble upon yourself? Why do you not tell the king the cause of your laughter?" "I am quite happy here," he said; "you need not fret about me."

The princess went away, and after a few days the King of Rúm sent two images to the King of Delhi with a message that if he could not distinguish which of them was solid and which was hollow he would invade his dominions. The King of Delhi was much distressed at this message, and that evening the princess passed by where the weaver was buried. She said: "Why don't you tell me the cause of your laughter and I will get you released." "Do not distress yourself for me" he answered. She went to her father and said: "Father, why have you buried this weaver? He seems to be a youth of sense." "Well," said the king, "let him distinguish between the two images and I will release him."

At the same time he made proclamation in the city that if any one could solve the problem, he would give him his daughter to wife and half his kingdom. The princess went again to the weaver and told him of all her father's trouble. He said: "This is an easy matter, and I can solve it easily." She went to the king and got the weaver brought to court. He was dressed in good clothes and brought before the king, and when he was shown the images he called for a straw and, finding a minute crack in the back of one of them, he put in the straw and thereby discovered which was solid and which hollow. So the King of Delhi wrote the answer to the King of Rúm, who was pleased, and the King of Delhi married his daughter to the weaver. Some time after the King of Rúm wrote to the King of Delhi calling on him to pay some arrears of tribute. The King of Delhi was perplexed, but his son-in-law said: "Do not be anxious. I will recover the money, or get it remitted by the King of Rúm." The King gave him five hundred men and he set out for Rúm. Then the astrologer of the King of Rúm announced to him that a thief was entering his dominions. The King of Rúm consulted the King of Delhi as to what should be done, and the King of Delhi advised him to send a thousand men to capture him. The weaver was also an astrologer, and knew that this army was coming against him: so he sent a letter to his father-in-law asking for a reinforcement of five hundred men, who were sent at once. The astrologer of the King of Rúm informed his master of this, and he sent a force of one thousand men in addition. When the weaver knew of this he sent back seven hundred and fifty of his men, and with the remainder concealed himself so that the General of the King of Rúm failed to catch him.

The weaver then came to the city of Rúm by himself and put up at the hut of a faqir. The astrologer told his master of his arrival and the King sent the Kotwál to search for him. The weaver came to where a man was hanging on the gallows, and he got up in the place of the corpse and arranged the rope so that he should not be strangled. The astrologer took the king to the place and showed him the thief. The king would not believe that he was not dead and had the rope untied from his neck. He fell down like a corpse and when the astrologer burned his leg with a piece of wood, even then he would not speak. At last the astologer said: "He will never speak until some reward is offered to him." The king said: "If he speaks I will grant him any reward he asks." The weaver then got up at once and said: "I ask no other reward but that the King of Delhi may be exempted from tribute."

The King was much pleased to see his faithfulness to his master and forgave him the tribute, and giving him his daughter in marriage sent him home with many horses and elephants. The King of Delhi made him ruler of half his kingdom, and he lived for many years in the utmost happiness with his two wives.

(A folktale told by Dwarika Prasad, a Bráhman cultivator of Bithalpur, Pargana Kariyát Shikar, Mirzapur.)

[The bride seen in a dream is common in folktales, e. g., *Katha Sarit Ságara* (Tawney Trans.) II, 365. This tale is rather mixed. It is not quite clear how the incident of the images is arranged and the latter part diverges into something like the Master Thief cycle.]

193. Why the boy laughed.

Once upon a time the Emperor of Rúm was asleep in his palace with the Empress beside him and a little boy, the son of one of his slaves, at his feet. The boy had a dream, and he thought that the daughter of the King of Balkh was shampooing his feet, while the daughter of the Emperor of Rúm was standing beside him with water in a golden bowl. When he woke he began to laugh, and the Emperor asked him the cause of his laughter. But he would not tell, and the Emperor was so angry that he ordered him to be hanged. But when he prayed for mercy the emperor contented himself with putting him in a dungeon under a guard.

Some time after the King of Balkh sent three mares to the Emperor, and with them came a letter to the effect that if he could not give an answer his kingdom would be taken from him. The Emperor knew not how to answer and was in despair. All his courtiers tried to solve the question, but in vain. At last the boy offered to give an answer, and he had the three mares drawn up beside the palace wall. He sent a *bhishti* to the roof of the palace and told him to drop some water on them. Now the three mares were daughter, mother, and grandmother. When the water fell on the oldest of the three she jumped only fifteen paces, her daughter jumped twenty, and the foal bounded into the air and gallopped round the palace; so the boy explained the relationship of the three, and the Emperor was much pleased, and sent the right answer to the King of Balkh.

Then the King of Balkh sent with a similar letter three sticks and ordered the Emperior to say what relation they bore to each other. The boy was sent for, and as the three sticks were exactly the same in appearance it was hard to identify them. But the boy had them placed in a vessel of water. One stick sank to the bottom at once, and the boy said: "This comes from the root of the tree." The second sank half way, and he said: "This came from the middle of the tree." The third floated on the top, and he said: "This comes from the upper branch." And so it was; and the King of Balkh had to accept the answer.

Then the King of Balkh wrote to the Emperor to say that he had a monkey the wisest in the world, and if he could not find some one to defeat the monkey he must be his servant. So the boy was sent to Balkh to contend with the monkey in wisdom. When he came there he asked what fruits grew in that land, and they told him that all fruits, except the orange, were to be found there. So the boy got an orange, and when he came before the king the monkey said: "If you do not give me the fruit I ask for you are beaten." The monkey asked for an orange, and the boy gave it to him, and the monkey had to admit that the boy was wiser than he. The King of Balkh was so delighted with the wisdom of the boy that he gave him his daughter in marriage.

The boy then returned to Rúm with a great equipage, and the Emperor thinking that this was some foreign King who had invaded his dominions went out to meet him. But the boy sent him a message to say that he was his servant who had won the daughter of the King of Balkh as his wife. The Emperor was so pleased with him that he built a palace for him and married him to his daughter. So the daughter of the King of Balkh used to shampoo his feet and the daughter of the Emperor of Rúm used to bring him water in a golden bowl. Then the boy said to the Emperor: "My dream is now fulfilled, and this is the reason of my laughter."

(Told by Mathura Prasad, Káyasth, and recorded by Abul Hasan Khan, a Teacher of the Karaili Village School, Pilibhit District.)

[The above is another and a rather better version of the same story.—ED.]

194. The Princess and the Thieves.

There was once a Rájá who was losing daily a bag of gold from his treasury. The guards became aware of this, and as they feared dismissal they thought it better to resign their posts. The Rájá asked the reason, and they told him. He allowed them to go, and appointed other men in their places, and from that day he used to watch the treasury himself.

The princess, hearing of this, also took her station in the room with a sword in her hand. At midnight the thieves came, but suspecting that something was wrong, they agreed that one man should go alone through the hole in the wall. When he put his head in the princess cut off his head. A second man went in to his assistance, and she cut off his head also. In this way she beheaded all the thieves except one, who had only one eye, and was too cunning to risk his life by going in. But he who saw her through the hole and said: "It is you, who have killed my companions. Some day I will roast and eat you."

When he went away the princess tied up all the heads in a sheet and next day laid them before the Rájá. When he saw the heads he asked who had killed them, and one after another the soldiers claimed the credit of it. But at last the princess told how she had killed them, and the Rájá was much pleased and said: "You are the true daughter of a Rájá."

The same night the one-eyed thief broke into the private room of the princess with some of his compainions, and taking up her bed as she slept carried her off into the jungle. She was much terrified, but as they passed under a spreading fig tree she caught hold of a branch and swung herself up. When they had gone some distance the one-eyed thief said: "How is this? The bed seems lighter than it was before." And when they looked they could not find the princess. So they came back to the tree, and seeing her perched in the branches told her to come down. She said: "It is the rule with us women that when a man is fond of us he kisses us." So the one-eyed thief climbed up the tree, and when he put out his tongue to kiss her she cut it off with a knife and in the confusion ran off to the palace.

That night she waited for them again, and when they broke through the wall and one thief put in his head she cut off his nose. He called for help and a second put in his head, and she dealt likewise with him, and so with all of them in succession. They were all much ashamed at their misfortune, and agreed to meet at a garden near the city. The princess heard this, and next morning got herself up as a physician and went to the place where they were staying. She took with her a full sér of pounded glass, and coming into the garden cried out, "Vaid! Vaid!" (A physician. Who wants a doctor?) They asked her if she knew the treatment for noses, and she said that she knew it well. "But," said she, "my medicine is so powerful that whoever takes a dose remains senseless for four hours." "Never mind that," said they, "provided you cure us." Then she put some pounded glass into the nose of each of them, and they all immediately expired. She took all their property, which she divided among the poor, and then returned to the palace.

(A folktale told by Ramchandra, student, Mirzapur.)

195. The Contest of Good and Evil.

The two brothers Neki and Badi (Good and Evil) were one day disputing. Neki said: "The result of good is good and of evil evil." Badi denied this, so they agreed to appoint an arbitrator, and whichever of them was defeated was to have his hands and feet cut off. When they had gone some distance they saw a ním tree and Badi said: "Let us refer our case to the tree. Many travellers sit daily beneath its shade, and it must have wide experience." When they referred the case to the ním tree it said: "In my opinion the result of good is evil and of evil good, because every one sits under my shade and they are refreshed; but when they are going away one says, 'What excellent fire-wood this old tree would make;' and another says, 'I will come some day soon and cut it down to make a box.' Thus do they return me evil for good."

When Badi heard the judgment of the ním tree, he promptly cut off Neki's hands and feet and left him there. In his agony he rolled himself to a well close by and threw himself in. Now in that well there was a couch and on each of its legs sat a Deo. They used to go out in search of food and meet in the well at midnight. That night, when they met, Neki heard them talking. They were asking each other where they had been and what they had seen. One Deo said "Brothers! I have seen to-day a field the clay of which has this virtue, that it can restore the limbs of a cripple." The second said: "I have seen a treasure which is buried in such and such a place. I watch it all night long and leave it during the day when there is no danger of any one touching it:" The fourth Deo said: "The Rájá of this land is sick unto death. There is no man in the world who knows that if he were to bring a he-goat from such and such a village and sacrifice it and pour a drop of the blood on the Rájá he would recover."

Neki heard what the Deos were saying, and soon after a man came to the well and helped him out and then on promise of a reward took him on his shoulders to the field of which the Deo had spoken. When he touched the earth of the field his limbs were restored whole as before; Then he dug up the treasure and cured the Rájá by means of the goat as the Deo had said. The Rájá was so pleased that he gave him half his ráj. Some time after Badi happened to come to the city where Neki ruled, and when he saw his prosperity he was forced to admit that the fruit of good is good and the fruit of evil is evil.

(A folktale told by Surya Bala Sukl, village accountant, Mirzapur.)

[This corresponds in some ways with the well known story of the Bráhman and the Lion, for which see Clouston: *Group of Eastern Romances,* 254 and note 531. But in the main it corresponds with the famous cycle of the "Good Man and the Bad Man," for which see Clouston: *Popular Tales and Fictions,* I, 249 *sqq.*]

196. The fortunate Wood-cutter.

There were once two boys who earned a poor living by cutting wood in the jungle. One day they went out together and agreed to meet under a large banyan tree. The younger brother finished his work first, and when he came to the tree he saw a Sádhu sitting there. He bowed at his feet and the Sádhu blessed him and said: "My son, you shall be married to-day to the Ráni of Singaldíp."

Saying this he disappeared and when the boy went to his load of wood he saw a very pretty bird perched upon it which had an iron chain fixed to its leg so long that it trailed on the ground. The boy took hold of the chain, and the moment he did so the bird flew away with him to Singaldíp, and leaving him there, disappeared. He walked along, and suddenly saw a wedding procession (*bárát*) passing by. The bridegroom who was going to be married was not only lame but blind of an eye, and his father thought to himself:

"If the Rajá of Singaldíp sees that the bridegroom is lame and blind of an eye he will never marry his daughter to him. It would be better for me to hire a boy and let him act the part of the groom at the wedding, and when it is all over he can go away and my son will have his wife." He told his plan to the clansmen who were with him and they approved. Just then they met the woodcutter and asked him who he was and where he was going. When he told them that his home was in Jambudíp they were much pleased, because they thought that, being a stranger, he would keep the secret. So they told him their plan and he agreed to go with them. They dressed him in the wedding robe and brought him before the Rájá. All the people assembled, and the marriage was duly performed. Then the bride and bridegroom were sent into the marriage chamber (*kohbar*). When they were together the bride was very happy, but the bridegroom was in low spirits. She asked him what was the matter and he answered: "How can I admire your beauty when I am starving?" She said: "What do you mean? Thousands were fed here to-day, and were you, the Rája's son-in-law, alone left to starve?" Then he told her the whole story, which she wrote down, and then out of her box of dolls she took some sweetmeats which she gave him and they lay down to sleep. In the morning he want to bathe, and there he saw the same bird with the chain hanging to its leg.

He recognised the bird and took hold of the chain, when the bird in a moment flew away with him and brought him back to the jungle where he was before. Then it disappeared. He was overcome by grief, but putting off his wedding dress, he shut it up in an earthen pot and buried it in a dung heap behind his house. When he came back he said to his mother: "Mother I have been all night in a jungle so dense that no one ever saw it even in his dreams."

When the princess saw that it was getting late and that her husband did not return she was plunged in grief and told her mother, and her mother told the Rájá. For five years the princess never ceased searching for him but in vain. At last she gave notice that she would reward any one who could tell the best stories. Many came and told her stories, but she got no trace. Finally she asked her father to allow her to travel in search of him, and she assumed the dress of a prince and started. After many days she came to Jambudíp where the woodcutter lived. One day the woodcutter heard that this prince was in search of stories. He went to her and told her his own tale. Then with tears in her eyes she embraced him and said: "You are my dear husband for whom I have been searching so many years, but I want more proof." He went and dug up the pot which contained his wedding robe which, when she saw, she was convinced. She took her husband home with her and told her father how she had found him. He received him gladly, and after he had been there some days loaded him with wealth, horses, elephants, and sepoys and sent him home with his wife and they enjoyed many years of happiness.

May Parameswar restore the fate of all of us as he restored that of them!

(A folktale told by Ramanandan Lal, vilhage accountant of Kon, Mirzapur.)

[The sudden disappearance of the bridegroom just after the wedding is rather like Nur-al-din Ali and his son.—*Arabian Nights*, Lady Burton's Edition I., 172, *sqq.* The bird which carries him off is akin to the Rukh of Sindbad.]

197. *The Dhobi and his Ass.*

There was once a dhobi who had four asses: one of them he called Bhura or "the brown one," the second Khaira or "reddish," the third Lila or "blue," the fourth Mangala "the lucky one." One evening Mangala strayed away and the dhobi began to consult with his wife about it.

"'You had better go and look for him at once," said she. "But take care a tiger does not catch you."

"I don't mind a tiger," he answered, "I am more afraid of a wetting (*tapakwa*)."

Just then, it so happened, that a tiger had been wandering about, and when he heard the dhobi speak of *tapakwa*, he thought that it must be some demon or other. So the dhobi went into his stable, and in the dark saw some animal which he thought was, one of his asses; so he took a bludgeon, and mounting him started off in search of his missing ass. All the night he went on beating the tiger and rode all over the country on his back. When the dawn began to break he found that it was a tiger he had been riding; so he got green with fright and seeing a cave close by jumped off his back and ran in to save his life.

The tiger was only too happy to escape; so he went on till he met a hare, and to him he told all he had suffered at the hands of the dreaded *tapakwa*. The hare promised to revenge him so he called all the other hares, and they all went to the cave into which the dhobi had made his escape. They began to consult, and at last the king of the hares said:—

"Whichever of us has the longest tail must thrust it inside the cave to see what this *tapakwa* really is."

No sooner did the hare thrust his tail inside the cave, than the dhobi pulled it out by the roots, and all the hares ran away in terror.

The tiger, too, ran away into the jungle, and there he came across Mangala, the missing ass.

"Who are you?" asked the ass.

"I am the tiger," he replied.

"Well, if you are I am one and a quarter (*sawaiya*)."

So they went on together. Soon they came into a river and the ass fell in. The tiger caught him by the neck and pulled him out.

"What do you mean by interfering with me asked the ass indignantly."

"I only went into the water to catch some fish."

The tiger was so astonished that he ran away, and just then up came the dhobi and drove Mangala before him to the stable.

(A folktale told by Siu Narayan, Master of the Tahsil School, Kalpi, Jalaun District.)

198. The Pillars of the Sky.

Once upon a time Akbar said to Birbal: "My palace is supported on pillars of wood and stone, but on what does the sky rest?"

Birbal answered: "The sky, too, is supported on columns."

"Why then do we not see them," asked the king.

Birbal replied: "Give me money and time and I will show them to your majesty."

So the king gave Birbal a lakh of rupees and six months' leave, and he started on his travels through the world. He went toward the south and whenever he came to a city he used to shout out in the streets: "Whoever will stand five hundred blows of a shoe to him will I give five hundred rupees reward."

But no man would accept the condition. At last a man hearing his cry came out and said: "Give me five hundred shoe blows, and I will give you five hundred rupees." And then and there he produced the money.

Birbal said: "You will die after one hundred blows, and who is to bear the remainder?"

"My wife," he answered.

"But she must be weaker than you and fifty blows will kill her."

"Then my son will bear the rest."

"And if he die too?"

"Then my daughter, who is all I have, will stand the rest, for I know you come in the name of Allah and the Emperor, and their wishes are a law unto me."

Akbar, when he heard the devotion of the man, was astonished.

"Such, your majesty, are the pillars on which the heavens rest."

(A tale of Akbar and Birbal told by Bechau Kasera of Mirzapur.)

199. *A tale of Akbar and Birbal.*

Akbar once said to Birbal: "If you are such a wise man, what must your father be. Let me see him." Now Birbal 's father was an ignorant villager, and he feared that he would be disgraced before the court. So he told his father not to answer a single question. When the old man appeared Akbar said: "How are you?" But he answered not a word, and though Akbar asked him many questions he made no reply. Enraged at this Akbar said to Birbal: "How should one deal with an idiot?" "When a person comes before an idiot, your majesty," was his answer, "the best way is to hold one's tongue."

(Told by Pándit Janardan Joshi.)

200. *The Man who ate Human Flesh.*

A patient once went to a physician to be treated.

"The only thing which will do you good," said he, "is to eat the flesh of a man."

Some days after the physician met his patient and found him quite restored to health. He asked him where he got the human flesh, and when the physician got the address of the butcher he went and informed the king. The king, who was desirous of ascertaining the truth of the matter, dressed himself as a labourer and took service with the butcher who employed him in taking meat from his slaughter place to his shop.

One evening when the stock of human meat ran low the butcher called the king into the slaughterhouse, and drawing a long knife made preparations to kill him. The king was in sore fear and said: "If you let me write a line to the king's wazír he will give you five thousand rupees, which is more than you will make by selling my flesh."

The butcher agreed, and the king wrote a note to his wazír, who came at once with a body of troops, arrested the rascally butcher and hanged him forthwith.

(A folktale told by Syam Lal of Srinagar, Hamirpur District.)

[This story is interesting only as a reminiscence of the common belief that human flesh is useful as a remedy in various varieties of disease. See the Editor's *Introduction to Popular Religion and Folklore*, pp. 295, *sqq.*]

201. *The Fruit of Charity.*

The Lord Moses, on whom be peace, was once going into the court of the Almighty, when he met a poor man who said: "Find out what is to be my fate in this life." So Moses asked the Lord Almighty, and he answered: "His fate is to receive seven dirams in this life, of which he has received half already." So when Moses came out from the presence, he gave the poor man three and a half dirams and said: "This is awarded thee by the Lord Almighty."

With the money the poor man bought a cow and he used to give of her milk in charity; so he prospered and his income came to be seven dirams daily. Then the Lord Moses came to the Almighty and said: "You promised this man seven dirams in his whole life and now he makes seven dirams daily. How is this?"

"This," said the Lord Almighty, "is the fruit of charity."

(A folktale told by Abdullah Khan, Teacher of the Village School, Dholipur, Azamgarh District.)

202. *The Old Man's wisdom.*

It happened once that a rich man betrothed his daughter much against his will, and though he was very anxious to break the engagement he was bound by his word. Finally he sent a message to the bridegroom to come with exactly one hundred young men with him when he came to fetch the bride, and that if any of them failed to comply with the conditions imposed, the match should be broken off. The young man selected his companions, but had the wisdom to bring, one old man with him concealed in a drúm.

When they arrived at the bride's house her father produced a hundred goats and gave one to each of the party, and said that if each man could not eat his goat without leaving any scraps the marriage would not take place. They were all confounded until the bridegroom went and consulted the old man. "You must do this," he said; "first kill one goat and serve out a little to each of your men; then kill a second goat and act in the same way until all are consumed." In this way the condition was satisfied and he won his bride.—*Pandit Janardan Joshi.*

203. *The Princess and the Sepoy.*

There was once a sepoy who had a very beautiful wife and he used to do nothing all day long but look at her and did nothing to earn his living. One day his wife said to him: "What a fool you are to keep looking at me all day. Why do you not do something to earn your living?"

So he took some food from his wife and started on his travels. Now the king of the land had a daughter and though many envoys came to ask her hand in marriage she said that she would marry no one but the man who should prove himself faithful to her. At last she set out on horseback alone to find a husband. When night fell she came to a jungle and stayed near where the sepoy was halting. They fell into conversation and she shot a deer. Then the sepoy told her to go and bring fire and that he meanwhile would clean the meat. But she was a long time away and the sepoy was hungry, so he lit a fire with the flint of his gun and roasted the liver and kidneys of the deer which he ate. When the Princess came she asked about the meat and he showed her all; but when she asked him for the liver and kidneys he said that this animal had none. She was very angry and said: "You shall suffer for this some day."

So they went on together and came to the city of the king, the father of the Princess. As they had no money the Princess said to the sepoy: "Let us break into the palace of the king and rob him." The sepoy agreed and they both broke into the palace and there they saw two chests. The Princess took the smaller of the two chests and telling the sepoy to take nothing else they came away.

Next morning there was great confusion in the palace at the loss of the chest, but no trace of the thief could be found. Next night they broke again into the palace and this time the Princess tied the sepoy with a rope to the large chest and taking the clothes and jewelery of the queen went away and left him there. Next morning he was seized and brought before the king. The king asked him who had tied him there. He answered:

"Your Majesty has tied me." Again the king asked him who was with him and he said: "No one." "Who then took away the other box," and he said: "I know not." So the king ordered him to be executed. But as they were taking him to the scaffold the Princess came up and said: "Release this man." Then she went to the king and said: "This is a very brave, trustworthy man and you must marry him to me."

This was done; and when they were together that night she asked: "where are the liver and kidney of the deer?" "Be silent," said he, "or I will kill you. What I said once I shall go on saying till the end of my days." She replied; "Had you told me the truth I should have divorced you. I was merely testing your fidelity."

So he sent for his first wife and all three lived happily ever after.

(A folktale told by Lalle Kahan, Student, Village School, Robertsganj, Mirzapur District.)

204. *How the wise man learned experience.*

There was once a wise man who, when he came to an old age, determined to make over the cares of his business to his son and travel to holy places in search of divine wisdom. After many days he reached a great city where he saw a splendid palace of the Raja. He halted at the gate and meanwhile a woman of the cowherd caste came up and began to listen to the sound of the drum which the Raja's musicians were playing at the gate. She was so much interested in the music that she let her pot of curds fall on the ground. Her companion asked her why she was so careless. "What matter does it make?" she replied. "But will not your husband be angry when you come home without the price of the curds?" "If you had an experience like mine," she answered "you would not care much what happened to you." "What was that?" they asked. So she told her story thus:—

"In my early days I was the wife of the *guru* of the Raja of Angadesa. On account of my beauty the Raja fell in love with me and I consented to his wish. As he left me I took up a sword, severed his head from his body and went to my own house. I then determined to take my life and I jumped into the river. I floated down a long way till I came to a camp of Banjaras who saw me and dragged me out of the water. For a long time I wandered with them until at last they sold me to the mistress of a gang of dancing girls. She taught me to sing and dance and many lovers visited me. One day a man came to me and as he was going away I felt a desire to know who he was and he said: 'I am the son of the *guru* of the Raja of Angadesa. My father died of snakebite and my mother ran away from home. I was young and was adopted by a rich man and I am now wandering about the world in search of amusement.'

"When I heard this and knew him to be my own son I was almost dead with shame and so I determined to take my life in the jungle; but when I got there some cowherds took me into their house and I have stayed there ever since. Thus my friend, when I call to mind my sins and my adventures the loss of a pot of curds does not matter much."

The wise man when he heard this was so horror-stricken that he returned home and never again went abroad in search of knowledge.

(A folktale told by Pandit Vidya Dhar, Headmaster, Tehsili School, Jhansi, Hamirpur District.)

205. *Why Narada Muni laughed.*

Once upon a time Narada Muni was walking along and saw a man carrying a he-goat, which he had tied by the neck with a rope and was hauling along. The goat said to the man in its own language which Narada Muni understood, but the owner did not: "Why, friend, are you giving me so much trouble? In my former life I gave you much comfort." At this Narada Muni laughed. Now the Raja of that land had ordered that if any one was seen to laugh he was to be brought into his presence. So Narada Muni was arrested and brought before the Raja. The Raja asked him why he laughed and he answered "Because it is my pleasure." So the Raja fined him a lakh of rupees.

Narada Muni had no money to pay the fine, but a banker paid it for him. As he was going home with the Muni the banker ordered one of his men to realise a debt from a creditor. At this Narada began to laugh again and he was again arrested and brought before the Raja who fined him a second lakh of rupees. This the banker also paid.

As they were leaving the court the banker again ordered one of his men to collect a debt and again Narada laughed and as before he was again fined and the banker paid the fine on his behalf. Then the son of the banker asked Narada why he had laughed three times without any apparent reason. He replied:—"What have you to do with it? If you want your money I can repay you." He answered: "I do not want the money but I will not let you go until you tell me the cause of your laughter."

Narada Muni said: "The reason I laughed was because when I saw your father so busy collecting money I thought that he did not know that the money would be no use to him as he is to die to night," The boy asked him by what death his father was fated to die and the saint answered "By snakebite." The boy asked: "Is there any means by which this misfortune may be averted? I will not let you go until you tell me."

Narada answered: "I cannot avert the stroke of death, but there is one means of escape. Get a tank dug at the cost of a lakh and a quarter of rupees. Plant a garden round it and place a bed in the midst. When your father dies of snakebite make it known that Parameswar has killed him. Then your father's life will be saved; but never say that he died of snakebite."

Having thus said Narada Muni departed to Vaikuntha, the heaven of Parameswar, but when he saw Parameswar he did not salute him. Parameswar asked the saint why he did not give him the usual blessing. Narada answered: "Thou art a slayer of men (*hatyara*) in as much as thou hast slain a man. Hence I do not pronounce a blessing on thee." Parameswar answered: "I have slain no man." "If this be so," replied Narada, "Come down with me to Mrityaloka, the land of men, and I will show thee what thou hast done."

Meanwhile the son of the banker did as Narada had ordered and he made the tank and planted the garden and made his father sleep on a bed within it. During the night the banker felt cold and sent for a shawl. The servant shook it before he gave it to his master, but a snake stuck inside it and when the banker laid it over him he was bitten. Then he died and the snake disappeared out of the garden. When his son found his father dead he cried out that Parameswar had killed him. When Parameswar came down to earth with Narada he heard every one crying that he had killed the banker. And when he asked the son of the dead iman he heard the same story. So out of shame be brought him to life again and Narada blessed him. So Narada and Parameswar returned to Vaikuntha.

(A folktale told by Gokul Prasad, Kayasth, of Adinathpur district Jaunpur, and recorded by Raghunath Sahay, Master, High School, Jaunpur.)

[A curious example of the manner in which these great saints bully and control the greater gods.—ED.]

206. *The fate of the Shrewish Wife.*

There was once a wife who was such a shrew that every morning she used to say to her mother-in-law: "You wretched widow! May I see the day when your face is blackened, your hair shaved and you led round the city mounted on an ass." To this the old woman would say: "As long as my son is kind to me you can do nothing. Parameswar grant that he may never come under your influence." One day the wife began to moan and complained of internal pain. When her husband came and asked what he could do for her she said: "This disease is very difficult to cure. The only remedy is that you get your mother's head shaven, her face blackened and she led round the city on the back of an ass."

The husband went at once to his wife's mother and said: "Your daughter is sick unto death and it has been announced by the astrologers that she will never recover unless you allow your head to be shaved, your face blackened and are carried on the back of an ass around the city."

When she heard this the old woman wept sore; but her love for her daughter was great so she allowed to be done to her as her son-in-law had said. When the procession reached the house of her daughter, her husband went in, and said to his wife: "Come out and see! We have done even as you desired." On this she pretended that the pain had left her and she came out. But when she saw that it was her own mother who had been thus disgraced she was overwhelmed with shame, and cried—

> *Dekh mai ki cháli.*
> *Sir mundi, munh káli.*

"See how my mother comes—hair shaven, face blackened."
To this her husband replied—

> *Dekh nári pher pheri.*
> *Má meri hai ki teri.*

"Look again wife whether it is my mother or thine."
From this time the wife gave up her shrewishness.
(A folktale told by Manna Sinh Awasthi of Faizullapur and recorded by Iqbal Bahadur of Umri, Cawnpore District.)

207. *The charity of the Lord Solomon.*

The Lord Solomon (on whom be peace!) was so renowned for his charity that no suppliant ever left him unsatisfied. One day a starving *faqir* came to his Court and Solomon conferred upon him precious stones and robes and gold. As he was going away, he met a second *faqir* in worse case than his own and to him he gave the gifts which he had received from Solomon.

Next day he again went to Solomon who rewarded him as before, and again as he left the palace he met a starving *faqir* to whom he gave his gifts. In this way he went five times to Solomon and received lordly gifts which he immediately gave to some beggar poorer than himself.

At last when Solomon heard his case he said "For you it only remains to pray to God for blessing. Man gives not and receives not; the Lord is the giver and he is the cause of charity."

(A folktale told by Abdulla Khan, Teacher of the Dholipur School, Azamgarh District.)

208. *How to please everybody.*

One day Mahadeva and Parvati were travelling through the world together and Parvati asked her spouse: "How can a man so rule his life as to escape the blame of others?" "No man" he answered "can pass his life free of blame. If he does good or if he does evil he is blamed." Parvati asked Mahadeva to illustrate this. So he said: "I will mount my ox Nandi and you can follow on foot." Soon they met a party of men on the road who said: "What a knave this old man must be. He rides himself and lets his wife follow on foot."

Then Mahadeva dismounted and made Parvati ride the ox. Soon they met another company who said: "What a fool this old man must be. He lets his wife ride and trudges along on foot himself."

Then Mahadeva mounted the ox and took Parvati behind him. By and by some men said: "What a brute this old man is to ride with his wife on this unfortunate ox."

Then Mahadeva led the ox by the halter and both he and Parvati went on foot. Soon some people said: "What a stupid old man this is. He pampers his rascally ox and he and his wife march afoot."

Then Mahadeva said to Parvati: "You see now what an evil place this world is. Whatever you do you cannot escape the tongue of censure."

So they left this world and went to their abode in the Himalayas and were so disgusted that they never visited this world since.

(A folktale told by Devi Prasad, Teacher of the School, Unao.)

209. *The Wise Pandit.*

There was once a Raja who was blessed with a son in his old age; and when the boy grew up his father appointed the most learned Pandits to instruct him; but in vain, because the boy took to disorderly courses and spent all his time flying kites and pigeons and other disreputable amusements. At last the Raja promised a large reward to any Pandit who would reform his son. One day a Pandit passed through the city and seeing the notice agreed to attempt the task. So he bought a lot of pigeons and used to spend the whole day flying them. At last the prince struck up an acquaintance with him and one day he said: "Panditji tell me a story." The Pandit said:—"The words of the elders should be obeyed as you will learn from the following tale:—There were once seventy pigeons who lived on a tree and one of them was their *guru*. One day a fowler came to the foot of the tree, scattered some grain there and laid a snare. The pigeons were about to fly down and pick up the grain when the *guru* warned them; but they would not mind his words and when they flew down the fowler drew the string and they were all caught in the net. When they were caught they implored the *guru* to save them and at last he said: "My advice is this. The net weighs only a quarter *ser* of thread, you had better all rise at once and fly away with it to an island beyond the ocean."

So the pigeons flew away with the net and where they alighted was the hole of a rat. So they implored the rat to cut the net with his teeth and when he had done so all the pigeons were released. Thus you may learn to obey the advice of the experienced.

Again the Pandit related another tale:—"In a jungle lived many elephants and one of them was their *guru*. One day be saw two chameleons fighting on a tree and he said to the other elephants: "Brethren, fighting has commenced here and we would do well to leave this forest!" But one said: "Why should we leave this excellent forest for fear of these small creatures?" So they stayed there and as the chameleons were fighting one of them was defeated and ran for shelter into the trunk of one of the elephants to whom he caused excruciating pain. The elephant in terror went to the *guru* and implored his protection. At last the *guru* said: "Go into yonder deep tank and draw up a quantity of water with your trunk. Then discharge it violently and you will get rid of the chamelion." He did so and got relief. By this you should learn to obey the advice of the wise."

When the boy again asked the Pandit for a story he put him off on pretence that he was too much occupied with his pigeons. The boy was angry at this and sold all the pigeons he possessed and finally induced the

Pandit to do the same. Thus, by the cleverness of the Pandit he was induced to give up his evil companion, and devote himself to the acquisition of wisdom.

(A folktale told by Narayan, Bráhman, of Khakra, Meerut District.)

210. *The tale of the Raja Sarat Chandra.*

One night the son of a Raja was asleep near the palace and on a tree close by were perched a Chakwa and a Chakwi (a Bráhmani duck and his mate). Said the Chakwa to the Chakwi: "Tell me a story to make the night pass pleasantly." But she said: "You must tell me a story" and they had such a quarrel over this that the Chakwi would stay with the Chakwa no longer and flew away to another country.

She came and sat on a *nim* tree close to the Raja's palace. Now the Raja of that land had a daughter who was of the most perfect beauty and every morning she used to pour out water on the ground in the name of the Sun god, Suraj Narayan, and pray to him: "O Lord I grant that I may marry the prince, Sarat Chandra."

When the Chakwi heard her prayer she said to the princess: "The prince of my country is Sarat Chandra, the son of Megha Chandra. I will go and inform him of your desires."

So the Chakwi flew back to her mate and told him what she had heard and said: "How can I tell the prince of this?" But her mate said: "You must tell him at once."

The prince Sarat Chandra was sleeping close by and as he understood the language of birds he knew what they were saying. So he called the Chakwi and asked her how he could gain the princess. She said: "Go to the shores of the ocean and begin to bale out the water of the sea."

So he began to bale out the water of the sea and by this the throne of Bhagwán began to shake and he in fear sent one of his heavenly messengers to the prince and asked him why he was drying up the sea. The prince answered: "What is that to you. I shall do as it pleases me."

The messenger returned and said:—"He says that he cares not and will do as it pleases him."

Bhagwán sent a second and a third messenger and they received the same answer.

Then Bhagwán went himself and the prince said: "Why are you interrupting me? I will do as it pleases me."

So Bhagwán was sore afraid and sent for all the gods to save his throne and at last Mahádeva came and seating the prince on the *hansa* or sacred swan sent him off under the guidance of a parrot to the palace of the princess. When he arrived he halted in a garden and the parrot went and sat on a tree close to the palace. When the princess came out in the morning and made her usual prayer and offering to the sun, the parrot called to her and said: "He whom you love is in the garden of the king, your father."

When the princess heard this news she was overwhelmed with joy and went and told the queen, her mother, who told the king, her husband. He was much pleased, went and fetched the prince and married him at once to his daughter. When the wedding was over they again mounted the *hansa* and he carried them off to the banks of the Ganges. There they lived many days and the princess gave birth to a son.

One day the prince went to get fire. Now it was the custom of that land that whenever the king of the country died the first stranger who appeared at the city gate was elected Raja in his room. Just then the princess left her boy near the Ganges bank and went to bathe when a merchant who was passing by carried her off in his boat. Meanwhile a jungle cow used daily to give suck to the child and the master of the cow saw her, so he took the boy and reared him as his own son. When the boy grew up the servants of Raja Sarat Chandra heard of this and brought the boy to him. Not knowing him to be his son the Raja kept him in his palace. One day the boat of the merchant came to that city and the boy with some of his friends went on board and as he was telling them the story of his life his mother heard them and rushing out embraced the boy and claimed him as her son. So they were all taken to the Raja Sarat Chandra who acknowledged the lady as his Ráni and the boy as his son. The merchant was executed and the cowherd who reared the prince was rewarded and they all lived happily ever after.

May Parameswar restore us as he restored them.

(A folktale told by Ramsarup, a student of the school at Farrah, Mainpuri District.)

211. *Raja Vena and Raja Vikramaditya.*

Raja Vena was once playing with his little daughter on the roof of his palace and seeing a vulture flying by he said to her in fun: "I will marry you to that vulture." Immediately the vulture who was really Raja Vikramaditya swooped down and the Raja was so much frightened that he had to fulfil his promise and give him his daughter to wife.

After they were married the princess and the vulture went on together and she began to think: "Death is better than to live with this abominable bird." So when she came to a well she jumped in and Vikramaditya after her. By an underground channel they floated on to Ajudhya and there Vikramaditya assumed his real form and lived happily with the princess as her husband.

Meanwhile Raja Vena began to think about the fate of his daughter and went in search of her. When he came to the well he heard that his daughter and her husband had jumped into it, so he jumped in too and by and by came to Ajudhya where he found the pair living happily together.

As he explored the palace of Vikramaditya he found one room full of the hands of men; a second full of casks of human blood and a third full of the tongues of men. When he asked Vikramaditya the cause of this, he said:—"These are the hands of men who clasp the hands of men and then forget their promises; this is the blood of those who clap their breasts and then break their pledge; these are the tongues of those who tell lies. If you had not given me your daughter when you promised her to me your tongue would have been with these."

Then Raja Vena, when he heard these words, blessed himself that he had carried out his promise to Raja Vikramaditya.

(A folktale told by Bihari Lal of Awarekhi, Jagamanpur, Jalaun District.)

212. The Raja and the Bear.

One day a Raja went out hunting and going in pursuit of a deer lost his way in the jungle. The deer went out of sight and then the Raja saw a bear being hunted by a tiger. The Raja in fear climbed up a tree and the bear followed him. The Raja was frightened when he saw the bear following him. But the bear said: "Do not fear me; the tiger is the enemy of both of us. You help me and I will help you." The Raja agreed and when it was night the bear said: "I will take the first watch and you can sleep." When the Raja went on watch the tiger said from below: "Throw down the bear and I will devour him." The Raja gave the bear a shove and tried to throw him down, but the bear had his claws well fixed in the tree and woke when he was touched. "You are a false friend," said he, "but I will forgive you this time."

Next morning the bear took the Raja on his back and brought him to his palace. When he got to his gate the Raja called his dogs and set them at the bear. Then the bear ran at him and bit him to death. As he was going away he spoke in this verse:—

Marante ko máriye, ká Rája ká Ráo.

"When a man attacks you kill him whether he be king or prince."
(Told by Akbar Sháh, Manjhi of Manbasa, Dudhi, Mirzapur.)

213. Adam and the Prince.

There was once a king who was much displeased with his daughter because she would not marry according to his wishes. So he had her sent to live in a hut in the jungle. There by chance the son of another king came to hunt and seeing the princess fell in love with her. They were married and in due time a son was born to her. When her father heard of the birth of the child he sent men into the forest with orders to kill it. One of these men came and took service with the princess and when he got an opportunity he killed the child.

When the mother came home and found the child dead she was half mad with grief. Just then Adam and Eve were flying through the air and heard her cries. They asked her the cause of her grief. Then Adam cut his ring finger and let two drops of blood fall into the mouth of the child which immediately revived. Then Adam and Eve flew away and the prince and princess lived in perfect happiness.—*Pándit Rám Gharib Chaubé.*

214. The Boasting of Nárada Muni the Rishi.

Once Nárada Muni boasted that no one could sing as well as he could. He went to Bhagwan and made the same boast to him.

Bhagwan said: "You had better not say this to your father Bráhma." Nárada, however, went to Bráhma and said the same to him. Bráhma said: "You may say this to me, but do not say it to Siva the All-knowing."

But he went to Siva and made the same boast. When Bhagwan knew that he had boasted in this way to all the greater gods, he said to him: "O Nárada! it is a long time since we had any news of the Northern world. Go there and find out its state."

So he started, and by and bye he came to a city where he found the people wailing and lamenting. When he asked them the cause, they answered "We are the Ragas and the Raginis, the personification of melody, and when any one sings out of tune we suffer tortures. There is a certain Nárada, the son of Bráhma, who always sings out of time and tune and causes us great annoyance." "How can you be relieved?" asked Nárada.

"If Siva were to come and sing to us and the other great gods sit and listen, then we may be relieved."

Nárada was ashamed and went to Bhagwan and, telling him the case, said: "I have been guilty of foolish boasting. How can I be pardoned?"

Bhagwan ordered him to go into the forest and remain absorbed for ten years in devotion to Siva. As he was worshipping, Siva appeared in the form of a terrible tiger. Nárada ran to Bhagwan and asked what he should do. Bhagwan ordered him not to fear but to continue his worship. After many years Siva was appeased and came to him and asked him what he wanted. When she heard his case Siva told him to call Bráhma, Bhagwan and the other greater gods. They implored Siva to grant the prayer of Narada. So all the gods went to the city of the Ragas and Raginis and Siva played and sang before them. They were so pleased that all the trouble they had suffered through the singing of Narada passed away. From that time he ceased to boast of his skill in music.

(A folktale told by Juala Prasad, Teacher of the School at Rampur, Sitapur district.)

215. *The Tale of the Thakur and the Barber.*

There was once a Thakur in a village and his barber was Gukul Nai. One day the Thakur made up his mind to go on a pilgrimage to the Ganges and he ordered the barber to accompany him. The barber was tired of always having to attend on the Thakur for nothing, so he said: "The only condition on which I agree to go with you is this, that you must be able to give an answer to any question I put to you on the road, and as soon as you fail I will leave you."

The Thakur agreed to this and they started. In the evening they came to a town and the Thakur gave the barber some money and told him to go and buy some provisions. When he went into the bazar he met a man who was shedding tears and crying: "*Hae! meri nagin; Hae! meri nagin.*" (Alas my female snake!) The barber came back to the Thakur and began to pack up his things. The Thakur asked him the reason, and he said: "I have just seen something which I am sure you cannot explain."

When the Thakur heard the facts he began:—"There was once a Rája, who was very sad, because his Ráni brought forth only girls and he had no male heir. When she next became in child the Rája said: 'If it is a girl this time I will kill both mother and child.'

"In due time the Ráni gave birth to a girl, but she feared her husband and pretended that the child was a boy. She called the Pandits and induced them to tell the Rája that the child had been born in the asterism of Mul and that he must not see his son for twelve years. So the matter was kept secret for that time, and when the boy was nearly twelve years old his father arranged his marriage. When the procession started with the girl dressed up as a bridegroom, her mother was half dead with fear, because she knew that the matter could be concealed no longer. When the procession had gone some distance the Kahars put the palanquin down by the side of a tank and went to cook their food. All the women of the village collected to see the supposed bridegroom, but she lay weeping in the palanquin and hid her face from them. When all the women had gone the Rája of the snakes, who lived in that tank, came out in human form, and when he saw her weeping he insisted on knowing the cause. When she told him her trouble he promised to help her. So he dived into the tank and having summoned all the snakes, his subjects, he told them the case of the Ráni and her daughter and asked their advice in the matter. The snakes said: 'Why should we help these mortals who are always ready to injure us?' But the Rája of the snakes would not mind them, and again assuming the form of a man he came out to where the girl was lying in her palanquin. He took her out and seated himself and went off and was married in her place.

Meanwhile the old Ráni was consumed with terror and was ready to take poison as soon as her fraud should be discovered. But when she was called to receive the pair at the door of the palace she was delighted to find the bridegroom like the Sun and the bride like the Moon.

The Snake Rája and his Ráni continued to live together for some time and he quite forgot his home and his real wife. When he did not return the Snake Ráni set out in search of her husband. At last she found where he was and came to the girl whom he had married and asked her if her husband loved her. She answered that her husband loved her greatly. The Snake Ráni then said to her: "Ask him to eat with you and then enquire of what caste he is."

She did so; but when he sat down to eat he could not eat after the manner of men, but he took some food out of the dish and placing it on his hand managed somehow or other to eat it. But when she asked him to what caste he belonged, he warned her to cease her questions or the result would be evil. When she would not desist he took her to the tank and, assuming his original snake form, dived beneath the water. She was heartbroken at the loss of her husband and made a little hut near the tank and continued to live there. Now there was a *mali* woman who lived near, who used to supply flowers to the Snake Rája, and when she saw the grief of the deserted wife she went to him and told him that if he did not return to his bride she would commit suicide. So the Snake Rája tore himself away from his Snake Rání and returned to the girl who was overcome with joy. But the Snake Rání followed them and hid under their couch intending to bite the girl. The Snake Rája knew this and he applied some poisonous gum to the leg of the couch and to this she stuck and died. When he found she was dead he began to lament her in the words *Hae! nagin; Hae! nagin.* "Alas! my Snake-wife."

The barber was satisfied and went on with the Thakur. Next day they came to another town, and again the Thakur sent the barber to a bazar to buy food. There he saw the head of a he-goat hanging over the door of a shop and sometimes it used to laugh and sometimes wept. When he saw this he returned to the Thakur and said that he would leave him if he could not explain this mystery. When they had eaten, the Thakur said "Once upon a time Raja Vikramaditya was going to the house of his father-in-law and he came across a temple of Mahadeva which had no door, but dancing was going on inside. He knew the art of infusing his life into the body of another creature and close by lay the dead body of a parrot; so Vikramaditya infused his life into it and flying up to a window was able to look in and see what was going on. The servant of Vikramaditya was also skilled in the arts of his master, so he entered his body and went off to Ujjain and took his place as Rája. But the Rání would not recognise him and refused to admit him into her apartments. When the Rája, in the form of the parrot after seeing the dancing, came down and looked for his own body he could not find it, and in grief and amazement went and perched on a tree, and there a fowler caught him. He took him to the bázár and sold him to a *banya* for a large sum of money. The parrot showed so much wisdom that all the people of the land used to come to get their cases decided by the bird. One day two persons with a suit passed that way, and when people asked them where they were going they said that as Rája Vikramaditya was absent they were going to the parrot to get their cause decided. When the Rání heard this she asked them on their return to come and inform her of the result. When they came and told her the result of the case she knew that the parrot must be Rája Vikramaditya, and she sent for the Kotwal and giving him ten thousand rupees sent him to buy the parrot, and ordered that if the *banya* would not sell the parrot it was to be taken from him by main force. The Kotwal bought the parrot and brought it to the Ráni, and at night the bird told her the whole matter. She told him not to fear and that she would turn him into a man again. So she bought a he-goat and tied it up in the palace. She cut off the head of the goat and then sent for the servant who had personated the Rája. She asked him to bring the goat to life. He asked how he could do this, but she told him that once he had in the same way bought a lamb to life. The servant thought that this must really have been done some time or other by Vikramaditya. So afraid of his fraud being detected, he put his life into the body of the goat. Then the Ráni asked the parrot to put his life in the body of the Rája, and at once Vikramaditya assumed his original form. Then she cut off the head of the goat, hung it up in the bazar, and sometimes it laughs when it thinks how the country was ruled by the servant as Rája, and sometimes weeps when it thinks how it fell by the treachery of the Ráni."

When the tale was ended the barber took the Thakur to the Ganges and after he had bathed brought him home in safety.

(A folktale told by Menhdi Lal of Bibipur, Bara-Banki district.)

216. Budh Sen and his Monkey Army.

Once upon a time there was a king of the monkeys, named Budh Sen, and as famine raged in his own dominions, he determined to remove to some other land where the people were at peace with each other and settle there. At last he came to a land where all creatures were friendly to each other, except one maid-servant of the Rája and a ram. So by the leave of the Rája Budh Sen settled there with his monkey arms. One day as the maid-servant was going along with some fire in her hand the ram batted her and the fire fell among some straw and raised a great conflagration, so that the palace and much property were consumed and some of the horses of the Rája were half burned. After the fire was put out one of the Pandits of the court, who was unfriendly to Budh Sen, suggested that the blood of monkeys would be useful as a remedy for the horses. So the Rája had the whole army of Budh Sen beheaded and their blood was used for this purpose.

Budh Sen, when he heard of the destruction of his army, said nothing to the Rája, except that he was pleased that his men had been of some service. Then he brought an ear-ring and presented it to the Rája, who took it to the Rání; but she said that it was no use to her until she got the pair to it. The Rája asked Budh Sen to get a second ear-ring. He replied: "It is very difiicult to get a second to match it, but I will go in search of one."

So saying, he went with some of his companions into the jungle. At last they came to a tank where lived a demon (*deo*) whose habit it was to drag beneath the water any person whose shadow fell on the surface. Budh Sen climbed a tree and threw in a branch which the demon pulled under water at once. Then Budh Sen went back to the Rája and said: "Come with me to a certain place and you may find as many ear-rings as you please."

So the Rája with all his men came to the tank, and Budh Sen said: "Tell your men to search in the grass and reeds on the banks."

No sooner did they come within sight of the water than the demon pulled them all in. Then Budh Sen said: "I am a Rája as well as your majesty. As you destroyed my army so I have destroyed thine."

(A folktate told by Siva Prasad, Teacher of the Sarosa School, Sitapar district.)

217. Akbar and Birbal's Daughter.

When Birbal was appointed to be Prime Minister of Akbar many persons, and particularly Muhammadans, were jealous of him. One day a Muhammadan came to court and endeavoured to supplant him by a show of superior wisdom. Akbar asked him first—"Which is the best of flowers?" He replies the *genda* or marigold, which is used in daily Hindu worship. Next he was asked—"Whose son earns most?" His answer was "the *banya*." Then he was asked—"Who is a great man?" He replied, "the King," and to the last question—which is the sweetest thing in the world? he said: "Nothing is sweeter than sugarcane."

When the daughter of Birbal heard of this contest of wisdom, she instructed her father how to answer. When he came to court and was asked what was the best flower, he answered "The cotton flower"; the son who earns most is that of the cow; the virtuous are the great; the sweetest thing in the world is one's own interest.

The Muhammadan sage was worsted and left the court in disgrace.

(A folktale told by Narayan Das, Teacher of the Shahpura School, Etah district.)

218. The Raja and the Swans.

One year there was no rain in the asterism of Swati and the sea produced no pearls. The swans (*hansa*), who lived on pearls, began to starve, and they came to the Rája and asked for food. He asked them how much they could eat, and they replied a *ser* each. So he ordered that they should each get a *ser* of pearls. So they stayed there till, in the next rainy season, pearls were again produced in the sea, and then they took leave of the Rája and went to their home by the ocean.

On the way they chanced upon a certain city, the Rája of which was then preparing for the marriage of his son. When they saw the preparations, the male swan said to his mate: "Me thinks this Rája is very rich." "He is not so rich," she replies, "as that Rája who used to give us each a *ser* of pearls daily."

Now the Rája understood the speech of birds, and when he heard what the swans said, he sent his fowlers to catch them. The male swan was caught, but his mate escaped and flew away to the Rája who had so generously protected them. He, when he saw her, asked her why she had returned, and she related the misfortune which had come upon them. The Rája ordered that she should receive a *ser* of pearls as long as she stayed there, and he himself set out at once to effect the release of the male swan. After many days he reached the city of the Rája who had captured the swan and stayed there. Now it so happened that a Rakshasa had beset that city and was demanding a tribute of a human being daily, whom he used to devour. After he had devoured five or six of his subjects, the Rája became exceedingly sorrowful and sat at the great gate of his palace, plunged in grief. Then the Rája, the benefactor of the swans, came and asked him the cause of his misery. The Rája said: "If this Rakshasa continues to devour one of my subjects daily, my kingdom will soon become a waste."

The other Rája promised to overcome the Rakshasa, so he went to the place where he used to devour a human being daily and collecting some leaves under a tree threw a sheet over them. In the meantime the Rakshasa came up and asked where was his victim. The Rája answered: "He is coming. Kindly sit down on these leaves."

He sat down, and falling asleep, ordered the Rája to wake him when the victim arrived. Then the Rája set fire to the leaves and in a moment the Rakshasa was consumed to ashes. When the Rája of the land heard of the death of his enemy he was overwhelmed with joy and asked the other Rája to claim any reward he desired. He said: "I want nothing but the release of the swan whom you have captured."

The Rája of the land did as he desired. The Rája returned to his city, and the swans flew off to their home on the shores of the ocean.

(A folktale told by Makund Lal, Kayasth, of Mirzapur.)

219. *The Old Woman and the Crow.*

An old woman was one day frying rich cakes (*púri*) in a frying-pan, when a crow came and said: "Mother, give me a cake!" "Go and wash your bill first," she said. So the crow went to the water and said:—

> *Pannar, pannar, tum pannar dás!*
> *Do panariya, dhowai mundariya,*
> *Matkáwen púri pánch.*

"Water, water, thou art water's slave! Give me water and let me wash my bill. Then I'll ogle the five cakes." The water replied: "Bring an earthen pot from the potter and you can take water and wash thy bill." So the crow went to the potter and said:—

> *Kumhár, kumhár, tum kumhár dás!*
> *Tum do handaria, khinchai panariya,*
> *Dhowai mundariya, matkáwen púri pánch.*

"Potter, potter, thou art the potter's slave! Give me a pot, I will take water, wash my bill and ogle cakes five." But the potter said: "Bring earth and I will make an earthen pot for thee." So the crow went to the earth and said:—

> *Matar, matar, tum matar dás!*
> *Tum do matariya, banai handariya, khínchai*
> *   pandariya;*
> *Dhowai mundariya, matkáwen púri pánch.*

The earth said: "Bring the deer's horn and dig the earth." So the crow went to the deer and said:—

> *Hiraniya, hiraniya, tuns hiran dás!*
> *Tum do singariya, khodai matariya*
> *Banai mandariya, khinchai panariya,*
> *Dhowai mundariya, matkáwen púri pánch.*

But the deer said: "Go to the dog and he will fight me and break my horn; then I will give it to thee." So the crow went to the dog and said:—

> *Kuttur, kuttur, tum kuttur dás!*
> *Tum laro hiraniya, tútai singariya, &c.**

But the dog said: "Bring me some milk, and when I drink it I will fight the deer." So the crow went to the cow and said:—

> *Gaur, gaur, tum gaur dás!*
> *Tum do dudhariya, piái kutariya, larai*
> *hiráníya, &c.**

But the cow said: "Bring me some grass, and when I eat it I will give you plenty of milk." So the crow went to the grass and said:—

> *Ghasar, ghasar, tum ghasar das!*
> *Deo ghasariya khawai gauriya;*
> *Dewai dudhariya, &c.**

But the grass said: "Bring a spade (*khurpa*) and you may collect as much grass as you wish." So the crow went to the blacksmith and said:—

> *Lohar, lohar, tum lohar das!*
> *Tum do khurpiya, khodai ghasariya;*
> *Kháwai gauriya, &c.**

The blacksmith said: "How will you take the spade?" The crow said: "Put it round my neck and I will manage to carry it away." So the black-smith heated the spade and hung it round the neck of the crow, and when he tried to fly away with it his neck was burnt and his head fell off and that was the end of him.

(A nursery rhyme told by Brij Lal, Student of the High School, Bulandsháhr.)

[This is one of the cumulative rhymes on the model of—"This is the House that Jack built." Mr. Clouston gives other examples in *Popular Tales and Fictions*, II, 289 *sqq.*—ED.]

*The refrain as before.

220. *Which is better—Wealth or Wisdom?*

Two men were once disputing which was better—wealth or wisdom. They went to the Emperor to decide the case, and he sent them with a letter to the King of Balkh. In the letter it was written—"Hang these men at once." So they were thrown into a dungeon. The advocate of wealth admitted to the other that he could do nothing to save their lives. The other said: "Write these words on a piece of paper and I will procure our release." So he demanded an audience with the King, and when he came in the presence, he said "Does not your Majesty know why we have been sent hither? The Emperor of Hindustan is your greatest enemy, and his astrologers have foretold that if our corpses are buried in your city it will become a ruin. It is for this reason that he desires to have us executed here." When the King of Balkh heard these words he released them. The advocate of wealth then admitted that wisdom was superior.

(A folktale by Shadi Khan, Pathan, of Kasganj, Etah district.)

221. *The Goddess of Poverty.*

There was once a Bráhman so poor, that he could scarcely support himself by begging. The goddess of poverty had beset him. One day he was bathing at the Ganges, when a friend advised him to go to the Rájá, who would surely relieve his wants. He went to the Rájá, and when he stood before him he cried out:—"Victory to the Rájá," and the Rájá gave him ten thousand rupees. As he was going home with the money the goddess of poverty met him in the guise of the Rájá and ordered him, on pain of his life, to surrender the money, so he laid it down and went home empty-handed.

Next day he went to the Rájá, got the same present as before and lost it in the same way. And so it happened a third time also. Then the Rájá was surprised and determined to go himself and see what the Bráhman did with the money. When he saw the goddess take the money he went to her and asked her who she was. She answered:—"I am the goddess of poverty, and I am now besetting this Bráhman. Whatever he receives I take from him." The Rájá asked if there was any way by which this poor Bráhman could be relieved, and she said:—"If you take me upon yourself, then he will be relieved." The Rájá agreed and the goddess came to live with him, and when he went home the Bráhman found all the money which the Rájá had given to him at his house. When the Rájá returned to his palace he sent the Ráni with her children to her mother's house and he stayed at night in the palace. Suddenly a terrible storm arose and the palace was demolished, and all the horses, elephants and other goods of the Rájá were buried beneath the ruins. So next day the Rájá started for the jungle and another Rájá ruled in his stead. The Rájá went along begging his bread, and at last he came to a city and began to cut wood, which he used to sell daily to a confectioner. When the confectioner cut up the wood a lot of diamonds came out of it, whereat he was much pleased. He offered some to the Rájá, but he said that they were of no use to him, and that all he wanted was the bare price of the wood. The confectioner wished to give him a share, so he put some of the jewels in a *laddu* (sweetmeat) and gave them to the Rájá. On the way he met a Bráhman, who asked for alms, and to him he gave the *laddu*. The Bráhman did not care for the *laddu,* so he brought it back to the confectioner and changed it for some parched barley flour. When the confectioner examined the *laddu* he found the diamonds within it; so he said:—"It is my fate to keep them."

The Rájá then went out to the jungle. There some thieves were planning to commit a theft and they, thinking the Rájá to be a Sádhu, bowed before him and asked him to bless their enterprise. After committing a burglary in the palace they returned to where the Rájá was, and by force made him accept a diamond necklace which was part of the booty. He left it lying near him and the thieves went away. Meanwhile some sepoys of the Rájá, who were in pursuit of the thieves, came up and finding the necklace with the Rájá seized him and brought him before the Rájá. He protested that he had no share in the robbery, but without further enquiry the Rájá had both his hands struck off.

In this miserable state the Rájá took refuge in the house of an oilman who, when he heard what had befallen him, said:—"I cannot give you charity; but if you will sit on the beam of my mill and drive the ox, I will give you food."

There the Rájá remained many days. Meanwhile the Rájá of the land was performing the *swayamvara* of his daughter, and the Rájá having by chance gone to the assembly, the princess put the garland of victory round his neck. They tried to make her change her mind, but she refused; and they were married, and the Rájá, her father, allotted a mansion in which they lived.

This went on for three years, and one day a pair of swans came and sat on a tree, near where the Rájá lived. They began talking together and the male said to his mate: "This is a very virtuous Rájá, who has taken upon himself the poverty of another man." His mate asked:—"Is there any medicine by which he may be cured?" "If he procure a certain root from the jungle, and having powdered it apply it to his hands, they will be restored." The other swan said: "It is impossible for him to get the root, unless you go and fetch it." So the swan fetched the root and the Rájá, who knew the speech of birds, heard what they said, and having applied the root, his hands were restored to him.

When his father-in-law heard of his recovery he enquired into his case, and then he gave him a great army and he returned and won his kingdom from the other Rájá and lived with his Rání and children many years in happiness.

(A folktale told by Bhawani Din, Bráhman, of Faizabad.)

222. *How the Banya's wife went to heaven.*

There was once a very miserly Banya who had a pious wife. One day she went to attend a recitation of the sacred books and there she heard that if she gave a cow of gold to a Bráhman she would have no difficulty in crossing the Vaitarani, or river of hell. So she came back and told this to her husband. But he said:—

"What nonsense. If you make a cow of earth and give it to a Bráhman on the banks of the Ganges it will do just as well."

The woman did not believe him and had a cow of gold made, but in order that her husband should know nothing about it she plastered it over with mud and the Banya had an earthen cow made for himself. They both went to the Ganges and each made his offering to a Bráhman. Time passed and the Banya and his wife both died. When they came to the banks of the Vaitarani they found two cows awaiting them, one of gold, which the woman seized by the tail and the other of earth for her husband. They attempted to cross the river of hell. The woman crossed in safety and was received into the heaven of Vishnu, but half way across the cow of earth dissolved and the Banya sank in the waters.

(A folktale told by Ramadhin, Kalwar of Gasainganj, Sultanpur district.)

223. *The four friends and the Princess.*

There were once four youths, one the son of a Banya, the second of a Patwa, the third of a Pathán and the fourth of a Mína, who were excellent friends and used to spend all their time amusing themselves. At last their fathers remonstrated with them for their idleness and they started with some money for the city of Delhi.

The Patwa bought some gold thread and made a splendid necklace, which he took round the city to sell. As he stood at the Lál Darwáza, the princess saw him and fell in love with him. She called him in and after asking the price of the necklace told him to come next day. That night she began to think of him and determined to go and see him. So she put on a disguise and came to the room in the inn where he was staying. She went in and found that he was not there; so she put on the necklace which was hanging to a peg and lay down on the bed. As she moved in, the sword that was hanging on the wall fell and she died.

When the Patwa came back and found the girl lying dead in his room he was overcome with grief and fear. So he took a large earthen jar and putting the body into it threw it into a ravine close by. Next morning some one found it there and when enquiries were made it was found to be the corpse of the Princess. So the Emperor called the Kumhars and asked them to identify the pot. One man said that he had made four of that pattern, which he had sold to four friends. The four youths were arrested and three of them were able to produce their jars; but the Patwa's jar was recognised and be was ordered for execution.

After the order was passed, the Emperor was desirous of finding the true facts of the case; so he went in disguise to the cell in which the Patwa lay and asked him if he would care to see his friends before he died. He went first to the Banya who said:

"You need not be frightened. I will spend all I have to get you released."

When they came to the Mína he said:

"Fear not, I will give my life sooner than that you should be executed."

When they went to the Pathán boy he said:

"Do not be afraid. I have a relative in the Emperor's service. We are arranging to get the Emperor blown from a gun sooner than that you should lose your life."

When the Emperor saw the devotion of the three friends he was much pleased and when he investigated the matter and found that the Patwa was innocent of the murder, he made the Banya his Treasurer, the Pathán his Commander-in-chief, the Mína his Brigadier and to the Patwa he gave ten villages.

(Told by Mangal Prasad, Dikhshit Brahman, and recorded by Pandit Hanuman Din, Master of Lawal School, Lucknow district.)

224. *The Rájá and the Physician.*

There was once a Rájá who was much oppressed by increasing fatness, so that he began to despair of his life. He called many physicians, but there was none who could give him relief. Now in a distant city there was a poor physician who was sore pressed to make a living by his profession, and at last he determined to go elsewhere in search of employment. By chance he came to the city where the Rájá lived and as he was walking about he heard a herald going about proclaiming: "Whoever can cure the Rájá his fee shall be a lakh of rupees; but if he fail he shall be put to death with the most extreme tortures."

When the physician heard this notice he began to reflect that his future state could not be worse than it was then. So he went to the Rájá and accepted his conditions, but first he demanded a lakh of rupees as an advance for the preparation of the necessary medicine which he said it would take six months to prepare. When he got the money he at once sent it home, so that in case he came to an untimely end, the support of his family might be assured.

When six months passed he was no nearer having the medicine ready than he was at the beginning, and his heart sank within him when he began to think what the Rájá would do to him when he failed to perform his engagement. So he made a plan and at night he began to wail and cry and dashed himself so violently against the walls of his room that his whole body was a mass of bruises. When the messengers of the Rájá came, he said:

"I am so wounded that I cannot appear before the Rájá unless you bring a conveyance."

So they brought a palanquin and brought him before the Rájá, who demanded his medicine and threatened that if it was not ready the physician would be delivered over to the executioner. When he heard this the physician began to weep and said:

"Last night, your Majesty, I was compounding the drugs for you when 'Azrail,' the angel of death, appeared and asked me why I was preparing a potion for a Rájá who would die within a week. When I remonstrated with him he fell upon me and beat me sorely, as you see me now. Even now 'Azrail' is hovering over your Majesty's palace, waiting to carry you off. What then avail the drugs of your servant?"

When he heard the words of the physician the Rájá was overcome with fear and lay on his couch and wept and thus he continued for the space of a week, until by reason of his fears and neglect of food his fatness left him and he regained his original form.

When the week had passed he sent again for the physician and said:

"You see that 'Azrail' has spared me so far and lo! my fatness has disappeared."

"This is the result of my strategem" replied the physician, "You have to thank me for your recovery."

The Rájá admitted the truth of his words and dismissed the physician with a handsome present.

(A folktale told by Abdul Ghani, Teacher of the Muhammadi School, Kheri district.)

225. *The rival Castes.*

Four men, a Dhuniya, a Máli, a Juláha and a Ját, once went to a Rájá for employment. When he asked the Juláha who he was, he said:

"I am a Khaták Pathán."

The Dhuniya said: "I am a Tank Pathán."

The Mali said: "I am the arranger of melody. "(*Rág b ag Si dhawan.*)

When he asked the Ját what his caste was, he said:

"I am of the caste of Khuda. "

"You rascal," said the Rajá, "what do you mean?"

He answered—

"This Khaták Pathán does weaving in my village. This Tank Pathán cards cotton. This arranger of melody sings at the weddings of Chamárs. If they are of these noble castes then what is my caste but that of the Lord Almighty?"

(Told by Pandit Sri Ráma and recorded by Yubraj Sinh Student of the Dhaupur School; Bijnor district.)

226. *The Dom Rájá of Oudh.*

There was once a Bráhman boy who was sent to Benares to be educated. After some time when he was qualified to be a Pándit he started off to visit his father-in-law's house. On the way he came to a river which was in flood and as he was looking for a means of crossing it he saw a cow stuck in the mud. He had no pity for the sacred animal and instead of trying to extricate her he mounted on her back and made her carry him across. Then the cow cursed him and so he went onto his father's house.

When he arrived there and it was night, he went into a room with his wife. But no sooner did he come into the room than he was turned into an ass. When his wife saw this she tied him to the leg of the bed and sat weeping and bemoaning her fate.

In the morning she was ashamed to come out and the people began to mock and say:

"When a husband returns after a long absence he does not rise early."

At last the girl's parents went in and when they saw the ass they were sore grieved; but for shame they pretended that their son-in-law had been obliged to leave early and they left the ass in the house. At last the other Bráhmans went to them and said:

"We cannot eat or smoke with people who keep a foul animal like an ass in their house. "

So they determined to turn out their son-in. law; but the girl said that where he went she would go too. So she took him with her and went to Benares. The Rájá of that city was then building a temple to Vishnu and the girl went there to work and with what she earned she used to support her husband and herself. But while she was at work the ass used always to go about with her and if any man tried to speak to her he would lash out and kick him. When the Rájá heard of this wonder he went to the place and asked the girl what it all meant. When he heard her sad case he summoned all the Pándits of Benares and consulted with them how the Bráhman could be restored to his former shape. After they had long consulted together, they said:—"Your Majesty must perform a great sacrifice according to the usage of the old kings of the land and then when each Rájá throws a drop of water on the youth he will recover his original shape."

Now at that time the Rájá of Ajudhya was on bad terms with the Rájá of Benares and when he was invited not only would he not come himself but he sent his Dom in his place. This he did not knowing that the Doms were the ancient lords of the land, so when the sacrifice was done and all the other Rájás stood round the youth and sprinkled water upon him, nothing happened till the Dom threw water on him and then at once he was restored to his former shape.

So the Bráhman girl brought her husband home in triumph and since then the proverb runs:—

> *Awadh des ka Domra aur des ka bhup;*
> *Inke sabar na karo; bhlao lagaen chup.*

"The Domra of Oudh is equal to the kings of other lands; nor should you vie with them; rather keep silence."

And they say that Domariya Dih about twenty miles from Ajudhya was the Domra capital in the old days.

(A folktale told by Ram Das, Master of the Zillah School, Partabgarh)

227. *How Shaikh Chilli made a fool of himself at the wedding.*

One day Shaikh Chilli was invited to the marriage of his sister-in-law, and while the rejoicings were going on a letter came which they gave him to read. As he was reading it he began to weep and lament and seeing him all the guests commenced to wail and beat their breasts. After a time when they came to their senses they asked him who was dead, and he answered:—"No one is dead. I wept only when I began to think of all our forefathers who have died in the evil days of old."

They were all so angry that they rushed at him and kicked him out of the house.

Another time he was invited to another wedding and he borrowed all the good clothes he could get from his neighbours and went off to the party. At the same time he borrowed a horse from a friend on which he mounted and set out. He put all his property in charge of the mistress of the inn and she seeing him to be a soft fool said:—"Take this scraper and rope and go out and cut some grass for my pony." So he went out with only a rag round his loins and meanwhile the woman escaped with his horse and clothes. In this wretched guise he was obliged to go on to the wedding, but he was ashamed to go in and, creeping in by the house drain, sat down where they were distributing rice water to the beggars. As he was trying to get some his foot slipped and he fell into the cess-pool which was close by. Hearing his cries his relatives came up with torches and pulled him out. But he was so ashamed that he ran away and came home.

(A folktale told by Muhammad Halim and recorded by M. Ram Sahai, Sub-editor, *Educational Gazette,* Lucknow.)

228. *The pious Prince.*

There was once a Rájá who had a son and a daughter. One day the Prince said to his sister: "I wish to become a Sadhu."

She replied: "Do not so. You are a Prince and the life of a Sadhu is hard."

But he would not be persuaded and started on his travels. He came to a city and asked the people where he could find a carpenter. When they pointed out his shop, he went to the carpenter and asked him to make the shape of a loaf of bread out of wood. He made it for him and then the Prince tied it to his waist-cloth and went his way. By and by he came to the palace of a Rájá who asked him to come in and eat. But he pointed to the loaf which hung at his waist and said: "This is sufficient for me." Then he came into the jungle and hung himself from a tree with his feet downwards. Soon a crow flew down and began to try and pick out his eyes. He said to the crow:

> *Kága, sab tan kháiyo, chun chun kháiyo más,*
> *Donon nain bacháiyo, ki priya milan ki ás.*

"Crow, you may eat any part of my body you please, but spare my eyes, because this is my only chance of seeing my beloved (the Creator).

Thus he became perfect (Siddhi) and Bhagwan came down himself and carried him off to his heaven.

(A folktale told by Girja Dayal, Kayasth, of Ahmedabad, Lucknow district.)

229 The wit of Muhammad Fazil.

The proverb runs—*Parhe na lihe, nám Muhammad Fázil.* "He can neither read nor write and he is called The Scholar."

This is how the proverb arose.

There was once a Rájá who employed a Persian teacher to instruct his sons and when he died he left a son whose name was Muhammad Fazil, who was as ignorant as his fattier had been learned. Him the Rájá summoned and ordered him to serve in the place of his father. He had to accept the post, but as he was totally ignorant, he began to think how he could ever discharge the duties. And such a fool was he that the boys used to shout after him and call him Tadda, or Fool, until he came to be known to every one by that name.

One day the Rájá sent for him and said:—"My ring has been stolen and you must from your books discover the name of the thief as your father used to do."

The teacher was in great distress and said: "Give me time to consult my books and I will give an answer to-morrow."

But the Rájá was wroth and cast him into prison and threatened to hang him next morning if he did not find out the thief.

The teacher lay down, but from sorrow he could not sleep, at last he called out:

Ao re sukh nindiya;
Subh ko kat jae mundiya.

"Come sweet sleep, for I shall lose my head by dawn."

Now the Rájá had a female slave named Nindiya and she was listening at the door of the cell. When she heard what she supposed was her own name, she was afraid, and goiug to the teacher told him that the ring was concealed under the Rájá's bed where she had placed it and implored him to save her life. The teacher promised to do as she asked and next morning when he was called by the Rájá, he showed him where the ring was hidden and thereby gained great honour.

One day the favourite riding camel of the Rájá was lost and Muhammad Fazil was ordered to trace it. He did not know what to do and went wandering in distress near the palace, when what should he see but the camel grazing in a ravine.

So he went to the Rájá and said:—"Your Majesty's camel is grazing in such a ravine with his head to the North. "

When they went to the place and found the camel as he had said, his renown still more increased.

Another day the Rájá was walking with the teacher in the garden and finding a worm known as Tadda he concealed it in his hand and asked the teacher what he had. He was confused and cried out "Tadda, Tadda, your time is now come."

The Rájá did not know that Tadda was his nickname and was astonished at his wisdom.

At last Muhammad Fazil was tired of running constant risk of his life, so one night he took a dagger and went into the room where the Rájá was asleep. He was about to stab him, when he thought to himself that it would be safer to drag the Rájá out into the courtyard and kill him there, where there was no chance of any one hearing the noise. Just as he dragged him out, the roof of the palace fell in and the Rájá fell on his knees before him and said:—"My preserver, I owe my life to you. Share with me half my kingdom."

And this was the way the idiot Muhammad Fazil prospered.

(A folktale told by Marizi Khan and recorded by Hashim Ali, Master of the School at Dharmpur, district Sultanpur.)

230. *The Prince and the Snake.*

There was once a Rájá who had seven sons, all of whom were married except the youngest and he had tamed a snake which he loved dearly and always kept with him. When the Wazír was going home from Darbar he saw the prince feeding the snake and he went and told the Rájá that the boy was taking to evil ways. The Rájá promised to look into the case next day and calling his son he took him in his lap and said:—

"You must give up keeping this snake."

The prince promised to get rid of it; so he came home and taking the pot in which he used to keep it, he started for the jungle. There he took out the snake and said:—

"O god, you have undergone much while you were with me. But as you are sprung from a high family you must pardon me on account of my great love for you."

The snake replied:—

"Prince, while I was with you I enjoyed perfect comfort. I will recompense you. Stay here while I go to Patala. There I will introduce you to Rájá Vasuki, the lord of the snakes."

So the snake went down a hole in the ground, and when the other snakes saw him they said:—

"Brother you have come back after a long absence."

They took him to the Dárbar of Rájá Vasuki and he saluted the Rájá and said:—

"Maharaj! the son of a great Rájá is waiting for an interview with your Majesty."

Meanwhile the prince got tired of waiting and was returning to his father's palace when the snake came up from behind and called him. The prince replied that he thought he had been forgotten; but the snake took him down to Patala and brought him before Rájá Vasuki. After a time, when he was about to leave, Rájá Vasuki gave him an iron chain. When the prince saw it he said:—

"Maharaj! In my father's house are many chains of gold. What is the use of this iron chain to me?"

Rájá Vasuki said:—

"Brother! Do not speak thus. This chain will be of great value to you. Mahádeva conferred it on me. The merits of it are these. Whenever you desire aught you must dig the earth to the depth of one and a quarter cubits and put the chain thrice into the hole. Then cover it with earth and four Birs will attend and do your bidding."

So the prince came home and took the chain with him; but he grieved greatly at parting from the snake.

One day he went into the inner apartments and began to joke with his sisters-in-law. They said:

"You may say what you like when you get the Mute Princess (Anbola Ráni) as your wife."

These words inflamed his mind and he mounted his horse and at once set out in search of Anbola Ráni. He passed through a forest and there he saw a tigress lying on the path. He tried to avoid her, but she saw him and called to him, and said:—

"If you do not come and ease my pain I will curse thee."

He was afraid and came to the tigress, who said:

"I have a thorn in my foot. Pull it out and earn my blessing." The prince agreed to attempt to relieve her pain; but she said:—

"You are the son of a king, but you are destitute of wisdom. If you try to extract the thorn and give pain, I will surely kill you; bring a large log and place it near me. When I am mad with the pain I will gnaw that and spare you."

The prince placed the log before the tigress and by its help he managed to extract the thorn frorn her foot. Next day as he was going away, the two sons of the tigress appeared, and when they saw the prince they said:—

"We shall have a dinner today without the trouble of hunting for it."

Saying thus, they were about to devour the prince, when the tigress abused them and said:—

"This man has saved my life and you must not attempt to seize him."

As the prince was going away she said:—

"I shall never see you again; but as a mark of my gratitude I will give you a son of mine. He will serve you faithfuly."

So the prince took the cub and started, and on the way he halted under a tree. Suddenly his eyes fell on a snake creeping up the tree on which was the nest of the bird Garuda. The young birds began to cry with fear and the prince at once shot the snake. The prince put the dead snake under his shield and resting his head upon it lay down to sleep. By and by Garuda and his mate returned, and when they saw the prince, Garuda said to her that she should kill him. She said:—

"I, a female, cannot kill a male, but you may do so if you please."

Garuda said:—

"I will not kill him as it is a sin to kill a man asleep."

Meanwhile the young ones cried out:—

"Do not kill him. He has just saved our lives from the snake and if you doubt it look under his shield."

When Garuda saw the dead snake he was very grateful and gave him food and brought a goat for the young tiger that was with him. When the prince asked leave to go they said to him:—

"You must take one of our young ones with you."

So they gave him one of their young ones, and he went away. As he went along the bird went flying over him and kept off the heat of the sun. The tiger walked behind him and the dog in front. Next day they came to a garden which was guarded by a Rakshasi. The prince was suffering from thirst and said to her:

"Mother, tell me where I can get water, as am athirst."

She said:—

"My son, go into such a place in the garden; raise a stone, and you shall find water beneath it.

When he raised the stone he found that beneath it flowed the river of gold. When he bathed therein he found that he had become the colour of gold. So he bathed his horse, his dog, the tiger and Garuda in the water and they all became golden. Then he came into a city and he appeared like the rising moon in beauty. The Rájá of that land was going through the city and when he beheld him he was astonished. The princess was looking from an upper chamber and, when they saw each other, they fell in love, and he lost his senses with passion. When he came to his senses he returned to the garden, and, leaving his goods in charge of the Rakshasi, he went again to the city. He came to the shop of a grain parcher, and said:—

"Give me food and I will collect leaves for your oven."

Thus he lived for some time and then the Rájá held the Swayamvara of his daughter. All the princes of the land were assembled and the princess went round with the garland of victory. She looked everywhere for the prince who, clothed in rags, was sitting in a corner, and when she did not find him she gave the garland to none. The assembly broke up. When she came back to the palace she prayed for aid to the Lord Ganesa. At the next meeting Ganesa pointed the prince out to her and she threw the garland round his neck. But the assembly cried that there was a mistake and it was not till she threw it thrice that they believed her. So the Rájá had to marry her to the prince, but he gave them only a hut to live in and the coarsest food to eat. Then her brothers planned to take the prince into the jungle and slay him. So they asked him to go hunting with them. But he said that he had neither horse nor weapons. Then the princess went to her mother for advice, but she turned her back upon her. And her brothers would not speak to her, so she returned home in tears. But the prince said:—

"I am going to bathe."

So he went back to the garden where he took his horse, tiger, dog and Garuda, and, mounting went into the jungle. His wife's brothers had been hunting there before he came. He shot a deer and sitting near a tank began to roast the meat. The brothers of the princess came to the same place and when they saw them the dog and the tiger were about to devour them. So they fell before the prince and asked forgiveness and he gave them water and some of the venison. Then he said:—

"I must brand you with a hot iron on your loins; if not my faithful animals will devour you."

So he branded them and let them go. Then he tied them on their horses with their faces to their tails and let them go. Next day he went to the Darbar of the Rájá. But the princess had gone to the Rání and told her how the prince had branded her brothers and would surely slay them. The Rání told this to the Rájá and the Rájá was grieved and came to the Darbar. The prince came in guarded by his animals and they were all the colour of gold. The Rájá and all his court saluted him and he said:—

"In your court are five thieves whom I have branded on the loins. Let them appear before me."

Then the Rájá bowed before him and begged forgiveness.

But the prince took over the kingdom and ruled as Rájá. After a time he began to consider that he had not attained his desire of gaining the Rání Anbola, and when he told the princess, she agreed to join him in the search for her. The Rájá also tried to dissuade him, but next day he started with a singe groom. After many days he came to the palace of Anbola Rání. At the gate was placed a great drúm which any one who wished to marry the Rání had to strike. The prince struck the drúm a hundred times. A servant came out to see who had struck the drúm. She brought the princess before the Rání who, seeing him, fell in love with him, and swooned. When she recovered her senses she asked him who he was and what he desired. When he explained his case she said:—

"You must fulfil the conditions, which are these;—On the first night you must bridge the stream near the palace; and secondly you must make a garden such as the world has never seen."

Then the prince invoked the aid of the iron chain and at once four mighty Birs appeared to do his bidding. He told them what they had to do. They began to reflect that a bridge could not be built in a single night. So they determined to lay the mountain Kailása across the river as a bridge, and for a garden, to bring down the garden of Rájá Indra and place it there. They did so, and next day the prince sent his groom to inform the Ráni Anbola that the conditions were fulfilled. The Ráni was satisfied and returned to the palace. Then she said to the prince:—

"The conditions for the second night are—That you shall make me speak at the end of each watch."

The prince caused them to disguise themselves so as to see all and be seen of none. He went to the palace and a couch was spread for him beside that of the Ráni. Then he seated the demons—one on the Ráni's lamp, one on her couch, one on her water-vessel and one on her necklace. She covered her face with a sheet and lay down. Then the prince said to the water-vessel:—

"Brother! Let me pass part of the night in talking to you."

The vessel replied:—

"Prince! What can I say? I am in great trouble. I have been made by a workman who has not his equal in the world for cleverness, but I have the misfortune to live with a wretched woman who never takes the trouble to clean me. She washes herself with the water I hold but she is too lazy to wash me."

Hearing this the Ráni cried out:—

"You lie, you wretch! I wash you four times a day."

So saying she took up the vessel and flung it on the ground so that it was broken. But the prince said:—

"The Ráni has spoken:"

"She answered:—

"I spoke to the vessel, not to you."

"Well!" said he "you have spoken now to me."

So he ordered the drum to be beaten. And so the first watch passed. In the second watch the prince said to the Ráni's necklace:

"Necklace! Help me to fulfil the conditions of the second watch and tell me something."

The necklace said:—

"What can I say? I have been made by a famous artist, but this wretched woman never wears or cleans me, and since I came to her she has kept me hanging on this peg."

The Ráni was wroth, and said:—

"Miserable one! I wear you daily and you will go lying about me."

So saying she flung away the necklace and it was broken. But the prince said:—

"The Ráni has spoken."

"I spoke, not to you but to the necklace," she said.

"At any rate you have now spoken to me," he cried and he struck the drum for the second time. Then the prince said to the couch:—

"Say something to me that the conditions of the third watch also may be fulfilled."

The couch answered:—

"O prince! What can I say to you? I was made by the cleverest carpenter in the world, but woe to me that I have come into the hands of this miserable Ráni. She never moves me, or cleans the dust from beneath me. She must have been a she-ass in her former life."

The Ráni said:—

"Wretch! Why do you make these lying charges against me?"

"This is a means for your correction," the couch replied. Then the Ráni kicked the couch, but the demon who was on it, pressed with all his might, and the couch was broken. The Ráni slipped and fell and the prince said:—

"The Ráni has spoken."

She answered:—

"I did not speak to you."

"Well you have spoken to me now," he said and he struck the drum for the third time.

Then the prince said to the lamp:—

"O lamp! Relate to me something so that I may fulfil the condition of the last watch."

The lamp said:—

"Friend! What can I say? I was cast by a famous workman; but I fell into the hands of this most miserable princess. On me is accumulated the filth of years, and she never takes the trouble to clean and trim me."

The Ráni was wroth and, dashing the lamp on the ground so that it was broken to pieces, said:

"Miserable creature; I have you cleaned daily and yet you tell lies like these!"

The prince said:—

"The Ráni has spoken."

"I did not speak to you," she said.

"Well! You have spoken now," and with that he had the drum beaten, that the Ráni had spoken four times. When the news spread through the city the people were delighted, and the marriage preparations began at once.

So they were duly married, and the prince stayed there some time. One day he went to the river bank and saw two rubies in the water. When he put in his hand and picked them up, he saw two more, and when he picked these up he saw two more; so he threw away all of them and resolved to go to the place where all these rubies came from. He followed the stream to its source and there he saw a splendid building, and from beneath it there came a stream of rubies. He ordered his demons to take him into the house, and there he saw a fairy (*Pári*) lying dead. The demons rubbed on the forehead of the fairy the consecrated ashes of Mahádeva, so that she might not see them and they rubbed it on their own foreheads so that they might see all and be seen of none. In the evening a Rákshasa appeared. He took up a bottle from the shelf and sprinkled some magical essence (*áraq*) on the fairy, and she awake. The Rákshasa said in his own tongue:—

"*Khan man sain.*" "I smell a human being."

The fairy answered:—

"I know naught of this. You must have caught many men to-day as your prey, and these you smell."

The Rákshasa passed the night playing dice with her and in the morning he went off to the world to hunt for men. When he had started the prince sprinkled the magical essence on the fairy, and she awoke and asked him why he had come and where he was going. He told her all his story, and she warned him to escape before the Rákshasa returned. But he said:—

"As, I have come, I do not wish to go away and I will face any danger that may happen" and he added:—

"Fairy! If you wish me to stay always with you, you must tell me in what dwells the life of the Rákshasa."

She answered:—

"You must promise that if you will kill him, his funeral rites will be duly fulfilled. His life lives in a parrot, which is on the topmost branch of a banyan tree; but this branch swarms with snakes innumerable, and in every leaf there are countless scorpions. This tree is in the midst of the seven oceans, and is guarded by hosts of demons. If any one can kill the parrot then he can get me."

The prince said to his demons:—

"Take me to that tree."

So he was taken there and by the help of the demons he overcame the snakes and scorpions and the demon guard. Finally he seized the parrot and tore its limbs asunder. The Rákshasa rushed up; but as the parrot died, he died also. Then the prince took the fairy on his shoulders, and his demons carried them through the air to the palace of Anbola Ráni. Thence with his two wives he started to recover his third wife. He also brought with him his horse and dog and tiger and Garuda. On the way he gave over his animals to their parents, and when he came home the wives of his brothers were put to shame to witness his success and he lived with his three wives for many years in the utmost happiness.

May Parameswar deal with us, as he dealt with him!

[Told by Yubraj Sinh Barhai of Dhanpur, Bijnor District.]

231. Prince Nilkanth.

There was once a Rájá who had come to old age and had no son. One day he was sitting at the gate of his palace lamenting his trouble, when a *Sádhu* came up and asked him the cause of his grief. The Rájá said "What have you to do with it? Take your alms and leave me." But the *Sádhu* persisted in asking, and at last the Rájá said:—"If I tell you my trouble, will you promise to remove it?" The *Sádhu* made the promise and the Rájá made him repeat the promise three times. Then he said "The cause of my grief is that I have no heir." The *Sádhu* said:—"The cause of your having no heir is that *Bhagwán* has not written it so in your fate." " But," said the Rájá "as you have promised me an heir you must give me one."

So the *Sádhu* had to fulfil his promise and as he was going away he met a sparrow and said to him:—"Go and live in the Ráni's womb for a year." The sparrow replied:—"How can I do this? When the time is over I shall have to come out and then go to Hell." The *Sádhu* went on and met a paddy bird (*bagula*) and made him the same proposal, but the paddy bird for the same reason refused. Next he met a jay (*nilkanth*) and ordered him to live for a year in the womb of the Ráni. The jay said:—"I have no objection, but how am I to get out again?" The *Sádhu* answered: "When you are twelve years of age you will be married and then you must sit on your wife's knee. When you do this you will die immediately. But as you are dying, you must tell your wife to put your body in the hollow of a *pipal* tree and then you will become a jay again."

The *Sádhu* departed and in due course the Ráni came to be in child. When her son was born, he quickly grew in strength and when he reached his twelfth year, he was married. When the ceremony was over he made his wife seat him on her knee, and said:—"I am about to die. When I am dead, put my body in the hollow of a *pipal* tree." When her friends heard that the newly-married bridegroom was dead, they were surprised to see the girl place it in the hollow of a *pipal* tree. She went the next day to see the corpse, but it was not there.

After this, her sisters were always taunting her with losing her husband on her wedding day. One day she went out with her companions to collect cow-dung fuel in the jungle. She got lost and happened to take refuge in the same *pipal* tree in which she had placed the body of her husband. At midnight her husband with a servant came into the hole in the same tree and cooked food. But instead of two, the food divided itself into three parts. He and the servant ate two shares and left the third in the hollow of the tree. The girl took her share of the food and in this way lived there for three months.

One day, as her husband was going away, she seized him by his feet. He recognised her, but said:—"Dear, you cannot get me back so easily as that. You must go to the bank of the Ganges and worship *Mahádeva* for twelve years, before you can recover me." She did as he ordered her and when the period of her worship was over, the god appeared to her and said:—"Ask any boon you desire." So she asked for her husband and got him back and they lived long and happily together.

(A folk-tale told by Ramnandan Tiwári, Bráhman, of Mirzapur.)

232. *The Clever Brahman Girl.*

There were once two Brahmans who lived in neighbouring cities, one of whom had a son and the other a daughter. The father of the girl sent a Brahman and a barber to search for a match for his daughther and by chance they selected the son of the other Brahman as her future husband. In due course they were married and after this the boy returned home at once leaving his wife with her father.

By and by his father who had wasted all his substance on the marriage, fell into extreme poverty. One day he said to his wife:—"We are starving and there is nothing for us but to sell the boy as a slave or eat his flesh." When the boy heard this he was afraid and ran away, and by chance came to the village in which his wife lived. But he did not know this and as her father was a very wealthy man and took pupils to whom he gave food and lodging, he went to stay in the house of his father-in-law. His wife too used to read with her father and the two, who knew not that they were husband and wife, became great friends and called each other brother and sister. Now in this city lived a reprobate Rájá who used to seize the wives and daughters of his subjects, and at last his servants came to the house of the Pándit and ordered him to send his daughter to the Rájá. He in his grief ordered his pupil to go with her. He was in great trouble but the girl told him to go to the Rájá and tell him that she would go to him if he would erect a palace with four gates facing the four corners of the sky and in one corner to put a leaf of *tulasi*, in a second water, in a third tire and in the fourth corn.

When the girl went to the Rájá after she sat with him for some time the Rájá who was chewing *pán* went into a corner of the room to spit; but when he saw the *tulasi* plant he did not dare defile the goddess and he went to the next corner, but in each he found a goddess sitting. So he came back to her, ashamed and she said:—"O foolish Rájá. You call inanimate objects gods and goddesses and fear to defile them, but you have no fear of Bhagwán and wish to dishonour a Bráhman girl."

The Rájá bowed before her in shame and the boy took her home; but believing that the Rájá had dishonoured her he left her with her father and ran off to his home. His parents were delighted to see him and determined to bring his wife home. So when he and his friends came to claim his bride, he found that she was the daughter of the Pándit. He would not eat food there and ran away to Benares. His relatives returned without the bride and when the boy heard this he came home. Then his father-in-law asked him to come over and see him for one day. He made his son-in-law play at dice with his wife's mother. He first threw the dice with the words:—

> *Bar kul biyáhi bar badhu, háth panw ek chitt;*
> *Kyún biyaho? Kyun pariharyo? Káran ka*
> *sumitt.*

"I married the high born girl of the noble family to a youth who resembled her in every way. Why did you marry her and why did you divorce her friend? If she be true let the throw be 12, if not let it be 17." The throw was 12. Then the Pándit asked his son-in-law to throw, but he refused and his mother-in-law threw the dice with the words:—

> *Mán Sarovar pánh gayon; chonch pánwa*
> *nahín dính.*
> *Upar se jal taulke gawan páchhi kinh.*

"I went to the Mán Sarovar lake but I did not dip my bill or feet in it. I merely measured the water from above and came back, Fall O dice on 12; if this be not so on 17. And the throw was 12."

Then the husband threw the dice with these words:—

> *Jehi márag kehari gayo; gayo Gang trin mánh;*
> *So gayo bhagat phirat; samujhi dekhu jiya*
> *mánh.*

"The elephant saw the tracks of the lion on the Ganges bank and runs away in fear; reflect on this in your mind. O dice if she be true let the throw be 12; if not 17." And the throw was 12.

Then the girl threw with these words:—

> *Kehari kesh, phanig maní aur súr ke astra;*
> *Sati payodhar, Bipra dhan, mue pai lágai hast.*

"You may seize the mane of the lion, the gem of the snake, the weapons of a hero and the breast of the chaste woman or the property of a Bráhman only when they are dead. O dice if I am true let the throw be 12; if not 17." And 12 was the throw.

The husband was then convinced of the innocence of his wife. He accepted food and water from her hands and brought her to his house.

(A folk-tale told by Motiram Pandit of Robertsganj, Mirzapur.)

[For chastity tests Mr. Jacobs (*Folklore Reports*, 1889) refers to Child's *English and Scotch ballads*. I, 266–71; II. 502.—ED.]

233. *The Wisdom of the Daughter of Bírbal.*

One day Akbar sent for Birbal and said: "Procure me masons who will build a house neither on the ground nor in the sky."

When Birbal heard this order he was overcome with grief and was unable to eat. But his daughter came to him and said:—"Father, do not be distressed. Take some leave from the Emperor and I will arrange all."

So Birbal got his leave and his daughter bought some parrots and every day she used to teach them to say—

> *Pahuncháo int gára*
> *Tab banai I mámabára.*

"Bring bricks and mortar and let us build the Imambara."

When they had fully learnt their lesson one day Birbal went to the Emperor and as they were sitting together a flock of parrots flew over the palace crying:—*Pahuncháo int gára, táb banai Imámbára.*

When Akbar heard them he asked what this meant and Birbal replied:—"The masons are ready. If your majesty orders the materials to be brought they will build you a mosque between the earth and the sky." The Emperor laughed and said:—"You may call your masons. Who wants such a mosque to be built?"

(A folk-tale told by Girja Dayal, Kayasth of Ahmedabad, Lucknow district.)

234. The Prince and the Angel of Death.[94]

There was once a king who reached old age and was never blessed with a son. At last when he was well stricken in years Khuda blessed him with an heir. He was much pleased and, summoning the astrologers, required them to calculate the fortune of the prince. They consulted their books and after much consideration said:—"The prince will be very fortunate, but he will die on the seventh day after his marriage."

At this the king was sore troubled and passed his days in care until his son grew up, and fearing calamity, he never married him. At last the prince grew up and asked his father to find a wife for him. Then the king told him the sentence of the astrologers. The prince said:—"All astrologers are liars. Trust not to them. No one but Khuda knows what a man's fate is." So the king found a wife for him, but when he was married the prince feared for his life and leaving his bride rode off to escape his fate.

On the road he saw some men digging a grave and asked them whose it was.

"This is the grave of the prince who has run away to escape his fate," they answered.

In great fear he rode on and found a grave being dug and received the same answer. This happened again a third time. At this his soul nearly left his body, but seeing at a distance a mosque he thought to himself:

"If I am to die, better would it be to die in the house of Khuda."

So he bathed, changed his garments and entered the mosque. There some followers of Islám were praying and when they saw him overcome with grief they asked the reason and he told them his story.

"Pray for me," he implored, "that I may be saved from the Angel of Death."[95]

They consoled him and began to offer up prayers on his behalf. By and by the Angel of Death peeped through the door of the mosque.

"Friends" said he, "you have in your midst one whom Khuda is calling from your world. I have come for him. Make him over to me."

The believers asked:—"Art thou the Angel of Death!"

"I am" he answered.

"We pity" said they, "the fate of this youth. Is there no means by which his life may be spared?"

The Angel answered:—"If each of you give a portion of his span of life to him he may escape." They agreed and prayed to Khuda to save him; and Khuda spared him. Then he started for home and on the road he found all the graves filled up. He recovered his bride, told the whole story to his father who prayed to Khuda with the prince and they all lived happily for many years.

235. *The Pandit and his children.*

There was a Bráhman who had a daughter whom he educated with his other pupils one of whom became a very learned Pandit. One day the old Bráhman said to him:—

"What is the use of my searching for a husband for my daughter? If you agree I will marry her to you."

The Pandit said that he agreed, provided the girl approved, and when she asserted they were married and the old Bráhman and his wife made over all their property to them and took to a life of asceticism. By and by the Pandit's wife had a son, and the moment it was born the Pandit took it into the jungle and said to the baby:—

"On account of our former lives do I owe you anything, or do you owe me?"

The baby replied that his father owed him a thousand rupees. When his father asked how he could repay the debt the child said:—

"Plant a grove and dig a tank and you will be free."

Immediately the child died and his father threw the corpse into the jungle, and going home commenced to plant the grove and dig the tank. The village people thought that the Pandit had intentionally got rid of the child, so they stopped saluting him.

A year after, the Pandit's wife brought forth a second son. In the same way his father took him to the jungle, and when he asked him did he owe him aught the child said:—

"Father, you owe me five hundred rupees." When he asked how he could pay the debt the child said:—

"Build a temple to Siva and sink a well and then you will be free."

So his father threw the child away in the jungle and when he came home began to build the temple and sink the well.

Again the Pandit's wife bore him a third son, and when he took the child into the jungle and asked him if he owed him aught, the child said:

"Father! I owe you a lakh of rupees."

His father began to think: He will hardly ever be able to pay the debt and he will surely live.

So the Pandit brought him home and in order to increase the debt he spent large sums on his teaching and marriage, and when his son became as great a Pandit as himself he one day said to his wife:—

"I am going to make a pilgrimage. If our son earns anything, mind you do not take anything from him."

Soon after the Ráni of that land had a son, and the young Pandit was called to cast his horoscope. After making his calculations the Pandit said to the Rája:—

"His fate is on the whole good, but there will be a time of danger (*kshepak.*) While he is walking round the holy fire at his wedding Rája Indra will shoot an arrow at him."

"Is there anyway of obviating this?" asked the Rája.

"I will announce it when his marriage comes on."

After some years the marriage of the boy was arranged, but the Pandit was not invited and he began to think that if he was not present the boy would surely die; so he went and reminded the Rája of what he had told him at the time of his birth. The Rája made excuses and asked the Pandit to save the life of his son. So the Pandit made an image of wax and dressed it in the clothes of the bridegroom, and as the rite of walking round the fire was being performed he hid the son of the Rája and moved the image round in his stead. Then Rája Indra shot his arrow; the image was consumed to ashes, but the life of the Rája's son was saved. Then the Rája gave the Pandit a lakh of rupees and sent him home with many other rich presents. When he came home with the money he offered it to his mother, but she said:—

"What does a blind woman like me want with money? Give it to your wife."

"O Mother, this is a large sum of money and I cannot give it to my wife. If you will not take it I shall die."

So she was forced to take the money and immediately her son died. Just then his father returned from his pilgrimage and his wife explained how her son had got a large sum of money from the Rája and had required her to take it. The father said:—

"Let us take the corpse to the Rája and die in his Darbar."

They all came with the body of the Pandit to the Rája and having erected a pyre were about to burn themselves with it. When the Rája and his son saw this they said:—

"What is the use of our living when these Bráhmans are going to die?"

So they too prepared to ascend the pyre. Then a voice came from heaven:

"Why are you losing your lives? It was written in his fate that he should die in this way."

The Rája said:

"If Parameswar will revive the Pandit none of us need die."

The old Bráhman said to him:

"If you will give half the life of your son my son will recover."

The Rája agreed and the Pandit arose and said: "Rám Rám" and the Rája after loading them with gifts sent them to their homes.—*Chhedi Sinh, head-master of the School, Partabgarh*

236. The luck of the youngest son.

There was a Banya in a village who had two sons. At one time he was very rich but he fell into poverty. One day he was sitting in his hut and said—

"If I had only a couple of cakes and salt daily I would be happy."

The elder son said—

"If I had only a pair of oxen to plough a field I would be happy."

But the younger son said—

"I will not be happy till I have four Ránis, one to shampoo my feet, another to fan me, a third to bring me a drink of water, and the fourth to cook for me."

"What nonsense for a beggar like you to talk such a folly" they said and beat him out of the hut.

So he ran away and came to a tank where the fairies of Indra were bathing. He seized their clothes and climbing up a tree refused to restore them until they promised to obey him.

Then he came to a palace where the son of a banker was sitting with a princess and they were reading together. The boy asked them to let him stay there and he soon was able to read as well as either of them. One day the princess wrote on her slate that she would run away with him. So they shut up the banker in a room and started. They took a lot of money with them and came to a city where they hired a fine house and lived together. Then he began to attend the Raja's Court and after some time the Raja offered to give him a post and fixed his pay at two lakhs of pies a day; so they called him Lakhtaki.

Lakhtaki and the Raja used to go out hunting and the princess made a contrivance by which he could carry food and drink behind him on the saddle. They wandered into a desert and the Raja would have died of hunger and thirst had not Lakhtaki relieved his need. So the Raja told the Ráni that they ought to give their daughter in marriage to Lakhtaki. The Ráni said.—

"I agree if he can make the fairies of Raja Indra dance before me."

The prince sent at once for the fairies and the princess became his wife. The night of the marriage the princess dropped her gem necklace and when her husband found it and was taking it up it turned into a snake and bit him. Just then up came a Bengalin who tamed snakes and she cured him. But he ran away to the house of a banker and took refuge there and when they asked the banker who he was he had to say from shame that he was his son-in-law and marry him to his daughter and at the same time he married the Bengalin also.

So now he had his four wives and he came home and said to his father and brother.—

"I have attained my desire. Now you may have what you wanted to make you happy."

And they were ashamed before him.

(Told by Gangaram, Brahman, of Kalyanpur, Etah District.)

237. *The witch and the boy.*

One day a porter's son was wandering about and seeing a Gular tree covered with fruit he climbed up and began eating. Just then an old woman came there and said—

"Pass down some of that fruit to me."

So he bent down the branch and when he came within her reach she caught hold of him and put him in her bag. This she threw on her shoulder and went off. By and by she sat down to rest and when he got the chance he popped out of the bag and putting some stones and thorns inside he hid himself. She soon got up and raised the bag on her shoulder. She was going off when a thorn pricked her. Then she called out—

"You young rascal, you may scratch me as you like with your nails, but when I get home I will make soup of you."

When she got home and found the boy had escaped from the bag she was much disgusted, but she was on the look out for him and a few days after she found him on the same tree.

So she caught him and put him in her bag and said—

"You won't escape me this time, my boy."

So she went home and called her daughter-in-law and said—

"You cut up this boy and put him in the soup-pot. I am going to the bázár for some pepper and salt and I will be back by the time he is cooked."

When the young woman took the boy and was going to cut him up she could not help admiring him and said—

"What nice eyes you have and what a pretty round head. How did you manage to be so?"

He answered—

"My mother arranged my eyes with a hot darning needle and she shaped my head with the rice-pounder."

"Will you make me like you?" she asked, and when he said he would she put down her head and he put out her eyes with a hot needle and smashed her head with the rice-pounder and then put her into the soup-pot. When he saw the old woman coming back he dressed himself in the young woman's clothes and sat modestly by the fire with the corner of her sheet over his face.

When the soup was ready the old woman shared it with her family, but when she gave some of the meat to the cat the cat said—

"Spit it out! The mother-in-law is eating her daughter-in-law."

"What is the cat saying?" the old witch asked.

"I will be back in a moment and tell you" said the boy and with that he bolted out of the house. And it was not till the old woman looked into the pot that she found that it was her own daughter-in-law that had been made into soup. I need hardly tell you that the boy kept away from that tree in future.

(Told by Raghunandan Prasad, student. High school, Bulandshahr.)

238. The Ahir's folly.

An Ahir was once going to see his wife at her father's house, and his mother advised him to maintain a grave and sober demeanour.[96] By way of carrying out her advice he put a large stone on his head and stalked up to the house. His mother-in-law asked him what on earth he meant, and when she heard, she said:—"What an awful fool you are!"

As he was taking his wife home he suddenly noticed that the parting of her hair was marked with red.[97] Just then another Ahir came up with an ox. Our friend said to him:—"Brother my wife's head is broken and I don't mind exchanging her for your ox." The man agreed and he drove away the ox. On the way it sat down and chewed the cud. "There is certainly something wrong with this beast's jaws" he thought to himself. Just then a Kurmi passed by with some radishes. "Friend" said the Ahir "My wife's head got broken and I swopped her for this ox and now I find that his jaws are all wrong. Do you mind swapping your radishes for him?" The Kurmi agreed and drove off the ox.

When his mother heard his story she exclaimed:—

"Better had it been that I were childless than cursed with a fool like you."

(A folktale, told by Nadu Kurmi, of Chopan Mirzapur.)

["In the second book of Afanassieff there is a story which speaks of the exchange of animals in the very same order as in the Aitareya Brahmanam i.e. the gold for a horse, the horse for a cow, the cow for a goat or sheep. The Russian peasant goes on with his unfortunate exchanges: he barters the sheep for a young pig, the young pig for a goose, the goose for a duck, the duck for the little stick with which he sees some children playing: and he takes the stick home to his wife who beats him with it." De Gubernatis's *Zoological Mythology* I. 176, who gives other instances].

239. How the Prince won his bride.

There was a Rája who had four sons, of whom three were married but the youngest could not find a wife. One day when the boy was eating he said that the food was badly cooked. One of his sisters-in-law said:—"When you marry the daughter of a king your food will be well cooked." He was angry, and taking a horse and arms, set out on his travels. When he had gone some distance he came to the cross roads and asked a man which way he should go. The man said:—"One road is a journey of six months and the other of twelve." The Prince chose the short road. On the way he met a Rákshasa who was an eater of men and was called Kamdeg or "Slow-foot." The Prince addressed him as "Uncle" and asked his help which he promised to give.

Further on they met another Rákshasa who was called Kamkhurák or "Little feeder." He also went with them. Further on they met a third who was called Kampiyás or "Little thirst" and he also joined their company. On they went and soon they met a multitude of rats, and these also they took with them.

They came to the city of a Rája and put up in a garden outside the town. The Rája had announced that whoever would eat as many cakes as would fill a room, cross a river in a single leap, and drink all the water of a tank, would get his daughter in marriage. So the Prince called the rats and told them to make an underground passage between the garden and the room of the Princess. When the passage was ready the Prince went along it and found her asleep. Her dinner was laid in a dish beneath her bed; of this the Prince ate half, and leaving one of his shoes there, went away. The next day he did the same and the third time he tried to take her ring from her finger but she woke and had him seized and taken to her father. The Rája said:—"If you wish to marry the Princess, you must fulfil the conditions."

So the Prince called Kamkhurák and ordered him to eat up all the cakes in a room at one meal; he told Kampiyás to drink up the water of the tank and Kamdeg to jump across the river in a single bound. These Rakshásas took the form of the Prince and did as the Rája required. So the Rája gave him his daughter and he brought her home and lived happily.

(A folktale told by Bháwáni Din Pánre Bráhman of Faizabad.)

[For the Skilful Companions in Celbic folklore see Mr. Nutt's note to MacInnes *Folk and Hero Tales from Argyleshire* 445 *sq*. In Afanassief the hero is helped in the same way by eating (Abicdalo) and by drinking (Apivalo) who do the eating and drinking for him: See Gubernati's *Zoological Mythology* l. 206.]

240. *The Ahír and the Cow of plenty.*

There was once a poor Ahír in whose herd the Cow of Plenty (*Surabhi gáe*) was reborn. The cow had six calves. The wife of the Ahír was a shrew and never gave him enough to eat, and used to be constantly abusing him. So he used to save a little of his food and take it to the field to eat while he was at work. One day the cow saw this and said to her master:—"Why do you conceal your food in this way? Give the scraps to my children and I will give you as much milk and sweetmeats as you desire." The Ahír did as the cow ordered, and she gave him as much of the choicest food and sweetmeats as he needed. Then she took him to the hole of a snake and said:—"Master, whenever I give you milk and sweets you must always put a little milk and one sweetmeat near the hole for the use of the snake."

The Ahír obeyed her orders.

One day the little son of the Ahír came to the field and his father gave him some of the food which he received from the cow. The boy tied up some of it in his waist cloth. His father said:—"Do not commit this folly. If your mother sees this she will kill me and the cow." The boy promised that he would not show it to his mother; but one day his mother saw some of the sweetmeats with him and asked him where he got them. He said:—"My father gave them to me and the Cow of Plenty gives them to him every day." She said:—"If the cow is such a fool I will have all her calves killed by the butcher and I am going to him this very moment."

When the Ahír heard from his son what his wife had said he was terrified and told the cow. She said:—"Don't be anxious. I am going to bring my children. Go and take leave of the snake and then we will all go to another country."

The Ahír went to the snake and told him what his wife had done. The snake said—"Do you wish me to do anything? I am always at your service." The Ahír answered:—"My mother, the cow has not told me to ask you for anything, but whatever she advises I will ask you to do." He went to the cow and asked her what service he should require from the snake. The cow said:—"Ask him to give you his flute and handkerchief." The snake gave him what he wanted. Then the cow seated the Ahír on her back and with the help of her children carried him off into a jungle. There she made a platform (*machán*) on a palm tree and seated him there, and used to feed him every day with milk and sweetmeats until as he ate this food his hair became the colour of gold. One day the cow ordered her children to take him to the river to bathe, but she warned them not to lose a single one of his hairs. By chance one of his hairs broke off and the calves put it in a leaf cup and let it float down the stream. It floated past a ghát where a princess was bathing and when she saw it, she took it to her father and said "If I cannot marry the man who owns this hair, I must die."

So the Rája sent out many messengers to trace the owner of the golden hair. One old woman came to the forest where he was staying with the cow and said she was the sister of his mother. The cow warned him against her wiles, but he would not heed, and one day the old woman induced him to go out with her in a boat and carried him off to the city of the princess.

The princess was delighted to see him and was about to marry him at once, but he blew his flute and the Cow of Plenty and her calves appeared at once and began to break down the palace of the Rája. He came out and implored the cow to take pity on him. He agreed to build a splendid house for her and she consented to live there with her calves. The Ahír then married the princess, and by reason of the Cow of Plenty, the Rája enjoyed the utmost prosperity.

A folktale told by Bhawani Din Panre Bráhman of Faizabad.

[This is a variant of the "Lucky Herdsman" of which numerous parallels are given by Major Temple and myself in *Indian Antiquary* March, 1893. *Surabhi gáe* is also known as Kámadhena, Kámadhuh, or Savalá. She belonged to the Sage Vasishtha: See Gubernati's *Zoological Mythology* l. 73.]

241. *The tale of the two Queens.*

There was a Rájá who had two wives, one of whom bore a son but the other was barren. One day while the mother of the boy was absent, the barren Rání choked the boy and each laid the blame upon the other. The Rájá was at a loss how to discover which of them had killed the boy, so he said:

"Whichever of you will stand naked before the whole Court I will be sure that she speaks the truth."

The murderess agreed to do as he ordered. Then he said: "Shameless wretch! if you have no regard for your Honour and mine you must have killed the boy."

So he handed her over to the executioner.

(Told by Akbar Sháh Manjhi of Mombasa, Dudhi, Mirzapur District.)

242. *Shaikh Chilli and the Fakir.*

One day Shaikh Chilli was very sick and he vowed that if he got well he would feed a fakir. When he recovered he went out and meeting a fakir he said:—"Will you kindly eat at my house to-day?"

The fakir agreed and when the Shaikh asked him what he would eat, he said he would like an ounce of mung pulse. Shaikh Chilli went back to his wife and said:—

"A fairk will eat here to-day. Cook an ounce of mung pulse and you can give it to him. I perhaps shall not be home as I am going to the mosque to pray."

She cooked the food and gave it to the fakir and then she asked:—

"Do you ever go to Khuda? If so perhaps you can tell me how my parents are getting on."

"I go every day to Khuda," he replied, "and see your parents. They are miserable and get only bones to chow; but the parents of your husband get plenty of *pulao*."

So she gave him five hundred rupees and said: "Please take this money to my parents and let them get better food in future."

When the Shaikh came back his wife said:—

"It is very hard that my parents should have to chew bones while yours get plenty of *pulao*."

When the Shaikh heard this he got on his horse and pursued the fakir. When the fakir saw him he climbed up a tree. The Shaikh climbed after him and shouted:

"Where is my money, you rascal?"

The fakir went out along the branch and the Shaikh followed him. When he came over the place where the horse was tied the fakir jumped on it and rode away. When he came back his wife said: "Where is the horse?"

"When I heard" said he "that my parents had such high rank in heaven, I thought it only proper that they should have a horse to ride there. So I sent them mine."

(Told by Muhammad Halim and recorded by M. Rám Sahay of Lucknow.)

243. *The young Bráhman and his Wife.*

Once upon a time a Rájá was sinking a tank and hard as the labourers worked not a drop of water would remain in it. The Rájá called the *pandits* and asked them how the tank could be filled with water. They told him that this would occur only when he sacrified a Bráhman boy at the tank. He gave them money and told them to buy a boy. With great difficulty they got a Bráhman to sell his son to be sacrificed. When the time to sacrifice him came he recited the following verse:—

> *Máta pita mál ke lobhi; Rájá lobhi ságara.*
> *Deva, Daitya rakta kar bhukha dhanya dhanya*
> *to ságara,*

"My parents covet wealth, the Rájá covets the tank; the gods and goblins covet blood; blessed is the tank."

When he had finished this verse the Rájá had the boy sacrificed. Immediately water appeared in the tank. Rejoicings were made and every one returned home.

After some days the boy appeared in the centre of the tank in the form of a lotus. Many people tried to pluck it, but when any one came near it, it used to disappear in the water. One day the boy's wife happened to go to the tank to bathe. She, too, saw the lotus and tried to pluck it. But the lotus disappeared and then she began to think that it was her husband who had been sacrificed. So she sat on the bank of the tank and determined to stay there until her husband was restored to her. At midnight her husband came out of the lotus and went into the hollow (*khokhra*) of the tree and sat down there. After some time a man came to him with a dish of food, and after eating and drinking with him went away. The girl saw all this, and when her husband returned to the lotus she went into another hole in the same tree and sat there. The next night the boy again came out and sat in the same place. The man again brought him food, and when they went to divide it into two parts it divided itself into three. They were astonished but did not trouble themselves to find out the reason. They left the third portion there and went away. The girl in this way lived on the share of her husband's food. One day she caught the feet of her husband as he was going back to the lotus; but he said:—"You cannot recover me in this way. Sit at the tank for seven days and then you will get me back for ever." She obeyed his words; and when six days had passed Parámeswar in the form of a Bráhman came to her and asked:—"Why are you sitting there?" She said:—"I am sitting here until I get that lotus flower." Parámeswar brought her the lotus flower. She at once bowed down in worship before it, when a boy twelve years old came out of it. The girl took the boy to the Rájá who had them married and gave them half his kingdom and she and her husband lived many years in happiness.

(A folktale told by Bhawani Din, Bráhman, of Faizabad.)

[This reviving of the dead in the form of plants is very common. See, for instance, the Comtesse d'Aulnay's *Fortunée;* Lang: *Blue Fairy Tale Book,* 148, sqq—Ed.]

244. Shaikh Chilli and his Turban.

One day Shaikh Chilli was going to see his wife at the house of her father and when he had gone a long way he was tired and sat down by a well to rest. He felt sleepy, but not wishing to disarrange his turban he lay down on the platform of the well with his head over the mouth and fell asleep. As he slept his turban fell into the well and when he woke he thought nothing of his bare head and went so on to the house of his father-in-law.

Now among his people to go about bareheaded was a sign of mourning and when his relatives saw him thus they began to wail and beat their breasts and called out—

"Which of our dear relations is dead?"

"What do you mean?" he replied. "No one that I know of is dead."

"Then why do you go about bareheaded?" they angrily asked.

"Is it a fact" said he, putting his hand to his head, "that I am without a turban?"

But they were so enraged at being taken in that they fell on him and beat him out of the village. So he lost his wife in the bargain.

A folktale told by Muhammad Halim and recorded by M. Rám Sahai, sub-editor, "Educational Gazette," Lucknow.

245. *The City of the Jinn.*

A fakir was once making a journey and saw a great city in ruins and the people living in huts on its borders. When he enquired the cause they said:—"This city is infested by the Jinn and we dare not live therein." So the fakir went into one of the deserted palaces and having killed two goats, cut them up and placing the flesh in two cauldrons with some rice proceeded to cook it for himself and his companions. But when he opened the cauldrons he found naught therein, because the Jinn had eaten the food. Three times he did the same and each time the Jinn devoured the food. Then he filled the cauldrons with oil and when it was boiled by the force of his spells, he consumed the Jinn therein. Only the leader of their host escaped and he came and kneeling before the fakir asked for mercy. The fakir pardoned him on condition that he left the city in peace. Then he called to the people of the city to return to their homes. But they refused to come unless the fakir remained to guard them. So he stayed in the city as long as he lived and thenceforth the people lived in safety.

Told by Urfan Ali, of Bhanwar, Bijnor.

246. *The Bard and his Wife.*[98]

Once upon a time a Bhát[99] and his wife lived in a village. On the day of the Godhan feast these people did not fast and curse their relations as the other villagers did.[100] The sister of the bard was very angry at this and told a snake who was her friend to bite the Bhát. He went to bathe in a tank and while he was in the water the snake came out and sat in his turban. The Bhát saw it and called to his companions to kill it. They did so.

When he came home, he told his wife what had happened. She went at once to the tank, and brought the dead body of the snake home. Then she cut it into pieces and distributed them as follows:—One she put into an earthen pot: a second in the frying-pan: a third in the locks of her hair: a fourth she tied round her waist, and the fifth she squeezed into oil and put it in the lamp saucer: and one piece she put under each leg of the bed. At night when she lay down to sleep near her husband she said:—"I will tell you a riddle and if you cannot give the answer I will kill you."

"Say on" he answered.

So she said—

"Some are in the locks: some round the waist some in the earthen pot: some in the frying-pan some under the four legs: some in the lamp: some in the wick which burns all night. Now read me the riddle.[101] The husband said:—"I cannot tell the answer now, but wait till to-morrow." Next morning he went to his sister, and told her all about it. They both went to the tank.

At midnight all the lamps of the village came to the tank and began burning there. Last of all, when one watch of night remained, the lamp which contained the snake oil came.

All the other lamps said to it:—

"Why are you so late?"

"I had terrible adventures and escaped only with the utmost difficulty," it replied. Then the lamp told what had happened: and when they heard it all the Bhát and his sister returned home. Then he told the answer of the riddle to his wife. She was much surprised and spared her husband's life.

247. *Women rule the World.*

One day a Raja said to his courtiers:—

"Who rules the world?"

They were unable to give an answer then and begged time for consideration. The Wazir was in great distress what answer to give, for he feared that if his answer turned out wrong, he would lose his office. As he was going home he saw the daughter of the Raja who was a very wise princess sitting at her window and when she saw the anxiety of the Wazir, she asked the reason. He told her the question which the Raja had proposed to his courtiers. She said—

"When you go before my father say that it is women who rule the world."

The Wazír trusted in her wisdom and when the Raja again summoned him he gave this reply. Now the Raja hoped that the Wazir would say that it was the Raja who ruled the world; so he was wroth and knowing that it must be some woman who had suggested the answer, he made the Wazir tell her name. When he heard that it was his daughter who had suggested the answer, he sent an officer with orders to her to strip off her dress and ornament and bring her to the court with one dirty rag to wear.

When she came, he sent for a loathsome beggar who used to beg about the city and he made her over to him, telling him that he might use her as he pleased.

The princess went in great distress to his hut with the beggar; but before she left the palace she managed to conceal one valuable jewel in a corner of her rags. When she got to the hut she took it out and said:—

"You must go with this to the quarter of the money changers and sell it. You must not say a word. I will write down the price of the jewel on a leaf and lay it and the jewel before the merchant and he will give you the value of it."

The beggar did as he was told and when the merchant saw that he kept silence he supposed that he was some great saint under a vow not to speak. So he was afraid and counted out the money as the princess had written on the leaf. This the beggar brought home to her.

Now it so chanced that two thieves saw the beggar getting the money from the merchant and determined to rob him. So they waited till the beggar was out of the hut and then they broke in. When the princess saw them she was afraid. But she made a plan and said to them—

"You are welcome. Here I a lady of high birth have been given by my father to this filthy beggar. Will you save me from him?"

One of them gladly agreed to marry her and she told them to go off at once and bring a litter that she would go with them as a bride. Meanwhile the beggar returned and she told him what had happened. She made him hide himself and by and by the thieves returned and brought with them a litter and bearers. Then she said to them—

"The first night I came here Devi sat on my breast and would have taken my life had I not vowed to offer to her a black goat on the eighth of every month and this is the day of the sacrifice. I dare not set out till it is done."

So one of the thieves went to get a goat and soon after she said to the other:—

"I am sorry that when I sent your brother for the goat I forgot to ask him to bring some flowers as well, for without them the sacrifice cannot be performed." So he went away to get the flowers and then she called the beggar and seating herself in it with him she told the bearers to take them to the house of the thieves. When they arrived there, they went in and bolted the door and told the bearers that the house was her's and if the thieves came up they were to beat them off.

When the thieves came and could not get into their house they made a great disturbance, but the people of the quarter who were sore afflicted by them came up and drove them out of the place. Then the thieves went and made a complaint to the Qazi.

When the princess heard that they had complained to the Qazi she went to him herself and told him that she had bought the house for two hundred rupees and if he wished he might come and see it that night at the first watch. When he saw that she was a handsome girl he readily agreed to come. Then in the same way she went to the Kotwal and asked him to come at the second watch; the Wazir she asked for the third watch and the Raja for the fourth watch of the night.

When the Qazi came she kept him talking about the thieves until the Kotwal knocked, when she told him to take off his clothes and hide behind the water-pots.

So she dealt with the Kotwal and when the Wazir knocked, she told him to take off his clothes and put on a woman's old ragged petticoat and sit in a corner and grind the flour-mill.

In the same way when the Wazir came and after he had been some time with her the Raja knocked, she made him take off his clothes and hide under the granaray. Meanwhile she went into another room and soon after the Raja felt thirsty and went to where the water was kept to get a drink. The Qazi was so frightened that he moved and knocked down the water-pots, and when the Raja saw him standing naked there he was sure he was a Rákshasa and began to scream for help. Then the princess came down and when she brought a light the Qazi, Kotwal and Wazíi, were all discovered to the Raja; they were all ashamed. But the girl said to her father—

"Do you not know that I am your daughter and it is women who rule the world."

So the Raja took her to the palace and had her duly married, but the thieves he made over to the Kotwal.

Told by Manna Lal, Awasthi, teacher of the Akbarpur School, Cawnpur.

[This is another version of the famous worldwide tale of the "Lady and her Suitors." We find it in the *Gesha Romanorum, Arabian Nights, Kattra Sarit Sagara*, and many other collections. See Clouston *Popular Tales and Fictions*, II, 289, Ed.]

248. *The Fool and his House.*

There was a fool whose roof was so shaky that he was always putting in posts to prop it up. At length his house became so full of posts that there was no room in it and he was obliged to sit outside. One day a neighbour passed and seeing him sitting outside said:—

"Why don't you sit inside."

"Had there been any room" quoth he "do you think I would have lost the chance of sticking in another post?"

Told by Khairati Lal, student, High school, Bulandshar.

249. *The story of a Banya's son.*

A Banya had a very promising son and suspecting that he would go on his travels when he got a chance married him to a beautiful girl, thinking that thus he would detain him at home. But the young man would not be persuaded: and started on his travels. He halted at the hut (*kuti*) of a fakir. The *sadhu* (ascetic) was absorbed in meditation. Then he asked the boy about his circumstances, and then he gave him three pieces of advice—first, that a man should not leave home alone, but should have a companion however weak or useless he may be; secondly, that a traveller should not take the middle but one of the side roads where three roads meet at a point; and thirdly, that a stranger should not take his seat on a couch however well adorned it may be without striking it first with his hand or with a stick. The Banya's son gave him a present and went on his way. In a shallow pool which lay near the road, he caught a crab (*kekra*) and put it into his turban. Then he came under a shady tree in the branches of which lived a serpent and a crow who were bosom friends. The youth was tired and went to sleep in the shade. The two friends wishing evil to the youth came down and the serpent bit him. The crow tried to pick out his eyes, but the crab in compassion caught the bird by the neck and refused to let it go until the serpent agreed to take back the poison which he had infused into the youth's body. The serpent did so and the youth recovered. Then by the crab's advice he killed the two treacherous friends and went on until he reached the sea shore. The crab asked to be allowed to go into the water and he dived in and soon came out with two gems. The Banya's son cut a hole in the flesh of his thighs and put in the gems, so that they might not be stolen. Then the crab left him and went into the sea and he pursued his journey. Next he came to the house of a *Dáin* or witch who had seven sons and a beautiful daughter who, on the first glance, knew that the youth had the gems. So she welcomed him and provided him with all he needed. But soon she began to pity him and when every one was asleep she went and advised him to escape before morning, lest her mother and brothers should kill and eat him. He was confounded and brought the girl to help him. Now the witch had two elephants, one worth a thousand and the other ten thousand rupees. They differed in this that while one took one step the other took ten. By mistake the girl mounted him on the slower elephant and did not perceive her mistake until her seven brothers mounted the swift elephant and started in pursuit of them. She saw a thicket and induced the youth to get down and conceal himself, intending while they were searching for him, to change the elephants. So she did and her brothers finding themselves outwitted turned back. The Banya's son returned home, built a house for the witch's daughter and took her to wife, and gave the jewels to his first wife who, in the meantime, had fallen in love with a goldsmith. She also gave him all the valuable stones which the Banya possessed. When he learned this he was overcome with grief, and all he could say was Hai Lal! Many doctors came, but none could cure him. Meanwhile his son's new wife busied herself in tracing out the thief. So at dead of night she pitched a splendid tent outside the town and announced herself to be a lovely dancing girl whose face no one could see without paying a heavy fee. The goldsmith offered anything she pleased. So he came and she seated him on a couch and asked his leave to take her food. In an earthen pot she put some water and began to heat it. She managed to put off cooking her food by various excuses and asked the goldsmith to come next evening. Disguised as a doctor she went to the house of her father-in-law and promised to cure him before long. She was allowed in and after encouraging him went away. Finally she induced the goldsmith to give her the jewels and when the Banya next called out *Hai Lál* "alas! my boy," she showed him the rubies (*lál*) and he recovered. So his son killed his faithless wife and lived happily with his new wife ever after.

A folktale worded by Lala Rajbahadur Lal of Mirzapur.

[Here we have the usual mixture of incidents. The faithful animal has appeared in several of these tales: see Temple, *Wideawake Stories* 412 for Indian instances, and for those from Europe Clouston: *Popular Tales and Fictions*, I, 223, *sqq;* who has collected various instances of concealing jewels in the thigh in *"A group of Eastern Romances,"* 541 *sqq.* For the aiding animals see also Jacob's *Proceedings Folklore Congress* 1891, p. 88.]

250. *Which is greater—Rama or Khuda.*

A Hindu and a Muhammadan fakir were once disputing. The Hindu said that Rámá and the Muhammadan said that Khudá was the greater. So they went to Rájá Vikramaditya to decide the dispute. The Rájá ordered the Hindu to climb up a palm tree and jump down. As he jumped he thought of Rámá and was not hurt. When the Muhammadan went up seeing how the Hindu had escaped he began to think that he had better invoke both the deities. So with an invocation to Rámá and Khudá he jumped and was dashed to pieces.

So Kabir Das writes:—

> *Do nawa na chariye;*
> *Doka phatke biche giriye.*

"Do not sit on two boats when crossing a stream. You will fall betwixt them and loose your life."

(Told by Devi Dayal Lal, Teacher of the Jamuni Mahadeva School, Basti District)

251. *The two Women and the Dog.*

There were once two sisters-in-law, the Jehani and the Devarani, who were cooking together. A dog came in and ate the food prepared by the younger woman; so she took up a bludgeon and broke his back. But the elder woman took pity on him and gave him food.

In the next birth both the women were re-born in the family of a Bráhman, and the elder sister became rich and prosperous while the younger was born to menial work. She had seven sons all of whom died one after the other. Then she went to a Pándit and explained her case. When he looked at his books he said:—"This is the result of your cruelty to the dog. Now you can procure release only by deeds of charity."

So she began to do charity, and one night the dog appeared to her in a dream and said to her:—"This is the result of your breaking my back. Now I have broken your back by being re-born seven times as your son who died. Go on doing works of charity and I shall be again re-born as your son and you will prosper."

(A folktale told by Siva Prasad, Teacher of the Orai School, Jalaun District.)

252. The wicked Queen and her Step-children.

A certain king had a son and a daughter, and when he married a second time their step-mother was displeased with them and induced their father to get rid of them. So he called the snake-catchers and told them to catch the smallest snake they could find. They brought a very little snake and this the king had put in the water goblet used by the children. When they returned from school the girl went to get a drink and soon after returned to her brother and said: "As I was drinking something went into my stomach." He said "nonsense! You drank too fast and so thought that something had gone down your throat."

So the children left home in grief, and wandering on they knew not where, came to a great jungle and there saw a great house, the door of which was shut. There they sat weeping. Now in front of the house a cow was tied and she took pity on the children and prayed to God (*khuda*) "O God! Give me only the power to speak and I will comfort them." So God heard her prayer and gave her the power of speech. The cow asked "why are you weeping?" The children told her who they were and how they had been driven from home. The cow said:—"I will open this house for you, stay here. Give me a little grass now and then and I will supply you with as much milk as you want." So the cow opened the house and then she lost the power of speech. The children slept in the house and in the morning milked the cow: they drank some and put the rest on the fire to boil. Then the boy said:—"Sister! I am going out to get grass for the cow and search for some fruits in the jungle." So he went out leaving his sister alone, and she lay down to sleep. Then the snake came out of her stomach and drank all the milk, and then went down her throat again. When the boy returned he woke his sister and said:—"Bring the milk, I am hungry." She said:—"I am hungry too," but when she went to look what did she see? that all the milk was gone. She told her brother and they had to fast till evening. In the evening they milked the cow and made their supper on milk and some fruits which the boy had brought. The rest of the milk they put in the fire to boil and when the girl went to sleep, the snake came again out of the stomach and drank the milk.

So it went on for many days. At last the boy thought "I will sit up and catch the thief who steals our milk." So he watched and saw the snake come out of his sister's throat, drink the milk and go back again. Next night he armed himself with a club and sat up again. When the snake came out the boy struck it with a stick and killed it. Then he took the dead snake and threw it into a pit, and went to cut grass for the cow.

When his sister got up and saw that the milk was safe she told her brother. He said:—"I killed the thief to-day." She asked—"What thief?" "A snake" he answered "used to come out of your mouth and drink the milk." "I told you" she said, "the day we left home that something went down my throat." "This must be the same snake," he said. After that the milk was not stolen. One day the girl said:—"I am very lonely while you are away. Take me with you." He agreed. So they went out togother to cut grass for the cow, and as they were returning the girl happened to look into the pit into which the boy had thrown the snake. But the snake had turned into a tree on which a beautiful flower was growing. When the girl saw the flower she said to her brother, "Pull it for me." When he saw the fruit he suspected that it was the snake, and thought that if he plucked it injury might result. So he began to make excuses to his sister. At last as she insisted he had to give her the fruit, she was very tired and said:—"Brother I am very tired." So he took her on his back, and as they went on she said to him:—"If I put this flower in your turban you will look so handsome." She then put the flower in his turban and he was immediately turned into a snake. As he was crawling away his sister kept calling out "Oh my brother! O my brother!" but he paid no attention to her, and at last they came to a river into which the snake jumped. His sister sat on the bank weeping until in three days she became dumb from dint of crying.

At last on the third day a king's son came up to the place, and saw the girl sitting there weeping. He asked her the cause of her distress, and she signed with her hand that her brother had been turned into a snake and had jumped into the river. But he could not understand what she meant, and pitying her took her home and said to his mother:—"This seems to be the daughter of some nobleman (*amir*) because though she is dumb she is very beautiful." At last he fell so much in love with her that he married her. On their marriage day her tongue was loosed, and she told how she was the daughter of a king and detailed the whole story and how her brother had become a snake and jumped into the river. Then the king of the land had many large earthen vessels (*nand*) sunk in the ground and filled with milk and made proclamation to the snake-catchers that whoever should seize the snake which the girl pointed out, would receive a great reward.

The first day many snakes came out of the river to drink the milk, but her brother was not among them. She looked at all the snakes and said:— "My brother is not here." Next day the King had the vessels again filled with milk and many snakes appeared; but even then her brother did not appear. On the fourth day, however, her brother came out of the river and the moment she saw him she cried out:—"This is my brother." At once the snake catchers trapped him and lo! the snake had a long loch (*chonti*) on his head. The moment the snake catchers pulled this out he turned into a man again, and embraced his sister.

The king asked him:—"How far is your home from here?" The young man replied:—"a week's journey." So the king took the brother and sister with him to their home. When the young man saw his father he said:— "Hail father!" (*báp ján, salám!*) and his fathier said:—"Why do you call me father? I had only two children, and these I turned out of my house. And when I heard that they were innocent I was much grieved and searched for them. Nay, I promised half my kingdom to whomsoever would recover them. But from that day to this there is no trace of them." The youth answered:—"I am the son whom you expelled from home." Then the king embraced his son and daughter and had his wife killed. Some days after he sent off his daughter with her husband. The youth remained with his father, succeeded to the kingdom on his death, and ruled his kingdom with wisdom and valour.—*Lal Behari De,* 117.

A folktale recorded by E. David, A Native Christian of Mirzapur, and literally translated.

NOTES

1. The word used was larná = to fight, contend, dispute.

2. The Pankas are aboriginal weavers and, like the Juláhas of the plain country, proverbially fools.—ED.

3. This is the common way of inviting guests.—ED.

4. In the original sat, *dharna*.—ED.

5. A folktale told by Akbar Sháh, Mánjhi, of Manbasa, Dudhi, Mirzapur, and recorded by Pandit Rámgharíb Chaubé.

6. *Suggá gayé hain Nandban,*
   Hansá Sarowar Tál: Mantrí hain ab kág, srig:
   Ihwán buri ahwál.
   Nandban is in Mathura,
   Mánsarowar lake on the Himálaya.

7. A folktale told by Ramanandan Lál, Village accountant, Kon, Mirzapur District, recorded by Pandit Rammgharíb Chaubé.

8. Folktale recorded by Lála Rajbahadur Lál of Mirzapur.

9. A folktale told by Ali Sajjad, Assistant Registrar of Mirzapur.

10. A respectful way of addressing a faqír.

11. *Takiyá*, the place where a Musalmán faqir stays.

12. The Rájputais' way of addressing her husband.

13. A folktale told by Akbar Sháh, Mánjhi, of Manbasa, Dudhi, Mirzapur, and recorded by Pandit Ramgharíb Chaubé.

14. A folktale told by Akbar Sháh, Manjhi, of Manbasa, Dudhi, Mirzapur, and recorded by Pandit Ramgharíb Chaubé.

15. In the original Nekí and Badi.

16. A folktale told by Shyam Sundar, a village accountant of Dudhi, Mirzapur District, recorded by Abmadullah.

[This lamenting for nothing appears in Temple's *Wideawake Stories*—"The death and burial of poor hen-sparrow."

Something like it is "The unwise schoolmaster who fell in love by report"(Lady Burton's *Arabian Nights*, III, 228) ; and "Telty Mouse and Talty Mouse" (Jacob's *English Fairy Tales* with note, p. 234, *sqq.*)—ED.].

17. A tale told by Waziran, a Muhammadan Ayah, and recorded by Mirza Mahmud Beg.

18. A folktale told by Setha Manjhi of Mahuli, Dudhi, Mirzapur.

[This is the usual cumulative cycle "This is the house that Jack built, etc." See Clouston, *Popular Tales and Fictions*, I, 289, *sqq.* Another version was given in *North Indian Notes and Queries*, II, para. 181.

19. A folktale told by Hazari Lal, a village accountant of Chopan, Mirzapur.

[For forbidden rooms of the Blue Beard cycle, see Clouston, *Popular Tales and Fictions*, I, 198 sqq; the faqir is deceived as Vetála is at the time of sacrifice in *Katha*

Sarit Ságara. (Translation, Tawney II, 359). For the gambling device of the cat and mouse the best parallel is Rája Rasálu (Temple: *Wideawake Stories*, p. 278)

20. A folktale told by Akbar Shah, Mánjhi, of Manbasa, *Dudhi* Mirzapur.

21. A folktale told by Akbar Shah, Mánjhi, of Manbasa, *Dudhi*, Mirzapur.

22. A folktale told by Akbar Shah, Mánjhi, of Manbasa, *Dudhi*, Mirzapur District.

23. A folktale told by Akbar Shah, Mánjhi, of Manbasa, Dudhi, Mirzapur District: recorded by Pandit Rám Gharib Chaubé.

[There is a similar story of a snake who gives a Bráhman, who is kind to him, a gold piece every day, in the Third Book of the *Panchatantra*. The tale of Pipa, the Bráhman (Tod, *Annals of Rajasthán*, I, 777, *sq.*), is very similar to this. Connected with it is the story of the "Goose and the Golden eggs" (*Exempla* of Jacques De Vitry, 78, *sq.*) and the references collected by Professor Crane, 209. Also see "The Gold-giving Serpent:" Jacob's *Indian Fairy Tales*, 246.—ED.].

24. A folktale told by Mádho Prasád, a clerk in the Collector's Office, Mirzapur.

25. A folktale told by Lachhman Ahir, a cultivator of Mirzapur, and recorded by E. David, Native Christian.

26. A folktale recorded by Baba Anumol Sinh, of Azamgarh.

27. Syáwa Karna appears often in folklore. Such a horse was used in the Asvamedha.

28. The analogy to Ali Baba in the *Arabian Nights* is obvious.

29. A folktale told by Waziran, a Muhammadan woman, and recorded by Mirza Mahmud Beg.

30. Told by Iláhi Bakhsh, bhishti, of Nadehra, Dholpur State.

31. A folktale told by Akbar Sháh, Mánjhí, of Manbasa, Dudh, Mirzapur District: recorded by Pandit Ramgharib Chaube.

32. A folktale told by Hira Lal, Village Accountant, of Haliya, Mirzapur.

33. A folktale told by Farzand Ali, of Rae-Bareli.

34. A folktale told by Akbar Shah, Manjhi, of Manbasa, Dudhi, Mirzapur.

35. A folktale told by Shiudan Chamar, of Chaukiya, Mirzapur.

36. A folktale told by Chatur Bihari Lál, of Narera, Pilibhit.

37. Told by Abdul Hasan Khán, teacher of Karaili Village School, Pilibhit District.

38. Told by Annie Solomon, a Native Christian woman of Mirzapur, and recorded by E. David, Native Christian.

39. Told by Ramnandan Lál, village accountant, Kon, Mirzapur

40. Told by Pritam Siuh, Sánsya, of Karaili, Pilibhit.

41. A folktale told by Mukand Lál, Káyasth, of Mirzapur.

42. A folktale told by Bachau Kasera, of Mirzapur.

43. A Folktale told by Shiu Sahái, Teacher of the Village School of Daghari Chakeri, Etah District.

44. A Folktale told by Shiudán Chamár, of Chaukiya, Mirzapur.

45. A Folktale and recorded by Nand Lál, Bráhman, of Nardaul, Etah District.

46. A Folktale told by Mazhar Husen, of Mirzapur.

47. A Folktale told by Faqír Chand, a Village School Teacher of the Pilibhit District.

48. A Folktale told by Bachau Kasera, of Mirzapur.

49. [For the variants of this famous Folktale, see Clouston: *Popular Tales and Fic-*

tions, II., 413 *sqq*: the Indian Tale is found in an early version in the *Katha Sarit Ságara* (Tawney: Translation, I., 272, with his note.—Ed.]

50. Told and recorded by Khadim Husen, a Musalmán tailor of Saháwar, Etah District.

51. Told and recorded by Maha ráj Swarúp, teacher of the village school, Jalesar, Etah District.

52. Told-by Hazari, Brahman, of Mirzapur, and recorded by Shekh Ahmadullah.

53. Told by Thakur Umráo Sinha, of Sonhár, Etah District.

54. Told and recorded by Babu Gandharab Sinha of Etah.

55. A folktale told by Ali Sajjad, qanungo, Mirzapur.

56. A folktale told by Bhawani Din, Brahman of Faizabad.

57. A folktale told by Ramnandan Lál, village accountant of Kon, Mirzapur District.

58. A folktale told by Mukund Lál, Káyasth, of Mirzapur.

59. A folktale told by Ramanand Tiwari, Brahman of Rám patti, Mirzapur.

60. A folktale told by Mukund Lál, Káyasth, of Mirzapur.

61. A folktale told by Sital Prasad, Brahman of Mirzapur.

62. A folktale told by Mukund Lál, Káyasth, of Mirzapur.

63. A folktale told by Mukund Lál, Káyasth, of Mirzapur.

64. A folktale told by Mukund Lál, Káyasth, of Mirzapur.

65. A folktale recorded by Mr. H. Finch, of Meuna, Shahahanpur.

66. A folktale told by Bhawáni Dín Panre Bráhmán, of Faizabad.

67. A folktale told by Jagat Pal Singh, of Chakritpur, Teacher, Akbarpur, Faizabad District.

68. A folktale told by Sital Prasad, Sukl Brahman, of Mirzapur.

69. A folktale told by Raghunandan Swami of Ramaipatti, Mirzapur.

70. A folktale told by Gopal Chand, Teacher of Dhirpara School, Agra District.

71. A folktale told by Nagnu Kurmi, of Chopan, Mirzapur.

72. A folktale told by Mukund Lal, Kayasth, of Mirzapur.

73. A folktale told by Mukund Lal, Kayasth, of Mirzapur.

74. Karnálpur as if from Sans *Karna*=ea: *Sunetra*=he with the lovely eyes.

75. Here, as in others of these tales, we have one of the Ali Bába incidents.

76. The arti or parachhan to repel evil spirits.

77. A respectful term for a Faqír.

78. A folktale told by Akbar Sháh Manjhi, of Manbasa, Dudhi, Mirzapur.

79. A folktale told by Akbar Sháh Mánjhi, of Manbasa, Dudhi, Mirzapur District.

80. *Swet, swet—sab ek sé jahán kapúr, kapás:*
    Aisé des kudes men kabhún na kijé bás.

81. A folktale told by Mádho Prasád, clerk in the Collector's Office, Mirzapur.

82. *Bharbhúnja.*

83. Great Devi, a title of respect.

84. *Jaymál.*

84. A folktale told by Pandit Rámgharib Chaubé.

85. Speak! speak!

86. The bitter leaves of the *aziderachta Indica*.

87. *Dauná.*

88. Told by Ali Sajjad, Registrar of Hallia, Mirzapur District: recorded by Pandit Rámgharíb Chaubé.

89. *Mausi*, a term of endearment.

90. A folktale told by Rahim Bakhsh, weaver, of Mirzapur: recorded by Pandit Rámgharíb Chaubé.

91. The *jámun* is the Eugenia jambolana, or black plum. The fruit is sub-acid and astringent, and generally eaten with a little salt.

92. The *gobraurá*, which is something like a *jamun* in appearance.

93. *Kali* means a fruit, or a pipe bowl.

94. A folk-tale told by Ashraf, weaver of Hallia, Mirzapur district. Recorded by Pándit Rám Gharib Chaubé.

95. Malaku'lmaut, also called lzráil. In the *Qurán, Surah* XXXII-14, we read: "The Angel of Death who is charged with you shall cause you to die: then ye shall be returned to your Lord."

96. The word in the original is *garhu gambhir*, which means "grave" or "heavy."

97. This is the steak of red lead (*sendur*) which every married woman wears in the parting (*máng*) of her hair.

98. A folktale told by the wife of Ramai Kharwár of Dudhi, Mirzapur District and recorded by Pandit Rám Ghárib Chaube.

99. A bard or genealogist.

100. The Godhan is a women's festival, held in the Eastern Districts of the North-Western Provinces two days after the *Diwáli* when women make clay figures of snakes, scorpions, &c. and beat them and abuse their friends to bring good luck on the house.

101. *Kuchh jurá; kuchh phurhurá*
Kuchh hándi, kuchh dali:
Kurchh chúon pawa:
Kuchh dryá, kuchh báti,
Jarai sari rati

FROM THE *INDIAN ANTIQUARY*

❧ *Folk-Tales from Northern India* ❧

[The following folk-tales and fables were collected by the late Dr. William Crooke, C.I.E., and were probably intended to be published in book-form. After his death, they were forwarded to Mr. S. M. Edwardes, on the chance that he might be able to make use of them. As the tales are numerous and possess a value for students of folk-lore, it has been decided to publish a selection of them in this Journal. In nearly every case Dr. Crooke had entered above each story the names of the persons who told it and recorded it. These names have accordingly been reproduced, as well as a few notes by Dr. Crooke appended to some of the stories.— ED.]

1. The slave discovered.

(Told by Lâla Sankar Lâl of Sahâranpur and recorded by Pandit Râm Gharîb Chaube.)

A nobleman once had a slave who absconded with a large sum of money. Some time later his master found him by chance in a distant city. When he took him before the Kâzi, the slave said:—"I am not this man's slave, but he is my slave." The master was confounded at his insolence. So the Kâzi sent his servant outside. Then he made the master and man put their heads through a slit in the wall, and he called to his servant:— "Cut off the slave's head with your sword." The slave blenched at the order and drew in his head, while his master remained unmoved. Thus the Kâzi decided which of them was the slave.

2. The man and the loaves.

(Told by Lâla Devî Prasâd of Aligarh and recorded by Pandit Râm Gharîb Chaube.)

A certain man used to buy six loaves daily at the baker's shop. To a friend who enquired how he consumed all this bread, he replied:—"One loaf I keep; one I throw away; two I give in discharge of a debt; and two

I lend." The friend asked him to explain, and he answered:—"The loaf which I keep, I eat myself; the loaf I throw away I give to my wife; the two for the discharge of debt I give to my parents; and the two which I lend I give to my children."

3. The cuckoo and the owl.

(Told by Ganesa Lâl, Schoolmaster, Digh, Fatehpur District.)

A cuckoo and an owl once dwelt in the same tree. One day the cuckoo flew to the court of Indra and sang so sweetly that he and all his fairies were delighted and gave him many presents. "Who are the other sweet singers in the land of men?" asked Indra Râja, and the cuckoo replied:— "The peacock, the bumble bee, the maina and the nightingale, the parrot and myself are the six great singers."

When the cuckoo returned and showed his presents to the owl, the latter was envious and flew himself to Indra's court, and alighting on a tree began to hoot. Indra, hearing him, thought some Râkshasa had come to trouble him. So he called him and said:—"Who are the great singers in the land of men?" The owl replied:—"The owl, the ass, the dog, the jackal, the crow and tire cat—these are the best singers in the world." So Indra drove him forth with blows, saying, "You with your hooting would alone destroy the land of fairies. The earth must be made of iron to stand you and your five friends."

4. The two Fakirs.

(Told by Misra Gomati Prasâd of Bânsi, Basti District.)

One day a Hindu fakir came to the court of Akbar and presented some holy ashes (râkh). Then came a Musalman fakir who presented some sweet basil (*sabz, sabja*). The Muhammadan courtiers remarked "How much better is the gift of the Musalman. He brought a green plant, but the Hindu ill-omened ashes." A Hindu answered them:—"*Râkh* is a lucky gift, for it signifies 'Keep all things safe'; but *sabja* means 'let everything go (*sab jâ*).'"

5. The defeated Pandit.

(Told by Dulâse Lâl Brahman and recorded by Jagat Bahâdur Lâl of Basitpur, Hardoi District.)

Two Pandits once had a dispute about capping one another's verses, and one of them, having defeated the other, took all his goods. The defeated Pandit then fetched his brother, who managed to defeat the other.

Then in view of the whole village he pulled a hair out of the moustache of his defeated rival, and when they asked why he did this, he said:— "The hair of the moustache of this Pandit is excellent for keeping demons out of the house." Hearing this, everyone in the village wanted a hair; and therefore, they fell upon the unfortunate Pandit and pulled out every hair of his beard and moustache.

6. Life as an inn.

(Told by Lâla Sankar Lâl of Sahâranpur and recorded by Pandit Râm Gharîb Chaube.)

The King of Balkh and Bukhara was sitting at the gateway of his palace, when an old Fakir appeared and insisted upon forcing his way in. When the attendants prevented him, he said:—"Why should I not enter an inn, if I please?" "This is not an inn," said the king. Then the Fakir asked him to whom the palace belonged before he was born, and he replied, "To my grandfather and to my father." "And to whom will it belong after you depart from the world?" "To my son and grandson," quoth the king. "Then," said the Fakir, "a house which has so many owners is naught but an inn."

7. The honest man and the rogue.

(Told by Gauri Sankar and recorded by Gopâl Sahai of Morâdabad.)

A good man and a rogue were friends, and the former recked not of the roguery of his friend, who was planning how he could injure him. The honest man was about to marry his son, and asked his friend to join the procession to fetch the bride. But the latter made an excuse, intending to rob the house while every one was absent. Only the wife of his friend was at home, and in the night she heard someone breaking through the wall. She rose, and when the thief came in, legs foremost, through the hole, she cut off his legs with a sword.

The thief crawled to his house and gave out that he had had to cut off his legs, because a snake had bitten him. When the husband returned from the wedding, his wife saw him mourning the misfortune which had overtaken his friend. So she took out the legs, which she had kept in a jar, told him the whole story and said:—

> "Kapati mit na hoya, bala sâncho shatru bhala:
> Yamen kachhu na goya, sab lahate nij karm
>   phala."

i.e., "May you never have a treacherous friend—An open enemy is better than he—Certain it is that everyone reaps the reward of his actions."

8. The two brothers.

(Told by M. Abdul Wâhid Khân, Sadr Qânungo, Sahâranpur.)

There were once two girls who said they would not marry anyone with money, but that their husbands should agree to submit to a daily shoe-beating from them. No one would consent to this, till two youths, who were very poor and could not get anyone else to marry them, agreed to the conditions.

So they were married and started for home with their brides. They halted at an inn, and during the night the elder brother heard an ass bray. So he arose, drew his sword and cut off its head. Soon afterwards he heard a cat mew under his bed: so he arose and killed it too. When his wife saw this, she realised that he had a hot temper, and made no attempt to beat him with shoes.

Meanwhile the younger brother used to be thrashed daily by his wife, and at last, finding his brother so much better off, he asked his advice. When his brother told him how he had managed, he ran home and forthwith killed the cat with his sword.

His wife laughed and said:—

"Garbah kushtan roz avval"

i.e., "If you go to kill the cat, it is better to do it the first day." After that she never troubled him.

[This story appears in Fallon's *Dictionary of Hindustani Proverbs.*—ED.]

9. The Brahman and the money-bags.

(Told by Râmdhan Misra, schoolmaster, Gonda.)

A Brahman, walking through a jungle one day, saw four bags of money. "These are four witches," he said and went his way. Soon after he met four sepoys who asked him if the road was safe. "There are four witches ahead," said he: "you had better be cautious." When the sepoys saw the bags of money, they exclaimed, "What a fool that Pandit was. He calls these money-bags witches." Two of them stayed with the treasure, and the other two went to the bazar to buy food. The two latter planned to put poison in the sweets, so that their companions should die and all the treasure be theirs. The other two made a similar plan, and when their comrades arrived with the sweets, they attacked them with their swords and slew them. Then they ate the sweets and died also.

After a while the Brahman returned to see how the sepoys had sped with the treasure, and found all four lying dead beside it. He took pity on them, and, cutting his little finger, poured some nectar into their mouths, and they came to life. They cast themselves at his feet and said, "Verily, these are witches indeed." So they gave up the world and became disciples of the Brahman.

10. The death of Sheikh Chilli.

(Told by Mukund Lâl, clerk, of Mirzapur.)

Once upon a time Sheikh Chilli asked a Pandit when he was likely to die. The Pandit replied, "You will die when a red thread comes out of your back." One day it happened that Sheikh Chilli entered the shop of a *Pathera* or silk thread maker, and a thread stuck to his back. Seeing it, he thought to himself, "I am now certainly dead." So he went to a grave-yard and dug himself a grave; then sat beside it and put a black pot on his head. A traveller who passed by asked Sheikh Chilli the way to the city. Replied the Sheikh, "I would gladly have told you, but don't you see that I really cannot, because I am dead." The traveller went his way, laughing at his folly.

["In the Turkish jest book which purports to relate the witless sayings of the Khoja Nasr-ed-dîn, he is persuaded to be dead and allows himself to be stretched on a bier and borne to the cemetery. On the way the bearers, coming to a miry place, said, "we will rest here," and began to converse; whereupon the Khoja, raising his head remarked, "If I were alive, I would get out of this place as soon as possible,"—"an incident which is also found in a Hindu story-book." Clouston, *Popular Tales and Fictions*, II. 33.—W. CROOKE.]

11. The Râni and the snake.

(Told by Gajâdhar Misra of Bhua Kalan and recorded by Chheda Lâl, Khapraha school, Jaunpur.)

There was once a Râja who had two wives; the elder he used to neglect, and loved the younger. One day the neglected Râni was sitting weeping in the courtyard, when a snake appeared before her. She took a jar and shut up the snake in it. She put the jar away and thought nothing of it, till one day she was looking for something in the house, and by chance she put her hand into the jar, and the snake bit her, so that she became insensible. When they went to the Râja and told him, he was much distressed and sent a message to say that he was coming at once to see her. Hearing this she recovered and said, "One never knows what may help one in trouble. The snake that I imprisoned has been the means of reconciling me to my husband."

12. The woman and her child.

(Told by Pandit Râmnâth of Sahâranpur.)

A woman with her child was once passing through a village notorious for the wickedness of its inhabitants. She was afraid, and putting the child on her shoulder walked along with her eyes downcast. A man saw her and quietly followed her. She did not hear him walking behind her, and as she went along he kept giving sweets to the child. After a time he shouted out, "Help, brethren! This woman is carrying off my child." She protested that the child was her own. So the elders of the village collected and said, "Make the man and woman sit down, and give the child to a third person; towards whichever of the two claimants the child stretches out its hands, to that one the child properly belongs." When the child saw the man who had given it sweets, it stretched out its hands to him, and all the people said, "Surely the child belongs to him." Soon after he gave the child back to the woman and said, "I merely wished to show you that the people here are both fools and knaves. It went to me because I gave it sweets—sweets are dearer to a child than its mother." Hence they say, *Khâi mîth; mâi nahîn mîth* (Food is sweeter than a mother).

13. How the dancing-girl was outwitted.

(Told by Pandit Chandrasêkhara, Zilla School, Cawnpore.)

There was once a dancing-girl, who lived in a Brahman village; and one morning when she looked outside her door, she saw all the Brahmans engaged in offering oblations to their dead ancestors. When she enquired what they were doing, they said:—"This is *Pitri-pâksha* or the fortnight sacred to the sainted dead, and we pour water in their honour." Thinking it would be a good thing if she did the same for her own ancestors, she sent for one of the Brahmans and asked him to officiate as her priest. He refused to act for so improper a person, and she could find no Brahman in the whole village who would perform the rites for her.

At last a *Bhânr* or buffoon thought he would take a rise out of her. So he dressed himself up as a learned Pandit, put on a big turban and a sacred thread, and with a bundle of books under his arm walked past her door. He fell into conversation with her and said, "I am a very learned Brahman just come from Benares—I am looking about for a wealthy client." So she induced him to stay in her house, and fed him well and gave him a handsome present. And daily he made her perform the oblations to her ancestors, while he mumbled some gibberish which she thought were the appropriate texts. At last when the ceremony was over and he had got as much as he could out of her, he departed, addressing her as he went in the following verse:—

> *"Kuâr badi pandravîn bhai, khûb urâi khâur;*
> *Ashikh de ghar jât hain, tum Vesya, ham*
> *Bhânr."*

i.e., "Up to the fifteenth of the month *Kuar* I enjoyed myself and was fed on sugar—I now leave you with my blessing. You are a dancing-wench and I a buffoon."

14. Iron and gold.

(Told by Kâzi Shamsu'ddin of Bâbugarh, Meerut District.)

Iron and gold once disputed which of them was the greater, and as they could not settle the matter themselves, they asked Râja Bhoj to arbitrate. Said Iron:—"What qualities dost thou possess, that thou dost not fall down and worship me?" Said Gold:—"Why should I fall down and worship thee, seeing that I am much superior to thee. I am measured by the *rati* and thou by the *ser*. I am the ruler and thou the slave." Said Iron:—"The reverse is the case. My shoes are on thy head. Of me the anvil and hammer are made, and between them thou art hammered and fashioned. When thou art made into coins, the moulds are formed of me. When thou art shut up, it is under my lock and key. How canst thou call me one of menial caste?" Said Gold: "How canst thou pretend to rival me, since it is of me jewels are made?" Said Iron:—"True, but these are the ornaments of women. Of me are made armour and the weapons of war. It is I and not thou, who conquer the world." Said Gold:—"Thou art a rogue, while I am a gentleman. Everyone curses thee, while all love me." Said Iron:—"At the first shower of rain in Asarh all thy votaries have to mortgage thee to buy cattle and seed-grain. I help my votaries to earn their bread by honest labour, and all respect me. If anyone takes me with him, he has no cause for fear. He may be sure of returning home in safety, while he who carries thee is in constant fear of the thief and the robber."

When the arguments were ended, Râja Bhoj said:—"Iron has proved his case."

Said Gold:—"This is only what might be expected from a Râja, but no Râjput shall ever possess me."

And this is the reason why Râjputs are usually thriftless and impoverished.

15. *The tale of the cuckoo.*

(Told by Akbar Shâh Mânjhi of Mirzapur District, and recorded by Hamid Husain.)

A certain Râja had a beautiful garden, in which lived a *koil* or cuckoo, which used to sing morning and evening, and keep silence all day while she sought food. This annoyed the Râja, and he sent for some fowlers and ordered them to catch the cuckoo. When they went in search of her, she was absent, and they caught a *kuchkuchiya* bird (the red-headed Trogon) and brought it to the Râja, who shut it up in a cage. The bird had only one note, "*Kaeh! Kaeh!*," which it kept repeating. Thereupon the Râja struck at it with a stick, whereupon the bird said:—

> *Kuh kuh bole koiliya nanda*
> *Bin aparadh paryon main phanda*

i.e., "The cuckoo sings sweetly; but I have been snared for no fault."

On this the Râja released the bird and punished the fowlers for their mistake.

16. *The Kori's dilemma.*

(Told by Râmnâth Tiwâri of Sarkandi, Fatehpur District.)

There was once a Kori weaver who was a great fool. One day his wife began to abuse him and said, "You are such a lazy fellow: You never do anything offhand." So he went away, saying "Offhand" to every one he met. He came across a fowler catching birds in a net. When he saw him the Kori shouted out "Offhand" and all the birds flew away. Then the fowler fell upon him and said, "When you meet anyone, you should say—'May two fall into one'—that is to say, may two birds fall into the snare at once."

He went on and saw two men carrying a corpse, and when he saw them, he spoke as the fowler told him; but they beat him and said, "You should always say 'If a thing has happened, who can cure it; but may it never occur again.'"

He came to a place where the Râja had just had a son, and when he said what had been told him, they beat him and said, "You should always say, 'May such a thing never occur again.'"

He came to a village where an Ahîr was milking his cow, which recently had not given any milk; but that day she was a little better and was giving a little. When he said, "May such a thing never occur again," the Ahîr gave him a beating.

So he said to himself, "Whatever I say brings me into trouble, so I had better go home"; and go home he did and stayed there.

[This noodle story is told all the world over—See Clouston, *Book of Noodles*, 128.—W. CROOKE. The Koris of the U.P. are supposed to be an offshoot of the Kols. In customs they approximate to the Chamârs and others of like social grade—ED.]

17. The Râja and the sharpers.

(Told by Râmlâl Kayasth of Mirzapur and recorded by Pandit Râm Gharîb Chaube.)

A Râja was once on a journey and came to a tank, where a Dhobi was washing clothes. The Râja shot a paddy-bird on the tank, and the Dhobi shouted out:—"What do you mean by killing my mother? You must come to the king and I will get redress."

So they went on, and on the way they met a one-eyed man. He said to the Râja, "My father once pledged my eye with you for a rupee. Here is the money, give me back my eye, or come to the king and I will get redress."

They went further and met a barber. "Shave me," said the Râja, "and I will satisfy you for your trouble." When he had done shaving him, the barber said, "Nothing but your kingdom will satisfy me. If you will not give it, come to the king, and I will get redress."

When they came to the king, the Râja sent a letter to the queen, asking her to help him out of his trouble. She wrote back, "When the Dhobi says you killed his mother, just say, 'And what about my father the fish, that your mother was eating when I killed her?' When the one-eyed man asks for his eye, say, 'I have a heap of eyes and I cannot match yours, unless you take out your remaining eye and let me measure it.' And when the barber asks you for your kingdom, say, 'You can have it when my son is married.'" Now the Râja had no son. In this way he escaped the wiles of the three sharpers.

18. The potter and his friends.

(Told by Râmdayâl, schoolmaster, Gonda.)

A certain potter had three brothers. One of them was a very powerful man, and his brothers were on the look out to kill him. The wife of one of the brothers was one day cooking, and her husband told her to put poison in the dish for his brother. When the latter came in to eat, the woman repented and began to weep. When asked the reason, she told him to throw some of the food to a dog. When the dog immediately died, he knew that his brothers had made a plot against him. So he thought he had best go abroad to earn his living.

When he had gone some distance, he saw a carpenter who was digging earth, and as he dug it, he threw it over a hill close by.

The potter said—"You are a very powerful man."

He answered—"I hear that there is a potter who is even stronger than I am."

So they started off together. When they had gone some distance, they saw a cowherd taking one of his buffaloes on his back to a tank to bathe her. Him also they made join their company. When they went a little further, they came upon a goldsmith who, when his anvil got out of shape, hammered it straight with his hand. He also joined them. Then they came to a well and they told the carpenter to go and draw some water. When he put in his *lota*, the fairies who were in the well caught hold of it. So he jumped in; and when he did not come out, they sent in the cowherd; and after him went in the goldsmith also. So the potter was left alone outside. Then up came a Râkshasa, who was lord of the well, and challenged the potter to fight him. The potter after a fierce fight killed him, and then he too went down into the well. There they found the palace of the fairies, who were of heavenly beauty; and they had a store of all manner of wealth. Here the heroes and the fairies lived ever after.

19. The Ahîr and his Guru.

(Told by Pandit Chandrasêkhara, Zilla school, Cawnpore.)

There was once an Ahîr, who was the ser cant of a Thâkur, and one day his master's Guru came to see him. This was in the month of *Baisakh*, when the weather was very hot. So the Thâkur gave the Guru a seat, bathed and fanned him, and gave him sherbet to drink. Just at that time the Thâkur was in trouble because his wife was barren, and he had a dispute with his relations; but soon after the Guru arrived, his wife conceived and the quarrel was settled.

When the Ahîr saw what had happened, he thought it would be much to his advantage to get initiated himself. So he went about looking for a Guru.

One day his younger brother came running to him in terror and said—

"I was just passing the river, when I saw a terrible animal chewing an enormous bone in its mouth and making an awful noise. Perchance he may injure our flocks, and we had better slay him." Now it was the month of *Magh* and very cold weather; and this was a poor Sanyâsi who was sitting by the river, making his *Sandhya* oblation and blowing his conch-shell. The Ahîrs stole up behind him and struck him a blow with a club. But when they saw that it was a Sanyâi, they were grieved, and making their excuses to him, carried him to their house. They wished to treat him with the utmost respect, and the Ahîr, remembering how his master had treated his Guru, seated him on a chair, poured a lot of water over him, though it was freezing, and made him drink a lot of sherbet.

In consequence the unfortunate Guru died, and the Ahîr was never able to find another.

20. *The Ahîr and his Guru.*

(Told by Hanumân Prasâd, teacher, Rai Barêli.)

There was once an Ahîr who thought that he was neglecting his religion; so he got himself initiated by a Guru. Soon after, the Guru came to see him, and the Ahîr gave him all the milk and butter there was in the house. The Guru thought the Ahîr a very liberal man; so he used to come every ten days or so; and whatever he found in the house the Ahîr would give him. The Ahîr's wife did not like this and said to herself, "Since this Babaji has taken to coming to the house, I might as well have no buffalo at all; for my husband gives him all the milk and butter." Soon after the Guru appeared and asked the woman where her husband was. She said— "Poor man, he has lost his wits and he cannot bear the sight of a beggar about the place. Just now a poor man came to the door, and my husband has gone hunting him through the village with the chaff-chopper." When he heard this, the Babaji was sore afraid and he ran away. Just then the Ahîr came back from his field and asked his wife if the Babaji had been to see him. "Yes," she said, "he was here just now and wanted our rice-pounder. But I did not dare to give it to him as you were not at home." The Ahîr seized the rice-pounder and ran after the Guru. "Babaji," he shouted, "stop! here is the rice-pounder." But the more he called to the Babaji to stop, the faster he ran; and that was the last the Ahîr and his wife ever saw of him.

21. *How the Ahîrin was outwitted.*

(Told by Ganga Sahai, schoolmaster, Hathras, Aligarh District.)

There was once an Ahîr, who had a very deceitful wife. When she was cooking, she used to make all the good flour into cakes and eat them herself, while those she made for her husband were only of chaff and refuse. Her husband, being an easy-going man, stood this for some time: but one day, as he found himself growing weaker, he said:—"How is it that when I give you plenty of good food, my cakes are made only of chaff and rubbish." She replied in verse:

> *Gangapar teri bahin basen,*
> *Jake jamhen kank uren,*
> *Pisen getun kukas khayan*
> *Is se balam latte jaen.*

i.e., "Your sister lives beyond the Ganges. When she yawns, all the good flour is blown away. I grind wheat and eat rubbish. Hence my husband is pining away."

When her husband heard this, he thought he would go and give his sister a beating. His wife tried to dissuade him; but he went. When he came to his sister's house, she received him hospitably and gave him a good dinner. Said she—"Alas! brother. I see that you are very weak. Why is this so?" "How can I be strong," he answered, "when every time you yawn, you blow away all the good flour and my poor wife is left with only the husks to cook?" She asked—"How did you find that this was so?" He said "My wife told me."

His sister knew that this was some roguery on the part of his wife. So she went to a carpenter, who was a neighbour of hers and a great wizard, and she got from him four magic pegs, which she gave to the husband and said, "When you reach home, plant one of these at each corner of your house."

The Ahîr did as she told him, and planted one of the pegs at each corner of his house. Next day, when the woman was cooking, and as usual taking all the good flour for her own cakes, one peg said—"What are you doing?" The second said—"This is what she does every day." The third said—"Has she no fear of Nârâyan? "The fourth replied—"If she feared him, she would not act in this way."

When the Ahîrin heard these words, she did not know who was talking, and thought that some of her neighbours had seen her. So she cooked the bread in an honest way that day, and when her husband came home, she set it before him. Said he—"I am pleased to see that my sister did not yawn to-day."

After this the pegs used to speak whenever she tried to do any roguery, and though she searched everywhere, she could never find out who was watching her, and she became so stricken with fear that she was forced to amend her ways and give her husband his fair share of the food.

22. *The Brahman and his Guru.*

(Told by Hira Halwâi and recorded by Bhagwân Prasâd, Nizâmâbâd, Azamgarh District.)

There was once a Brahman who was initiated by his Guru, and he asked him to give him a Mantra, which none but himself could know. So the Guru whispered the usual Mantra into the ear of his disciple and departed.

Soon after the Brahman went to bathe at Benares, and hearing many other pilgrims reciting the same Mantra, he thought that his Guru had deceived him. So he went to him and charged him with trickery. The Guru was wroth and said:

"Take this scrap of paper and put it at the root of a Banyan tree and bring me whatever you find there."

The disciple did as he was ordered, and found a small ball. He brought it to his Guru, who said:

"Take this to the bazar and sell it; but whoever buys it must give all his wealth in exchange."

He took it to several shops, but no one would buy it on such terms. At last he came to a goldsmith, who saw that it was of wondrous value and gave all his wealth in exchange for it. When he opened it, the whole of his house was filled with a marvellous light, and the king, thinking that the moon had come down, went there with his troops. The goldsmith was afraid, and buried the ball in the ground; and when the king saw that the light was quenched, he went away. Then the goldsmith called the Brahman and said:—

"Take away your ball. I am afraid to keep it any longer." The Brahman went back to the Guru, who said:—

"This is like the Mantra which I gave you. It has wondrous powers, which none but I know. Go in peace."

The Brahman fell at his feet and worshipped him.

23. The Biter Bit.

(Told by Ajudhya Prasâd Dube of Bhonpapur, Benares District.)

There was once a very poor Brahman, who was sore pressed to marry his daughter. Having no means, he decided to go to the Râja and see if he could make something towards the marriage expenses. The porters at the Râja's gate would not let him enter; so he asked them to show him the house of the Râja's Pandit. The Pandit was at his prayers; but when he came out and learnt what the Brahman wanted, he said:—"There is no use in your going before the Râja unless you can answer the questions he puts. Now what learning do you possess?" The Brahman was obliged to admit that he was an ignorant man. So the Pandit said, "If you cannot say anything else, say, when you are addressed, *Dharm ki jay, Pâp ki chhai*" (*i.e.*, "Victory to Religion and Ruin to Vice.")

When they came to the court, the Râja asked the Brahman to recite some verses, and all he could say was:—"*Dharm ki jay, Pâp ki chhai.*" The Râja could understand this, which he could never do when his own Pandit spoke: so he was pleased and gave the Brahman a thousand rupees. As he was going away, the Pandit asked him for half the gift, and when he refused, the Pandit went straight to the Râja and told him what an impostor the Brahman was.

The Râja said nothing; but next day when the Brahman came to court, he gave him a scrap of paper and said:—"Take this to my Treasurer and he will give you your reward." Now on the paper was written—"Cut off this rascal's nose."

As the Brahman was walking to the Treasury, he met the Pandit, who demanded his share. Said the Brahman, "I fear the Treasurer. You go and get this money, and then we will divide it." When the Treasurer read the message, he cut off the Pandit's nose, despite all his protestations. Next day, when the Râja sent again for the Brahman he was surprised to see him unhurt. When he heard the story and sent for the Pandit, all he could say was "*Dharm ki jay, Pâp ki chhai.*"

So the Râja dismissed the Pandit from his service, and appointed the Brahman Pandit in his place.

24. *The Craft of the Barber.*

(Told by Pandit Chandrasekhara, Zilla School, Cawnpore.)

There was once an old Mahâjan who was a widower, blind, deaf and lame, and he had no son. One day he called his chief agent and said:—"I am very anxious to marry again and have an heir. If you can arrange this, I will reward you handsomely."

Now in that village lived a very cunning barber, to whom the agent went and said, "If you can arrange a wife for the Lâlaji, you will receive two hundred rupees, and be appointed also his family barber." Delighted with this offer, the barber went to a village some way off, where lived a number of Banias. "There is," said he, "a wealthy Mahâjan who is my client, and I am off to Ujjain to find a bride for him." Hearing this, the Banias began to think there was a chance of profit, and so they came to him and said:—"Worthy barber! why should we send you to Ujjain? Perchance the marriage can be arranged nearer home, and if you could bring it about, we would make it worth your while."

The barber raised sundry objections, till they gave him a handsome present, when he agreed to marry his client to the daughter of one of them. Now he knew they would be asking all sorts of questions about the bridegroom, which he could not safely answer. So he pretended to be very hungry, and when the women took him inside and began to feed and question him, he stuffed his mouth full of rice, so that he could not talk properly. Said one woman to him:—"How old is the youth?" "Twenty, twenty, twenty," said he. "Does he care about seeing nautches?" asked a second. "He sees nobody but himself," said the barber. "Does he care for singing?" asked a third. "He never listens to anyone," said the barber. "Has he a conveyance?" asked a fourth. "He never moves anywhere without a conveyance" was his reply.

The barber then left. When the marriage procession arrived and they saw what the bridegroom was like, they seized the barber and cried, "What a lying rogue you are!" But he replied, "If you think well, you will find that I never deceived you. When I was asked his age, I said "twenty" three times, which makes sixty. I said he never looked at dances or listened to singing, by which, of course, I meant that he was blind and deaf, and when I said that he never moved without a conveyance, you might have understood that he was lame."

But they would not listen to his excuses, and drove him and the procession out of their village.

25. The Affliction of Devi.

(Told by Râm Sahai and recorded by Siu Darsan Sinh, schoolmaster, Aurai, Fatehpur District.)

There were once a Bania and a Lodha in a certain village, and neither of them had a son. So they went to the shrine of Devi, and the Bania vowed that if a son were born unto him, he would offer a gold *mohur*, and the Lodha promised a buffalo as his offering. In due time by the grace of Devi a son was born to each of them. After the children were named, the Bania and the Lodha went to the shrine with their friends, beating drums and making merry. The Mali, who was the priest of the shrine, thought to himself—"To-day for certain we shall get two valuable offerings." The Bania went in first, and after making a prayer touched the image with a gold *mohur*. Then he took it up, and coming home to his wife, said—"This is a blessed coin. Tie it round the neck of our son, and he will be safe from the attacks of demons and the Evil Eye."

The Lodha, when he went in, also prayed. Then he tied his buffalo by the neck-rope to the image of the goddess and came home. The Mali was well pleased, but just as he was going to loose the beast, it jumped and made a rush for home, and dragged the image by the rope along the ground to the door of the Lodha's house. Just then Mahadeva came up and, seeing the goddess in this wretched plight, asked her what had happened. She answered—"This is the result of conferring blessings on the base. The Bania robbed me of the offering, and this rascally Lodha has caused me to be dragged through the thorns and disgraced." So Mahadeva appeased her, and carried her off to his seat on Mount Kailasa, and there he comforted her.

26. The Age of Man.

(Told by Kâzi Waqar-ullah and recorded by Faizullah, schoolmaster, Budaun.)

On the day of Creation Allah called all creatures into his presence and began to allot their ages on the earth. First came the Ass, and Allah said, "Thy age shall be forty years." Next came the Owl, and to him the same age was given. And so with the Dog. Last came Man, and to him Allah said, "Thy age shall be forty years."

The Man said—"O Almighty Father, Thou hast made me lord of all thy creatures and thou hast fixed forty years as the space of my life. In twenty years I shall gain maturity. Twenty years will be spent in acquiring wisdom and knowledge. What time is then left in which I may do thee service?"

In the meantime the Ass came into the presence of Allah crying bitterly and said "O Lord, Thou hast given me an age of forty years. To me has been allotted the duty of carrying bricks and mortar and the foul raiment of men. My food is only the scraps of dry grass I pick up on the wayside, and my master has been allowed to thrash me with a club and torment me in various ways. How shall I be able to bear such hardship for the space of forty years? Of thy mercy reduce the span of my years." Allah said to his *Peshkar*—"Lessen the age of this creature by twenty years and give it to Man, who claims that the allotted span of his age is too small."

Then the Dog came into the Presence and said—"O Lord, Thou hast fixed my age at forty years, and thou hast given as my food dead animals and all kinds of carrion and the leavings of men. My business is to lie awake at night, and by day to watch the person and property of my master. How can I pass such a length of time in affliction like this? I pray thee reduce my age. Allah said to the *Peshkar*—"Reduce the age of this creature by twenty years and add them to the age of Man, who prays that his life be increased." And it was so.

Then came the Owl into the Presence and said—"Almighty Lord, my age has been fixed at forty years. But it has been ordained that my presence in any house is ill-omened. Hence men will ever hate and curse me and abuse me. How can I pass such a long time in this misery? I pray thee shorten my life." And Allah said to his *Peshkar*—"Take twenty years from his life and add it to that of Man, who says that his age is too short." And it was so.

Thus the limit of man's age was fixed at one hundred years; and all the animals came down to this mortal world. This is the reason why up to the age of forty years Man is a man indeed, active and vigorous, courageous and vigilant. After that, for the space of twenty years he is as an ass, idle and slothful and content with what he can get. Then for twenty years he is as a dog, weak in strength and sharp of tongue. He is easily provoked to anger and greedy for everything he sees. After that he acquires the faculties of an owl. His eyes become weak and, as his teeth drop, he speaks in a croaking voice. He loses his power of hearing and sits silent in the house, blinking at his friends, who hate and curse him and long for the day of his death.

27. *The Founding of the Dom Kingdom of Gorakhpur.*

(Told by Khâdim Husain, village schoolmaster, Dulhipur, Benares District.)

There was once a Râja in Benares, who had no child, and he grieved much on that account. One day a Fakîr came to his palace and begged alms. The Râja gave him much money, and when the Fakîr asked what boon the Râja desired in return, the latter said, "Pray that I may have a child."

By and by, through God's grace, the Râni had a daughter. The Râja called the Pandits to draw her horoscope, and when he asked them to explain it to him, they said, "We cannot tell you one thing." But on his insisting that they should tell him, they said, "Your daughter will marry the son of Raghu the Dom."

The Râja sent at once for the Dom boy and had him exposed in the jungle, which swarmed with beasts of prey. As the boy sat alone, the tree above him said, "Dig here, and you will find a treasure." So he dug there and found an underground palace, filled with the treasures of seven kings. He stayed there for some time and then returned to Benares with an army. The Râja, who knew him not, was afraid of his power and gave him his daughter in wedlock. On the wedding night the bride discovered that the prophecy had been fulfilled and that she was the wife of a Dom. So the old Râja drove out his son-in-law, and he went with his force and wealth to Gorakhpur, and there he founded the well-known Dom kingdom.

28. *Alexander and the Sea People.*

(Told and recorded by Sheikh Waliullah, Mulla of Sahaswan, Budaun District.)

When Alexander had subdued all the people of the world, he desired to conquer also the people of the sea, and he enquired of Aristotle how this could be done. Aristotle, after many days' reflection, came to the king and said:—"My advice is this. Have a palace built on the shore of the sea, and collect a party of the loveliest maidens of the earth and make them live there. Let them go daily to the shore and sing the sweetest songs, and order them to treat with the utmost kindness any who come from the sea, be they men, beasts, demons or angels."

Alexander did as Aristotle advised; and when the maidens came to the palace, they used daily to sit and sing by the shore of the sea. One day they suddenly saw a head appearing above the surface of the water. As long as they continued to sing, the head remained above the water; when they ceased, it sank beneath the waves. In appearance it was as the head of an ape. Day by day the head came nearer to the shore. At last, when the sea-man saw that there was nought to fear, he came on land and sat beside them. So he came and went as he pleased and none forbade him. He lived and ate there and chose the loveliest of the girls to stay with him; and in due course a child was born to them. And the man of the sea loved his son dearly, and he used to dive into the water and bring precious stones and jewels, such as man never saw, from his treasure beneath the waves. He also taught him the speech of the people of the sea, and his mother taught him that of the people of the land. And the boy would often go with his father and visit the kingdom of the sea.

When Alexander heard what had happened, he came to the palace and rewarded the boy and his mother with costly gifts. Then he consulted Aristotle on what was next to be done. Aristotle went to the girl and asked her to request her husband to take her king to the kingdom of the sea. "If he refuses," said Aristotle, "the king of the land will slay thee and thy son." When the man of the sea heard this, he agreed to the order of Alexander. He came next day with a boat, and placed in it Alexander, Aristotle, his wife and son. Then the boat sank in the water, and they landed in the kingdom of the sea. There he showed them all the wonders, and Alexander ordered the boy to write a letter to the king of the sea, which he sent by the man of the sea. When the king of the sea saw the boy and read the letter, he was much pleased and told him to bring his king to his court.

So Alexander went with the boy to the king of the sea, who received them with the utmost respect and seated Alexander on a throne equal to his own, and said to him—"O Alexander! You are now my guest. I will do what pleases you. But is the income of the land too small that you desire tribute from me?" Then he said—"I will give you this little box of wood. If you can fill it with anything, I will own that I am bound to give you tribute. If you fail, you must return to your kingdom as you came."

Alexander returned to the land and told Aristotle to fill the box with something. Aristotle put into it all the things which the world contained, but still it remained empty. All the wise men of the earth tried with all their skill to fill the box, but they failed. So Alexander and Aristotle returned to the king of the sea and admitted that they could not fill the box. The king of the sea said—"Return to your own land and speak not again of levying tribute from me."

As he was going, Alexander said—"Pray tell me now of what this box is made and how it can be filled." The king of the sea said—"This box is made of the eye of covetousness. Nought but the dust of the grave can fill it."

Alexander and Aristotle were abashed and returned to their own land.

29. *The dream of the Sadhu.*

(Told by Gokul Sinh Thakur of Nârâyanpur, Cawnpore District.)

A certain Sadhu was wandering about begging, and reached a village just as a grand marriage procession was passing. Seeing the bride and the rejoicings, the Sadhu thought to himself:—"After all, the lot of the married man is the best." And with that he fell asleep on the edge of a well. He dreamed that he was married and had a lovely wife, and that when he called her she came and sat on his bed. Whereupon he cried, "What insolence to sit on my bed," and gave her a slap in the face. At that moment the Sadhu fell into the well and the people had much ado to fish him out with a rope. "After all," said the Sadhu, "the life of the unmarried man is best."

30. *The Mulla and the Boors.*

(Told by Nârâyan Das and recorded by Rahmatulla, schoolmaster, Baksiya, Budaun District.)

One day a Mulla went to preach in a rude village. "To-morrow," said he, "Ramzan Sharif will come and you must all fast." The rough villagers were much put out at this, and next day, when a stray camel with a young one entered the village, they cried: "Here is that rascal Ramzan Sharif. Let us kill and eat him." The following day the Mulla returned and seeing them eating meat, asked them what they meant by it. They replied:— "We killed that scoundrel Ramzan and are eating him." Said the Mulla:—"*La haulawa la quvvata illahi'l lahi*" (There is no strength or power save in God). "Never mind," said they, "we killed the brute *La haula* with its mother." The Mulla gave up teaching them their duty as a bad job.

31. *The Liar tricked.*

(Told by Kedarnâth Kayasth and recorded by Jang Bahadur Sinh, Basitnagar, Hardoi District.)

There was once a man who was a noted liar. One of the villagers happened to say that his house was too small for his family. Said the liar:— "My grandfather's house was so big that it would hold the whole village."

No one replied to this, except an old man, who remarked:—"My father's spear was so long that whenever he pleased, he used to pierce the clouds with it and cause the rain to fall." "And where did he keep such a long spear as that," asked the liar. "In the house of your grandfather," was the answer.

32. Honesty is the best policy.

(Told by M. Durga Prasâd Bhârgava, Banda.)

A Brahman, who had a grown-up daughter, was so hard pressed to procure money for her marriage that he broke by night into the palace of the Râja. Entering a room, he saw a box full of jewels, but when he seized it, his conscience reproved him, and he laid it down. He entered another room, where he found more valuables, but again he left them untouched. At last he came into a room where the Râja lay asleep on a couch, with a monkey squatting on guard with a drawn sword in its hand. As soon as the monkey saw the shadow of the Brahman fall on the Râja, it raised the sword and would have slain the Râja, had not the Brahman seized the weapon and killed it.

Then the Brahman wrote the following couplet in Sanskrit on the wall of the room:—

> *Pandita shatru bhalo na murkha hitkârka*
> *Bandro nahdapi Râja Bipra choure na rakshita.*

i.e., "It is better to have a learned man for an enemy than an illiterate man for a friend. If a monkey be even a Râja, and a Brahman a thief, they should not be protected."

When the Râja awoke next morning and saw the dead monkey and the verses written on the wall, he was amazed and called on all his learned men to interpret the mystery. But they failed. So he issued a proclamation that anyone who could explain it should be liberally rewarded. At last the Brahman appeared and explained the matter, and the Râja dismissed him with a royal present.

33. The tale of Nobody.

(Told by Râm Gharîb Chaube.)

There was once a woman, whose husband went away to a far country, and during his absence she took another man as her lover. Whenever she spoke of this man to her little boy, she called him "Na koi"—"Mr. Nobody." After a time the husband returned, and he called his child and asked him whether anyone had been visiting his mother in his absence. He replied:—"Na koi used to come." At which the fool was satisfied.

Hence they repeat the following verse:—

Na koi jâta tha, na koi âta tha,
Na koi god men lekar khelâta tha.

i.e., "Nobody came and Nobody went: Nobody used to take me on his knee and play with me."

[The old tale of Outis and the Cyclops.—W. CROOKE.]

34. The old woman and Satan.

(Told by Abdulla Julaha of Man, Azamgarh District, and recorded by Pandit Jadunandan Lâl.)

An old woman, who was barren and was very anxious to have a child, used to visit every Fakîr and wiseacre whom she heard of. One day, while on her way to another village, she saw an old woman sitting by the roadside. Now this old woman was Satan (may he be stoned!) in disguise. The old woman approached Satan and explained her case. Satan replied: "Make water in that well over there, and you will have a child." The old woman said:—"I cannot do this, because the water of this well is used by mankind for drinking and bathing." "Very well," said Satan, "there is no other way: and if you do not do as I advise you, you will have neither chick nor child." At length the old woman yielded to Satan's advice. When she had done so, a terrible flame rose from the well, the glare of which mounted to the heavens. Her eyes were dazzled and she called to the Almighty to deliver her. Then she returned to the old woman who had given her the advice, but could not see her anywhere. To an old man who happened to be standing near she said:—"Babaji, where is the old woman who was sitting here just now?" He laughed and answered:—"That was not a woman, but His Holiness Satan himself. He wished to test your honesty and virtue: and now you will have neither son nor daughter."

When the old woman's husband heard what she had done, he divorced her. She then said:—*Gaye donon jahân se, na idhar ke hue, na udhar ke hue,* "I have been ruined in this world and the next. I am neither on this side nor on that."

35. The Pandit and the Rakshasa.

(Told by Beni Mâdho Pandit of Hargâm, Sîtapur, and recorded by Kunj Bihâri Lâl, Hargâm School.)

A Râkshasa and a Râkshasi once lived in a forest near a certain city. One day the Râkshasi said to her husband, "I long for the flesh of a man." The Rakshasa promised to fetch her some soon, and so went to the court of the Râja, dressed as a learned Brahman, and said:—"I will ask a question. If any Pandit of the Court fails to answer it, he must die; and if I fail to answer, I will kill myself."

The Râja agreed, and the Râkshasa then asked the meaning of the following words:—

> *Na panch Mi na panch Si*
> *Panch Mi aur panch Si.*

None of the Pandits could answer this, and the Râja gave them a week to think over it. Only one day remained and still they had not solved the riddle. The Râkshasa used to attend the court daily and go home in the evening. Finally, one of the Pandits, despairing of life, followed the Râkshasa and overheard him talking to his wife. Said she: "You have been a long time getting me the flesh of a man, and now there is little hope left." So he told her about the riddle, and she asked him for the answer. For a long time he would not tell her, but at last, when she pressed him hard, he said:—

> "In the Hindu fortnight there are 15 days. Of these five end in *Mi*, the *Panchami* (5th), *Saptami* (7th), *Ashtami* (8th), *Naumi* (9th) and *Dasmi* (10th). Five end in *Si*; the *Ekadasi* (11th), *Duâdasi* (12th), *Triyodasi* (13th), *Chaturdasi* (14th) and *Purnamasi* (full moon day). The five which have neither *Mi* nor *Si* for their ending are the *Parîva* (1st), *Dvîj* (2nd), *Tîj* (3rd), *Chaturthi* (4th) and *Shashti* (6th)."

The Pandit, having heard this, returned home, and when the Râkshasa received the correct answer, he was confounded and killed himself on the spot. The Râja then had the Râkshasi put to death.

[This story is somewhat on the lines of the English "Tom Tit Tot" and Grimm's "Rumpelstiltskin."—W. CROOKE.]

36. How the pious ploughman escaped death.

(Told by Sayyid Khâdim Husani, Benares District.)

There was once a very pious man who fell into poverty and was obliged at last to work as a ploughman. While at work, he used to keep a copy of the Holy Koran, at the side of the field, so that he could read a line or two as he came to the end of each furrow. One day an astrologer passed by and said to his comrade:—"This man is doubtless very pious: but if he is not married within a week, he will die." When the pious man heard this, he was dismayed, and having tethered his oxen went about the place, crying, "For the love of God, will anyone give me his daughter to wife and save my life." For sometime none would agree: but at last the pious daughter of a merchant consented to marry him for the love of God.

So they were married, and in the middle of the night the bridegroom said to his wife:—"I have been in such fear of my approaching death that I have not eaten aught to-day. Rise and get me some food, lest I die." So she got up and cooked for him some of the wedding rice, and just as it was ready, a beggar came by and asked for alms. The pious man, though starving himself, gave him the food, and the Fakîr blessed him in the following words:

"May you live a year for every grain of rice you have given me!"

And so it turned out; for he lived to a great old age.

[This story resembles one of the incidents in the life of Râja Harischandra.— W. Crooke.]

37. True Love.

(Told by Pandit Nârâyan Das of Kangra and recorded by Râm Gharîb Chaube.)

A woman was walking along the road and saw a man following her. She asked him what he wanted, and he said:—"I have fallen in love with you." She replied:—"My sister, who is much prettier than I am, is behind me." So he went back and saw the sister, and lo! she was very ill-favoured. So he ran back to the first woman and said:—"You lied unto me." And she answered:—"Nay, you lied unto me. Had you truly loved me, you would not have gone after the other."

38. How the Pandit was taught to lie.

(Told by M. Gaurîshankar Lâl, Unao.)

A Pandit was on his way to give a recitation of the sacred Bhâgavata Purâna, when he met the Kali Yuga or Iron Age on the road, who asked him whither he was going. When the Pandit told him and asked him to join the audience, he said:—"I care not for such meetings; but if you wish to please me, tell one good lie in the course of the service."

The Pandit was a very pious man and could not bring himself to tell a lie. So, just as he was going home, the Kali Yuga in the guise of a dancing girl's musician appeared, and when the people asked what such a low fellow as he wanted at a religious service, he said:—"This Pandit of yours owes one of my girls fifty rupees, and he said he would pay me out of what he made by this recital." When the people heard this scandal, many of them ceased attending the service.

The next night Kali Yuga appeared in the guise of a butcher, with the head of a goat under his arm; and when the audience asked what he wanted, he said:—"Your worthy Pandit owes me twenty rupees for meat, which he promised to pay me out of this night's fees, and he also bade me have a goat's head ready for him when he left the service." With this he showed them the goat's head, and many, who believed that their Pandit never touched meat, left the place.

The third night there were very few people present, and Kali Yuga came as a liquor-seller. When they asked him why he had come, he replied:—"Your Pandit owes me ten rupees for spirits and I have come for it, and I have brought a bottle for him to drink when he goes home." When they heard this, they all left the place. As the Pandit was going home, Kali Yuga said to him:—"It would have been better for you to do as I asked you." The Pandit replied:—"Don't disgrace me any more and I will tell as many lies as you like." From that day forth the Pandit became the greatest liar in the village.

39. *The Quest of Managori.*

(Told by Naurang Sinh, Tahsil School, Fatehpur.)

There was once a Râja who dreamed that in the city of Ajudhya was a maiden, Managori by name, the like of whom the world never saw. In the morning he put five packets of *pan* in front of his *gadi* and said to his courtiers:—"I saw last night in a dream the maiden Managori of Ajudhya. There is no woman in the world so beautiful as she. Whoever brings her to me shall receive the half of my kingdom." When the courtiers reflected on the danger of the task none dared to attempt it. But one named Dariya Rathaur raised the *pan* and said: "Mahârâj, if thou givest me thy charger to ride and thy five suits of raiment to wear, I will bring thee the maiden."

The Râja agreed and gave him all he asked. The Rathaur went to bid his mother good-bye and told her that he was going in quest of Managori. His mother said:—"Let me give you food for the road." But when she went to look for flour wherewith to cook the cakes, she put her hand into a jar and took up a handful of salt. She was distressed and said:—"How can a journey prosper with an omen such as this?"

The Rathaur did not heed her words and went off. When he had gone a little distance, he saw a snake crossing his path and on the other side lay a broken vessel of curd. When he saw this he spake these lines:—

> Dahine to phuti sar ki matukiya, bayen
>   phenkara siyar;
> Rah kate ka nikra hai kalwa, kaise ke lagihai
>   par?

i.e., "On the right lies a broken curd pot, on the left howl the jackals. The snake crosses my path. How can I return successful?"

When he neared Ajudhya he came on several roads and he could not discover which was the proper path. He saw a cowherd sitting on a tree and watching his cattle. To him he said:—

> Rukh charante chhuhara re bhaiyya, tu awat aur
>   jat,
> Awadnagari ki bhali dagariya utari ke dewa
>   bataya.

i.e., "Brother, you climb the tree and go one way and another. I have missed the way to Awadhnagari. Come down and point it out."

The herd came down and showed him the road, and by and by he came to the garden of Managori. There he met the gardener and to him he said:—

> Khirki ke jhakwaiya re bhaiyya, it awat aur jat.
> Sitalgarh ki talkh tamaku, tanik tumhun lai
>   jawa.

i.e., "Brother, you peep into every window and go from one place to another. The tobacco of Sitalgarh is tasty; take a little."

The Rathaur gave him a smoke and then he gave him an *ashrafi*, and the gardener asked him what his errand was. He said:—"I have come here in search of Managori, the fairest of women." The gardener answered:—"Managori comes here daily with her maidens." The Rathaur remained in the garden, and by and by Managori came there. The Rathaur followed her and tried to speak to her. Then a sister of Managori, who had only one eye, said to the maidens:—"I am going to speak to this stranger." They said:—"It is not proper to speak to a stranger;" but she answered thus:—

> *Ek lakh ki mor gagari ghailwa, du lakh meri*
> *dor;*
> *Tin lakh ki mori sir ki gudariya; panch lakh*
> *mera mol.*

i.e., "My pitcher is worth a lakh and the rope is worth two lakhs. My head pad is worth three lakhs and my own price is five."

To this the Rathaur replied:—

> *Mati ki tori gagari, san ki tori dor;*
> *Lattan gundhi tere sir ki genduriya, kani*
> *kauriya ki mol.*

i.e., "Thy pitcher is but of clay; thy rope of hemp; thy head-pad is but of twisted rags and thou thyself art worth a cracked cowry."

To this she replied:—

> *Ek lakh ki beni, aur dui lakh ka jhunna sar*
> *Tin lakh ka mora bana hai ghaghra, sat lakh*
> *mora mol.*

i.e., "My hair-plait is worth a lakh, my pitcher two lakhs, my skirt three lakhs and I myself seven lakhs."

To which he replied:—

> *Ek lakh ki beniya, do lakh ki jhunnasar,*
> *Tin lakh ka jobana, ek panahiya ki nok.*

i.e., "Thy hair-plait is worth a lakh, thy pitcher two lakhs and thy beauty three, but I would not give the point of my shoe for any of them."

When he said this, he ran away and left one of his shoes behind him; and when the girl picked it up she saw that the coins of seven kingdoms were broidered upon it. Managori then said her maidens:—"This must be the son of a Râja; and none of you should speak to him."

She returned to her palace; and the Rathaur, not knowing he might have to wait for her return, composed the following verse:—

> *Sun agili, sun pacchil Râni, sun majhili*
> *panaihar.*
> *Tora ghara ka thanda ho pani, to ek lota dehu*
> *piyaya.*

i.e., "Listen, Râni, whether thou be late or whether thou be early. Listen, water-bearer, who comest between. If the water in thy jar be cool give me a drink."

The one-eyed damsel answered:—

> *Pani piyasapani piu pyare, nain dekhi jani bhul;*
> *Jin ghar ki chhail chhabili, tum as lage majur*

i.e., "Drink, dear one, drink, if thou art athirst. But be not enamoured of the eyes thou lookest on. I am a maid of a house in which such as thou art hinds."

The Rathaur answered:—

> *Râjan ke ham chhokra, bhule des kudes;*
> *Jin ghar ke ham chhokra, tum as lagi panihari.*

i.e., "I am the son of a Râja and have lost my way in an evil land. In my house girls like you draw our water."

Then Managori said to the one-eyed maid: "Thou shouldst not exchange words with one who is a stranger and has lost his way. I will give him to drink." So she went to the Rathhaur with a *lota* of water, but the one-eyed snatched it from her hand. And when she took him the vessel, he smote her on the back with his riding whip and raised a grievous weal. He took the *lota* and washed his hands and feet with the water. Managori took up the *lota* and said to him:—"Come to my house and I will tell thee what I desire." To her the Rathaur answered:—

> *Tumhara to gori naihara, hamara hawai pardes;*
> *Kal baja koi mar darai, to kaun kahai ghar*
> *bandes.*

i.e., "Fair one, this is the house of thy mother and mine is in a strange land. If anyone should kill me, who will carry the news to my home?"

Managori went into the palace and from the upper window she let down a rope, and the Rathaur climbed up and came unto her. In the morning she let him down into the garden, but she forgot to raise the rope. Just then her husband came home from a journey in a distant land, and when he saw the rope he doubted the honour of his wife. He saw the Rathaur in the garden and rushed at him to slay him with his sword. Long they fought, and at the last the Rathaur was slain.

When Managori heard of this, she raised a funeral pyre and, laying the corpse of her lover upon it, she fell upon his breast and both were burned to ashes. When her husband heard of this, he went and bound up the ashes in a sheet. But as he attempted to tie it up, the bundle became larger and larger. Bind it as he would, he could not tie the ashes up. He was amazed at this miracle and sat on the ground and wept. Just then Mahâdeva appeared and asked the cause of his sorrow. When he heard the tale he pierced his little finger and a drop of his nectar fell on the ashes and lo! Managori and the Rathaur stood before them.

Then the Rathaur carried off Managori and brought her to his master. Her husband sat mourning the loss of his wife; but Mahâdeva poured water on the ground and a second Managori, equal to the first, was formed and he gave her to him as his wife. When the Râja received Managori he was filled with joy and gave the Rathaur noble largesse, even half his kingdom, and they all lived happily ever after.

40. *The Wit of the Rânis*

(Told by Harcharan Lâl, Musaha, and recorded by Karamat Ali.)

There was once a Râja who had four wives, but he was so occupied with business and amusement that he never visited them; and they grieved because none of them bore a son. The youngest Râni was the cleverest of them all, and she made a plan. She got a parrot and taught him to say "Thua, Thua;" "Fie, Fie;" and then he flew away and sat on a tree in the courtyard of the palace and spoke as he had been taught, When the Râja heard what he said, he was perplexed and called the Pandits of his court to explain. They said:—"Mahârâj, the time is evil and it is proper for you to make sacrifices and feed holy Brahmans." The Râja was not such a fool as to accept this advice. So he called the Diwân and consulted him. He said:—"Have you consulted the Rânis in the case?" The Râja answered:—"What can foolish women know of such matters?

Why should I consult them?" Just the the Rânis sent the Râja a message to say that, if he wished, they could explain the matter. So he sent for them and the eldest said:—

> *Gaya jaya pinda na parai;*
> *Bairi ke sir kharag na jharai;*
> *Pati, pani, pokhar na kuan,*
> *To lako tota pukarai thua.*

i.e., "The son who does not go to Gaya and offer holy cakes to his dead father, he who does not take vengeance on his enemy, he who does not sink tanks and wells and maintain the honour of his house, to him the parrot calls Fie, Fie."

The second Râni said:—

> *Nahin de bhojan, chhajan, basa,*
> *Brat ekadasi nahin upwasa.*
> *Sankar bhagat, na Sursar chhua.*
> *To tota bhi pukarai thua.*

i.e., "He who does not give food and shelter to the needy, who does not keep the fast of the eleventh, who is not a votary of Siva, and touches not the Ganges, to him the parrot says, Fie."

The third Râni said:—

> *Sadhu ki sangat nahin dwij dana,*
> *Ram ka nam nahin sunana,*
> *Jotish, Ved, Puran na chhua*
> *Tota tahi pukarai thua.*

i.e., "He that keeps not company with the saints, who repeats not the name of Râma, who reads not the books of astrology, the Vedas and the Purânas, to him the parrot says, Fie."

Now the Râja knew that he had done all these duties, and turning to his Diwân he said:—"Said I not that the race of women knew not the affairs of state!" Then the youngest Râni said:—

> *Charto rang kumkum nahin lai,*
> *Khatras se mukh suad na pai,*
> *Jo naina mukh adhar na chhua,*
> *Tota tahi pukarasi thua.*

i.e., "He who in youth dyes not his garments with saffron, who tastes not the six flavours of food, who regards not the face and eyes of beauty, to him the parrot says, Fie."

"This I have not done," said the Râja. So he embraced his wives and lived happily with them ever after.

41. The Warning of the Dancing Girl.

(Told by Muhammad Muhib Ali of Nasirabad and recorded by Râm Sarup of Budaun.)

There was once a Râja who had a son and a daughter who were possessed of great widsom. His son was of a wilful nature, and one day he went to the superintendent of the Râja's stables and asked him for a horse to go hunting. The officer answered that he could not give it without the leave of the Râja. The prince was wroth and said:—"How long can I stand the tyranny of my father. This very night will I slay him."

That night he went into the Darbar, armed with a dagger, and sat near the Râja, intending to kill him when he got an opportunity. As the night passed, most of the audience was overcome with sleep, and the dancing-girl, in order to rouse them and her drummers, sang:—

Bahut gai, thori rahi, aur yah bhi pal pal jat;
Thore der ke waste kahe kalank lagat?

i.e., "Most part is spent and little now remains. Why on account of a little time dost thou bring disgrace upon thyself?"

On hearing this the prince jumped up and gave his shawl to the dancer. The princess gave her a necklace worth nine lakhs, and the daughter of the Wazir gave her father a slap in the face, and he jumped up and began to dance with her in the midst of the assembly.

When the Râja saw this unusual and improper conduct, he was much enraged and called on all of them to explain why they had acted thus.

First the princess said:—"My father, three years ago I was married and the time draws near when my husband will fetch me home. But in the meantime I had fallen in love with another, and this night I intended to abscond with him. When I heard the words of the dancer, I thought that it would be ill to lose my honour when such a short time now remains."

The prince said:—"Father, I was impatient to rule in thy stead, and this night I purposed to slay thee. But when I heard the words of the dancer,

I repented of my evil design; and I knew that in the usual course of things it could not be long before I succeeded to the throne. So I forbore."

The daughter of the Wazir said: "My father up to this has taken no thought for my education; and when I heard her words, I thought that soon I would be married and the time for learning would be past. So I struck my father to remind him of his duty."

The Wazir said:—"When my daughter struck me, I thought that perchance she might slay me. For who can tell what an ignorant woman may do. So I thought it wise to feign to be a madman and disturb the assembly, that I might save my life."

Then the dancer said:—"I meant only that it was time for the drummers to wake and for the audience to listen to my song, as the night was far spent."

The Râja was pleased and gave her royal largesse.

42. *The Test of Honesty.*

(Told by Girwar Lâl and recorded by Mulchand of Kakuba, Agra District.)

There was once a Bania who was going on a pilgrimage, and hearing that the road was beset by thieves, he thought it well to leave his money with some honest person until his return. He saw a shopkeeper sitting in his shop and wondered if he was a proper person with whom to leave the money. As he sat at the shop considering the matter, the servant of a dancing girl came up to buy some *ghi*. The shopkeeper was a rogue at heart and thought that this was the servant of some rich man. So wishing to ingratiate himself with her, he gave her three pica worth of *ghi* for two pice. This still more convinced the Bania that the shopkeeper was a very honest man and he was the more inclined to give him the money. Meanwhile the girl went home with the *ghi*, and when her mistress saw it she said:—"You have brought more than the right amount. It must be some lover of your's who has sold it to you." The girl angrily denied it and brought it back at once to the shopkeeper saying:—"My mistress has sent back this *ghi* because you gave her too much." The Bania thought that the girl's mistress must be a most honest woman. So he went to her house, thinking that he would leave his money with her.

He was talking to the dancing girl about the matter, when a Sadhu came in. The dancing girl gave him at once three cakes and said to him:—"Be off at once." The Sadhu said to himself:—"There must be some roguery afoot, because this woman never before gave me a single cake willingly; but now, the moment I enter her house, she offers me

338

three." So he said: "What can I do with all these cakes. Take back the rest and give me only one which suffices me." The Bania thought the Sadhu must be a most honest man, and that he would leave his money with him.

When he came to the hut of the Sadhu, he said to him: "Mahâraj, I have a large sum of money with me and I wish to leave it with you, till I return from my pilgrimage." The Sadhu, who was a very rogue at heart, pretended not to care whether the Bania left the money there or not. So he flung his tongs into a corner of his hut and said: "You can bury your money there if you wish, and come and dig it up when you return." The Bania did so and went his way.

When he had gone, the Sadhu dug up the money and then he changed the appearance of his house; so that when the Bania returned, he could hardly believe that this was the same place. But he knew the Sadhu and went to him and asked for his money. The Sadhu addressed him angrily, saying:—"Why do you talk of money? I never saw you before in my life."

The Bania was in despair when he found that he had been tricked. So he went to the dancing girl and asked her advice. She said:—"I will do a trick and recover your money. But you must give me half of what you get back." The Bania agreed and she said:—"Go to the Sadhu and dun him for the money until I come." So she went and filled several boxes with bricks, and putting them on the heads of her servants, came disguised to the Sadhu and said:—"I am the Râni of Gwalior, and I want to leave all these valuables with you." The Sadhu was just then arguing with the Bania about the money, and he thought it unwise, just when another matter was on foot, to quarrel about a trifling sum. So he paid him the amount of his deposit. Just then the maid of the dancing girl came running up and said:—"Râni Sahiba, you need not mind leaving your things here, as the Râja Sahib himself has come." So the Bania went off after thus outwitting the Sadhu.

Then the maid-servant began to laugh and her mistress said:—"What are you laughing at?" She replied:—"I remember the proverb:—

Jo dhan disai jat,
Adhi dijai bant.

i.e., "When you see that you are losing something, compound for half."

43. *Sujan Chand and Nitikala.*

(Told by Bâldeo Sinh, schoolmaster, Sayyidnagar, Jalaun District.)

Sujan Chand was the Râja of the western land and Nitikala was his

Râni. One night the Râja and his Râni were sleeping on a bed of flowers, and that day the Mâlin had left among the rose leaves a single thorn which pricked the tender skin of the Râni. She told her husband and abused the Mâlin for her lack of care. Then the lamp which hung in the room laughed and said to her:—"You fret to-day for a thorn among the rose leaves; but to-morrow, when you have to carry bricks and mortar on your head, what will you say?"

They slept through the night, and in the morning the Râni reminded the Râja of what the lamp had said. He knew that its words would come true, and knowing that he could not bear the sight of the affliction of his loved one, he determined to remove her from his sight. So he got a box and shut up the Râni in it, leaving a hole to admit the air, and then he took the box and flung it into the river.

The box went floating down the stream till it came opposite the palace, where lived the sister of the Râja Sujan Chand. Her husband was bathing in the river, and when he saw the box floating down, he sent his servants and they drew it to land. He did not open the box, but, making it over to his Râni, he went to the Darbar and busied himself in the affairs of his kingdom. The Râni opened the box and found inside a damsel so lovely that the world did not hold her equal, and she thought to herself that, if her husband saw the maiden, his love for her would change. So she blackened the girl's face with charcoal, took off her gorgeous apparel, and gave her a suit of rags. When the Râja came and saw her, he deemed her some foul slut, who had been sent away for her foulness, and he made her a servant in his household. He was then building a new palace, so he set Nitikala to carry the bricks and mortar for the masons. Some years were spent in this manner.

One day the Râni was keeping her fast in honour of the Disha Râni, and Nitakala, following her example, fasted also in honour of the goddess. The deity was pleased at her devotion and determined to mend her state and end her days of sorrow. So she brought to the mind of Sujan Chand the Râni whom he had loved, and he set out at once to seek her. By and by he reached the palace of his sister, where his Râni was a maidservant; and his sister received him with love and entertained him with all due respect.

One day it happened that his sister was sitting in the courtyard. Beside her sat her brother, and near them Nitikala was carrying the bricks and stones to the workmen.

The Râni said to Nitikala:—"Go and shampoo the feet of my brother." She went and began to press his feet, and as she pressed them she saw on his feet the marks of royal birth, the lotus sign which marks a king, and the moonlike brightness of his face; and she began to think of her husband and how she too had loved a king and lost his love. So she began to weep, and the eyes of the Râja were opened and he asked her why she wept. She said:—"O Mahârâj, when evil days come, they bring trouble in their train." And then she repeated these lines:—

> *Barhat nir sampati bibhan man barij barhi hoe;*
> *Ghatat nir puni ghatat nahin, kauj dukh sukh*
> > *joe.*

i.e., "When the water of fortune rises, the lotus of the heart also rises. But the heart, like the lotus, does not sink low."

By this she meant that it is impossible for one used to happiness to accustom himself to trouble. Again she said:—

> *Kabahun palau shakh men kabhun mahi*
> > *dikhahin;*
> *Aise he dukh sukh sakal, yah tan gudarat jahin.*

i.e., "Sometimes the shoots of the tree grow and sometimes they fall upon the ground. So pleasure and sorrow come and go betimes."

Then she cried:—"Mahârâj, I wept to see the marks of royalty upon thy feet," and she added:—

"I think of how the lamps laughed when I complained of the single thorn among the rose leaves." Then he told his sister the whole tale of Nitikala, and she begged her forgiveness for her despiteful treatment of her. Then Sujan Chand took his Râni home and they lived many days in happiness.

44. Half a lie.

(Told by Thakur Pohap Sinh of Kota, Budaun District.)

There was once a very respectable Kâzi who hired as his servant a man named Pira. Now Pira was given to lying, and whenever the Kâzi sent him on any business he used to shirk it, and, when he came home, would tell all kinds of lies to his master. At last the Kâzi could stand him no longer and sent for him and warned him. Then Pira said:—"When you took me into your service, you knew that I could not help telling a lie now and then." "But," said the Kâzi, "there is a measure in lying. I do not mind your telling half a lie now and then; but to lie always is bad."

Some business took the Kâzi from home and after some time Pira went to see him. "Is all well at home?" asked his master. Tears began to drop from Pira's eyes and he said:—"All is well save that your brown dog died suddenly." "What matter," said the Kâzi, "dogs die every day." Then he asked "Of what disease did he die?" "He had no disease," said Pira, "but when he began to chew the bones of your ox he got choked." "And what happened to the ox?" "He died from the labour of carrying the bricks." "What were the bricks wanted for?" "For building the grave of your wife, the Bibi Sâhiba." Then the Kâzi was overwhelmed with grief and said:—"What happened to the Bîbî Sâhiba?" "She died of grief at the death of your eldest son." Then the Kâzi fell down senseless with grief.

"Tell the syce," said he "to saddle my horse at once." Pira went out and said to the syce:—"Your master will not go out riding today. Take out the horse for a long airing along the road outside the village." The Kâzi waited for a long time for the horse; but when it did not come, he was perforce obliged to walk, and he was quite worn out when he came to the neighbourhood of his house.

"Let me go in advance," said Pira, "and make all ready that your worship may join in the mourning." So he went on to the Kâzi's house and began to weep and beat his breast. "What is the matter?" asked the Bîbî Sâhiba. "Alas, alas," cried Pira, "your respected husband, the Kâzi Sâhiba, has just dropped down dead." On this the lady began to weep and lament, and when all the neighbours heard the sound of lamentation in the Kâzi's house, they all crowded round the place. But when they saw the Kâzi arrive mourning and beating his breast, they were filled with astonishment and asked what had happened. "O fools," cried the Kâzi, "is it not enough that my wife and son and ox are dead? Why should I not lament?" With these words he entered the house, and what was his surprise to find his wife and family lamenting him. When he was somewhat comforted, he asked where Pira was; but he had by this time made his escape. Then he went out and saw his syce standing outside with his horse. "Where have you been all this time, you ruffian?" asked the angry Kâzi. And he was about to flog his servant, when the syce managed to convince him that it was all the fault of Pira.

After some time Pira came back, when the anger of the Kâzi was somewhat appeased. "What do you mean by this?" enquired the Kâzi. Then Pira said:—"This is but the half lie which your worship told me I might tell now and again." "If this be only half a lie, God preserve us from a whole one," prayed the Kâzi. But he so much admired his cleverness that he took him back again into his service.

45. *Râja Bhoj and his Râni.*

(Told by Nathu Mal, Bania, of Sahâranpur.)

Râja Bhoj was noted for his deeds of piety. Every day he used to feed one hundred and one Brahmans. One day a Brahman came in to eat, and as he left he did not bless the Râja as the other Brahmans did. This astonished Râja Bhoj, and the next day, when the Brahman came and acted in the same way, the Râja seized his hand and asked him the reason. "I cannot tell," he answered. "And if you want an answer you had better go to Bandu Patwa." Now Bandu Patwa was a noted magician.

When Râja Bhoj went to Bandu, he found that Bandu had just cut off the nose of his wife and the forelegs of his dog. The woman came out and saluted the Râja, and the Râja asked Bandu why he had done this thing. "Had I not cut off my wife's nose, such is her pride that she would not have come out to salute you; and my dog is always barking and trying to bite visitors; so I cut off his legs that he might not be able to move out of the corner." Then the Râja asked Bandu why the Brahman had not saluted him. He said:—"I cannot tell you; and if you want to learn, you must go to the Sadhu who lives in the forest."

The Râja went to see the Sadhu in disguise. Now Bhanmati, the Râni of Râja Bhoj, was unfaithful to him, and just as the Râja was going along the road he saw a palanquin coming along. As they came near him, one of the bearers fell down in a fit, and the Râni called out and offered a gold *mohur* to any one who would take his place. He helped to carry her to the hut where the Sadhu lived, and there she got out and stayed for the night.

The Râja determined to watch her. So one day he slept, intending to keep awake at night. When the Râni saw him sleeping, she woke him, and he said:—"Why did you wake me out of such a pleasant dream?" She said:—"What was the dream?" He replied:—"I dreamed that I saw you with the Sadhu in the forest." She knew that her secret was discovered. So she sent a message to the Sadhu telling him what the Râja had said. The Sadhu sent her a cord and said:—"When he is not watching you, tie this cord round the Râja's neck." She did so, and the Râja was forthwith turned into a dog.

The Râni tried to shut up the dog in a closet, but he escaped and ran off to the house of Bandu Patwa. He knew the device of the Sadhu. So he loosed the string off the neck of the dog and the Râja recovered his original form. Bandu Patwa shut the Râja up for some days in his house. Meanwhile the Sadhu had taken the form of the Râja and sat on his throne and lived with the Râni as her husband. One day the Sadhu sat in Darbar and gave an order that every one was to attend with his dog. Bandu Patwa went with the dog whose legs he had cut off. The Sadhu said:—"You rascal, where is your second dog?" Bandu answered:—"I have no other dog and you may search my house if you please." Then he went home and said to the Râja:—"You had better leave this and go a hundred *kos* off, lest the Sadhu finds and slays you." Râja Bhoj said:—"I never walked a *kos* in my life. How can I go a hundred *kos?*"

Then Bandu Patwa made a magic chariot, and mounting the Râja in it, sent him to a place which was one hundred and fifty *kos* distant.

The chariot halted in a garden, where the daughter of the Râja of the land was swinging. She soon went to her palace, and Râja Bhoj got into the swing and fell asleep. When the princess returned and found a man asleep in her swing, she was wroth and was about to slay him with a sword. But one of her maidens said:—"It is wrong to slay a sleeping man. When he wakes, slay him if you please." Then the princess woke the Râja and asked him who he was. When she heard the tale, she went to her father and said:—"I desire to marry the man whom I have found in my garden." Her father was angry and said:—"Marry him if you choose." So they were married, but her father gave them no dowry and they left him in poverty. The Râja was obliged to go and borrow some flour from the woodcutters to make a meal for his wife and himself. He then wished to go to his own land, but the Râni said:—"We cannot go till we have returned the flour to the woodcutters." The Râja went into the forest to cut wood, and the first tree he touched turned out to be a sandal tree. This he sold, and every day he used to cut a sandal tree, till he gained great wealth and his father-in-law recognised him and gave him half his kingdom.

One day two swans were sitting on a tree above the original palace of Râja Bhoj, and one said to the other:—"This is a splendid palace." The other said:—"The palace of Râja Bhoj is much finer." The Sadhu was listening and knew that Râja Bhoj must be alive. So he and the Râni disguised themselves and went in search of Râja Bhoj to slay him. Bandu Patwa knew their plan and he followed them. He said to Râja Bhoj:— "The Sadhu and your Râni are coming to this city, disguised as dancers, and they have planned to turn you into some vile beast and slay you. When they come and dance before you, they will ask as their reward your

Naulakha (necklace). Do not give them the whole necklace, but keep two beads of it."

He did as Bandu Patwa advised, and when he had given the Sadhu and his Râni the necklace, all but two beads, he threw one bead at the Sadhu and the other at Bandu Patwa, whereupon the Sadhu became a fowl and Bandu a cat, which devoured the fowl. And that was the end of the Sadhu.

Then Râja Bhoj said to Bandu Patwa:—"What should be done to my false Râni?" He said:—"Slay her and bury her at the cross roads, that every one's feet may fall upon her."

So it was done, and Râja Bhoj got back his kingdom and lived long and happily with his new Râni.

46. The Quest of the Princess.

(Told by Lâla Hardwari Mal, teacher, Fatehpur.)

There was once a Râja who had a son, and in his old age he said to him:—"I am shutting up two rooms in thy presence. Open them when I am dead." A few days later the Râja died; and when they saw that the prince was only a youth, the soldiers and the courtiers began to loot every thing which was in the palace. An old man was standing close by, and the prince said to him:—"Why do you not take the chance and plunder something?" The old man answered:—"I have eaten thy salt and I cannot do this." A short time after, the prince remembered the words of his father, and he called the old man and told him to open the rooms. When he opened one room they found it full of old shoes. Then the prince told him to open the other room, and when they unlocked the door, they found a cock tied by its legs to one of the roof beams. When the cock saw them, it began to crow, and the old man said to the prince:—"It is possessed by a demon; do not touch it." The prince untied the cock and gave it to the old man to sell in the bazar.

The old man sat in the bazar by the wayside with the cock in his lap. The people began to jest at him, and one said: "For how many cowries will you sell this cock?" He answered:—"Give me your daughter or sister for the bird and take it away." The old man did all he could to sell the cock, but no one would buy it. Then a Râja came into the bazar and asked the price of the cock. "A thousand rupees," said the old man. The Râja paid down the money and gave it to the Bhathiyârin of an inn close by. She asked:—"Who will buy the flesh of this cock?" The Râja replied:— "He of the bald head, the cripple, the blind and the deaf and dumb."

Then the old man got his hair shaved, bent his back and put on his eyes the web of a spider and came to the Bhathiyârin and said:—" Bîbî, give me the meat of the cock. The Râja wants it," She was very glad to get rid of it, and she gave the old man the meat and the pot in which she had cooked it. He bought some food and went to the prince. The prince was very hungry and began to eat the flesh of the cock and the old man said:—"When you have done, throw the bones to me." As the prince was eating the meat he found in it a ring, and when he put it on his finger, two demons stood before him. When the prince asked who they were, they said:—"We are the slaves of thy finger." The prince said:—"Go and call the old man, my servant." When the old man came, the prince told him with delight how the demons had become his slaves. But he said:— "I will not live with these demons." "Do not mind them," answered the prince. "They are now members of our household."

Said the old man: "We have naught in the house to feed so many mouths as these. Let us go out hunting and kill something for food." Then one demon rolled on the ground, and at once he was turned into a horse with splendid trappings, and the other rolled on the ground and became a servant finely dressed and armed. The prince mounted the horse and rode off to the forest. By and by he came to a fort in the forest, and from it there came a piteous cry. The prince rode on and, entering the fort, he saw a Sadhu crying and a crowd of men stood watching him. The prince asked the Sadhu why he was lamenting, and he said:— "Will you share my trouble?" "I will share it," said the prince. Then the Sadhu said:—"In a certain land a girl has been born, and from the day of her birth twenty-five maunds of food are daily cooked. A great pan is full of boiling *ghi*. There are eighty-eight million tanks full of water, and the garden is in charge of a Mâlin who lives two hundred million miles away. If anyone were to consume the food, drink the water, and go to the Mâlin and come back in the space of eight minutes with a garland of flowers, the girl will be given to him in marriage. But if anyone attempt these tasks and fail, he will be ground to pieces in a sugarcane-mill."

The prince determined to attempt the task. When he came to the palace in which the girl lived, he saw a mighty drum hanging at the gate and this he struck to announce his coming. When the maid-servant of the girl heard the sound of the drum, she said to her mistress: "Some one has come to sacrifice his life for thee." The girl told her maid to bring him, and he was taken into her presence. The girl said:—"Eat all this mass of food which has been cooked since the day I was born." The prince and the demons began to eat it, and so quickly was it eaten that they ate it all in eight mouthfuls. Then she said to them:—"Drink the water of all the tanks." They drank it all up in one gulp. Then she said to the prince:—"Jump into the pan of boiling *ghi*." The prince was about to jump, when the demons made a sign to him, and the prince said: "Any-one can do this. Let my servant do it." The princess agreed, and the demon spat into the pan and all the heat left the *ghi*. Then he told the prince to jump in and he did so.

Then the princess said:—"Only one deed remains to be done. Bhura Deo (The Brown Demon) is holding a cup in the sky. You must strike it with an arrow and cause it to fall." The prince shot three arrows, but Bhura Deo held the cup so tightly that he could not make it fall. Then one of the demons flew up to the sky and broke the hands of Bhura Deo, and the other demon told the prince to shoot one arrow more. The prince did so and immediately the cup fell on the ground. Then the princess said:—"You must now bring the garland of flowers from the Mâlin." He said:—"Let one of my servants do this." The princess consented, and one of the demons flew away. Hardly a moment had passed when he returned with the garland.

So the prince married the princess. Great store of wealth she had, and they lived long in happiness.

47. *The punishment of Râja Indra.*

(Told by Bansidhar, schoolmaster, Bah, Agra District.)

Once upon a time there were a swan and his wife, and the land in which they lived was ruined by famine. So the swan said to his mate:—"Let us seek another land." They flew on and on, till they came to a lovely garden, in the midst of which was a lake. The swan said:—"Let us halt here." Now the master of the garden was a crow, and he received them hospitably. They stayed a few days, and as they were going away the crow said to the swan:—"Why are you taking your mate away with you? She belongs to me, because she was my mate in a former life." The swan re-fused to give her up, and the crow said: "Let us call a *Panchayat* of the birds." Now there were in that land no other birds but crows. So, before the council met, the crow went round to all his brethren and asked them to give a decree in his favour. The trial came on, and when both sides had stated their case, the council gave a verdict in favour of the crow and made over the female swan to him. The swan said:—"I appeal to Râja Indra." So to Râja Indra they went, and before the case came on, the crow went to Râja Indra and said:—"If you give the case in my favour, I will bring you the fruit of immortality." Through his longing for the fruit, Râja Indra gave the case in favour of the crow. The crow took the swan, and they nested on a tree over the palace of Râja Indra. One day Râja Indra was going to worship his god, when the crow, who had just been rooting in a dunghill, flew by and dropped a piece of filth on the head of the idol. When Râja Indra saw that his worship was defiled, he cursed the crow and said:—"Faithless wretch, you promised me the fruit of immortality. Not only did you break your word, but you have defiled the deity as I am worshipping him." The crow answered:—"Who art thou to claim the fruit of immortality, when thou hast lost thy virtue and doest injustice?" Râja Indra was ashamed, and the crow called the swan and said:— "Take your mate. I did this only to prove that even among the gods there are liars."

48. The Pound of Flesh.

(Told by Rasul Baksh, combmaker, Sahâranpur.)

Two men, who were gambling with dice, made a wager that the loser was to allow the other to cut off a *ser* of flesh. One of them having lost, the other was preparing to cut his flesh, when the loser objected. So they both referred the matter to the Kâzi. After considering the case, the Kâzi said to the winner: "Bring your knife and cut off a *ser* of flesh. But if you take even the weight of a *rati* more or less and spill a single drop of blood, your life will be forfeited." The winner, fearing to violate this condition, abandoned the wager.

[The pound of flesh, of which the tale of Shylock is the most famous instance, has been bibliographised by R. Kohler in *Orient and Occident*, 315 ff. It is possibly of Oriental origin; but whether the above version is original is another matter.—W. Crooke.]

49. The Sweeper Youth and the Râni.

(Told by Pandit Tej Râja and recorded by Munshi Har Prasâd, Dânaganj, Budaun District.)

There was once an old sweeper woman who used to clean the courts of the Râja's palace. One day she fell ill, and being unable to work, she dressed up her son in woman's clothes and sent him to sweep the palace instead. As the lad was sweeping, he saw the Râni sitting at the window of her chamber combing her hair: and when his eyes beheld her, he was overcome with love, and crying, "Alas for the Râni! Alas for the Râni!" he ran home and lay there as if dead.

His mother seeing this, was amazed and feared the wrath of the Râja, if the matter came to light. So she went secretly to the Râni, told her what had happened, and implored her forgiveness, pleading that her son had been attacked with sudden madness. The Râni said:—"Let him give up his sweeper's trade and go into the forest and devote himself to the worship of Mahadeva."

The boy went into the forest and devoted himself to meditation, so that he became a mighty saint, and all the great ones of the land used to go to him and procure the realization of their desires. After a while the Râni said to the Râja:—"Let me too visit this famous saint, that I may pray for the long life of thee and my children." The Râja gave her leave, and she approached the saint. "I am she," said she, "whom thou sawest in the upper chamber." The saint replied:—"I am not the same. The great ones of the land honour me; and this is all through devotion to the Almighty." Thus he became a real saint, and his fame spread abroad.

50. *Vishnu Sarma and His Wife.*

(Told by Pandit Gore Lâl of Kailganwa, Lalipur, and recorded by Pandit Râdhika Prasâd.)

There was once a Pandit named Vishnu Sarma, who for a long time refused to marry. At last, under pressure from his friends, he married a blind Brahman girl. When she became pregnant, he went to her, and after reciting *mantras* threw some rice over her; whereupon the child in her womb spoke and said that he was indeed his son. So he was wont to do, whenever she became with child: and the child always spoke from her womb and testified to its legitimacy.

The other women used to laugh at her, saying: "If your husband is as learned as this, why does he not cure your blindness?" So she told her husband that if he would not give her her sight, she would commit suicide. Hereupon he threw rice over her and repeated *mantras,* and she recovered her sight.

One day after the time of her purification, she was bathing on the roof of her house, when her eyes fell on a groom, and she conceived. Then the Pandit threw rice over her, according to the usual practice; but the child made no reply. When he asked his wife, she would not tell him how matters stood. So for very grief and shame he fell ill and died.

After his death a son was born, who claimed a share in the estate, which the others refused to give. The case came before Râja Vikramâditya, and he asked his queen to test the matter. So she donned her royal robes and called all the sons to her. She asked each in turn to sit beside her on the couch, and those who were the legitimate sons of Vishnu Sarma refused by reason of the modesty of noble birth, while he that was the son of the groom took his seat beside her. Thus she knew that he was not the legal heir, and his claim was disallowed by the Râja.

[For instances of these supernatural births, see *The Legend of Perseus* by Hartland.—W. CROOKE.]

51. The Rogue and the Goat.

A goat once strayed into the house of a rogue, who forthwith killed and ate it. The owner came to him soon afterwards and asked him if he had seen his goat. The rogue replied:—"Not only have I seen it, but I have eaten it." "Then you must give me one as good or pay the price," said the owner. "Why should I pay for it?" said the rogue. "If you don't," answered the other, "I will claim it from you on the Day of Judgment." "But suppose I deny the matter." "Then the goat itself will come and give testimony against you." "Well," said the rogue, "when I see the goat coming before the Almighty, I will catch it by its ear and say to you, 'Take your goat and don't come annoying me with false charges.'"

52. The Weaver Bird and the Elephant.

(Told by Râm Sahai, Brahman of Audharanpur, and recorded by Jang Bahâdur Kayasth, Basitnagar, Hardoi District.)

A *Phadka* or weaver bird and his wife, the *Phadki*, once built their nest on an acacia tree, and close by lived an elephant and his wife. Now the elephant used to come daily and rub himself against the acacia tree so violently that it was almost uprooted. One day, when the tree was shaking violently, the *Phadki* said to the *Phadka*:—"My dear husband, if this goes on much longer the tree will fall, our nest will be thrown down, and our eggs broken. You must see to it at once." "What can I do against such a great beast as this?" said he.

So the *Phadki* went herself to the Elephant's wife and said, "Great trouble will soon befall your husband if he goes on rubbing himself against our tree." The female elephant warned her husband, but all he said was, "Let me once get the wretched creature under my foot and I will crush him to powder." Next day he went as usual to the tree, and as he was rubbing himself against it, the *Phadki* flew down, got into his ear, and began to scratch and tear with her claws and beak. The elephant howled for mercy, and from inside his ear the *Phadki* cried, "Did I not warn you that one day evil would befall you?" Then, when the Elephant besought her to desist, she repeated the following verse:—

> *Ari chhoto ganiye nahîn jâte hot bigâr*
> *Trin samuh ko chhinak men chinagi deti bigâr.*

i.e., "Never despise an enemy, however insignificant. A little spark destroys a great pile of hay in a moment."

[This is one of the cycle of tales in which the inferior animal overcomes the mightier one.—W. Crooke.]

53. *The Result of Charity.*

(Told by Thakur Sinh, Ahîr, of Sahâranpur.)

There was a princess who was so haughty that she said, "I will marry none save him who can bring Airâvati, the elephant of Râja Indra, and all the fairies of Indrasân to the wedding." In that city lived a poor Brahmani who was in the most bitter poverty. One day an old Brahman, who was Bhagwân in disguise, came to her door and asked for food. Her son was given to charity and he said, "Mother, there is naught in the house wherewith we may feed this poor Brahman. Cook my dinner and let him have it." So the old woman cooked her son's dinner and gave it to the Brahman. But by the grace of Bhagwân the food doubled in quantity, and when the Brahman had eaten, there was enough to spare for the boy and his mother. What was saved they gave to the needy.

Bhagwân was pleased with the boy; so that night he appeared to him in a dream and said, "Go and demand the princess as your wife." Next morning the boy went to the palace and demanded the princess. Her father and the courtiers were wroth at his presumption and the Râja ordered that he should be slain. But Bhagwân appeared to the Râja and said, "Do not slay the boy. To-morrow the elephant Airâvati and the fairies of Indrasân will accompany his marriage procession."

And so it was; the Brahman boy married the princess amid the utmost splendour.

So may Bhagwân reward all who do good.

54. The Fruits of Covetousness.

(Told by Thakur Sinh, Ahîr, of Sahâranpur.)

There was once a Chamâr who wanted a cocoanut to offer to his god. So he went to the bazar to buy one. He asked the price, and the Banya said, "An anna apiece." "And whence and at what rate do you buy them?" asked the Chamâr. "They come from Kahnpur," he replied, "and they cost half an anna each." The Chamâr thought he would save his money and buy at Kahnpur. So he went there and asked the Bania the price. "Half an anna each," he answered. "And whence and at what rate do you get them?" "They come," he replied, "from Calcutta and the price is a pice apiece." So the Chamâr went to Calcutta, and when he asked the merchant the price, he said, "The price is a pice apiece, but if you go out to the forest close by, you can pluck as many as you like for nothing." The Chamâr went to the forest and saw the cocoanuts growing on the trees, but they were so high from the ground that his wits were bewildered. At last he took courage and climbed to the top of one of the trees and tried to break off the nuts; but the stems were very strong, and as he used his strength to break them, he slipped, but was lucky enough to cling to a branch lower down. Then he looked out for someone to help him down; and by and by a camelman came up, and the Chamâr offered him a reward if he would help him. So the camelman brought his camel to the foot of the tree, hoping to jump down on its back. But as he climbed up, the camel ran away and was lost in the forest. So the two remained clinging to the branch until a horseman passed that way. They implored him to help them down. Seeing them in this strait, he made them promise him all they possessed. So he drew up his horse to the foot of the tree, hoping to jump down on his back. But when the horseman climbed up, the horse ran away and was lost, and the three remained hanging to the branch. But it was too weak to bear the weight of all of them, and it broke, and they all fell down and were killed. Such is the fate of the covetous.

55. How the Râja suffered Misfortune.

(Told by Ajal Bihâri Lâl and recorded by Sayyid Imdâd Husain, Kunwârpur, Fatehpur District.)

There was once a Râja who was famed for his glory and piety. He had a Rânî whom he loved dearly, and she bore him two sons. One day the Râja was hunting in the forest, when Ill Fortune in the guise of a man met him. When the Râja asked who he was, he said, "I am Ill Fortune.

Many a Râja have I reduced to poverty and now I am come upon thy head." When the Râja heard this, he was sore grieved and thought to himself, "It is well that Ill Fortune has come upon me while I am still young and able to work for my living." So he said, "Thou art welcome." Just then a tiger rushed out and fell upon him. He was sore wounded. His horse was killed, but he escaped with his life. When he recovered, he went to his capital, and on the way met a faithful servant of his house, who said, "Venture not into thy city. In thy absence the Diwân has seized the kingdom and turned thy Râni and sons out of the palace. It were well that thou shouldest not enter the city, where a reward is set upon thy head. Wait in this garden, and if it be possible, I will bring thy wife and sons to thee."

The Râja waited in the garden in sore plight, and the servant went and found the Râni and her sons in a miserable hovel in the most extreme distress. He told her of the arrival of the Râja, and she said, "If it be possible, bring me to him, and when the days of sorrow have passed I will reward thee." The servant brought the Râni and her children to her husband, and she found him lamenting his changed condition. She said, "What is the use of mourning when Paramesvar is displeased with us? Let us go to another land and work for our living."

They wandered long and far, and at last were exhausted with hunger. They came to a river, where a kindly fisherman gave them a couple of hooks, and the princes went to the bank to catch fish. As they were fishing, a crocodile came out of the water and devoured them. Their parents searched for the boys but could not find them, and went their way sorrowing. So they came to a city, where a grain-parcher took them into his service, and for many days they worked, stoking his furnace.

After the boys were lost, some fishermen were dragging the river, and by chance the crocodile fell into the net. When they cut him open, the two boys came out of his belly safe and sound, and the fishermen took them home and kept them as their own sons.

Now the Râja of that land was an old man and he had no son. So he sent his Wazîr to search for a boy to be his heir, who should be possessed of the marks of royalty. The Wazîr found the youths with the fisherman, and when he examined them, he found the marks of royalty upon them. So the Râja took them as his sons, and by chance he appointed their own father to teach them. He did not know that they were his sons, until they came to be married and repeated the names of their forefathers. Then he knew them, and when he told the Râja of his misfortunes, he provided him with an army. So he came to his own land, overcame his faithless Diwân and they all lived in complete happiness.

May Parameswar change the fate of all as he changed theirs.

56. *The Prince who would not marry.*

(Told by Mukund Lâl Kayasth of Mirzapur.)

There was once a widow who lived near the hermitage of some Sadhus, and she was always in attendance on them. One day one of the Sadhus blessed her and said, "Woman, for thy care of us thou shalt be rewarded with a son." She said, "How can I, a widow, have a son and what will the folk say of me?" He answered, "I cannot withdraw my blessing; but I can change it somewhat." So he took her hand and made a mark on it with his finger; and she conceived. And when the days were full, a son was born from her hand. She took the babe, and through fear of the folk laid it on the river-bank and went her way.

Soon after a Brahman came there to bathe, and seeing the babe, being himself childless, he took it home and reared it as his own son. Time passed, and the boy became a noted Pandit. His adopted father wished him to marry. But he said "I will not marry as long as you and my mother are alive."

When the Brahman died, he divided his substance among the poor and needy, and went to a forest, where he remained twelve years repeating the name of Râma. Then he came to a city and stood before the house of a banker. The banker asked him who he was and he said—"I am a wandering Sadhu and have come to see your city." The banker replied "My house is a mere hut. It is to the Râja's palace that you should go." He came to the Râja's palace, and the daughter of the Râja saw him and gave him food. "Ask a blessing," he said. She answered, "I love a certain prince, but he refuses to marry me. Go to him and induce him to take me."

The Sadhu went to the Prince and said—"Why do you refuse to marry the daughter of the Râja?" He replied, "In a former life she was my mate and we were both deer. One day the hunters came upon us, and she escaped and left me in their hands. Hence I will have no more to do with her." The Sadhu answered—"Dost thou not know the tale of Jaratkaru?" The prince said—"Say on."

Said the Sadhu—"Jaratkaru, like yourself, refused to marry. One day he went into the forest, and suddenly he came to a well in which five men were hanging. He asked them who they were. They said—'We are thy five ancestors, and we must hang here until you marry and beget a son.' Hearing this, Jaratkaru agreed to marry."

Hearing the words of the Sadhu, the prince was afraid, and consented to marry the princess. The Sadhu retired to the forest, whence he was shortly afterwards translated to Vaikuntha.

57. The Power of Fate.

(Told by Hasan Khân Pathan of Sahâranpur.)

There was once an astrologer who said to the King of Shâm (Syria), "Thou shalt meet thy death at the hand of the King of Rûm." Hearing this, the king stayed at home through fear. One day he went into the bath chamber, and lo! a golden bird appeared with a chain which hung to the ground. The king grasped the chain to seize the bird, when it flew away with him and landed him on the parade-ground, where the King of Rûm was exercising his troops. The King of Rûm recognised him and showed him due hospitality, asking him what food he needed. "I like no food as much as the cucumber," he answered. The King of Rûm then called for a cucumber and began cutting it in pieces and feeding his guest. But all of a sudden the King of Shâm sneezed, and the knife by mischance pierced his nose and entered his brain. Such is the power of Fate.

58. The Thakur and the Koli.

(Told by Makkhan Jat of Hatkauli, Mathura District, and recorded by Bhala Bania of that village.)

A Koli once took service with a Thâkur. One day the Koli said to his wife:—"I am going to my master. Do you need aught?" She replied, "Ask your master to give me a petticoat and a sheet." Her husband promised to do so. He found the Thâkur just ready to set forth to the house of his father-in-law and was bidden by him to go with him and mind the horse. As they went along, the Thâkur said to the Koli, "Take my sword and be careful of it, as it is of great value." On arriving at a river, the Thâkur asked how they were to cross. "You ride on," said the Koli, "and I will hold on to the tail." When they reached mid-stream, the scabbard dropped into the water, and the Koli cried:—"Something black has fallen from the sword." "Where did it fall," shouted the Thâkur. "Just about there," said the Koli and flung the sword after it. Then he said, "I just remembered that my wife asked you to give her a petticoat and a sheet."

Said the Thâkur, "Be gone, accursed one! What a fool I was to take such a stupid lout as my servant."

59. *The Sadhu and the Rat.*

(Told by Shiba Sinh, Brahman, of Sahâranpur.)

A rat, who lived in the jungle, was one day chased by a cat. He took shelter in the hut of a Sadhu and begged his protection. The Sadhu blessed him and said, "Go, my son, and become a cat." So he was turned into a cat and lived by hunting the rats in the jungle. One day, being chased by a dog, he again ran to the Sadhu, who blessed him and said, "Go, my son, and become a dog." So he became a dog and used to hunt cats in the forest. One day he was attacked by a tiger and again sought the Sadhu's help. The Sadhu blessed him, and he became a tiger, spending his time in chasing and killing deer. At length the deer got to know him and left the jungle, so that he had nothing to eat and suffered from hunger. By chance the Sadhu passed that way, and the tiger sprang upon him. Then the Sadhu cursed him, saying "Go, my son, and become a rat again." He implored the Sadhu to allow him to remain a tiger. But the Sadhu left him saying, "Thou art an ungrateful beast. If I bless thee again, perchance thou mayest work me evil."

60. *The Prince and Pân Shâhzâdi.*

(Told by Jhuman Lâl of Dîdârganj, Azamgarh District, and recorded by Jadunandan Rae of Baswân.)

There was once a Prince, whose parents died after they had betrothed him to a princess in another land. One day, while hunting, he felt thirsty, and went to a river, on the surface of which he found a *pân* leaf floating. When he touched it, he lost his senses: and bringing the leaf home, he placed it on a shelf.

The Prince's food was prepared daily and placed near his couch; but every night some one came and ate it. At last he determined to watch, and he cut his finger and rubbed it with salt and pepper. At night when Pân Shâzâdi came out of the leaf on the shelf and began eating his food, he seized her and made her live with him as his wife. After many days the parents of his betrothed summoned him to come and marry his bride, whereat he was very sad and asked Pân Shâzâdi what to do. She said, "Go and marry her. But when will you return;" "I will come," said he, "when the dove that sits on the banyan tree has eggs, and the tree flowers."

So he departed; and the dove had eggs and the tree flowered, but he never returned. At last Pân Shâzâdi had a flying elephant made, which could also speak. In this she concealed herself and was borne to the Prince's palace. The Prince was delighted and had the elephant placed on the roof of the palace. There his wife found it, and while he was out hunting, she had it burnt. The Prince was sore grieved at the loss of the elephant; but a Sadhu took the ashes and prayed to Bhagwân, and lo! a lovely girl rose from the ashes. This was the Pân Shâzâdi.

She went to the palace, and hearing that the Prince was sick unto death at the burning of the elephant, she disguised herself as a beggar, boiled some oil, and threw it over him, whereupon he at once recovered. He asked her to enter and see his queen, and when he himself came in a little later he found two lovely princesses together. So he knew that this was Pân Shâzâdi; and he killed his other queen, and they lived happily ever after.

61. The Lion and the Jackal.

(Told by Ramdayâl, Khairagarh, Agra District.)

A lion, who lived with his wife in a cave, used to leave her daily and go forth to look for prey. One day up came a jackal, mounted on a fox and carrying a bow and arrow of reed. Finding the lion away from home, he said to the lioness, "Where is that wretched husband of yours?" "What do you want with him?" she asked. "Do you not know that I am the lord of this jungle, and that your husband owes me his house-tax. I am looking everywhere for him, and when I find him, I will kill him." The lioness was much afraid at these words, and to pacify the jackal she gave him some of the meat stored for the use of her family.

After this the jackal used to come every day and get meat, and used all kinds of threats and abuse against the lion. Through anxiety and annoyance the lioness grew quite lean, and at last the lion noticed it and asked her, "Why are you so lean, when I bring abundance of meat daily?" Then she told him of the visits of the jackal and what he used to say; and when he heard it, the lion was very wroth; and next morning, instead of going out to hunt as usual, he lay down in ambush close to the cave. Up came the jackal as usual and began to abuse and threaten the lioness. Then the lion rushed at him, and the jackal ran before him under the pillar shoots of a banyan tree. He managed to push his way through them, but the lion stuck between two branches and could not escape. In a few days he died there of hunger and thirst.

Some time after, the jackal went back to the place, and when he saw the lion dead he was delighted, and, going to the lioness, said, "It is not good for any female to remain a widow. You must come and live with me as my wife." So he took the lioness to his den. Now the lioness, when the lion died, was about to have cubs, and soon after she went to live with the jackal, they were born. She was so much afraid of the jackal that she said nothing; but when her cubs were six months old, one day they asked her who their father was. She told them the jackal was their father.

Then the cubs went to him and said, "Father, teach us the language you speak." He answered, "I cannot teach you my language, because, if you learnt it, you would be the masters of the three worlds." But at last they persuaded him to teach them, and when he gave one howl, they knew that he was only a jackal after all. So they fell upon him and tore him to pieces.

May Parameswar so deal with all rogues like him!

62. The Magic Fish.

(Told by Lakshman Prasâd, Brahman, Jalesar, Etah District.)

Famine broke out in the land and grain sold at the price of pearls. All the people began to die of starvation, when one day in the river beneath the city there appeared an enormous fish. Many thousand maunds in weight was he, and so large that he could not be covered by the water, and his body stretched from bank to bank. When the people saw the fish, they all ran to the river and began to cut off pieces of his flesh, which they cooked and ate. Now there were in the city an old Brahman and his wife, and they too were sore afflicted by the famine. The old woman said to her husband—"Why should we die of hunger, when all the people of the city feed on the flesh of this fish? Go you and get a share." The old Brahman went at the order of his wife, and he took with him a basket and a knife. When he came to the place where the fish lay, he saw that much of his flesh had been cut off and there were great holes in his body; but he was still alive. When the Brahman saw his state he was moved to pity, and the fish said—"Why do not you, like all the other men of the city, cut off some of my flesh?" The Brahman answered—"I fear the Lord Nârâyan, who has ordered me to eat no flesh and to touch naught save the fruits of the earth." The fish answered—"Thou art a man of piety I will now give thee two rubies, one of which sell and buy food; the other keep for me, until I demand it from thee."

The Brahman took the rubies and went to another city. One of them he sold and gave food to his family, until the famine had passed. Then he came back to his own city; and meanwhile the fish had been reborn and become the Râja of the city. He, remembering how the people had treated him, began to treat them with the most extreme cruelty. When the Brahman returned, he was going to salute the Râja; but the people said—"Why do you approach this tyrant? He will surely do thee mischief." But he went and stood before the Râja who said—"Where is that which I entrusted to thee?" The Brahman knew not what he meant. At last the Râja said—"Where is the ruby, which I gave thee by the river bank?" The Brahman knew that the fish had become a Râja and gave him the ruby. The Râja said—"Thou alone of all my subjects didst treat me with mercy in the days of my affliction. Now I will make you my chief Pandit. As for my people, I will revenge my wrongs upon them all the days of my life." But the Brahman besought him in the name of Nârâyan, and he forgave their offence.

63. *The Fate of the Slattern Wife.*

(Told by Dharm Dâs, Schoolmaster, Lalitpur).

The wife of a certain Bania was a wretched slattern, and did not know how to cook anything. One day, as he was setting out for his shop, he said, "Cook some curry for dinner." So she procured all the materials and put them in a pot to boil. By and by the stuff began to boil over, and as she did not know what to do, she ran to a neighbour and asked her advice. "Put a little pebble in the pot," said she. But the slattern wife put in a big stone which smashed the pot, and all the curry was spilt on the floor.

On her husband's return, she scraped up as much as she could and placed it before him; but it was so full of mud that he could not touch it. Being a good-natured man, he said, "You must do better next time. I will take away the pieces of the broken pot." She would not let him do this, but put the broken pieces on her head and tried to go out. Now the door was so low that she had to bend her head, and so the pot slipped and a lot of curry ran over her clothes. "Wait," cried her husband, "I will call a washerman, and he will clean it for you."

But she paid no heed, and walked down to the river-bank, where she took off all her clothes, intending to wash them. But a dog smelt the curry on her sheet, and when she took it off and laid it down, he promptly ran off with it, and she was left naked and ashamed on the bank. Her husband heard her lamentations, and brought her another covering, and then took her home.

64. The Cunning of the Bania.

(Told by Lâla Mukund Lâl of Mirzapur.)

There was once a Bania who was about to go on a pilgrimage, and he did not know what to do with his money. So he went to a Mahâjan and asked him to keep it. The Mahâjan said—"You must give it to me in private." So they went into the jungle, and the Mahâjan said—"If any one sees me take this money, perchance he may rob me. Are you quite certain that nobody is watching us?" "I am sure no one is watching us save Parameswar and the trees and the animals of the jungle." "That will not do for me," said the Mahâjan, and refused to have anything to do with the money.

Then the Bania went to his Guru and asked him to keep the money, but the Guruji refused. The Bania said to his wife—"No course remains but that we take the money with us." Just then a thief was behind the house and watched the Bania tie up the money in his bundle. When every one was asleep, he broke in and was just laying his hands on the bundle, when the Bania woke and saw him. But he was afraid to try and catch him, lest the thief might do him an injury. So he called out to his wife, "After all I won't go on pilgrimage to-day." "What a fool you are," she answered, "just when you paid the Pandit and he fixed the lucky moment for your departure." "Is this the proper language to use to your husband?" and with that he caught up the bundle and threw it at her, and shouted—"Help brethren! my wife is killing me!" Immediately all the neighbours rushed in and said, "What are you fools fighting about?" Said the Bania—"I only wanted to show you that thief in the corner." When the thief was caught, even the Bania's own wife admitted that he was a very crafty fellow.

65. The Cunning of the Paddy Bird.

(Told by Râmnâth, Student, Musanagar, Cawnpore District.)

There was once a paddybird, which lived on the bank of a tank; and so cunning was he that he never tried to catch the fish in the tank, but lived on the worms and grubs he found on the bank. One day the fish came near him in the water, and one of them said "We see that, unlike your kind, you make no attempt to kill us. Why is this so? "The paddybird an-swered—"You must know that I have made the pilgrimage to Jaggan-nâth, where no one takes life; and now I have become pious, and in this way I rule my life." The fish answered—"We approve of your pious life. May none but you inhabit the banks of our tank." The summer came on and the water in the tank began to dry up. The paddybird went away for a couple of days, and the fish were very anxious about their friend. When he came back, he said—"As the summer is coming, I have been very anx-ious about your safety, and I have been thinking that perchance when the water dries, some evil-minded bird may attack you. Now just at the other side of yonder mound I have found another tank, in which the water is deep, and I will, if you approve, take you there one by one. The fish agreed to the proposal and the paddybird began taking them out one by one. But when he took them to the other side of the mound he ate them. This went on, until in the tank there remained but a single crab. The pad-dybird took him in his beak and was just about to eat him, when the crab thrust his claws into the bird's mouth and choked him and that was the end of the hypocrite.

66. *The Frog's Cunning.*

(Told by Ganesa Lâl, Schoolmaster, Digh, Fatehpur District.)

In a certain well there lived the frog Ganga Datta, who was the wisest of all the frogs in the land. And in the same well lived the serpent Priya Darsan and the biscobra Bhadre. Now Priya Darsan used to prey on the small frogs of the well until they were all consumed, and there remained only the master frog Ganga Datta, who began to reflect that one day Priya Darsan would devour him. So he planned how he could avoid calamity and save his life. One day he went to Priya Darsan and said with folded hands—"Mahâraj, I have been considering the case of this well, and I am full of fear lest thou shouldst one day starve, as all the small frogs have now been devoured." "Thy words are true," replied Priya Darsan, "I too am anxious about the future. Hast thou any plan whereby this danger may be removed?" "My plan is this," answered Ganga Datta, "Close to this well is a tank, in which there are many frogs. If I could only get out of this well, I would go there and on some pretence induce them to come into this well, and thus Your Highness would have a store of food for many years." Priya Darsan replied—"This device of thine is wise. But how can you ascend the wall of this well?" He said—"Thou hast only to order thy servant Bhadre the biscobra, who flieth, to take me on his back and fly to the top of the well. It is then my part to complete the business."

Priya Darsan agreed and called the biscobra Bhadre and ordered him to carry the frog Ganga Datta to the top of the well. When Ganga Datta reached the upper ground, he was overwhelmed with joy at his escape. So he hastened to the tank and sat on a log and loudly croaked to his brethren, and when they came before him, he told them of the wickedness of the serpent, Priya Darsan. They blessed him for the subtlety of his wit, and just then Bhadre called out—"Ganga Datta, our lord Priya Darsan waits for thy return and the fulfilment of thy promise." But Ganga Datta laughed and answered—"What sin is there which a hungry man will not commit for the sake of food, and what chance have the poor in the presence of the great? Tell him that now I have escaped, I will never return to the well again."

Bhadre took this message to the serpent Priya Darsan, who lamented that he had been beguiled by the device of the frog Ganga Datta.

67. The Three Wishes.

Thera was once a very poor man who made his living by cutting wood in the forest. One day, as he was working hard in the utmost misery, Mahâdeva and Pârvati passed by, and Pârvati said to her spouse—"You are always blessing some one. Now give a blessing to this poor creature." Mahâdeva said—"In this life everyone gets his due, and it is useless conferring favours on a boor like this." But Pârvati insisted; and at last Mahâdeva said to the wood-cutter—"Ask any boon you please." The man said—"My wife is a shrew, and I dare not ask a boon without consulting her." Mahâdeva answered—"You can consult her; and when you want to ask a boon, plaster a piece of ground, wash, and sit within the enclosure and make your request. But you can only ask once, and your wife and son may ask too."

The wood-cutter went home and told his wife what had happened. She said—"I must have my wish first." So she did as the god had ordered, and she prayed—"O Lord, may my body be turned into gold." And it was as she prayed.

Just then the Râja was passing by on his elephant, and looking into the house of the wood-cutter, he saw this woman of gold and he loved her. So he sent his servants and they seized her, placed her in a litter, and carried her off to the palace.

When the wood-cutter saw that he had lost his wife, he too did as the god had ordered and prayed—"O Lord, may my wife be turned into a sow;" and so it was. When they opened the litter to take her to the Râja, they found within it only a foul sow; and when the door was opened, she ran away and returned to her own house. When the son of the wood-cutter saw this loathsome animal enter the house, he rushed at her with a bludgeon. But his father stopped him and said—"This is your mother, who has been turned into a sow by my prayers, to save her from the Râja. Now you can make your prayer."

Then the boy prayed—"O Lord, turn my mother into her original shape." And so it was.

Then Mahâdeva said to Pârvati—"Now you see that it is useless trying to help boors like these."

68. Mir Kusro and the Kachhi.

(Told by Shankar Sinh Thakur of Ravi, Fatehpur District.)

One day the Emperor Akbar went out hunting, and in the chase he was separated from his companions and became very hungry. He came on a field where a Kachhi was watching his crop of melons and said to the man, "Give me one." "I can give to none," said the Kachhi, "until I offer the first-fruits to the Emperor." This he said, not knowing that it was the Emperor who stood before him. The Emperor offered him money, but the Kachhi would not part with one of the melons.

Akbar was pleased with his honesty, and on returning to the palace he said to Mir Khusro:—"When a Kachhi comes with a present of melons, see that he is at once conducted into my presence." Mir Khusro knew that the Emperor was pleased with the Kachhi and proposed to reward him handsomely. So a day or two later, when the Kachhi came with his melons, he said to him:—"I will take you to the Presence; but you must promise to give me half the reward which the Emperor confers on you." Mir Khusro was then summoned by the Emperor. Meanwhile Bîrbal passed by and asked the Kachhi what his case was. When he heard of the covetousness of Mir Khusro, he said to the Kachhi:—"Get him to give you a written undertaking that he is to take half of what the Emperor awards you." This being done, Bîrbal advised the Kachhi what to do when the Emperor summoned him. Accordingly when he appeared before Akbar and was asked what boon he desired, the Kachhi said:—"Swear thrice that you will give me what I ask." Akbar swore thrice and the Kachhi then said:—"Give me a hundred blows of a shoe." Akbar was amazed and tried to make him withdraw his request. But he would not; and when he had duly received fifty strokes, he said:—"Stop! I have a partner who is to share with me," and he pointed to Mir Khusro. When Akbar heard the tale, he was amazed at the rude strength of the man, and said to Mir Khusro:—"Now you have the reward of your covetousness. Fifty strokes with the shoe will end your life. Better will it be for you to settle with your partner." So Mir Khusro had to pay an enormous sum to escape, and the Emperor gave the Kachhi a village, which is still known as Kachhpurwa in the neighbourhood of Agra.

69. The Evil of Covetousness.

(Told by Ram Singh, Constable of Kuthaund, Jalaun District.)

One day Akbar and Bîrbal were out hunting on an elephant, when Akbar noticed something sparkling on the ground, which looked like a pearl. So he made some excuse and got down. But on touching it, he found that it was only a drop of spittle glistening in the sunshine. Being ashamed, he said nothing; but on returning to the palace, he asked Bîrbal what was the meanest thing in the world. Bîrbal asked for a month's grace to find out, and went and stayed in a village in the hope of learning the answer from the people.

He asked the women what was the meanest thing in the world, and they said:—"Ask our husbands;" and when he asked the husbands, they said, "Ask our women." Then an old Ahîr woman invited Bîrbal to stay with her. So he went and found food ready cooked for the household. When she asked Bîrbal to share their meal, he said:—"How can I, a Brahman, eat with an Ahîr?" "What does it matter," said she, "no one will know." But as he still refused, she brought a purse of two hundred rupees and gave it to him. Then he put out his hand to take the food. But she drew the food away from him, saying:—"How evil a thing is covetousness, when a man like you will lose his caste for such a petty sum." Bîrbal was ashamed, and returning to the Emperor, said:—"Covetousness is the vilest thing in the world."

70. The greatest leaf in the world.

(Recorded by Hazâri Lâl of Agra.)

One day Akbar asked his courtiers which was the greatest leaf in the world. They named various kinds of leaves; but Bîrbal said:—"The leaf of the *Nâgar Bel* is the greatest in the world, because it reaches as high as Your Majesty's lips." Now the betel leaf is called *Nâgar Bel* or *Indra Bel*, because it is believed to grow in Nandana, the garden of Râja Indra.

71. *The fruit of good wishes.*

(Recorded by Hazâri Lâl of Agra.)

Akbar once asked Bîrbal, "How much do you love me?" Bîrbal replied:—"*Dil ko dil pahchânta hai,*" or in other words "I love you as much as you love me."

They went forth and met a milkmaid tripping along in the pride of her beauty. "Look at this silly girl," said the Emperor, "she can hardly walk straight, she thinks so much of herself." When she came up to them, Bîrbal said to her, "The Emperor is dead." She began to laugh and said, "What matters it to me? He that buys my milk is Emperor."

By and by they met an old woman staggering under a load of wood. "How miserable a thing is poverty," said Akbar. Then said Bîrbal to her, "The Emperor is dead," on hearing which she began to wail and fell down on the road. "Now," said Bîrbal, "Your Majesty will see that people think of you as you think of them."

72. *Akbar's questions.*

(Recorded by Hazâri Lâl of Agra.)

Akbar said once to Bîrbal, "I will ask two questions, to each of which you must give the same answer." The questions were:—

"Why is the Brahman thirsty?"

"Why is an ass disconsolate?"

To both Bîrbal replied, "*Lota nahîn,*" meaning in the case of the Brahman "He has no water-vessel," and in the case of the ass, "He has not had a roll."

73. *Birbal's wit.*

(Recorded by Hazâri Lâl of Agra.)

Bîrbal once quarrelled with Akbar and went and hid himself in the city. Akbar could not discover his whereabouts. So at length he issued an order that two or three men should appear before him at noon, and stand half in the sun and half in the shade. No one understood how to comply with this order; so they went and consulted Bîrbal, who said:—"Put a bed on your heads and go to court, and you will be half in the shade and half in the sun," Akbar knew that they must have done this by Bîrbal's advice, and in this way discovered where he was and recalled him to court.

On another occasion Akbar asked Bîrbal, "Was there anyone born at exactly the same moment that I was?" "Thousands," replied Bîrbal. "Then why am I an emperor," said Akbar, "and they poverty-stricken?" Bîrbal took a number of betel-leaves and asked Akbar to thread them on a string. Then he told him to unthread them and see if there was the same sized hole in each leaf. When Akbar found that every hole differed in size, Bîrbal said, "Even so are there all sorts and conditions of men."

74. The result of Good Intentions.

(Recorded by Hazâri Lâl of Agra.)

One day, when Akbar was talking with his courtiers, Bîrbal said, "Intention (*niyat*) is everything." "Prove it," said Akbar. Soon after Akbar went hunting, and losing his way, was attacked by thirst. He saw an old woman watching a field of sugar-cane and asked her for a drink. She broke one of the canes and filled a cup for the Emperor.

Next day, when Akbar and Bîrbal were conversing, the former asked what was the revenue rate on sugar-cane, and when he was told it was only one rupee per acre, he thought what profits the old woman must be making out of her field. So he sent for the Revenue Minister and ordered the rate to be doubled.

Again Akbar went to the field and asked the old woman for a drink. This time she had to cut half a dozen canes before she could fill a pot with the juice. He asked her the reason, and she said, "This is the result of the evil thoughts of the Emperor, who has doubled our assessment." The Emperor took her words to heart and had the assessment reduced to the former rate.

[For another version, see Burton, *Arabian Nights,* IV, 51—W. CROOKE.]

75. Birbal and tobacco.

(Told by Bânsgopâl Lâl of Bansi, Basti District.)

Akbar and Bîrbal were once on the roof of the palace, when Akbar saw an ass grazing near a field of tobacco, but not touching the plants. Now Bîrbal used to chew tobacco. Akbar then remarked, "Even an ass does not touch tobacco." "No, Your Majesty," replied Bîrbal, "no one who is an ass touches tobacco."

76. *Akbar and Birbal's daughter.*

(Recorded by Hazâri Lâl of Agra.)

Akbar once told Bîrbal that he wished to become a Hindu. Bîrbal remonstrated, and said that the religious duties of a Hindu were very onerous. But Akbar paid no heed and said, "I give you a fortnight to make me a Hindu." Bîrbal went home very sorrowful and confided in his daughter. Said she, "Do not be anxious. I will give him a fitting answer." So next day she went to Court and came in tears before the Emperor, who enquired the reason of her grief. "Pardon me," she said, "I have committed a gross error. I am Your Majesty's washerwoman, and yesterday when I put the clothes of Your Majesty and the Empress into water, the water caught fire, and the clothes were burned." "Are you mad?" said Akbar, "Who ever heard of water catching fire?" "And who ever heard," she replied," of a Musalman becoming a Hindu?" Akbar was pleased and dismissed her with a present.

77. *How Birbal sowed Pearls.*

(Recorded by Hazâri Lâl of Agra.)

One day the Emperor and Bîrbal were in Darbar, when the latter spat. The courtiers informed Akbar, who was much offended at this breach of good manners, and had the Vazîr turned out of the palace. As he was leaving, Bîrbal said to his enemies: "If I am Bîrbal, before long I shall see your houses overthrown."

He departed to an outlying village and commenced working in the fields. One day the Emperor met him, and the old affection for Bîrbal revived. Said he, "What have you learnt, since you took to farming?" "I have learnt to grow pearls." "Then you must grow them for me," quoth Akbar. "It is only in special places that they can be grown," replied Bîrbal.

So Bîrbal returned to Court and Akbar gave him seed-pearls from the royal treasury; and Bîrbal selected as the site for his sowing the place where the houses of his rivals stood. The Emperor had them straightway razed to the ground. There Bîrbal sowed some *dûb* grass and the Arwi yam. When they had grown, he took Akbar there one morning and showed him the dew-drops on the plants, which looked like pearls in the sunlight. Akbar was delighted and said, "Go and pick some for me." Bîrbal replied, "None can pick these pearls save him who in all his life has never spat." Akbar understood the moral and restored him to favour.

78. How Birbal capped verses.

(Recorded by Hazâri Lâl of Agra.)

One day Akbar spoke the following lines and asked Bîrbal to cap them:—

> *Jal to Gangajal, aur jal kâh rê*
> *Phal to Âmphal, aur phal kâh rê*
> *Bhog to stri bhog, aur bhog kâh rê*
> *Jot men nain jot, our jot kâh rê.*

"Ganges water is best, all other water is naught. The mango is the only fruit, all other fruit is naught. Woman's love is the only joy, all other joy is naught. The light of the eyes is the real light, all other light is naught."

Then answered Bîrbal:—

> *Jal to Indrâjal, aur jal kâh rê*
> *Phal to putra phal, aur phal kâh rê*
> *Bhog to anna bhog, aur bhog kâh rê*
> *Jot to Surya jot, aur jot kâh rê.*

"The real water is that of Heaven, all else is naught. The son fruit is the real fruit, all else is naught. The real pleasure is eating, all else is naught. The light of the Sun is the real light, all else is naught."

Akbar was pleased and rewarded Bîrbal.

79. How Akbar was befooled.

(Recorded by Hazâri Lâl of Agra.)

One day Akbar said to Bîrbal "Is there any place where, if a man goes thither, he becomes a fool?" "Yes," said Bîrbal, "there is such a village called Mogâm, just across the Jamna, and I will take you there some day."

Bîrbal then went to the village and, calling up the elders, said, "The Emperor is coming here and you must make a verse in his honour."

One said, "I will say—*Sab peran men bargad bar.*" Another said—*Akâsh wâki chutiya, Pâtâl wâki jar.* The third—*Harê harê pattê, lâl lâl phar.* The fourth knew no verse, so Bîrbal taught him to say, *Akbar Bâdshâh gîdi khar.*

Then he told them to be sure and present the Emperor with a basket of onions, of which he was very fond. When Bîrbal conducted Akbar to Mogâm, he said, "You must go there bareheaded, as the people dislike seeing anyone with a cap or turban." So Akbar rode bareheaded, and on the way he said to Bîrbal, "Now am I a fool after all?" "Anyone who rides bareheaded in the sun is a fool," said Bîrbal.

Then the village-elders assembled under the village banyan tree and spoke the lines given above:—

"Of all trees the Banyan is the greatest,
Its top is in the sky and its roots in Hell,
Its leaves are green and its fruit is red,
The Emperor Akbar is a timid ass."

Then they produced the onions and presented them to Akbar, who was wroth and said, "Verily these are the greatest fools on earth."

80. *Akbar's Riddle.*

(Told by Janhâri Lâl Bania and recorded by Bhûp Sinh, schoolmaster, Agra District.)

Akbar once asked Bîrbal to interpret the following riddle: "A lid above and a lid below, and between them a melon cut with a waxen knife." Bîrbal asked for time and wandered in the fields seeking an answer. He saw a girl cooking, and when he asked her what she was doing, she said, "I am cooking the daughter and burning the mother. My father has gone to mix earth with earth and my mother is making one two." When her father returned, Bîrbal asked him to explain. "It is plain enough," said he: "My daughter is boiling arhar pulse with dead arhar stalks. I went to bury a corpse, and my wife is crushing peas, when each grain is split in two." "These are the people to answer Akbar's riddle," thought Bîrbal. So he repeated it, and the man said: "The upper lid is the sky and the lower the earth. Between them is the melon, Man, which can be cut in pieces by a knife of wax, because the least thing destroys his life."

Akbar accepted the answer and loaded Bîrbal and the poor man's family with gifts.

81. *How Akbar became Emperor.*

(Told by Râm Bihâri Misra of Amapur and recorded by Sankar Datt, Rae Bareli District.)

There was once a leper who lay by the tank of Somnâth, and Jagannath appeared unto him in a dream and said:—"Bathe in this tank and thou shalt be made whole." So he bathed and was cured of his leprosy. When he came out of the water, he began to laugh, and a fox who was standing near said:—"Why are you laughing at me?" "I am not laughing at you," the man replied. "I laugh because this tank cures the leprous." "Perhaps," said the fox, "if I were to bathe, I might become a human being." "Try," said the other; and lo! when the fox went into the water, he turned into a lovely girl. An old woman who was picking cowdung close by then came up and said to the girl, who was laughing, "You were a fox a minute ago; what right have you to laugh at me?" "I was not laughing at you," said the girl, "I was only laughing to think that the tank can turn a fox into a human being." "Perhaps if I were to bathe," said the woman, "my son who is in a distant land may come back to me." "Try," said the girl; and lo! when the old woman entered the water, her son stood on the bank. At this she laughed and her son said, "When a man comes home from afar, his mother gives him a drink of water and a smoke, and does not laugh at him." "I did not laugh at you," she said, "I was only laughing because bathing in this tank causes distant friends to return." "Perhaps if I were to bathe," said he, "I might get married." "Try," said his mother. And lo! the moment he entered the water, a bride and a grand marriage procession stood before him. Then he began to laugh, and the bride said:—"Is this the way for a man to welcome his bride, by laughing at her?" "I was not laughing at you," said he. "I was laughing to think that a man gets a bride by bathing here." "Were I to bathe here," said the bride, "perchance I might bear a son." "Try," said her husband. And lo! a son was born to her. When the babe was born, his mother laughed, and the child said:—"It is hard for a woman to laugh at her son when he is born." "I was not laughing at you," she said. "I was only laughing when I thought that bathing here brings a woman a son." "Perhaps if I were to bathe here, I might become Emperor," said the child. "Try," said his mother; and when he went into the water, he was carried off; and this was Akbar, the Emperor of Delhi.

82. Sulaiman the wood-cutter.

(Told by Shaikh Muhâmmad Kâsim and recorded by Kamaruddin of Sandîla, Hardoi District.)

There was once in the city of Agra a wood-cutter named Sulaiman, who was very poor and used to cut wood every day in the jungle, and thus he made his living.

One day, as he was walking in the jungle, he saw a whirlwind approaching; and out of it came a man dressed in green with a green lance; and when Sulaiman saw him, he bowed to the ground before him. The horseman asked him who he was and what was his business. When Sulaiman told him, he said:—"You need work at this trade no longer. I give you a ruby which you can take to a banker and sell. The proceeds of it will support you for the rest of your life."

The man gave him the ruby and disappeared. Sulaiman tied it in his turban, and with the bundle of wood on his head started for the city. On the way a kite swooped down and carried off his turban.

When he got to his house, his daughter asked him why he was so late in bringing the wood, and when he told her all that had happened, she said:—"No gift can make a man rich unless it is God who gives it."

Next day he went again into the jungle, and again a whirlwind appeared and the same horseman with it. He said to Sulaiman: "You wretch! You have broken your word and come here again, though I made you rich for life with the ruby."

Sulaiman told him how he had tied the ruby in his turban, and how the kite had carried it off. The horseman then gave him another ruby and disappeared. Sulaiman again tied it in his turban, and again, as he came near his house, a kite carried it off. When he told his daughter what had happened, she said: "Why do you trouble yourself about foolish things? It would have been better had you brought your wood and sold it. Now, what have we to eat to-day I told you that to become rich depends upon the will of God."

Next day again Sulaiman went to the jungle. Again the horseman appeared and upbraided him, and again Sulaiman told him how the kite had carried off the ruby. The horseman said:—"You should in future fast on the seventh, seventeenth and twenty-seventh days of the month; and when you eat, buy food only to the value of three pice."

"But where am I to get even three pice?" he asked. "Daily," said he, "put two cowries out of your earnings into an earthen pot, and by the day when you have to fast, you will have collected three pice which you can spend on food."

Sulaiman did as he was ordered, and next day when he went to the jungle, he found his two turbans under a tree and the rubies with them. So he took them home and commenced to fast as he had been directed. By the grace of the Almighty, he became by degrees a very rich man and after some time his daughter said to him: "It is time that you got honour from the Emperor."

So he prepared a vessel set with diamonds and presented himself before the Emperor Akbar, who, after he had enquired about him, took him into favour and made him one of his Vazîrs. And his daughter was received with honour in the palace.

One day he thought to himself that, now he was a rich man, it was folly to fast as he had been doing; so he gave up the practice, and, as he was walking through the bazar, he saw two splendid water-melons, which he bought as a present for the king. That day the son of the king had gone out hunting, and when the king opened the melon, what did he see within it but the head of the prince. So he had Sulaiman arrested and lodged in the prison, and at the same time all his wealth disappeared. As he lay in the prison, he began to reflect and knew that all the trouble which had befallen him was due to his having broken the rule of fasting. Just then the horseman appeared to him in a dream and said:

"I am the Khwaja Khizr. Have you been sufficiently punished for your sins?" "My punishment is great," he answered.

He replied: "Keep your fasts again. You will find three pice under the carpet on which you say your prayers."

Sulaiman looked under the carpet and found the money; and then he began to wonder how he could get someone to bring him three pice worth of food from the bazar. So he went up on to the roof of the prison, and then saw a man riding quickly past on a camel. He asked him to buy him food and he said: "I am hastening to buy dye for the feet of my son who is to be married to-day. I have no time to do your bidding."

By and by another man passed with tears in his eyes. When Sulaiman asked him to bring him food from the bazar he said: "My son has just died and I am going to buy his shroud. But, for the love of God I will do your bidding."

Just as he was buying the food, a man came up and told him that his son had come to life, while another man reported to the rider of the camel that his son had just died.

So the camelman went to the Emperor and said, "There is a wizard in thy prison. As I was going to buy dye for my son's wedding, he asked me to buy food for him: and when I refused, my son died; and the son of him who did his bidding came to life."

So Akbar sent for Sulaiman, and when the messengers went into the prison, they found him sitting quite happy, with the bonds loosed from his hands and feet. So they brought him to the Emperor. And just then the Prince, who was supposed to be dead, rode up safe and sound. Akbar asked Sulaiman to explain what had happened; and when he told the tale, he said: "All this happened through the might of the Lord Khwaja Khizr."

So Akbar restored him to favour and took his daughter to wife, and made him his Vazîr. And when he went home, he found his house full of wealth as it was before.

Thus was he warned of the sin of disobeying the Lord and the merit of serving him.

83. *The Sepoy and his faithless wife.*

(Recorded by Muhammad Husein of Chunar.)

There was once a sepoy who had a faithless wife, who fell into evil courses and had seven lovers. She wished to enjoy their society without trouble, so she went to the tomb of a saint close to her house and prayed to him: "Lord, make my husband blind, and I will offer thee sweet cakes and an embroidered sheet." Every day she used to go and make the same prayer, until one day her husband missed her; and when she went to the tomb, he followed her and hid himself in a pit close by. When she made her usual prayer, he called out from the pit:—"Feed your husband on chicken broth for forty days and he will lose his sight."

When she heard this, she was delighted and sent for her lovers and ordered each of them to provide a chicken by turns, till the forty days were over. Her husband had an excellent dinner every day, and when the forty days were nearly over, he began to grope about and feel his way with a staff, so that his wife believed that he was really losing his sight. She sent for her lovers and cooked a dinner for them and went to the tomb to make her thank-offering. Meanwhile her husband dosed the food with poison, and when her lovers came and ate it, they immediately died. The woman was sore afraid and knew not how to get rid of their corpses. Just then a beggar passed by, and she called him and said:—"Shâhji, remove this corpse for me and I will give you five rupees." He agreed, and she gave him one of the corpses, which he carried off on his back. Meanwhile she propped up another by the door, and when he came back for the money, she said:—"You did not put the corpse in the right place and he has come back." He went off with the second corpse, and in this way she made him remove all the seven.

Just as dawn was breaking, he took the last corpse to a well and threw it in, and at that moment a water-carrier came to the well. When the

Fakîr saw him in the dark, he said:—"You are the rascal that has been worrying me all night. Now I have you at last." And with these words he pitched the poor wretch into the well.

When he came back for his money, the sepoy was on the watch and slew him and his faithless wife with a sword. Then he left his house and became a Fakîr himself.

84. The folly of the Cuckold.

(Told by Nâzir Khân, Râjpût of Sahâranpur.)

There was once a man who had a very pretty wife, of whom he was exceedingly jealous. So he used to lock her up every day in his house, when he went out on business. One day, as the woman was locked up in the house, she heard a man in the street calling out:—"Mangoes to sell! Who will buy my mangoes?" So she went on the balcony and threw down some money, and asked the mango-seller to fling her up some mangoes. As she was buying the fruit, her husband returned and he was very angry.

"When a respectable woman talks to people in the street, what will people think of her?" "Why do you watch me so carefully?" said she: "If a woman chooses, she can make her husband bring her lover to her and take him away." "I defy you to do so," he retorted.

She was after this continually devising means to carry out her plan, and one day she complained of a severe internal pain. Physicians were called and all sorts of remedies employed, but to no avail. At last an old woman was sent for, and to her the woman explained the state of the case.

The old woman said that she would charm away the disease. So she went to her son and got him to get into a large earthen pot, which she made the husband bring to his wife. The pair remained together for the night, and in the morning the wife told her husband to take away the charm, as she was now quite recovered.

He went off with the pot on his head, and as he was walking along the bazar, his feet slipped on a place where a sweetmeat-maker had thrown the washings of his pots. The jar was smashed and out came the youth, who ran at the husband, shoe in hand, and cried out:—"What do you mean by throwing your jars on quiet passengers?"

But the husband remembered the words of his wife, and he knew that she had carried out her threat. So he was abashed and let her do as she pleased in future.

85. *The Shâlimar Bâgh at Lahore.*

(The following traditional account of the origin of the name of the famous Shâlimâr garden at Lahore was told by Shibba Sinh, Brahman of Sahâranpur.)

The queen of the Emperor Akbar had a brother, who was a useless, dissipated man. She was always pressing her husband to advance her brother to some high dignity, and at last when the Subahdar of Lahore died, she got Akbar to appoint him to the place.

When he reached Lahore, he continued his vicious practices. One day he heard of the beauty of the daughter of a great Mahâjan, and sent his emissaries to try and induce her to enter his harem. His love increased when he managed one day to see her bathing. But she resisted all his inducements. At last he sent for her and forced her to consent to name a day for their union.

The girl managed to escape to Delhi, and when she arrived there, she went round the city in a palanquin, with men shouting before her that the Emperor was dead. Akbar heard of this and summoned her before him, when she said:—"An Emperor who does not protect the honour of his subjects from the lust of his officers is as good as dead."

Akbar was interested in her story and took her with him to Lahore. He interrogated the Governor, who denied the charge. Then he had him and the girl locked up in adjoining cells and placed a guard on the watch. During the night the Governor spoke to her, admitting his fault and promising her his favour, if she would withdraw the charge.

His confession was reported to Akbar, who ordered the execution of his brother-in-law.

Hence the garden was called "the place where the brother-in-law was slain" (*sâlamâr*).

86. *A Woman's wit.*

(Told by Lâla Khayali Râm of Aligarh.)

There was once a woman who was taking a dish of soaked gram flour (*sattu*) to her husband in the field. On the way she met her lover and they passed some time together. While she was looking another way, he moulded the dough into the image of an elephant and put the cover on the dish. When she brought the dish to her husband and he opened it, he saw the dough elephant and was angry.

Said he: "How can I eat the image of Ganeshji?"

She said: "I will tell the truth. I dreamed last night that you were pursued and nearly killed by a wild elephant. So I consulted a Pandit and he told me to make an image of an elephant in dough and give it to you to eat, and that this would save you from the evil effects of the dream." Her foolish husband believed her and ate the dough elephant.

87. The neglect of good advice.

(Told by Tikaram Brahman of Mirakhar, Agra District.)

Four men were once journeying together and came to a forest in which lived a great saint. When they came to his hermitage he said:—

"Take my advice and do not go farther into the forest. Not far off lives a witch who will be your ruin."

But they would not heed his words and came to the house of the witch, who was exceedingly beautiful. She sent two of them to a village close by, and the other two remained with her. To them she said:—"When your comrades come, I counsel you to slay them with your swords, and then I will be yours."

The other two, as they came back with the food, consulted together.

"Let us kill our comrades and then the woman will be ours."

So they put poison in the food. As they came to the door, their companions cut off their heads with their swords. Then they brought the food to the woman, who cooked it and said:—

"Eat, and I will eat the leavings." When they ate, they fell down dead. So the four died because they would not listen to the advice of the saint. As the poet writes:—

Jo tâkon kânta bowai, tâhi bou tûn phûl;
Tâkon phûl ko phal hai, wâko hai trisûl.

"Sow flowers for those who sow thorns for thee. So shalt thou find flowers scattered in thy path, and thine enemy a spear."

88. The Kayasth and the Soldier.

(Told by Narâyan Dâs and recorded by Har Prasâd, teacher, Danaganj, Budaun District.)

There was once a Kayasth in a Râja's service, who had a quarrel with one of the Râja's Sipâhîs. The soldier in his rage threatened to give the Kayasth a sound beating. "I will knock out your teeth," replied the Kayasth. It was the custom that in the pay-bill a descriptive roll of each soldier was drawn up, and next time, when the Kayasth was drawing up the roll, he added opposite the Sipâhî's name, "two teeth missing."

When the Sipâhî came to draw his pay, the Bakhshi looked at him, and seeing his teeth sound, said:—"Your description does not tally and I cannot pay you." The Sipâhî made many attempts to draw his pay, but this objection was constantly made, and at last he had to knock out two of his teeth, and then his pay was passed. When the Kayasth next met the Sipâhî he said:—"Beware of Kayasths! They always do what they threaten."

89. *Wisdom inferior to learning.*

(Told by Kishori Lâl Bania of Mirakhar, Agra District.)

There was once a very learned Pandit who set out from home in search of employment. On the way he met a man who was noted for his wisdom, and he suggested that they should journey together.

On the way they halted under a Pipal tree in the forest and the Pandit said to his companion:—"In this world nothing is superior to learning."

"Nay," said the wise man, "wisdom is greater still."

Said the Pandit: "I know a charm whereby I can raise the dead to life."

The wise man answered: "Here is the bone of a tiger. Try your skill on it."

So the Pandit went up to the bone, repeated many incantations and poured some water on it from his *lota*. Whereupon the tiger came to life and immediately devoured the Pandit, leaving only a bone or two unbroken. All this time the wise man was looking on from the top of the Pipal tree, up which he had climbed in terror when the tiger appeared. When the animal went away, he began to consider what he could do for his unfortunate friend. So he repeated the incantations and poured on the bones of the Pandit some water from the *lota*, and he immediately came to life again.

Then the Pandit stood before him with folded hands and thanked him saying:—

"Learning is one thing and wisdom is another. A learned man destitute of wisdom is naught. Well did the poet write:—

> *Ek lâkh vidya, sawa lâkh chaturâi;*
> *Ek or châri Ved, ek or châturi.*

"Learning is worth a lakh, and wisdom a lakh and a quarter. On one side are the four Vedas and cleverness on the other."

90. *The Fate of the Uncharitable.*

(Told by Râm Ganesa, Dûbê Brahman of Mirzapur.)

There was once a beggar who used constantly to beg in the city. One day he came to the house of a woman, whose son and husband were absent from home on a journey. He stood at the door and cried: "Good luck to the charitable housewife. Give a poor man alms."

The woman said: "This rascal is always worrying me by asking alms every day. I will give him something which will prevent him from bothering me again."

So she put poison in some cakes which she gave to the beggar. He went back to his hut and put the cakes on a shelf, but he did not eat them, as he had other food which he had received as charity.

In the night the woman's husband and son came to his hut and said:—

"Give us to eat, as there is no food in our house."

So he gave them the poisoned cakes, and when they had eaten them, they fell down dead. The beggar man raised an alarm and the neighbours assembled; and when the woman arrived, she recognised her husband and son lying there dead. So she complained to the Râja that the beggar man had poisoned them. The Râja asked him why he had done so and he answered:—

"I did not poison them. I only gave them the cakes which this woman had given me." The Râja had her house searched and found poison there: so he sentenced her to death. But the beggar man implored him to spare her life, as she had been sufficiently punished already. As the poet writes:—

> *Jaisa karai, so taisa pâwai;*
> *Put bhatâr ke âge âwai;*
> *Sânghê karai sakârê pâwai.*

"As thou sowest, so shalt thou reap. It will come on thy husband and son. What thou doest in the evening, thou shalt receive next morning."

91. *The saint and the dancing girl.*

(Told by Brindâban, Brahman of Agra, and recorded by Kundan Lâl, teacher of Mirakhur, Agra District.)

There was once a saint who used to practise austerities in a forest. One day a dancing girl was passing that way and said: "*Jo ant men mati ho hai, soi gati prâni ki hai.*" "What a person thinks of at the time of death, he becomes in the next life."

This she said every day as she passed the saint, till one day he was wroth and struck her with his tongs. She complained to the Râja, who, when he heard her story, asked what she meant by her words. She said:— "In my former life I was a Brahman girl and became a widow. I fell sick unto death and my mother sent for a physician. As he felt my pulse, I had evil thoughts, and so I died, and in the next birth I was born a dancer."

The Râja and the saint knew her words were true. So she was dismissed.

92. *The wit of the Kayasth.*

(Told by Bhola Ram, Bania, and recorded by Chiranji Lâl, Brahman, of Mirakhur, Agra Dist.)

The Râja was once passing through a village where a very wily Kayasth lived, and the Kayasth came up to him and said:—"Your kingdom is hollow."

"Then you get into the hollow of it, and be hanged to you," replied the Râja angrily. The Kayasth got the Râja to write down what he had said, and then took it to the Râja's Manager and said: "The Râja means that I am to dispossess you and take your place."

It was not till long after, when the Manager came in rags before the Râja, that the trick was discovered.

93. *The dishonesty of the Shroff.*

(Told by Parmanand, Brahman of Jataul, Sahâranpur District.)

A man once deposited a sum of money with a Shroff, and when he went to ask for it, the Shroff denied having received it. So he went to the Kâzi. The Kâzi summoned the Shroff and said:—"I am getting old and the work is too heavy for me. I am thinking of appointing you to be my Assistant."

Then the owner of the money went to the Shroff and said:—

"If you do not pay me, I will lay a suit before the Kâzi."

The Shroff when he heard this, feared that he would lose his appointment: so he restored his deposit. When he went to the Kâzi to see about the place, the Kâzi said:—

"My health has much improved, and I do not want an Assistant just at present."

94. The dishonest Kâzi.

(Told by Aziz Khân, Râjpût of Sahâranpur.)

There was once a rich merchant who had a clever wife; and one day she said to him:—

"This world is always changing. You may come some day to poverty. It would be wise to deposit some of your treasure with an honest man."

So the banker changed a lakh of rupees into gold coins and deposited them with the Kâzi of the city. Time passed and the merchant lost his money by speculation; but when he went to recover his deposit, the Kâzi denied the receipt of it and abused him.

The merchant went and complained to the Nawâb Alivardi Khân. The Nawâb asked if he had any witnesses, and when the merchant admitted that no one was present when the deposit was made, the Nawâb sent for the Kâzi and said:

"You know that the Emperor sometimes makes sudden demands on his officers. I wish to deposit with you nine lakhs of rupees that I may have them on the evil day."

The Kâzi was pleased, and as he was preparing a vault to receive the treasure of the Nawâb, the merchant came again and demanded his money. The Kâzi feared that if he refused to pay, the merchant would complain to the Nawâb, who would withhold his treasure. So he paid the money; and then the Nawâb turned him out of the city.

95. The pride of the Jackal.

(Told by Kundan Sinh, Jât, and recorded by Ayub Hasan of Manglaur, Sahâranpur District.)

One day a jackal and his wife were out at night foraging, and he found a piece of paper with some writing on it. He took it to his wife and said: "Here is a *Firmân* of the Emperor Akbar, making me headman (*Choudari*) of all the jackals."

"All right," said she, "but you should also carry a badge in proof of your dignity." "You are right," he replied, "so tie a stick to my tail."

She did so, and just then up came a dog and chased them. The female jackal escaped into a drain, but as her mate followed her, his tail stuck in the opening, and the dog caught him and tore him to pieces.

So the poet writes:—

Baro na hajê gunan binu birad barâi pâi;
Jo nahîn mati yah hiya dharai shrig sam turat
nashây.

"Do not listen to flatterers and claim importance which you do not deserve. He who does not mind this advice will share the fate of the jackal."

96. The Wiles of Women.

(Told by Lâla Khayâli Râm, Kayasth of Aligarh.)

A man one day sent his wife, who was a beautiful woman, to buy some sugar in the bazar. She went to the shop of a Bania, who fell in love with her, and when he had enjoyed her favours, gave her some sugar for nothing. As she was going home, a boy followed her, and opening the knot of her sheet, stole the sugar, and tied up some earth in its place. Reaching home, she laid her sheet aside, and when her husband looked for the sugar, he found only earth.

Then her husband abused her, but she said:—

"I will tell you the truth. As I was coming home, a mad bull escaped in the bazar, and I dropped the sugar. In my hurry I picked up earth instead."

"Thank heaven, my love, that your life at least was saved," he replied, and believed her.

97. The Dream of the Opium-eater.

(Told by Parmânand, Gaud Brahman of Jataul, Sahâranpur District.)

An opium-eater once lay in his drunken sleep on the roof of his house, and he dreamed that a river was rising in flood all round him and that he and his household would be carried away. So he jumped on a chair and shouted out to his wife:—"Dear one, mind the little ones. The river is rising. There is neither boat nor raft to save us and we shall lose our lives."

With that, in hopes of saving himself, he jumped from the roof and fell to the ground.

A friend came and helped him up, but the opium-eater pulled himself away angrily and said, "What is the good of saving me when the danger is over? If you had come when the flood reached the roof of my house, you would have been a true friend!"

98. The Opium-eater's Dispute.

(Told by Thâkur Sinh, Ahîr of Sahâranpur.)

Two opium-eaters were once sitting together, half intoxicated by the drug, and one said to the other:—

"Let us be partners and start a sweetmeat shop. We can eat some sweets when we come to our senses every evening, and we shall also be able to support our families."

"I have a better plan," said the other. "Let us sow our field near the river bank with sugar-cane, and you and I can sell it to a greengrocer. But we will make it a condition that we may each cut a cane every day; and we can sit there and peel and eat it."

"Who am I," said the first, "that I should eat only one sugar-cane. I must have two."

On this the other in a rage hit him on the head, and they went to the Kotwâl for justice. He sent them to the Vazîr. The Vazîr said: "Apparently you have not paid the rent for your field."

So they had to pawn their clothes and pay the rent. But when they went to sell their sugar-cane, they could find it nowhere and came home naked and ashamed.

99. The dishonest Perfumer.

(Told by Azîz Khân, Râjpût of Sahâranpur.)

There was once a man who had some money; and as he was going on a journey and was afraid he might lose it, he made it over to an Attâr who lived near him, who promised to keep it safely until his return.

When he returned and demanded the deposit, the Attâr angrily denied having received any money from him, and when the neighbours came up, on hearing the quarrel, they said: "This man must be a rogue. Who ever heard of his having any money? Besides, the Attâr is a most respectable man."

So, as he could get nothing out of the Attâr, he went to the Nawâb, who asked him if he had any witness of the deposit. He said, "None but God Almighty."

So the Nawâb said: "Go every evening and sit near the shop of the Attâr, and when you see me coming out in my carriage for my daily airing, come up and whisper something, no matter what, in my ear."

This went on for a few days, and the Attâr began to think:—

"This man must be a friend of the Nawâb. Heaven only knows what he says to him. Perhaps it may be to my harm."

So he called his debtor and said:—"Tell me something more about your deposit. Perchance I may remember something about it."

And in the end he paid up the money.

100. The Fate of the boastful Jackal.

(Told and recorded by Shaikh Ali Ahmad, teacher, of Fatehpur Sikri, Agra District.)

There was once a jackal who, as he was wandering in the jungle, chanced to come across the den of a tiger. So he used to stay about the place, and whenever the tiger chanced to bring home any prey, the jackal would get some scraps to eat. After many days he went back to his wife, who was surprised at seeing him so fat and sleek, and said: "Where on earth have you been all this time, and what have you been eating that you have got so fat?"

"You must remember," he answered "that I am no longer a common jackal; I have now taken to killing mighty beasts of the forest whenever I am hungry."

"Let me see you kill one," she said, "because I and the young ones have had little to eat for a long time."

Next day as she looked out of her hole, she saw a great ox grazing outside. So she woke her husband and said: "Here is an animal worth killing. Don't delay any longer." The Jackal ran out and came back in a short time and said:—

"Are my eyes red with rage?"

"No," she said, "your eyes are much as usual."

Again he ran out; and when he returned, he asked:—

"Are my eyes now red enough?"

"I think they are," said his wife.

So with that he sprang on the back of the ox and seized his tail in his teeth. But the ox turned round, butted at him and never ceased tossing him with his horns till his life departed. So this was the end of his boasting. As the wise say:—

> *Apnê bal son adhik jo, karai murh koû kâj:*
> *So srigal sam binsai, hansain bhi sakal samâj.*

"When one attempts what is beyond his power, he is destroyed like the jackal and the folk mock at him."

101. The Dancing-girl and the Parrot.

(Told by Daulat Râm, teacher, Lalipur.)

There was once in the Court of Vikramâditya a dancing-girl, who was called Lâkho, because she was so famous that whoever visited her had to pay a lakh of rupees. One night she dreamed that a certain Brahman was with her, and next day she went to him and demanded her usual fee. He refused to pay, as he had never been with her, and when she appealed to the elders, they could not settle the case and took the parties to the king. He was also perplexed, and finally a very wise parrot of the king offered to settle the matter. So he brought a lakh of rupees into the Court and a looking-glass. He laid the rupees before the glass and said to the girl:—

"As you only dreamed that the Brahman was with you, you may take the shadow of the rupees in the looking-glass as your reward."

Lâkho was thus defeated by the wit of the parrot, but she vowed vengeance against him. So one day when she had danced and sung before the king, and he offered her what she pleased, she asked for the parrot. She took the bird home and gave it to her servant, and told her to cook it at once for her dinner. The servant plucked the parrot and laid it down for a moment, and went for a knife to cut its throat, when the parrot, seeing a chance of saving its life, crept into the house drain and hid there. When the servant came back, she thought that a cat must have carried off the bird, so she bought another parrot in the bazar and cooked it for her mistress.

By and by the parrot grew his feathers again and flew into a tree near the house of Lâkho. One night he called out to her from the tree, and she thought that it was the voice of an angel from heaven. The parrot said:—

"Lâkho! I am an angel of the Lord, and if you obey my words, a heavenly chariot will come down from heaven and fetch you up. First, you must give all your wealth to the poor and leave yourself not a single rag. Then you must go at night naked to the palace of the king and there the heavenly chariot will come to fetch you."

She obeyed the heavenly voice, and when all her wealth was gone, she went at night to the palace of the king. But the heavenly chariot never came; and in the morning the servants found her lying naked there, and she was mocked of all the city. Thus the parrot was revenged of her; and when he told the tale to the king, he was received back into the Court.

102. The Dog and the Brahman.

(Told by Pandit Râm Gharîb Chaube.)

Once upon a time a Brahman was passing along the road, and seeing a dog sleeping there, struck at it with his bludgeon and broke its back. The dog went to the Court of Râmachandra and made his complaint against the Brahman. When the king called on him to make his defence, he said:—"It is true I struck the dog and yet I did not intend to hurt it so severely. Further, had I not struck it when it was lying on the road, it might have bitten someone who stumbled against it. Thus I acted for the public good and I am blameless."

The Râja consulted his ministers and they said:—

"The Brahman is surely to blame, but it is a rule of the State that no heavy punishment shall be inflicted on a Brahman. It is best that the dog be asked to fix the penalty. So shall we be free from blame."

Râmachandra asked the dog what punishment should be awarded to the Brahman, and he said:—"Give him a number of villages and let him become the head of a monastery and escort him to his new charge on an elephant."

"But" said the Râja, "this is no punishment at all."

"It is the greatest punishment in the world," said the dog, "and I will tell you why. I was in my former life a Brahman, and this Brahman was a *Mathdhari Atith* or abbot of a monastery. One day I was sitting with him, and the time came for him to cook his food. He sat down to cook in the sacred cooking square, but he had forgotten the *ghi,* and he asked me to bring him some. I went up and took out a little *ghi* with my finger and brought it to him. Then I went home and bathed, but a little morsel of the *ghi* stuck inside the point of my nail, and when I was eating, it went down my throat. This so defiled me that when I came before Yama Râja, the Lord of the dead, he ordered that I should for one thousand successive births be reborn as a dog. The same will be the fate of this cruel Brahman and he will be reborn a dog for a thousand births."

So Râmachandra was convinced and awarded the Brahman the punishment assigned by the dog.

[The tale curiously illustrates the abhorrence felt by Brahmans for the class of so-called ascetics who live worldly lives as the heads of monasteries.—ED.]

103. A Fatal Compact.

(Recorded by Miss Ida Casabon of Aligarh.)

One day a Thakur boy was herding his buffaloes, and near him a sweeper lad was grazing his pigs. The Thakur for a joke said:—"If I jump over one of your pigs, you must give me your sister to wife. If you jump over my buffalo, I will give you my sister." They agreed, and the Thakur tried to jump over the pig, but the pig always ran out of his way, and he failed. Then the sweeper lad easily jumped over the back of the buffalo, and when he had done the feat, he said:—"Now marry me to your sister."

The Thakur did not know how to escape carrying out his promise: so he said:—"Go across the river: turn yourself into a marigold and you shall have my sister." The sweeper went across the stream and became a marigold at once.

By and by the Thakur's sister came with his breakfast, and he said to her:—"I won't eat my breakfast till you go across the river and pick that marigold." She objected, but when he would not eat, she went into the water. When the water reached her knees, she was afraid and called out:—"The water is up to my knees." But he told her to go on. When it reached her waist, she cried out again; but he spoke as before. Then it came to her shoulders and then to her neck; but her brother would not let her come back. At last she sank and was drowned.

Then he went home, and his mother said:—"Where is your sister? Why did she not come home with you?" He answered:—"She was in a hurry and started before me." But the parrot, who was in a cage close by, suspected him and said:—"Open my cage and I will go and look for her." So they opened his cage and he went to the river-bank and called out:— "Hiriya, Hiriya, where are you?" She called out from under the water. "Go and tell my mother that I was drowned, because my brother rashly promised to marry me to the sweeper."

The parrot went and told her mother, who turned her son out of doors.

104. The Pandit and the Princess.

(Told by Sivarâm, teacher, Madhoganj, Hardoi District.)

There was once a Râja, who had a lovely daughter; and as she grew up, the Pandit fell in love with her and began to plan how he could get her into his power. One day he sat down near the Râja in his court, and the Râja said:—"Panditji, my daughter is now coming of age. Search and find a suitable match for her." The Pandit asked to see her horoscope, and when he read it, he said:—"I have terrible news to tell you. When the princess is seventeen, a great trouble will come upon you, and you will be expelled from your kingdom." The Râja was overcome with fear and asked the Pandit to devise some means for his protection.

Next day the Pandit came to the Râja and said:—"I have considered the matter. You must get rid of the princess before the fatal day arrives. It is not well for you to kill her with your own hand. So you should shut her up in a box and let her float down the river, and the animals of the river will devour her." Then the Pandit called his disciples and said:—"I am going to recite the great witchcraft spell (*Dankini Mantra*). I shall throw the objects used in the sacrifice into the river. So you should watch on the bank, and if you see anything floating down, pick it up and bring it to me, as it is of the greatest efficacy."

They put the princess in the box and let her float down the river. Just then a Râja, who had a most vicious monkey, came to the bank of the river where he intended to release the animal; and when he saw the box floating down, he had it taken out and found the princess. When he heard her story, he mounted her on one of his horses and rode away with her; but first he shut up the monkey in the box.

When the box had floated some way down, the disciples of the Pandit saw it and brought it to him. He had arranged the inner room; and there he took the box, intending to open it when he was alone. So he said to his disciples:—"I am going to do some more witchcraft; and when the witches come, they will make a great disturbance. But you should remain outside and go on blowing the conch shell, and do not pay any attention to whatever you may hear."

They promised to obey him and went on blowing the conch shell. When the Pandit opened the box, the monkey came out and jumped on his back and began to tear him to pieces. He shouted for help, but no one minded him; and a long time after, when they opened the inner room, the monkey rushed out and they found the Pandit on the point of death. When they asked him what had occurred, all he could do was to scratch this verse on the wall with his nail and then he died:

Jo jaisê karni karê; so taisa phal pâe;
Râja bhogê sundari, Biprahin bandar khâê.

"Everyone reaps the fruit of his deeds; the Râja gets the damsel and the Pandit is devoured by the monkey."

105. The Banker's Wife.

(Told by Lakshman Prasâd, Bijpauri, and recorded by Kundan Lâl, Pithauli, Agra District.)

A certain banker had a very beautiful wife, who was seen one day by the king, as she stood on the upper storey of her house. The king became greatly enamoured of her, had her carried off by stealth, and married her. In grief at her departure, her husband and her son abandoned their home and became religious mendicants: but some little time afterwards the son obtained the post of city *Kotwâl,* while his father sought some means of recovering his wife. One day, as the latter was passing the palace, his wife espied him and called to him; and on his approaching, she said, "Go and wait by the temple outside the town, and I will come to you." Now the woman was devoted to her husband; and so, when the king came to sleep with her that night, she cut off his head and went with it to her husband. But unfortunately he had been bitten by a snake, while waiting for her, and was dead. Thereupon in great distress she ran away, and on the road she fell in with a Banjârâ, who kept her as his wife. Arriving with him at a city, she was forcibly seized by the Nâyaks and made a prostitute. Now it chanced that this was the city in which her son was the *Kotwâl.*

Her son happened to see her and fell in love with her beauty, but did not recognise her as his mother. But by degrees, as they became intimate, the truth dawned upon them both. Thereupon in shame she fled to the river-bank and mounted a funeral pyre, in the hope of ending her miserable life. But the river could not brook this, and rose and flooded the pyre; and she, balancing herself on a log, floated away on the flood-tide to a spot where some Gujars were grazing their cattle. They seized her and one of them took her to wife. He used to send her to the market to sell curd, and there the men of the market began to cut jokes at her expense; whereupon in anger and distress she threw down her vessel of curd and smashed it. The Gujar, hearing of this, was very angry and exclaimed: "This woman will be the ruin of my home at this rate." Then did she retort in the following words:—

> *"Nrip mâri chali apnê piya kûn piya kâl daso*
> *dukh mên parihô;*
> *Bhâgi chali, banjâr lai, tab bênchi dai ganikâ*
> *ghar hô;*
> *Sut sang bhai jari bê ko chali nadiyâ parwâ*
> *bahi tirihô;*

*Itnê dukh pâi bhai gujari, teri chhâchh kô sôch
kahâ karihô.*

i.e., "Having killed the king, I went to my lawful husband. But a snake bit him and I was in sore distress. So I fled, and a Banjârâ caught me, and after that I was sold to a prostitute. When I met my own son, I sought to burn myself; but the river rose in flood and I was cast upon its bank. It is after all these sorrows that I have become a Gujari. Why then should I care aught for your curd?"

106. A Wife's disappointment.

(Told and recorded by Chaube Braj Kishor, schoolmaster, Pinâhat, Agra District.)

A certain man left his home for work and was absent on duty for twelve years. When he returned, his wife was overjoyed, made special food for him, and did all she could to celebrate his home-coming. At night she placed his cot on the upper storey, and when he lay down, she set to shampooing his feet and legs, in the hope that he would give her the money he had brought back with him. But the husband, who was tired, fell fast asleep without offering a single cowrie to her. In the morning his wife helped him to perform his ablutions, and when these were finished, he ordered her to boil some water for his bath. Then said she:—

> *Bârah baras bîtê sajjan âyê;*
> *Unchî atâ par palang bichhâyê;*
> *Sarî shâm se rahê wê sôya;*
> *Lênâ êk na denâ dôya.*
> *Huâ fazra tab hukm farmâyâ*
> *Thandhâ pâni tatta karwâyâ.*
> *Jhûnghat mânjh tiriyâ musukâni;*
> *Kis biratê par tattâ pâni.*

i.e., "The husband returned after twelve years. The cot was set on an upper storey. In the evening he fell asleep, but he neither took one nor gave two (he gave nothing). When morning dawned, he ordered cold water to be heated. Hearing this the woman turned her face and muttered, 'What mighty deed have you done that you want hot water?'"

[This tale gives the origin of the common saying, *Kis biratê par tattâ pâni.*—Ed.].

107. The Musalman's error.

(Told and recorded by Pandit Chandra Sekhara, Zilla school, Cawnpore.)

A certain Muhammadan made friends with a Brahman, who had many clients. The Brahman used to take food at his clients' homes, and when he came back, used to tell the Muhammadan what an excellent dinner he had had. Hearing his friend's praise of the various delicacies, the Muhammadan felt curious, and one day said to the Brahman, "My friend, you are constantly praising the food you eat with your friends, but you give no thought to me, who have never tasted such delicacies." The Brahman answered, "Miyân Sâheb, if this is so, I will arrange to get a seat for you among the Brahmans at the next *Nagar Bhoj* (a feast to the Brahmans of a village)."

Soon after a merchant prepared a *Nagar Bhoj*. Then the Brahman put a sacred thread on the Muhammadan, marked his forehead with sandal-paste, put a turban on his head, and in one hand a vessel and in the other a *sâlagrâma*. He also showed him how to conduct himself as a Brahman. Accordingly, when the Brahmans crowded into the merchant's house, the Muhammadan went with them, sat on the plastered ground, and began to eat with them. When his leaf-plate was getting empty, the pseudo-Brahman called out:—"*Aji miyân, zarâ idhar lâo.*" This startled the Brahmans, who asked him who he was. "Be silent," replied he, "*Khûdâ* (God) has given food to you and me. Why grudge it? Take your food and go your ways." This made the Brahmans very suspicious, and several of them gathered round him and demanded to know who he was. Said he, "I am a Gaud Brahman." "Which Gaud?" said they. The Musalman replied:— "*Ya Khudâ, kya Gaudon men bhi Gaud hote hain* (O Heaven, are there Gaudas within Gaudas)?"

Hearing this, the Brahmans shouted out, "He is not a Brahman." The Muhammadan said, "Why do you say that I am not a Brahman? Don't you see that I have here *Sâle ghulâm* (instead of *Sâlagrâm*) in the small wooden box?" That settled the matter, and they drove him out of the house.

[This story illustrates the Hindi proverb, *Sikhâe put darbâr ko nahîn jâte hain, i.e* "Tutors' sons do not suit a Darbâr."—ED.]

108. The Bee's Secret.

(Told and recorded by Durga Prasâd, teacher, Aligarh District.)

Four women, drawing water at a well, saw a bee rolling in the dust, and said to one another, "Why should this bee, who inhabits fair gardens and enjoys the honey of flowers, be thus rolling in the dirt?"

Then the first woman said:—

> *Ban nahîn belâ nahin, nahîn Kêtaki sang;*
> *Madhukar kaun sê karmê bhasm lapêtê ang.*

i.e., "Nor forest, nor *bêlâ* blossom, nor kêtaki are with you. Why then, O Bee, do you smear your body with ashes?"

Then said the second woman:

> *Pahilê hi yahân Kêtaki jar gai dhaun kê sang;*
> *Prit purânî karat hain, jâsê bhasm lapêtê ang.*

i.e., "Perhaps Kêtakî burnt herself here with some one in old days, and the bee smears himself with ashes in memory of the old love."

The third woman said:—

> *Jab to jarî thî Kêtakî, tab to jaryô na sang;*
> *Log hansâî karat hain, yâ tên bhasm lapêtê ang.*

i.e., "When Kêtakî burnt herself, he did not share her fate. The world laughs now at his unfaithfulness, and therefore he smears his body with ashes."

The fourth woman then said:—

> *Jab to jarî thî Kêtakî, tab to nâ hô sang;*
> *Prit purânî karat hain, lai pahuchâwain Gang.*

i.e., "When Kêtakî burnt herself, he was absent. So now he testifies to his ancient love by bearing her ashes to the Ganges."

109. The Fruit of Immortality.

(Told by Thâkur Prasâd Pujâri, Sitâpur.)

Once on a time Râja Vikrama performed so much penance that Bhagwân as a reward gave him a fruit, which caused whosoever ate it to become immortal. The charitable Râja gave it to a Brahman, who sold it to Râja Bhartrihari for a large sum. Bhartrihari in turn gave the fruit to his beloved wife, who conferred it upon the Kotwâl, who happened to be her paramour. Now the Kotwâl at the time was enamoured of a prostitute and therefore gave her the fruit. This girl used to dance in the Râja's palace, and one day he saw the fruit in her possession and enquired how she had come by it. When he heard the whole story, he exclaimed:—

Yâm chintyâmi sat tam mayi sâ biraktâ
  sâpanyam
ichhati janam jan nonya saktah.
Asmat krite cha paritushyati kâchi danyâ,
  dhaktân cha
tan cha madanam cha imâm cha mân cha.

i.e., "She, of whom I am always thinking, is averse from me. She thinks of another man, who loves another, and another woman finds delight in me. So fie upon her; fie upon lust; fie upon her and fie on me!"

They say that from that day Bhartrihari decided to renounce the world.

110. *The Râja and the Cowherd.*

(Told and recorded by Jagat Sinh, Meerut District.)

A king and his minister were once out hunting, and as they were conversing together, they met a cowherd grazing his cattle. Just as they were passing, the minister spoke as follows:—

Râjâ to pâg bân ke, thân bân kî ghôrî;
Gây bhains sing bânkî nain ban kî gôrî.

i.e., "A Râja looks well with a turban on, and a mare when she is tied in the stable. A buffalo looks beautiful when it has good horns, and a fair lady when she has large eyes."

The young cowherd overheard this and said to a cow, which was going astray: "O cow, if you wander away I will break your legs, even as this prince has broken the legs of the verse." Hearing this remark, the Râja asked the boy what he said, whereupon the boy repeated his remark to the cow. "But how did the minister break the legs of the verse?" said the Râja. Said the boy: "Does a turban make a Râja look well? No! This is wrong. The verse should run thus:—

Râjâ to ran bân ke, pîth ban kî ghôrî;
Gaya bhains dudh ban kî, kak bân kî gôrî."

i.e., "A Râja looks well who is equipped for battle, and a mare when she has a strong back (to carry her rider). A buffalo looks beautiful when it is in milk, and a fair woman when she has sweet speech."

III. The Parrots Reproof.

(Told by Akbar Shâh, Dudhi, South Mirzapur.)

A woman was going after her marriage to her husband's house, when she saw her lover standing a little way off and weeping. Then she said:—

> *Gori chali gawanâ kê jankhan lâgê mit kyâ?*
> *Jhankho kya jhurwâ? kya jhurwâ kêo?*
> *Dahi rahâ so tum khâyô, au manthâ chalâ bidês.*
> *Bhar ângan sab sabhâ rahi, kaise bidâ batâwon;*
> *Gâon ke uttar pokharâ wahân pâni bharne âwôn;*
> *Tum dhani ghorâ daurâye awo to hamen wahâ pâyo.*

i.e., "The fair one started for her husband's home and her lover began to mourn. Why mourn for the beloved and her hair? You ate the good curd; the curd which has been mixed with water and adulterated is going to another country. How could I let you know that my father would send me away on such and such a day? You know that during these days our courtyard was full of clansmen. To the north of the village lies a tank, on the bank of which is a pipal tree. If you ride quickly there on horseback, you may find me, as I shall go there to draw water."

Hearing this, the lover retired, and in the evening he went to the tank, but did not find his beloved. So he returned home, heavy of heart. Seeing a parrot on a tree, he exclaimed:

> *Sugâ tor lâl thor, piar thor, tore mukh men*
> *   amrit ghariyâ;*
> *Yah bâtên gôrî dêkhê, sîr par gagariyâ.*

i.e., "O Parrot, thou hast a red and yellow bill. In thy mouth is the cup of nectar. Sawest thou my fair one pass this way with a pitcher on her head?"
The Parrot answered:

> *Gori âya rahî, gori jâya rahi, aur bhari*
> *   gâgariyâ;*
> *Chand, suraj donon chhapit bhayê, torê mukh*
> *   men lâgî karikhâ.*

i.e., "The fair one came and drew water and went away. The sun and moon have now set. Thy face, O my friend, has been blackened (*i.e.,* You came too late)." The lover was ashamed of his folly and went home.

INDEX

ABOUT THE VOLUME EDITOR

Dr. Sadhana Naithani is assistant professor at the Center of German Studies, Jawaharlal Nehru University, New Delhi. Her doctoral thesis, "Politics of Love," is a study of German folk songs. Her postdoctoral research and publication in the history of folklore research have focused on the interface between nineteenth-century European folkloristics and colonial folklore collections compiled in India by British colonial administrators. The postcolonial perspective in her writing has brought forth the role of native scholars in the compilation of those volumes. *Folktales from Northern India* is the first volume ever to be published under the joint authorship of a colonial administrator-scholar—William Crooke—and his Indian scholar-associate—Pandit Ram Gharib Chaube. Sadhana Naithani's articles have been published in the *Journal of Folklore Research* and in *Folklore*.